BRISTOL
BEYOND THE BRIDGE

'Beyond the Bridge a second city grows'
W. Goldwin—Master of the Grammar School, Bristol, 1712

MICHAEL MANSON

REDCLIFFE
Bristol

First published in 1988 by
Redcliffe Press Ltd, 49 Park Street, Bristol 1

© Michael Manson 1988

**For Hannah
Born Bristol 25/3/86
and Matthew
Born Bristol 6/1/88**

ISBN 0 948265 96 5

*Typeset and printed in Great Britain by
Penwell Ltd, Parkwood, Callington, Cornwall*

Contents

Continued over

Foreword

From my bedroom window in Redcliffe Parade, I had a spectacular view looking down onto Bristol's Floating Harbour. It was a vista of endless fascination; Redcliffe Bridge in the foreground, the warehouses of Redcliffe Back and Welsh Back to the right and left and in the far distance a glimpse of Bristol Bridge. I relied on St Nicholas' church clock for the time and, with the aid of a telescope, could even read its unique second hand.

After a while, something struck me about this view—the difference between Bristol north and south of the water. The Bristol that I could see to the north of the float was grandly prosperous. Whilst to the south, Redcliffe Back with its hulking empty warehouses was a derelict wasteland. I knew much of the centre of Bristol had been devastated during the Second World War, and even in the 1970s the city still bore the scars, but this contrast started me thinking. I wondered, had there always been such an obvious divide between north and south of the Avon? And why? It was from these thoughts that *Beyond the Bridge* grew.

Acknowledgements

Many people have assisted in various ways in the writing of *Bristol: Beyond the Bridge*. For help along the way I am grateful to Chris Challis, Marion Dyer, Trevor Fry of GWR, Mike Hallet of DRG, the staff of Bristol Central Reference Library, Sheena Stoddard, Mike Ponsford and Andy King of the City of Bristol Museum and Art Gallery and Sarah Barnes and John Sansom of Redcliffe Press. Also a tip of the hat to the Redcliffe Paraders who were there at the beginning: Dennis, Digby, Fiona, Fred, Hilary, Karen, Liz, Lucy, Mick, Nick, Nancy and Rosie. And finally thanks to Maggie Moss without whose encouragement and faith the book would never have been completed.

Bristol Bridge, built 1247. Despite its narrowness, its potential for trade was quickly realised and buildings soon sprang up on both sides of the roadway.

Introduction

Crossing Bristol Bridge after a pleasant stroll along Corn Street and through St Nicholas Market one enters a bleak area of office blocks, warehouses and car parks. Today it is difficult to believe that Redcliffe, Temple and Thomas Streets were once amongst the liveliest thoroughfares in Bristol. From the present surroundings there is little indication that an important community thrived in this area for over 800 years. Nobody lives there now—at night-time and weekends the area is deserted.

But if one takes the time to look there are signs of a greater past than is immediately apparent. Continue walking down Victoria Street and the building that grabs attention is Temple Church with its ornate leaning tower. Though now sadly gutted, it still reflects the prosperity of its builders. The name Temple is a reminder that this area was once governed by the Knights Templar, the fierce crusading order whose history dates back to 1118. Look around further and many other names give clues to the past; Portwall Lane runs alongside the former site of the invincible thirteenth century city wall, whilst the name Temple Gate speaks for itself. Nearby, sitting sadly on the edge of a car park is Chatterton's House, the birth place of the marvellous boy poet who died so young. Across the road, hidden by a modern hotel, stand the remains of a truncated glass cone representative of one of the area's staple industries. And then, of course, there is the beautiful St Mary Redcliffe Church. 'In all respects the finest parochial church in all England' as Queen Elizabeth I so rightly described it. This magnificent church, the size of a small cathedral, gives an idea of the wealth of Redcliffe's inhabitants during the middle ages. Up until the twentieth century much of Bristol's prosperity came from its trade through the docks. Although the docks are now quiet, the massive warehouses and mills (some at last undergoing restoration) along Redcliffe Back are nevertheless reminders of the scale of trade handled by the port in the nineteenth century.

But why a history of just these Southern Parishes when there are already many excellent histories of the city? South Bristol, in an indefinable way has always had its own distinct identity. Like many other cities divided by a river—the north and south of the Thames at London or the left and the right banks of the Seine at Paris—the transpontine area has a character all its own. The Southern perspective is a side of Bristol's history that has largely been ignored. Perhaps it is because, at first sight, the South was where much of Bristol's grimy industry was based. Usually Bristol's history is presented as a glamorous tale of rich merchants, far off exotic overseas travel, exploration and adventure. However, back home in Bristol, in the Southern Parishes, there were equally exciting, though admittedly less exotic adventures going on in the world of industry—an industry that fed products to the new colonies and made both Bristol great and Britain a force to be reckoned with.

Beyond the Bridge is a history of the three original southern parishes of Bristol—Redcliffe, Temple and St Thomas. Geographically it covers roughly the area enclosed in the loop of the Floating Harbour southwards to The Cut. There are, however, exceptions, notably the section on the New Gaol.

Yet, of course, no parish is an island, and although divided by a river the Southern Parishes are in many matters inseparable from the remainder of Bristol. Indeed, in some ways *Beyond the Bridge* comprises personal and capricious vignettes of the history of Bristol told with a view from the steps of St Mary Redcliffe.

Although *Beyond the Bridge* makes no attempt to be a definitive record it will, I hope, give a feel of the times and a glimpse at the characters that have shaped this neglected area of Bristol.

The Early Days

One thousand years ago the area that we now know as Redcliffe was little more than a swampy uninviting patch of land. Nobody lived there; it was inhabited only by grazing animals and wildfowl. Even so, there were two tracks, raised on a wattle causeway in the most sodden places, that led away from a timber bridge that crossed the Avon. One of these tracks went along the wooded river valley to Keynsham, the other, disappearing over a low red cliff, led to the Somerset village of Bedminster.

The early settlement of Redcliffe, named after this reddish sandstone cliff first grew after the Norman conquest. A ribbon of wooden and wattle and daub dwellings gradually appeared alongside the two trackways. Indeed, in early charters this string of houses was merely called Radeclivestret (Redcliffe Street).

But apart from its track side position what was it that encouraged settlement in such a damp, uninviting and defenceless place? The answer can be found in the quay that we now call Redcliffe Back. Here, through the natural flow of the river there was a deep waterfrontage. In time, the fact that ships from as far afield as Ireland, France and even Iceland could moor here was the key to Redcliffe's development. It is crucial when looking at the early history of Redcliffe to understand that it existed not merely as a suburb of Bristol but as a distinct community in its own right. The reason for this division lay not only in the divide created by the River Avon but also in the fact that Bristol and Redcliffe lay in different administrative areas. To the south of the Avon, Redcliffe on its soggy river flood plane, was in the manor of Bedminister, while to the north of the river Bristol lay in Gloucestershire. Consequently, despite their proximity both areas grew up and were governed independently. It was an independence that over the years was to cause problems between two such youthful and vigorous communities.

Apart from administration it would be ridiculous to deny that Redcliffe and Bristol had affinities. Geographically, socially and economically there was an evident closeness between them. Like reflections in the river dividing them, events in one community were mirrored in the other.

The Redcliffe land was gradually divided between owners. The feudal system was such that the King, who owned all the land in the country, would parcel out his property to tenants as gifts in return for certain services—such as the loan of money or manpower. Once they were given property, tenants still had no absolute right to this land and, as we shall shortly see, if they failed in their duties were liable to forfeiture.

In 1145 the eastern part of Redcliffe was granted to the heroic group, the Knights Templar. This eastern strip came to be known as Temple Fee and was soon established as the Templars' administrative centre in the West Country. And so Temple Fee with its own market, its settlement of weavers and its peculiar round chapel was soon also a community in its own right.

In the early Norman period Redcliffe, as part of the manor of Bedminster, was under the charge of Robert, Earl of Gloucester—an illegitimate son of Henry I and potential heir to the throne. Robert of Gloucester owned vast tracts of land in both England and France and through his wide ranging connections he did much to promote Redcliffe's development.

Alongside Robert of Gloucester another powerful local figure of the period was Robert Fitz Harding (died 1171). Fitz Harding held the post of King's Reeve—the official royal representative in Bristol. A perceptive businessman, he invested much of his not insubstantial income in the purchase of land and estates. To this end, some time in the 1140s, Fitz Harding bought the manor of Bedminster, which of course included Redcliffe, from the Earl of Gloucester. And in the next few years, thanks largely to the troubles of King Stephen's reign (1135-1154) Fitz Harding's good fortunes were to take an even greater, and unforeseen, turn for the better.

With Henry I's daughter, Matilda, vying with Stephen for the throne, Stephen's reign collapsed into a prolonged period of baronial anarchy. Redcliffe and Bristol, like much of the West Country, offered allegiance to Matilda. Her son, Henry, even spent four years of his childhood in Bristol. When Stephen died it was this Henry who, unopposed, took over the throne.

After the insecurity of Stephen's reign, Henry II's wise and lively rule brought with it a new direction for Redcliffe's economy. For when Henry II came to the throne he inherited a vast empire, the Angevin Empire, that stretched from the Scottish borders down to the Pyrenees. Indeed, the interests of Henry and his French wife, Eleanor of Aquitaine, lay as much with France as they did with England—so much so that of the thirty-four years of his reign Henry spent twenty-one of these abroad. Nevertheless such strong links with Anjou and Aquitaine could only be of benefit to local trade.

Henry was eager to reward those who had been faithful to his mother Matilda. Thus Robert Fitz Harding, who already owned Redcliffe, was awarded the valuable fiefdom of the Berkeley estates which centred on Severn Valley in Gloucestershire. This grant of both Berkeley land and title laid the foundations for a remarkable dynasty that would rule over Redcliffe for the next two hundred years.

However, there was one problem. The previous baron of the estates, Roger De Berkeley, who had sided with Stephen in the civil war, was meanwhile banished to a dark and dank castle in the shadow of the Cotswold escarpment at Dursley. Needless to say Roger was not pleased to look across the wide Severn Valley and see land that had once been his in the hands of another man. So 'vexed and troubled' was Roger that his discontented rumblings had eventually to be quelled by Henry II with a masterstroke of marriage diplomacy. At the command of the King, Robert Fitz Harding's eldest son, Maurice (1117-1189) married Roger De Berkeley's daughter Alice. It was a fruitful union: not only was the rift between the two families healed, but Alice also bore six sons and a daughter.[1]

Even with his new clutch of land in the Severn Valley, Redcliffe was still Robert Fitz Harding's most valuable asset. If he and the people of Redcliffe were to benefit fully from the new expanded trading connections with France—and also Ireland (even in those days there is mention of Bristol's penchant for the trading of slaves—especially young girls) a charter was needed giving freedom from tolls in other areas. Bristol had had such a dispensation since 1155. So some time between 1164 and 1170 Fitz Harding duly sought, and was awarded by Henry II, a charter which granted freedom of customs throughout the land to the men who dwell in the 'marsh near the bridge of Bristol'.[2]

An indication of any community's standing and wealth was given by its ecclesiastical buildings. In a society where everyday life was dominated by the church, a fundamental requirement of even the smallest hamlet was a place of worship. As the settlement of Redcliffe grew, so we find reference to two chapels—those of St Mary and of St Thomas the Martyr. Both were attached to St John's parish church in Bedminster. The humble Norman chapel of St Mary Redcliffe was first mentioned in 1158 when it was given to the cathedral at Salisbury. The foundation of the less famous church of St Thomas came later, probably in the 1170s. Thomas a Becket was martyred on December 29th, 1170; the scandalous manner of his death, murdered by four knights before the altar of Canterbury Cathedral, would account for the dedication.

With time, the Berkeleys moved out of Bristol to their land in the Severn valley and took up residence in Berkeley Castle. They nevertheless continued to look after the needs of the Redclivians. In 1207 Robert Berkeley (1165-1221) granted a supply of fresh clean water to his people by providing a pipe line from the hillside at Knowle to bring spring water down to St Mary Redcliffe. Part of the original conduit still exists and the fountain head can be seen today in the churchyard wall on Redcliffe Hill. From there, there was also a pipeline, the dimensions of a medium sized thumb, that supplied the Hospital of St John in nearby Redcliffe Pit, an institution for the poor also partly supported by the Berkeleys.

So by the beginning of the thirteenth century, Redcliffe with its Berkeley patronage, its charter and its deep waterfrontage looked all set to equal, if not overtake, neighbouring Bristol. Indeed when King John levied aid in 1210 for war in Ireland, both Redcliffe and Bristol contributed the same amount of money.[3] Although Bristol may have been established earlier (the first written mention of Bristol is in 1051 but the fact that the borough had a mint by 1020 shows its importance at a much earlier date) Redcliffe, the late starter had caught up.

The Great Works

It was during the thirteenth century that Redcliffe and Temple Fee united with Bristol to undertake civil engineering works of gargantuan proportions and of such permanence that the city still bears their stamp seven hundred years later.

They were days of boundless energy; the greater part of Bristol had been burnt to the ground in an accident in 1237 yet at the same time the people on both sides of the River Avon were embarking upon costly operations that over the years would involve the building of a new harbour, the construction of a new stone bridge across the river and the extension and strengthening of the town walls.

The business transacted in the harbour had grown to such an extent that, despite its position up a twisting river and through a gorge that took the wind out of your sails, by 1230 the port facilities were becoming overcrowded. Bulky cargo ships carrying anything up to 200 tons—50,000 gallons—of wine from Gascony were sailing up the River Avon and finding berthing awkward. If Bristol was to thrive as a port—albeit a port that at this time relied on imports rather than exports—a new harbour was needed. It was not an easy facility to provide 10 miles from the sea. The plan, however, was this: an enormous trench 2,400 feet long, 120 feet wide and 18 feet deep was to be dug—redirecting the River Frome from its curving entry into the Avon just below Bristol Bridge (the Frome ran roughly parallel with today's Baldwin Street) to a more direct route southwards creating new deep water berthing facilities. But to the merchants of Redcliffe and St Thomas there was one catastrophic fault with this bold scheme. It would rob them of their premier waterfrontage. They therefore withheld their support from this grandiose work and were only coaxed into action by a sharply worded writ from the King asserting that the diversion of the Frome was 'for the common good of the whole town' and could not be completed without 'great costs'.[4]

Eight years later and at a massive expense of £5,000 the new reach of the Frome, strengthened with stone, was completed and ready to receive the largest ships of the day. Redcliffe and St Thomas' ace card had been trumped; after a brief supremacy their moorings were now eclipsed into second place.

The next great work, the building of a stone bridge across the Avon was of benefit to both communities. Although a wooden bridge had spanned the river for perhaps two hundred years (Bristol is a corruption of the name Brig-Stow—fenced place of the Bridge) it was now felt that a new, more stable, even fashionable structure that could cope with increased traffic was needed to link the two sides of the Avon. After all, London's great multi-arched bridge had been erected over fifty years before.

The construction of the bridge in 1247 called for some of the expertise that had already been used in the remodelling of the harbour. The builders' first task was to divert the Avon so that the bridge's foundations could be safely and satisfactorily laid. This was achieved by truncating the loop of the Avon that encompasses Redcliffe, Temple and St Thomas parishes and redirecting it along a ditch. Until 1965 it had been assumed that the full flow of the Avon was able to course along this channel, but excavations in that year have shown that this was unlikely as the Portwall ditch, as it came to be known, would certainly have been inadequate for this purpose.[5] Even so, if only part of the waters of the river were directed it would still have made construction easier—especially at low tide.

The completed bridge was a sturdy structure on four arches, the columns of which were so thick that they impeded the flow of the water and, like London Bridge, created a small waterfall. Despite the narrowness of the 19 feet wide bridge its superb potential for trade was soon realised and buildings quickly sprang up on both sides of the roadway. To make the most of the very limited space, this accommodation was partly built on trusses jutting out over the water. The roadway across the bridge took on the aspect of a dark street, its dinginess further increased by the chapel of the Assumption of the Blessed Virgin Mary which was built on an archway straddling the centre of the bridge.

Because ordinances forbade the use of any other material these buildings were built entirely of wood and to lessen the fire risk, roofed with slate. Although the rooms were tiny, the houses were often as many as four storeys high. The ground floor would contain a shop, with perhaps a tiny room behind, a staircase would lead up to a small parlour and kitchen, with two further floors above this and sometimes even an attic. Several houses also had cellars built into the piers of the bridge. Although it was a popular trading site there were some particular disadvantages to it. It was not unknown for animals being led across the bridge to panic, crash into a shop and run amok. On one occasion a large and powerful ox lumbered through the ground floor of a house and jumped out of its back window, splashing heavily into the water below. Also in times of flood cellars would be awash and there are tales of ships' masts forcing themselves through floor boards with the rising tide.[6]

It was hoped that the new bridge would bring about a spirit of unity, it being mentioned by one optimistic chronicler that 'this year the bridge of Bristow began to be founded and the inhabitants of Redcliffe, Temple and Thomas were incorporated with the town of Bristol . . .'[7] It was a peace that was not to last for long: squabbles soon broke out over the funding of the third and last 'great work', the improvement of the fortifications.

The inhabitants of Redcliffe, Temple and St Thomas were not happy with the system whereby the murage, a tax collected on goods entering and leaving the town, was pooled. They jealously demanded that the money collected on the southern routes of entry into the town should be put only towards the construction of the southern walls, (walls were important not only for defence but also as a means of regulating the collection of tolls). Despite this haggling, the walls to the north of the town were extended and new fortifications enclosing an area of 70 acres (ten more acres than the north) were erected to protect the vulnerable south. To create a hopefully impregnable defensive system the new south wall flanked the north side of the ditch that had originally been dug for the diversion of the Avon.

There were two gateways, Redcliffe and Temple Gate, and an illustration from the seventeenth century indicates that the 8 feet thick walls were further strengthened by a series of eight bastions. When Henry VIII's topographer, John Leland, visited Bristol in the 1540s, he was able to report that the Portwall, as it was called, 'is the highest and strongest piece of all the town walls'.[8] He was not wrong; the wall was to stand for many years and indeed was so solidly built that it remained, as we shall see, invincible to all attack until its demolition in the eighteenth century. Interestingly, St Mary Redcliffe, not yet splendid, was stranded outside the fortifications. To direct the defences up Redcliffe Hill would not only have been needlessly expensive but also strategically unwise.

The Templars

Temple Fee, like Redcliffe, was also administered separately from Bristol. Here the Templars raised their own taxes, held their own courts and ran their own market round their own market cross, the stallenge, at the north end of Temple Street.

But who were the Templars? Founded in 1118 they first made a name for themselves defending the pilgrim routes to the Holy Land. The twelfth and thirteenth centuries were the era of the crusades—a time that offered a unique opportunity for exotic travel and adventure subsidised by ecclesiastical tithes. The initial impetus for the crusades had arisen in 1098 when Pope Urban II had preached in France that Jerusalem should be rescued from the grip of its moslem conquerors. From that time on, in a remarkable example of early international cooperation, much money and time was spent transporting armies from north western Europe to the far end of the Mediterranean. It was a long, long way to go and not all those who set out made it. Neither were the intentions of the crusaders always noble—all too often their initial worthy ideals were submerged in an orgy of drunkeness, pillage and rape.

After crossing the choppy seas of the Biscay most crusaders from England would stop off at Oporto. Whilst establishing useful trade links with Portugal this break in the journey also offered a first taste of adventure, as down the coast Lisbon was in the hands of the Moors.

It was during the second crusade in 1147 that the men of Bristol made a particularly bad example of themselves. It is recorded that whilst attacking Lisbon their zeal seemed inspired not so much by christianity as by piracy.[9] The Bristolians were far more interested in the immediate pleasures of looting rather than liberating the Holy Land.

Despite such transgressions, the crusaders and the military orders such as the Templars that backed them were deemed a worthy cause of support; so in 1145 Robert Earl of Gloucester granted the eastern part of Redcliffe to the Knights Templar.

Temple Fee soon became the Templars' headquarters in the south west of England. The order also built itself a small chapel, typical of the Templars in that it was round—the shape reminiscent of the Holy Sepulchre in Jerusalem.

Although these 'Poor Knights of Christ' as the Templars liked to call themselves, started from venerable beginnings—they took the same vows as monks; poverty, chastity and obedience—through their spectacular military achievements they soon became very rich. And in time the Templars, dressed in their distinctive white robes with a red cross emblazoned on the shoulder, became associated more with high handed arrogance than the humility expected of a quasi-religious order. In England and France they acted as a law unto themselves, recognising only the authority of the Pope. In

12

The knights of St. John made their mark on Temple Fee by building the Church of the Holy Cross. They did not, however, account for the softness of the alluvial soil and soon found their church tower leaning at an alarming angle.

Temple Fee they certainly paid scant regard to the laws of their neighbours. Not surprisingly such behaviour was to cause their eventual downfall. By 1306, King Phillipe of France was anxious to rid his territory of the Templars. He used heresy as a convenient excuse. The Grand Master and several of the knights were burnt at the stake for alleged witchcraft. By 1312, on order of the Pope, The Knights Templar were disbanded. In England, although the Templars were spared the vicious persecution that they received in France, their possessions, which included Temple Fee, were handed over to their rivals, the Hospitaller Knights of St John.

The Knights of St John made their mark on Temple Fee by demolishing the Templars' chapel and on the same spot building their own church. They did not, however, account for the softness of the alluvial ground upon which they were building and soon found that the first stage of their church tower was leaning alarmingly out of skew. Sixty years later, after strengthening the foundations, a second tier was added which also housed a peal of bells. Apocryphal tales abound of how these bells upset the stability of the fine tower even more. On a visit in 1568, the Duke of Norfolk observed the tower's giddy swaying, whilst many years later in the nineteenth century the 'Rural Church Goer' Joseph Leech wrote of a man he met as a boy who used to sit beneath the belfry inserting nuts into the corner stones having them 'incontinently and cleverly cracked as the superstructure swayed with the vibration on the bells'. Leech's comment was that 'the man's sang-froid must be great who could enjoy salt and filberts under such circumstances'.[10]

Woollen Cloth

Apart from its leaning tower, Temple Fee was also famous for its cloth. From the early days of the Templars, Temple Fee had been well known for its settlement of weavers. Even so, it was not until the reign of Edward III that the full potential of the cloth trade was realised and the industry given encouragement to expand. In 1337 the export of raw wool (England's raw wool was acknowledged to be the best in Europe and was eagerly bought by the famous Flemish clothiers) was for a time forbidden. The purpose of this prohibition was two fold: first, to stifle the Italian cloth producers, and second, to encourage the expansion of home production. Additionally, to increase the skilled workforce on the home front, foreign weavers were encouraged to settle and carry out their craft in England. Accordingly Thomas Blanket and a workforce of foreign weavers set up production in Temple Fee in the 1340s. Not surprisingly this foreign, guild-breaking workforce was unpopular. Blanket had to seek protection from the King, who also confirmed that it was in order for the continental weavers to be employed.

It ought to be mentioned that the names of Bristol's woollen products can be misleading. There was a stripped cloth known as Bristol Cotton that did not contain any cotton whilst the connection between Thomas Blanket and the cloth that bears his name is tenuous. The tale that Blanket was the originator of the cloth is unlikely; in French, blanchette means white cloth.

Although cloth workers were to be found on both sides of the river it was in Temple Fee where the majority of them—both indigenous and immigrant—lived. In Temple Fee there was a Tucker Street (tucker being the west country name for a fuller) and in the new buildings of Temple Church—itself evidence of local prosperity—there was a chapel dedicated to the patron saint of weavers, St Katherine. In fact the manufacture of cloth was so widespread in the parishes of Redcliffe, Temple and Thomas that archaeological investigations into the medieval period invariably uncover related remains. In Cart Lane in

1974 the stumps of the cloth drying racks were uncovered while in 1980 excavations in Redcliffe Street revealed a workshop that had been used by dyers and possibly fullers as well.[11]

So how was the cloth produced? The production of woollen cloth was a relatively complex process involving many operations which would be farmed to different domestic premises. Much of the combing, carding, cleaning and spinning of the raw fleece would already have been done elsewhere—it was for its weavers that Temple Fee was famous. Once woven, the woollen cloth had to be washed and then tentered, that is hung out to dry and stretched to the correct length on racks. Just south of Temple church was an area called the Rack Close, equipped with numerous racks set aside for this specific purpose. In 1673 Millerd's map of Bristol showed the Rack Close to still be in existence. Other processes followed: the nap of the cloth had to be raised with the aid of teasels; it was then sheared several times to produce a soft finish, the finest of which was called 'doe skin'. The most popular agent for dying was woad and we find that after wine, woad was the import most mentioned in thirteenth century port records.

But the steady increase in the manufacture of woollen cloth was brought to an abrupt, albeit temporary, halt by the arrival of that curse of medieval and renaissance Europe, the black death. Being a port, Bristol was especially vulnerable to such epidemics and with the great mortality of 1349 it suffered badly. Across the country the black death killed nine out of ten of its victims. In Bristol local calendars tell how the living were scarcely able to bury the dead.[12] For a while Bristol was a ghost town and on streets that had once been so busy grass began to sprout. 'There died in a manner the whole strength of the town.'

Some of the effects of the black death were unexpected. For those who survived, it was an age of opportunity. Remarkably, after the pestilence, the upside down economy of the country caused the production of wool not to decline but to increase. With fewer people to farm the land, large areas of the countryside were turned over to sheep tracts. The 1350s and 1360s were an outstanding time for Bristol's entrepreneurs with cloth being exported as far afield as Denmark, the Baltic coast, Iceland, France, Spain and other Mediterranean countries.

In short, Edward III's aspirations for a country that produced its own cloth were bearing fruit—though how much his protectionist policies contributed to this is open to speculation. Whatever the reason, England had emerged from the position of Europe's prime wool producer to the more sophisticated role of manufacturer of woollen cloth. In 1348-1349 only 900 cloths had been shipped from Bristol but by 1360 this figure had soared to four and a half thousand.[13] What is more, Bristol was not just a cloth port, it was now the major cloth port of the realm.

Trouble with the Berkeleys

The arrest and imprisonment of a Bristolian in Redcliffe Gaol in 1303 triggered off a series of unexpected and far reaching events.

As we have already seen, the relationship between Redcliffe and Bristol was frequently strained. The roots of this antagonism lay partly in the differing laws governing the two areas—whilst Redcliffe was under the control of the Lords of Berkeley, Bristol was ruled by an elected mayor. The Lords of Berkeley held their own court, established a prison and gallows and maintained the right to collect certain taxes. Because of these differences Redcliffe and Bristol looked upon each other with suspicion. Indeed at the beginning of the fourteenth century a state of near civil war existed for a while between the two communities.

Matters came to a head when Richard of Cornwall, a Bristolian, was incarcerated in Redcliffe Street Gaol pending his trial for murder. Some Bristolians may have heard how, forty years before, a fellow burgess was imprisoned by the Berkeleys and promptly, without trial, hanged. Even if they had not heard this tale they were still uncertain that Richard would have a fair trial under the direction of the Berkeleys. So at a meeting hastily summoned by the ringing of the common bell it was resolved to take immediate action to prevent any miscarriage of justice. A large number of people, headed by the Mayor, swarmed across Bristol Bridge and forcibly rescued the prisoner, plundering 500 marks worth of Berkeley property as they went.

The Berkeleys were, of course, furious at this outright disregard for their authority. Not only was it a blatant invasion of their rights, it also posed a wider long term threat to their rule over Redcliffe. Measures had to be taken swiftly to reassert their supremacy. An appeal to the King was therefore lodged, requesting that he appoint a jury to investigate the raid.

Unfortunately no record survives of the outcome of this appeal. Two years later, however, the Bristolians voiced a series of retaliatory petitions, which if they are to be believed show the Berkeleys to be brutal, bullying and corrupt. In comparison, the previous complaints of the Berkeleys fade into triviality.

The tables were turned, it was now the Berkeleys' turn to come under scrutiny. The King appointed two men who, along with the constable of Bristol castle, were to enquire into the accusation and if they had any difficulty in coming to a decision they were to present their findings to Parliament.

First the Berkeley's court had to be examined; it would appear that not all Redclivians recognised the Berkeleys' jurisdiction and it was claimed that some of these dissenters were dragged from their homes, roughed up and thrown into a pit. In the commotion that followed, several people were trampled on and mortally wounded. The impartiality of the Berkeley courts was also in doubt, for it was alleged that 'three lewd thieves and wicked persons', who at Bristol had been imprisoned were taken and re-tried in Somerton, Somerset and there declared as 'honest men'.[14]

But that was not all: further complaints create a picture of the Berkeley family as the despots of the Severn Vale. In Frampton-upon-Severn, a Bristolian was so brutally assaulted by Lord Berkeley (died 1321) and his men that shortly afterwards he died. Whilst at Tetbury Fair there was an 'armed rout' of the burgesses of Bristol, many of whom were imprisoned and 'most wickedly . . . there intreated'. And finally, at Dundry Fair, it was vividly described how Lord Thomas Berkeley, Maurice his son (died 1326) and twenty-six henchmen set upon the unfortunate Adam the Cheeseman and 'brake his legs in such a pitiful manner that the marrow came out of his shin bones'.[15]

Not surprisingly, the judgement went against the Berkeleys. They were heavily fined, but more serious, Redcliffe and the rest of the Manor of Bedminster was confiscated.

Yet it was at this time that Robert the Bruce was marauding the Northern Borders of England and if there was one thing that the King needed as much as money it was good soldiers. It was therefore to the mutual advantage of both parishes to come to some agreement over this penalty. Accordingly the 1,000 mark fine was commuted in return for the supply by Lord Berkeley of ten armed horsemen under the command of his son or some other 'fit captayne'. The confiscation of the valuable Manor of Bedminster remained, however it was a severe blow to the Berkeleys, and they would do their utmost over the following years to secure its return.

For the next few years the Berkeleys made certain they were seen to be faithful allies to the crown. Father and son joined the fighting in the war against Scotland; Thomas himself was captured at Bannockburn but secured release with the payment of a ransom. Nearer home, Lord Thomas was sent to Bristol to enquire into a revolt over taxation that came to be known as 'the Great Insurrection'. Lord Thomas, not being the paragon of impartiality that the Bristolians had hoped for, was briefly held prisoner but later had the satisfaction of being a major force in the revolt's collapse by blockading the port of Bristol with his boats.

But even so, these displays of allegiance went unrewarded and by the end of Edward II's troubled reign the Berkeleys began to take a very different approach.

For the last few months of his life Edward II was deposed from the throne and held prisoner by his wife, Isabella, and her lover Mortimer. For a while the King was interned in Bristol but in the spring of 1327 he was escorted to Berkeley Castle for 'safe keeping'. Though tales of the manner of Edward's death vary they all have one element in common: extreme sadism. At Berkeley, Edward II was kept 'in a vault up to his knees in water, to which the channels of the castle run'. And it is told how, on a chill autumn night in 1327, the townsfolk of Berkeley were awoken from their sleep by terrible screams from the castle. Many 'prayed to God for the harmless soul which that night was departing in torture'. The next day Edward II was dead. His body, which is reputed to have had no outward signs of violence upon it, was buried some days later at Gloucester Cathedral.

Although the brutal deed occurred at Berkeley Castle, Lord Thomas (died 1361) was keen, not unnaturally, to be disassociated from it. He claimed to be ill at the time, six miles away at Bradley, near Wotton-under-Edge. He was so stricken that he said that he had lost his memory. This plea was subsequently accepted by Parliament and he was absolved of any involvement in the murder. However, Smyth, the Berkeleys' erudite historian, doubts this alibi and notes that Lord Thomas' recovery was swift, for on the day after the killing he was quick to send the news of the regicide to the treacherous Isabella and Mortimer.

Two years later, perhaps prompted by Isabella and Mortimer, the young King Edward III returned the Manor of Bedminster to the Berkeleys. After a twenty-five year lapse the Berkeleys were once again in control of their valued Redcliffe.

Southern Parishes United with Bristol

The administrative divide between north and south of what was now England's second largest town made little sense to anybody—apart from the Berkeleys and Templars, that is. Despite a charter of 1331[16], one of many which confirmed that Redcliffe should answer to the jurisdiction of Bristol, the Berkeleys determinedly held onto their loosely defined privileges.

On top of this Berkeley interference there were other problems. Merchants complained of arduous journeys through deep and dangerous roads to the county courts at Ilminster in Somerset and Gloucester. Such journeys could take two days each way and for those who had property on both sides of the Avon, matters could be even more tiresome.

So, the Mayor and people of Bristol, together with many merchants from the Southern Parishes, petitioned the King to resolve this hindrance to the smooth running of their businesses. With £400 on offer, a beleaguered Edward III, currently suffering financial hardship through war with France, was keen to listen. Though unprecedented, the answer to the merchants' problems was straightforward: turn Bristol and its dissenting suburbs of Redcliffe, Temple and St Thomas into a county in its own right. It would then hold its own courts and be governed by a body of its own councillors.

So the King sent letters patent to the Bishops of Bath and Wells and Worcester, and to the Abbots of Cirencester and Glastonbury and to six neighbouring gentry to pace the boundary and erect stones of demarcation. The ceremony was performed on September 30th, 1374 and the whole transaction ratified by Parliament two months later. The first Mayor of the new County of Bristol was William Canynges—a Redclivian.

The burgesses of Bristol had at last gained a resounding victory over the Lords of Berkeley, winning from them the rights of jurisdiction and assize that they had doggedly claimed for so long. It was a blow to the Berkeleys; with the forfeiture of Redcliffe and St Thomas it is claimed that they lost all chances of becoming one of the top ranking noble families in England. Yet Bristol's victory was not absolute. There was still one small, though niggling, thorn in the side of the new county—the Knights of St John of Jerusalem were to maintain independent control over Temple Fee for a good deal longer.

CHAPTER ONE: NOTES

1. J.F. Nichols and J. Taylor, *Bristol Past and Present* (Bristol, 1881), Vol 2, p.101
2. N. Dermott Harding (ed.), *Bristol Charters 1155-1373* (Bristol Record Society, 1930) p.4-5
3. S. Seyer, *Memoirs of Bristol* (Bristol, 1822) Vol 1, p.529
4. N. Dermott Harding, op cit, p.18-19
5. M. Hebditch, *Excavations on the Medieval Defences, Portwall Lane Bristol* (Bristol and Gloucestershire Archaeological Society) Vol 87, p.135
6. S. Seyer, *Memoirs of Bristol* (1823) Vol 11, p.38
7. Adams, *Chronicle of Bristol* (Bristol, 1910) p.21
8. J. Latimer, *Leland in Gloucestershire* (B.G.A.S., 1890) Vol 14, p.221
9. R. Macaulay, *They Went to Portugal* (Penguin, 1985) p.25
10. J. Leech, *The Rural Rides of the Bristol Church Goer* (Gloucester, 1982) p.88
11. B. Williams, *Excavations in the Medieval Suburb of Bristol* (Bristol, 1981) p.5
12. S. Seyer, op cit, p.143
13. J. Sherbourne, *William Canynges 1402-1474* (Bristol Branch of the Historical Association, 1985) p.3
14. S. Seyer, op cit, p.81
15. ibid, p.81
16. J. Latimer, *Bristol Charters* (1909) p.68

Other Sources
W. Hunt, *Bristol* (London, 1889)
J.W. Sherborne *Port of Bristol in the Middle Ages* (1965)
D. Walker, *Bristol in the Early Middle Ages* (1971)

2—The Great Merchants

The emergence of the woollen cloth trade was also accompanied by the rise of the great cloth merchants; wise and illustrious men such as Robert of Cheddar, Richard Le Spicer and, most famous of all, the Canynges family. They left an indelible mark, not only on the commercial records of Bristol, but also on the physical landscape.

The Canynges—no mere merchants but political figures whose influence spread as far as the King—were particularly associated with the Southern Parishes.

William (died 1396) and John Canynges (died c.1406) made their money mostly from the cloth trade—both producing cloth and selling it in the established markets of Ireland, Gascony and the Iberian Peninsula. William Canynges the Younger (1402-1474) was even bolder in his enterprise. At a time when trade was generally poor he made a very courageous move. According to James Sherbourne he withdrew from personal shipments of wine and cloth and took to using his own ships for transportation of the goods of others.[1] In other words he established his own shipping line. It was a gamble, but a gamble that paid off. By 1460 William Canynges the Younger had his own fleet of nine ships and was said to employ a colossal workforce of eight hundred people; one in eight of the adult population in Bristol was in Canynges' employ. He was involved in more trade in Northern Europe than anyone else in the country, dealing with the export of cloth, food and drink and the import of, among other things, dried and salted fish.

William Canynges the Younger was innovative in other ways. The pride of the Canynges' fleet was the giant 900 ton *Mary and John*, an absolute monster of a vessel when the average ship on the quay was only 200 tons.

The most successful merchants were also politicians. In Bristol they had to be if they were to get a fair share of the country's trade. William Canynges the Younger was five times Mayor of Bristol and twice represented the town in Parliament. Such was his power that when Henry VI pledged a protectionist treaty with the King of Denmark a special and unique licence was made excluding Canynges from the embargo.

We may know the names of Canynges' boats but of those who sailed in them we know nothing. This is one of the regrettable problems of medieval history: only a few exceptional characters are recorded—the everyday people, the mainstay of Bristol's maritime greatness, go unmentioned.

A unique and precise record does exist, however, of Bristol's medieval buildings. William of Worcester, a scholar who had been in the service of Sir John Falstaff, retired to Bristol and spent his last years recording in remarkable detail the fabric of the town. He must have appeared an eccentric figure pacing the streets, noting down in his little book the measurements of buildings, streets and even the bridge. He was obsessed by numbers, often to the exclusion of any aesthetic detail.

Although the Southern Parishes had been incorporated into Bristol in 1373, Redcliffe, Temple and St Thomas retained a character and spirit of their own. The Southern Parishes still had a rural feel about them—animals freely roamed the streets and once outside the town walls you were immediately in the king-cup meadows of Temple and Redcliffe Meads. And even within the walls there was still plenty of space. The bigger houses had gardens and orchards, some of which ran down to the river. It was not until 1470 that the busy main thoroughfares of Redcliffe, Temple, Thomas and Tucker Streets were paved; before this they would have been impossibly muddy during wet weather and dusty during dry. Most houses were timber framed structures filled in with wattle and daub and roofed with straw. There were exceptions though; the few people with money built with more permanent materials. Undoubtedly the most impressive private house in the Southern Parishes was William Canynges' residence in Redcliffe Street. Built of stone, it even broke away from the local vernacular styles by incorporating, as William of Worcester noted, 'baye wyndowes'.

The front rooms of Canynges' house looked out on Redcliffe Street, behind them stretched the great hall with its lofty roof supported on corbels carved in the shape of angels, and way beyond this, past two courtyards and many other rooms was a stone tower overlooking the river.[2] In an age when most buildings were of an insubstantial nature this one was made to last. Incredibly high up in a wall just off Redcliffe Street there remain today two small splayed windows that must once have belonged to this very house. Apart from bits and pieces of the old castle this wall of Canynges' house must be one of the earliest secular fragments of Bristol to survive to the present day. In fact much of the structure of Canynges house remained until the 1930s when in a shameless act of vandalism the Great Hall and other buildings were torn down. Fortunately the tiled floor, reputedly laid for a visit of Edward IV when he was a guest of Canynges in 1461, was saved and is now in the British Museum.

The Canynges were a rich family and, like their fellow merchants in such a God fearing age, were anxious to make donations towards philanthropic enterprises and ecclesiastical funds. After all, the dreadful pestilence of 1349 and its frequent recurrence was a constant reminder of God's omnipotence. The plague was interpreted by many as a sign of God's displeasure and it was conjectured that such charitable acts as church building and the endowment of almshouses might go some way to appease this wrath. Thus Richard Le Spicer established his almshouse just inside Temple Gate in the 1350s whilst Simon De Burton's almshouse opposite St Thomas's church in Long Row, founded in 1292, had already been long built. Somewhat less orthodox was Thomas Berkeley's quest for salvation. In 1347, he installed a hermit, John Sparkes, in a cave in Redcliffe Pit (the cave can still be seen in the Garden for the Blind) to pray for his redemption.

The Canynges family, along with other merchants, inaugurated a massive rebuilding scheme for St Mary Redcliffe. Over three generations the church was transformed from a small Norman chapel, an outlier of the Bedminster parish church, to the flower of perpendicular architecture, the 'pride of Bristowe and the Western land', that we know today.

The rebuilding in mellow Dundry stone started in earnest at the beginning of the fourteenth century when William Canynges the Elder and other citizens demolished most of the Norman structure and commenced the present building on the same site. The transformation took many years and evidence of a temporary roof indicates the suspension of the project for a while. In 1445 when the church was nearing completion there was a serious and most unexpected setback. During a violent thunderstorm the spire, nearly 300 feet of it, was struck by lightning. Blown by a strong west wind it came crashing down through the nave ruining a large part of the building. Rather than discourage Canynges this disaster merely inspired him to greater beneficence; he moved in a workforce of over one hundred people—masons, carpenters and labourers—to get on with the job. Eventually, the church was practically completed by 1480. The damaged nave was repaired but the steeple remained unfinished. For the next four hundred years the parishioners had to be content with merely a splendid gilded weathercock as a crown to the church's sadly truncated spire.

The church of St Thomas the Martyr was also closely connected with the Canynges family. Several generations of the family were buried there. The church itself—not the one we have today—was described by William Barrett as 'next to Redcliffe, the largest as well as the most elegant building'.[3] This was no mean compliment. Unfortunately we have little other evidence to confirm Barrett's opinion as no detailed or specific picture of

Above: St. Mary Redcliffe: for four hundred years the parishioners had to be content with a sadly truncated spire.

Right: The tomb of William Canynges (1402-1474), St. Mary Redcliffe Church. Canynges, a nationally influential merchant, was said to have employed over 800 people. *M. Manson.*

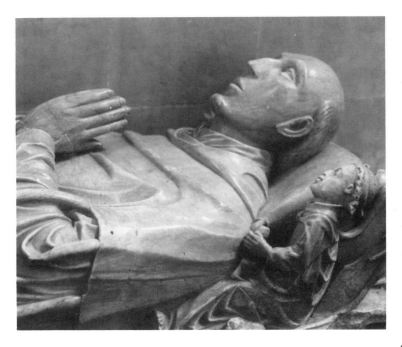

the early church survives.

William Canynges died, leaving no direct heir, six years before the building work on St Mary Redcliffe was concluded. His life being inextricably linked with St Mary Redcliffe, it comes as no surprise that his death in 1474, at the age of 72, is commemorated in the church. What is unusual though is that his memory is marked by not one altar tomb but two. Both tombs are placed in the south transept: one depicts Canynges in mayoral robes lying next to his wife, whilst the other represents him in the clothes of a priest. He has the features, wrote Bryan Little, 'of a Quaker business man . . . a devout and austere cleric.'[4]

The two tombs can be explained easily, as for the last seven years of his life Canynges turned his back on the world of commerce and sought holy orders. Records indicate that within days of the death of his wife, Joan, he entered the priesthood. One small shadow, however, hangs over the details of this retirement. In Ricart's Calendar there is a curious entry which states '. . . Mr Canynges should have been married by the King's command wherefore he in all haste took orders . . .'[5] This is indeed strange for apart from the Calendar which was written a long time after the event no other record exists to support this statement. Without further evidence it is perhaps best to take the view of the Victorian historian, Dallaway and dismiss this part of Ricart's writing as merely 'a silly tradition of malicious rumour'.

William Canynges eventually became Dean of Westbury College, a few miles north of Bristol. (It was from Westbury that the more austere of the two Redcliffe tombs came, being transferred when the college was dissolved in 1544.) It was a fitting retirement for someone who had publicly led such a devout life. And even today the event is commemorated in St Mary Redcliffe at Whitsun by the charming Rush Sunday service.

Decline of the Woollen Industry

The impetus of growth of the woollen manufacturing industry in the Southern Parishes did not last. As elsewhere in England, the woollen industry in Bristol was moving to the countryside where it could escape the stifling control of the guilds and also take advantage in Gloucestershire of the swift running water of the steep sided Cotswold valleys. This slow demise was a reflection of what was happening nationally to urban cloth manufacture.

But not only was the industry deserting the parishes of Redcliffe, Temple and St Thomas. In 1453 there was also a major shift of market when England lost its long cherished hold on Gascony. From then on the merchants of Bristol had to seek out new customers in Spain and Portugal. Luckily both these areas, like Gascony, produced strong wines to which the English palate was partial and which could be imported in return for the export of cloth.

Apart from the Iberian Peninsula, the loss of Gascony encouraged Bristolians to look even further afield for new markets. Through their voyages to Iceland they were as familiar with the tempestuous Atlantic as anybody else—it therefore seemed entirely natural that they should turn their attention to the mysteries of what lay beyond and try to discover a new way to the riches of the Orient.

As Spain, by treaty, had already annexed the Southern Hemisphere all explorers from England had to sail northwards.

In reality the finding of the new world must have been a bewildering disappointment. What the Genoese John Cabot and his Bristol-born son Sebastian found when they got to the other side of the Atlantic Ocean in 1497—one year before Christopher Columbus discovered South America—was a damp, misty, altogether uninviting continent. The navigators came back to Bristol not with valuable spices but with more cod—and also little immediate chance of a new market for the cloth industry. In Bristol's case the important discoveries of the New World were slow to bear fruit.

The loss of the woollen cloth market was, however, only a temporary setback. Trading relations were soon re-established when the Gascons realised that they needed a market for their wines as much as the West Country needed a market for their cloth. In fact by the end of the fifteenth century, Bristol was exporting three times as much cloth as in the period 1400-1420.[6] The difference was, however, that little of this cloth came from the Southern Parishes. The cloth market may have re-established itself, but in the process, right across the country, it had moved its manufacturing base from the towns to the countryside.

Reformation of the Church

Changes were also being brought about through the reformation of the church. This reformation, which had been going on for many years—the Protestant leader Latimer is reported to have preached in St Thomas church in 1528—was hastened by Henry VIII's own personal dispute with Rome. As Bristol was virtually surrounded by ecclesiastical land, Henry VIII's dissolution of the monasteries between 1536 and 1540 opened up new opportunities for development. The Parliament of 1540 passed, with little opposition, a bill that granted to the King all the lands, goods and houses of the abbeys, priories, nunneries and chantries that had been, or were about to be suppressed. Subsequently Henry VIII—ever short of money due to his extravagant and fruitless campaigns in France—sold these for knock-down prices. In South Bristol the Corporation, though lacking in funds, was keen to buy the Hospital of St John in Redcliffe Pit, just outside Redcliffe Gate.

St John's Hospital, founded by the Berkeleys in the late twelfth century for the aid of the sick and the dying, was a small establishment of a hall, cloisters with a fountain fed by the Redcliffe pipe and outbuildings. It had a somewhat uneventful history. Perhaps its main claim to fame was that Henry VI stayed there whilst visiting Bristol in 1446. Although merely a stone's throw across the road from St Mary Redcliffe its connections with the fine church are limited. St Mary Redcliffe was in the diocese of Salisbury whilst St John's Hospital came under the control of the Bishop of Wells. A strict agreement was made between the Hospital and St Mary Redcliffe that they should not poach each other's clientele.[7]

The Corporation was not immediately able to purchase St John's Hospital as Henry VIII had already granted it to his physician, George Owen. In 1553, however, Dr Owen granted a 99 year lease to the Corporation of numerous houses across the city belonging to the hospital and some time later granted them the hospital itself.

The Dissolution had other, more unexpected effects. For a start it put an end to the long disputed independence of Temple Fee. Even as late as 1532 the Corporation of Bristol, claiming that Temple Fee was a lawless area and a refuge for outlaws, had been contesting the authority of the Knights of St John of Jerusalem to exercise a jurisdiction independent of the city of Bristol. This trouble with the Knights came to an abrupt end with the dissolution.

More surprising, perhaps, was what happened to St Thomas Church. It had to change its name. By statute it was ordered that 'St Thomas of Canterbury should not be esteemed or called a saint; that all images of him should be destroyed, the festival in his honour be abolished, and his name and remembrance be erased out of all books under pain of his majesty's indignation and imprisonment at his grace's pleasure'.[8] Accordingly by 1566 we find that Apostle has been substituted for Martyr.

Poverty and Plague

The disbandment of St John's Hospital was yet another blow for the poor of South Bristol. By 1570, it was written that: 'The houses, structures and edifices are reduced to such a state of ruin and decay to the great nuisance to that part of the city; and the late inhabitants being forced by want, through the decay in their trade in making woollen cloths have suffered their homes to go to ruin; and that a certain almshouse situated near the said street for the support of many poor, and also a certain canal or pipe of water situated there which beyond the memory of man has been supported and maintained by the said inhabitants, are now in such a state on account of their poverty, that in a short time they will come to extreme ruin, if a remedy is not provided . . .'[9]

So Simon De Burton's almshouse was becoming dilapidated and perhaps more serious, the conduit, St Thomas' main source of water, was in bad repair. This decline is clearly emphasised in the parish returns of 1544 and 1574 which show a predominant position of wealth in the central parishes of Bristol to the north of the bridge. The Southern Parishes were no longer fashionable; there was a feeling of malaise in the air; the days when the wealthy merchants clamoured to live to the south of the Avon were long gone.

What could be done to revitalise the area? By 1570 matters were so bad that the Corporation took the very positive step of introducing a weekly market to strengthen the parishes' economy. The market, to be held on Thursdays, was for the sale of 'yarn cloth, cattle and all other things whatsoever'. With the money generated by it, it was expected that the parish of St Thomas 'may be better able to support and maintain' its houses, its almshouses and its conduit.

The grant of a market expressed a radical change in the thinking of the Corporation. Only thirty years before, extreme disapproval had been shown of another trading venture, the Candlemas Fair at Redcliffe. This fair had been held for thirteen years when the traditional rivalries between north and south brought it to an end. The people of the northern parishes complained, probably with some justification, that traders were only coming to the town at Candlemas to avoid tolls that would have been paid at any other time. Despite a petition of support bearing 629 signatures to the Star Chamber the Mayor had his way and in 1542 the Candlemas Fair was abandoned.[10]

However, after the tariff on gate-entry was abolished in 1546, the St Thomas market was looked upon as less of a threat and, indeed, became a more permanent affair; it was held regularly every Thursday until 1840 when it was transferred to Temple Meads.

Once the market was established, the vestry of the church got to work to build a rudimentary shelter for some of the more perishable products. A flat topped roof supported by stone pillars was constructed along the eastern side of the church of St Thomas. Many years later in 1691 four posts with brass caps upon them—similar to the famous and supposedly unique Nails in Corn Street—were donated for the telling of money.[11]

Although the Tudor era is generally regarded as the end of the Middle Ages and the dawn of modern times it is doubtful whether the people of the Southern Parishes noticed any such difference. The plague certainly had lost none of its potency and its occurrence

Simon De Burton's Almshouses. One of Bristol's earliest almshouses established in 1292 for the relief of 16 poor or aged women. By 1570 the almhouses were described as being in such a bad state of repair 'that in a short time they will come to extreme ruin if a remedy is not provided'. The buildings survived, however, until the blitz of 1940.
City of Bristol Museum and Art Gallery.

was just as frequent. There are records of its presence in Bristol in 1544, 1551, 1564, 1574 and at the beginning of the seventeenth century it appeared in Bristol five times in only eight years. Obviously the authorities were keen to take steps to avoid the spread of this dreadful pestilence, but with limited knowledge of medical science it was difficult. It was believed that the plague was carried by tiny creatures which infected the air making it denser than normal; dirty, dark and damp places were where these creatures could be found. To dispel the infection, enormous fires were lit in the streets, bells rung and cannons discharged to break up the density of the air. Precautions against the plague such as the wearing of amulets, the carrying of nosegays and the anointing of houses with oil were popular. It was advisable to remain cheerful at all times whilst music to dispel bad dreams was also recommended.

Fortunately there was at least some concept of quarantine—though not through any sound scientific reason. Travellers from areas of the country known to be affected were subjected, along with their possessions, to a lengthy 'air' before admission to the city. The house of anyone infected by plague was boarded up—with the occupants still inside. Those confined were given charitable relief and fed at the expense of the city. A watchman was also stationed outside to prevent entrance or exit. A cutler of St Thomas Street who contracted the illness in 1603 was accordingly imprisoned in such a manner. This course of action was unpopular and mostly ineffective. Householders were slow to report cases of infection and, indeed, would often disappear elsewhere before the outbreak was discovered by the authorities. Consequently the plague spread even further afield.

The beginning of the seventeenth century also brought with it the additional problems of particularly severe weather conditions. In 1606 there was an enormous flood when the lower part of the city was inundated. In Redcliffe, Temple and Thomas streets the water was as 'high as mens girdles', and in Temple and Thomas churches it was 'half way up the seats'.[12] At Treen Mills, (now the site of the Bathurst Basin) where the Malago Stream, or Bedminster Brook as it was then known, entered the Avon, the flood water was five feet deep. The following winter the whole country was gripped by a severe and prolonged frost. Unlike the Thames which at Westminster froze right over, the Avon with its large tidal fall remained free flowing. The streets however were slippery and dangerous. 'During this frost everyman was forced to strew stonecoal ashes before their doors to save the men and horses from falling; and the mayor sent about the bellman to command everyman to dig up ice and snow and cast it upon heaps and haul it away and over the Backe and the Quay'.[13]

In spite of the efforts of the Thomas Street market, hardship continued. Bristol had an additional problem with vagrants who came across the sea from Ireland looking for work. Every so often these sturdy beggars were rounded up, caged in the Newgate Goal and then shipped back to their mother country in 'a drove'.

Although the Irish vagrants were treated harshly there was a more sympathetic approach for the local poor. Vagrancy and poverty were national problems in the Tudor period. There was, however, a new more enlightened approach as it was beginning to be understood that poor relief was not just encumbent on charities and the church but on society as a whole. The law was beginning to recognise that there were different categories of poor—the sick, the old, the insane or those just temporarily down on their luck. In 1601 a new statute relating to poor relief was introduced which specified that overseers for the poor in every parish were to buy material to provide work for the unemployed. This statute was implemented locally in 1617 and 1618 when the Corporation opened a house in Temple Street for the employment of children in the manufacture of Kersey.

Statue of Elizabeth I in St. Mary Redcliffe. On her visit to Bristol in 1574 the Queen confirmed what every Redclivian had always known—that their church was the fairest in the land.

M. Manson.

Visit of Queen Elizabeth I

Poverty, plague and climatic hardship aside, there were times for celebration. One such occasion was the visit of Queen Elizabeth to the city in 1574. Although we know that the parish of St Thomas—amongst others—was down at heel this did not hinder the Corporation from pulling out all the stops to entertain the monarch. An unprecedented £1,000 was spent on the preparations, pageants and decorations; £200 of this being spent on gunpowder alone.

The roads were sanded and repaired, burgesses were given new uniforms and preparations were made for the novelty of the visit, the mock battle which was to be held on the Addercliffe (now the site of Redcliffe Parade) and below at Treen Mills. The entertainments were coordinated by the enthusiastic John Churchyard who saw to it that the Queen was met wherever she went by young men who would welcome her in elaborate verse. The Elizabethan age is justly famed for its lyrical verse, but unfortunately, in the words of John Latimer, this was 'tedious rhymned twaddle'. Indeed the speeches were delivered with more enthusiasm than they were received: several of the young orators were cut off in mid soliloquy on the pretext that time was short.

The undisputed highlight of the visit, however, was the staging of the mock battle on the scrubby Addercliffe. A scaffold was built across the river on the edge of the Marsh (now Queen Square) for viewing and over an exhausting three day period a war was waged. In fact it was enacted with such ferocity that several of the participants were injured. The battle was not only a display of military prowess, it also contained an allegorical message for Her Majesty with regards her dealings with the Spanish—a fort called 'Feble Pollecie' was quickly attacked and demolished. In later years, when there was a real threat of a Spanish invasion, Addercliffe was used for the more serious purpose of mustering able bodied men in readiness for attack by the Armada.

With all the excitement engendered by the royal visit it would seem that the care taken in the storage of the gunpowder to be used in the mock battle was somewhat slipshod. A day before the Queen's arrival some of the explosives, which were being kept at the Pelican Inn in St Thomas Street, ignited. In the explosion that followed five people were killed, another ten injured and the inn devastated. Further mishaps followed; 'about as many men were likewise burned by misfortune with gunpowder at Treene Mills'.

Apart from the accidents, the Queen's visit was a popular success. Surprisingly, it is by a casual remark attributed to Queen Elizabeth that she is most remembered in Bristol today. For in one sentence the Monarch confirmed what every true Redclivian had always believed: that their church, St Mary's, was the 'fairest, godliest and most famous Parish Church in England'.

CHAPTER TWO: NOTES

1. J. Sherborne, *William Canynges* (Bristol, 1985) p.9
2. J. Dallaway, *Antiquities of Bristol* (Bristol, 1834) p.145-146
3. W. Barrett, *The History and the Antiquities of Bristol* (1789), p.558
4. B. Little, *City and County of Bristol* (Bristol, 1954) p.85
5. Adams *Chronicle of Bristol* (Bristol, 1910) p.70
6. J. Sherborne, *The Port of Bristol in the Middle Ages* (Bristol, 1971) p.21-22
7. G. Parker, *The History of the Hospital of St John the Baptist, Redcliff Pit* (Bristol, 1925)
8. J. F. Nichols and J. Taylor *Bristol Past and Present* (Bristol, 1882) Vol 2, p.230-232
9. W. Barrett, op. cit, p.565
10. Jean Vanes, *The Port of Bristol in the Sixteenth Century* p.19
11. W. Barrett, op. cit, p.565
12. S. Seyer, *Memoirs of Bristol,* (1823) Vol 2, p.260
13. Adams, op. cit, p.183-184

Other Sources

J. Evans, *A Chronological Outline of the History of Bristol* (Bristol, 1924)

J. Latimer, *Sixteenth Century Bristol* (Bristol, 1908)

R. Latham, *Bristol Charters—1509-1899* (Bristol, 1947)

M. D. Lobel, E. M. Carus-Wilson, *Bristol* (London, 1975)

K. G. Ponting, *The Woollen Industry of South West England* (Bath 1971)

E. N. Simmons, *Into Unknown Waters: John and Sebastian Cabot* (London, 1964)

3—The Invincible Portwall

It was more by quirk of fate than design that Bristol found itself in support of the Parliamentary cause at the beginning of the Civil War. Indeed, like much of the country, the city would have preferred to stay neutral, for what use was a civil war—a war of ideas at that—to the merchants and traders of Bristol?

However, the protagonists of the war thought otherwise. Bristol, as second city in the country, would be of vital importance to whoever finally ruled England. The city was far too influential to be left alone.

So, with the arrival in Bristol of Colonel Essex, a Parliamentary figurehead and Governor of Gloucester, a neutral stance was no longer possible. Essex and his army marched into Bristol in 1642 and, with little opposition and no bloodshed, the city found itself host to the Roundhead garrison. For Bristol the Civil War was just beginning.

By the following spring, as the King's followers gained strength in the West Country, it became obvious that the city would soon be under attack. Preparations were made for the defence of the city. In the Southern Parishes cannons were mounted at strategic positions; Temple Gate and the eastern most bastion, Tower Harratz, had fourteen cannons between them, whilst in the vicinity of Redcliffe there were another fifteen. To the north of the Avon, however, the fortifications were more haphazard. Colonel Fiennes, the new Governor who had taken over from Colonel Essex who had been found to be drunk and unreliable, reluctantly admitted that 'Bristol was one of the hardest towns to be fortified'.

On Sunday July 23rd, Prince Rupert, the 24-year old nephew of King Charles, and his army set up quarters a couple of miles outside the city, at Westbury-on-Trym.

A little before dawn on the following Wednesday the attack on the city began. The Cornish Royalists were assigned the unenviable task of assailing the Portwall. They began their thrust at 3.00am—earlier than planned; an act that has been interpreted by some as eagerness but by others as dissatisfaction with being allocated such a difficult task. It was a short but determined attack. Against all odds the Cornishmen fought with 'a courage and resolution that nothing but death can control'.[1] Their first task was to fill the defensive ditch by driving carts into it. But the ditch proved deeper than expected, it was only at Temple Gate that some of the assailants were able to mount the city wall and even then they were quickly repelled. After half an hour of fighting, when 'the bodies lay on the ground like rotten sheep',[2] the Cornishmen retreated under a hail of bullets and stones to the safety of the hedgerows of Temple and Redcliffe Meads. Their losses were needlessly high as across the city, to the north of the river, the defences, although proving stronger than expected, with time were inevitably breached.

Thankfully there were no large scale massacres with the fall of the city—this was perhaps a reflection of the lack of commitment by Bristolians to any one side. Relationships between Royalists and Parliamentarians were as cordial as the conditions of war would permit. Indeed, the city fathers were as much concerned by the empty ships in the harbour and the loss of trade as they were with anything else. 'The governing body' as Patrick McGrath wrote 'would have preferred to adopt a policy of non involvement. When this proved impossible it cooperated without much fuss with whatever garrison occupied the city'.[3]

Certainly with the fall of Bristol to the Royalists there were no reported atrocities. But there was plundering. The shops on the bridge suffered most with the excuse that shopkeepers there harboured a particular hatred for the cavaliers.

The surrender of Bristol was seen as 'a fulltide of prosperity for the King'. But the victory cost him dear: 500 men fell in the assault.

The King's good fortune was short lived. Victory at Bristol was followed by a disastrous and unsuccessful siege at Gloucester. From then onwards the Royalists lost ground and by June 1645, after the battle of Naseby, the King held only the West of England. By the end of July, when the Royalists had lost Somerset and hardly had a field army to speak of, the capture of Bristol was seen by the Parliamentarians as a foregone conclusion.

Prince Rupert, however, had other ideas and certainly hoped that Bristol would evade capture. Since Fiennes' defeat Prince Rupert's garrison of 4,500 men had worked hard to improve the city's fortifications. In a letter to the King he felt confident enough to state that he had provisions and ammunition to last a long siege, Moreover, with the unseasonal wet and cold weather he knew that the morale of the Roundheads was low. To play on their low spirits Prince Rupert harrassed the besiegers with sudden attacks on their dispersed forces. One of several such spirited forays by the Cavaliers was a sally from Temple Gate into the Roundheads' Bedminster Camp; the Parliamentarians were caught unawares with ten people killed and a similar number taken hostage.

On September 6th, Cromwell dined in the fields near St Mary Redcliffe and reconnoitred the strong southern defences. To attract as little attention as possible the soldiers were ordered not to salute their general.

Bristol's defences—stretching four miles in all—might have been strengthened by Rupert's army, but the northern fortifications, twisting up and down the hills required a large number of solidiers to cover them adequately. Knowing this Cromwell and Fairfax decided upon a swift all out attack rather than a lengthy siege.

For over two weeks Prince Rupert played for time with hesitant negotiations, but by September 9th, Cromwell could stand the procrastination no longer and ordered the attack to begin at one in the morning of the following day.

Despite the obvious invincibility of the Portwall the attack upon it was fierce. Three 'forlorn hopes', each of two hundred men, were to lead the storm. This time the attackers brought ladders to scale the walls, but they misjudged the height and the ladders proved too short. They were quickly repulsed with a loss of one hundred men. Predictably the earth works to the north of the city proved to be the weak link and by evening Prince Rupert had surrendered.

The surrender was negotiated in a most gentlemanly manner. Rupert and his army were allowed to leave Bristol and were given eight days' freedom of passage to a garrison of their own choice. On the next day, September 11th, Rupert left the Royal Fort at Kingsdown for Oxford with '8 lords in his company, 500 horse and 1400 foot with their muskets and other arms'.[4] Fairfax accompanied him for two miles over Durdham Down and 'treated him with great courtesy'.[5]

The loss of Bristol to the Roundheads, in reality, indicated the end of the King's fight for England. Incensed at his nephew's conduct and overwhelmed by the loss, Charles wrote to Rupert reproaching him for 'submitting to so mean an action'. The King reminded Rupert of his letter 'whereby you assured me that if no mutiny happened you would keep Bristol for four months. Did you keep it four days? Was there anything like a mutiny?'[6] The King concluded his letter by dismissing Rupert from his service and ordering him to quit the country.

When Cromwell and Fairfax entered Bristol they were surprised by what they saw. With a large number of soldiers garrisoned in the city conditions had deteriorated. The plague had also been raging for some months. 'It looked more like a prison than a city and the people more like prisoners than citizens being brought so low by taxation, so poor in habit and so dejected in countenance; the streets so noisome and the houses so nasty that they were unfit to receive friends or freemen until they were cleansed.'[7]

With the fighting over, soldiers from the garrison visited the parish churches and destroyed what they called 'idolatrous sculpture'.[8] Included in the term was stained glass; in St Mary Redcliffe this was almost entirely smashed. Organs, which were also seen as 'objects illegal in the worship of God' were pulled down. The organ pipes of St Mary Redcliffe were carried through the streets and blown as trumpets.

Meanwhile, Prince Rupert followed the King to Newark, where he appealed against his expulsion from the country. A council of war subsequently found the Prince not guilty of treachery or cowardice but censured him for negligence.

The King surrendered in May 1646—he was beheaded in London before a silent crowd on January 30th, 1649.

Solemnity and Seriousness

Although the 1640s and 1650s were a period of expanding horizons for Bristol's overseas trade, at home there was a contraction of freedoms and a stifling of many activities that had always been taken for granted. This was the age of the Puritan: 'a narrow spirited, bigoted and fanatical age' when Bristolians found that many of their pleasures were banned or made illegal. It was a time of solemnity and seriousness; profane language was punishable by the stocks, Christmas Day was for fasting and to walk on the Sabbath, even to collect water, was a crime.

Puritan bigotry was at its worst when it came to the toleration of other religious groups. Indicative of these feelings was a bill read in Parliament in September 1646 stating that Unitarians and heretics could be put to death and Baptists and other sectarians jailed. In Bristol, the Quakers were constantly harrassed. Particularly distressing was the treatment of the 'mad messiah', James Naylor.

Before his arrival in Bristol, Naylor had been touring the West Country claiming to be a reincarnation of Christ. Although obviously mentally disturbed he was a charismatic figure and attracted a group of dedicated supporters. When Naylor arrived in Bristol in 1646, to the horror of the Puritan leaders, he was met at Redcliffe Gate by cries of rejoicing and hosannas. He was promptly arrested and sent to London to be tried for blasphemy. To the Puritans his guilt was in no doubt; difficulties arose, however, in devising a suitable chastisement. Finally, after thirteen days' deliberation, a sentence was declared which though it avoided execution was as cruel and gruesome as can be imagined. Two hours in the pillory at Westminster was to be followed by Naylor having his tongue severed through with a red hot iron and his forehead branded with a B. And this was only the beginning: he was then to be sent to Bristol to ride through the streets bare back and be whipped in St Thomas Street market and other parts of the city. Finally, it was proposed that he be returned to London and earn his living by hard labour in solitary confinement.

This punishment, authorised by Parliament without a voice raised against it, shocked the people of Bristol. The Mayor and other influential citizens presented a petition for remission but it was to no avail and the sentence was carried out.[9]

James Naylor claimed to belong to the Quakers, one of the new religious groups that arose out of the spiritual fervour engendered around the time of the Civil War. Very simply the Quakers advocated an absolutely spiritual approach to God unhindered by all the earthly trappings that went with the established church. Churches and priests, they argued, only served to distract attention away from, rather than focus on God. The

The Mad Messiah. James Naylor, sentenced in 1646 to have his tongue severed with a red hot iron, his forehead branded with a B and then whipped through the streets.

foundation of Quakerism is dated to 1652 and is first recorded in Bristol in 1654. From that date onwards the city became a centre for Quakerism in the South West. A perturbed commentator wrote in 1660: 'these monsters are more numerous in Bristol than the rest of the West Country, and hold meetings of 1,000 or 1,200 to the great alarm of the city'.

Though not officially outlawed during the period of the Commonwealth, the Quakers' strict lifestyle, their hatred of hypocrisy, their emotional and outspoken behaviour and their so-called lack of respect for authority made them targets for attack. Certainly the Quakers' popularity was hardly increased by their compulsion to interrupt Anglican church services and harangue both the 'hireling' priests, as they called them, and the congregation. Matters were also not helped by the brazen arrival in Bristol of the deranged James Naylor. Consequently, as the Quakers went about the city, they were, in the words of a contemporary writer (1660) 'openly abused, reproached, dirtied, stoned, pinched, kicked and grossly injured'.[10] It is as well to remember, however, that half a century before they would have been burnt at the stake.

Some Quakers, like William Penn, the son of Admiral Sir William Penn went to America to find their peace—many more stayed in England.

Although the Quakers held no formal church services they did need accommodation for their meetings. So they established a Meeting House first of all in 1656 to the North of the Avon, in Broadmead, and then another in 1667 in Temple Street. They also purchased land in 1665 for a burial ground in Redcliffe Pit (still there, a quiet, secluded spot below the Coliseum Pub on Redcliffe Hill).

Of course a society of strict conformity such as there was during the Commonwealth era must have its releases. One such safety valve was provided by the traditional festivals which offered a time of institutionalised disorder. Of these, the Shrove Tuesday festivities were celebrated with particular glee; whatever was lacking in the even more austere days of Lent was emphasised in that day's revelries. Amongst the most popular customs of the day were the sadistic games of cock throwing and dog tossing. Indeed, on Shrove Tuesday, it was dangerous to walk down some of the streets for fear of being hit by the shower of missiles flung at hapless cocks. These birds were tied by the leg and anyone willing to pay a penny was allowed to throw, from a distance, a stick or stone at it, the bird being theirs if it was killed. The nature of dog tossing is even more obscure. The diarist Samuel Pepys wrote in 1666 about dogs being tossed by bulls and commented that 'it is a very rude and nasty pleasure'. The present day substitute of a pancake is certainly preferable.

Needless to say, the Puritans found these Shrove Tuesday revelries offensive and in 1655 tried to ban them. The prohibition was ignored, however, and the 'sports' continued as usual. Equally ineffectual was a renewed ban in 1660. When the bellman attempted on March 5th (the day before Shrove Tuesday) to announce the outlawing of the 'sport' he was set upon, beaten up and had the livery torn off his back. But the next day the law was obeyed to the very letter. Certainly there was no cock throwing or dog tossing—for the animals had been changed to hens, geese, cats and bitches. The youths took particular delight in their hen throwing and bitch tossing carrying on with their fun directly outside the Mayor's house. A sheriff who tried to put a stop to this insult had his 'head broken for his labour'.[11]

Although the illegal celebrations were a minor protest they nevertheless indicate a growing disenchantment with the Puritan regime.

Nationally there was a feeling that Parliamentary rule must soon come to an end. Oliver Cromwell had died in 1658 and his son, Tumbledown Dick as he was called, proved an unworthy successor. The belief was slowly growing that the country would be safer in the hands of a monarch responsible to Parliament rather than armies answerable only to themselves.

So, just two months after the Shrove Tuesday riots, Charles II was rapturously welcomed off the ship, the *Naseby*, at Dover and a few days later proclaimed as King in London. For the first time in twenty years the people of England looked forward to a new found security. At least one thing was quickly restored to normal: having held their tongues for so long the people were once again able to give voice to strong language without fear of reprisal. Even Pepys, a man not noted for mincing his words, described the New Parliament of 1661 as 'the most profane, swearing fellows that I have ever heard in my life'.

On the other hand, Bristolians had found much that was admirable in the strict Puritan way of life: the dedication to hard work and the seriousness of intent were features that were attractive to Bristolian businessmen and were not to be quickly abandoned.

Bristol's Forgotten Hero

Accompanying Charles II on the *Naseby* on his triumphant return to England in 1660 was Admiral Sir William Penn—one of the most distinguished Bristolians of the seventeenth century.

Born in Bristol and christened in St Thomas Church, Penn joined the Navy at an early age and by the time he was 21 was captain of his own ship. In his portrait that hangs in the Painted Hall at Greenwich his looks—he was short, round faced, and sandy haired—belie his ambition. His rise through the ranks was meteoric and his career far reaching. Penn fought the Dutch in the North Sea (he was also commander of the troops, the only man ever to hold the dual role of Admiral and General), he hunted the exiled Prince Rupert in the Mediterranean and climaxed his career in the West Indies where, in a stunning and bloodless victory, he annexed Jamaica as an English Colony.

Although during the Civil War Penn was seen to support the Parliamentary side this was due more to his scheming ambition than to any personal commitment to Roundhead ideals. As he was to prove in later life, Penn was always a Royalist at heart.

The tale of Penn's battle with the Dutch under the command of Admiral Blake is in the best swashbuckling tradition. When the Dutch Admiral Van Tromp fixed a broom to the mast of his ship to imply that he would sweep the English fleet from the Channel, Penn retaliated by hoisting a riding whip above the rigging to warn the Dutch that they were due for a good thrashing. It was not an idle threat; after three days' fight the Dutch were beaten.

It was with the capture of Jamaica that Penn really made his mark. The assault upon the island was, in fact, an afterthought. Admiral Penn and the commander of the troops, General Venables, had been dispatched to 'assault the spaniard' on Hispaniola (now Haiti). Though Penn carried out his duties as required, Venables bungled his part and the English force withdrew from Hispaniola empty handed.

Fearing an ignominious return to England after such a profitless venture, Penn and Venables focused their attention on Jamaica. This island was far easier prey. On May 16th, 1655 Penn sailed into what is now known as Kingston Harbour and within a week, with only minor skirmishes, the island was captured. After staying six weeks to see that good order had been established, Penn and Venables set off to England hopeful of a hero's welcome.

City of Bristol Museum and Art Gallery

Part of James Millerd's map of 1673. Many houses still had gardens and orchards.

The capture of Jamaica, a sugar island which was soon to be a crucial base for the expansion of trade through the West Indies, was an important colonial triumph for both Bristol and the country as a whole. But far from receiving acclamation on their return, Penn and Venables were unexpectedly imprisoned in the Tower of London. Why? Had Cromwell discovered Penn's royalist tendencies? Was it because of the failure to capture Hispaniola? Or was it, perhaps, to cool the heels of both Penn and Venables who had had a personal dispute during the trip. The reason for the arrest has never been made clear.

Penn was detained in the Tower for six weeks and on release promptly retired from public life to his estate in Ireland. From there, no doubt provoked by his harsh treatment, he opened up correspondence with the royalists.

With the restoration of the monarchy in 1660 Charles II knighted Penn in gratitude for his support and also appointed him as commissioner for the Navy. In Penn's employ at the Admiralty was no less a person than Samuel Pepys. It has to be said that Pepys had a low regard for Penn, but the diarist, being an ambitious man himself, found it to his advantage to keep relations as cordial as possible. In his diary however, Pepys never misses a chance to vilify the Admiral. He frequently describes Penn as a 'false rogue' or a 'very villain' and constantly complains of his tightfistedness. Pepys wrote that the food at Penn's house was of miserly proportions and on one memorable occasion he was served by Penn with 'a damned venison pasty that stank like a devil'.[12]

It wasn't only Pepys who disliked Penn. Although the fruits of his victories were popular, Penn as a man was not. This was especially so in Bristol. Indeed he failed to be elected as member of Parliament for the city in 1660 and after his death, at the age of 49, in 1670, the Bristol Corporation refused to participate in his funeral ceremony at St Mary Redcliffe.

Naval historians rank Penn's achievements alongside those of Nelson, Blake and Rodney, yet today the City of Bristol does little to honour his memory. The only tangible reminders of this eminent Bristolian are his trophies—rotting flags, gauntlets and an age-blackened breast plate that is reputed to have been worn by Penn during the capture of Jamaica—which hang largely forgotten, high up in the nave of St Mary Redcliffe.

Monmouth threatens Bristol . . . Executions on Redcliffe Hill

The ill-fated West Country of 1685 was far from glorious; indeed, today it is remembered more than anything else for the retribution that followed.

With the intention of wresting the crown from the widely disliked James II, the Duke of Monmouth landed in Lyme Bay on June 11th, 1685. Already popular from previous exploits in the west, Monmouth, a bastard son of Charles II, was enthusiastically received during his march from the Dorset coast to Taunton. There, after a triumphant entry into the town, he was proclaimed King. From Taunton he moved to Bridgwater, and then on to Glastonbury, Wells and Shepton Mallet. The local support and loyalty that the dashing Duke received was remarkable; such dedication was unlike anything seen before—even during the years of the Civil War. All along the way his army swelled with excited volunteers, but despite this encouraging support Monmouth was perturbed. Few influential people had joined his cause. In reality his army comprised a peasant rabble.

Monmouth knew that if he was to hold any real influence in the West he would have to capture Bristol. This he was told would be an easy victory for he had been assured that there were thousands of sympathisers within the city.

There was little point in approaching Bristol from the south as the Portwall fortifications were known through the experience of the Civil War to be strong enough to withstand the most powerful attack. It was therefore decided to circumambulate the city and advance from the north. Ignorant of this plan the Duke of Beaufort had drawn up his troops outside Redcliffe Gate in readiness for battle. Suddenly, a pall of smoke was seen rising from the Quay. A ship was burning, the handiwork, it was surmised, of Monmouth's partisans. Equal to such skulduggery, the Duke of Beaufort forbade any of his men to leave their posts to fight the fire in case it was a diversion. Furthermore, to show that he meant business, he declared that if any insurrection was attempted by the inhabitants he would personally see that the city was incinerated about their ears.

Beaufort need not have worried, as evidence suggests that the burning boat was an accident unrelated to the revolt. Monmouth, meanwhile, was still pondering his plans whilst camped several miles away at Keynsham. On the night of June 24th, whilst Monmouth's forces were idling, a small group of horseguards dashed into the camp and caused a general panic amongst the bucolic insurgents. This minor attack was the first real resistance that Monmouth had encountered, yet it so disturbed him that he lost his nerve and abandoned his half hearted designs on Bristol.

So Monmouth's disillusioned army straggled back to Bridgwater. On July 6th, the rebels, equipped largely with makeshift weapons such as bill hooks and sickles, along with a few spears, were miserably defeated on the damp flats of Sedgemoor. It was the last battle to be fought on English soil. Monmouth lost all credibility by deserting his loyal followers before the end of the fray. He was captured a few days later in the New Forest, and after pleading in front of the King for forgiveness was clumsily beheaded by six blows of the axe.

The recriminations that followed Monmouth's misguided uprising against the Catholic King were so brutal that their memory has become part of West country folklore. Judge Jeffreys—'he'll rip yer guts out and show them to you afterwards'—held judgement over the rebels in a cruel and merciless manner. Even spectators of the uprising were condemned to death. In Bristol, typical of those who were executed was Edward Tippet. In his defence, Tippet said he only went to see Monmouth's army . . . 'he never had any aims to wrong any person in life or estate'. Despite his pleas Tippet was hung, along with two other men, on Redcliffe Hill, just outside the south western gate of St Mary Redcliffe. It is told how the simple Tippet could scarcely believe what was happening—'he continued cheerful, not changing his colour to the last moment'. Afterwards his body was drawn and quartered.[13]

Jeffreys, an unpleasant, peevish, and self righteous character, revelled in his blood-thirsty work. His dark moods were further inflamed by the pain he suffered from gall stones. In order to relieve his discomfort he drank inordinately. Bristol was the last stop of Jeffrey's tour of the West Country and he lost no time in revealing his abrupt character. At an official reception on September 22nd, Jeffreys was soon lashing out threats that had even the councillors shaking in their seats. His forceful monologue, full of venom and anger, gives a chilling impression of the Judge's mood. He gave the councillors a 'lick with the rough side of his tongue' as he put it. He scoffed at the splendours of his reception and declared that he had not come to make set speeches but to do the 'business of a gracious King'. Jeffreys continued with a torrent of attacks on the city; he jeered at the influence women were supposed to have over civic affairs and then burst into a denunciation of the execution of Charles I whom he claimed was the 'most blessed martyr after Jesus'. As to his task of punishing Monmouth's rebels, he asserted that rebellion 'is like the sin of witchcraft' and implied that the city was brimming over with rebels: 'Gentlemen, I must tell you, I am afraid that this city has too many of these people (rebels) in it, and it is your duty to search them out . . . I have brought a brush in my pocket and I shall be sure to rub the dirt wherever it lies, on whomsoever it sticks. Gentlemen, I shall not stand complementing with you: I shall talk with some of you before I part.' In conclusion to his speech, the Judge not only censured the magistrates for being corrupt in their dispensation of justice but also rounded on the Mayor and accused him of being a 'kidnapping knave', whom he would have hanged there and then had it not been for his respect of the city.[14]

Despite these threats only six people were condemned for high treason in Bristol: a small number in comparison to the hundreds he had executed elsewhere. The assize was a vivid warning of how perilous it was to contest the authority of the King. Even so, only three years after this pitchfork rebellion, William of Orange, a devout Protestant, was able to engineer a successful and bloodless insurrection, the Glorious Revolution of 1688. This time, in a remarkable fit of hysteria and nosebleeds, James II panicked and fled the country vacating the throne for the Dutch William and his wife Mary (James II's daughter).

Judge Jeffreys died three months later in the Tower of London—of natural causes.

Less Admirable Ventures

From the middle of the seventeenth century, new exotic imports such as tobacco, sugar and rum—products that were soon to become inextricably connected with Bristol's prosperity—were increasingly to be seen unloaded at the dockside.

Since the end of the Civil War, Bristolians had been able to concentrate on matters closer to their hearts—their trade and industry. At last Bristol was emerging from its economic doldrums. The 1650s was a time of economic growth; a growth particularly encouraged by a Parliament keen to see the expansion of the colonial trade—especially if it was carried in English ships. This Parliamentary support of trade, combined with the hardworking Puritan outlook and the increased contact with the New World seemed to provide an infallible recipe for Bristol's success.

After almost two centuries Cabot's discovery was proving its worth with opportunities in both North America and the West Indies being exploited. Although the traditional Irish, Spanish and Portuguese trades were still of considerable importance it was the trade with the West Indies, Virginia and Newfoundland that brought in riches. Merchants were able to prosper whichever way they turned as there were good profits to be made on both outward and inward journeys. Exports included cloth, groceries, cheese, bacon, nails, iron, glass and soap—in fact all those commodities that were needed to sustain the new colonies. On the homeward journey, further dividends could be made by returning via the Iberian Peninsula and exchanging fish for oil, wine and fruit.

This is not to say that those involved did not take risks: there were the ever present dangers from pirates, navigational error and shipwreck. Also tobacco and sugar cargoes were especially vulnerable to damp and salt water.

There was a darker side to the dawning of Bristol's so-called 'Golden Age'. Initially ships set their sights directly westwards but from the latter part of the seventeenth century the merchants' lust for profit became even more voracious. Ships increasingly sailed south to the African Coast to become involved in less admirable ventures.

In the opening years of the seventeenth century it had been the proud boast of Englishmen that, whatever other countries did, they abhorred the trade in human flesh. But with the demands for labour in the new colonies and the Eastern American seaboard these ideals rapidly changed. Greed overcame morality. For the outwardly respectable merchants, out of sight was out of mind; their lust for money defeated their scruples. Many years later in 1765, John Pinney a member of the famous Bristol merchant family, wrote about a visit to the West Indies that he was 'shocked at the first appearance of human flesh for sale'. But he reasoned that 'surely God ordained them for the use and benefit of us, otherwise his Divine Will would have made some particular sign or token.'[15]

In the early days of the slave trade, London had been granted a royal charter which specifically excluded all other ports from participating in this lucrative enterprise. But with such high stakes on offer Bristolians were unwilling to sit back on the sidelines. Small numbers traded with the African coast regardless. The trade was eventually authorised for Bristolians in 1698 and by 1725 it has been calculated that Bristol's ships were carrying yearly 17,000 slaves to the new world. Again, there were risks—for sailors it was a notoriously dangerous and pest ridden journey—estimates indicate that perhaps 25% of sailors leaving for the Golden Triangle would not return. Not for nothing did they sing:

> Beware and take care of the Bight of Benin
> There's one that comes out for forty went in.

So from the middle of the seventeenth century onwards it must always be borne in mind that Bristol's riches, directly or indirectly, came from slavery. Transported Africans and their enforced contribution to the production of tobacco, sugar and rum were to be the cornerstone of the city's great wealth in the eighteenth century.

Edward Colston

In present day Bristol, Edward Colston is a name one cannot ignore. There are Colston Streets and Colston Roads, there are Colston Schools, there is a Colston Hall and there is even a Colston Bun. Colston's name is everywhere but what do we actually know about the man himself?

Edward Colston, the eldest child of William Colston, a wealthy merchant of Wine Street was born in Temple Street in 1636. Initially, Colston made his money through a varied trade with Spain and other Mediterranean countries. His luck as a merchant was notorious—'he never insured a ship and he never lost one'.[16] Even so, for many years a mystery surrounded his wealth, it being remarked by the eighteenth century historian William Barrett that 'there has never yet been given any account how his fortune accumulated so fast.'[17]

Colston's true character is shielded by an armour of apocryphal tales. When asked why he never married, he is supposed to have retorted that 'every helpless widow is my wife and every distressed orphan is my child'. Then there is the fascinating tale of the dolphin that rescued one of Colston's ships by pressing its body against the holed vessel thereby plugging a leak. Colston is also credited with bringing the first pineapples to Britain.

Stories aside, there can be no doubt that Colston was a generous benefactor to the city of his birth. He was always keen to remember his roots and amongst the many charities that he supported he took a particular interest in the affairs of his native parish, founding a charity school in Temple Street and granting money to Temple Church. Even so, despite his benevolent gifts, his relationship with the City Corporation was often strained. Colston was a man of strong convictions; he was a dedicated Tory and a vehement hater of the Roman Catholic Church. When James II passed the Declaration of Indulgence in 1687 Colston felt that the Bristol Corporation was veering dangerously

Bristol's famous philanthropist Edward Colston (1636-1721) took an active part in the planning and financing of slaving ventures to West Africa. *Bust by Rysbrack, City of Bristol Museum and Art Gallery*

towards Catholicism and dissent.

Although for all practical purposes he was a Londoner—he had been living in London since he was eighteen—it is suggested that because of these threatened changes he sold his Bristol ships and closed down his local transactions.

By 1689 Colston had settled permanently in a modest mansion in Mortlake in Surrey. Here, amongst a number of servants, he had a black maid and grew oranges in the garden. He nevertheless continued to dispatch his benevolent gifts to Bristol—though only infrequently did he visit the city himself.

His charities did, however, have strings attached to them. At Temple School, children of Catholics or dissenters were not admitted whilst books containing any 'tincture of whiggism' were forbidden. On one occasion, Colston wrote to the governors of Temple School to denounce the energetic vicar of the parish, Arthur Bedford, claiming that his conduct was a scandal and that he was not a true son of the church. In Colston's view Bedford's low church beliefs were as obnoxious as anything preached by non-conformists.[18]

Over the following years such dogmatism was excused of a man who otherwise had such a generous reputation. Indeed on Colston's death several Colston Societies sprang up 'to keep his memory green'. And these societies performed their task well, for by the late Victorian era the esteem in which Colston was held had grown to such an extent that he seemed almost ripe for canonisation. In fact, Nichols and Taylor (Taylor was president in 1840 of the Colston-inspired Dolphin Society) whimsically wrote of Colston in their otherwise useful history of Bristol that 'the grand old man passed, on the 22nd October 1721, into the presence of his Lord, to be greeted with the words "well done, good and faithful servant." '[19]

But how had Colston made his money? It was only in the 1920s that the Colston myth came to be reassessed. At that time, a speaker to the Colston Society jokingly chided his audience by adding, when he toasted their patron 'of whom you know absolutely next to nothing.'[19] The speaker was right, for the benefactions of Colston are well known but the character of the man and his source of wealth continue to be clouded by mystery.

Colston's secret had remained well hidden, or ignored, for a long time. But subsequent research revealed that the bulk of his wealth came, of course, from his close involvement with the slave trade. In 1680 Edward Colston became a member of the Royal African Company and took an active part in the planning and financing of slaving ventures to East Africa, his name appearing in the company records for the following eleven years.

The paradox is that whilst Colston was closely involved with the slave trade he was undoubtedly a charitable and religious man. Even so, it is fitting that Colston's statue in the Centre of Bristol depicts him with his head bowed—bowed with humility or with shame? Yet it is unfair to single out only Colston for his dual morality. There were many other people whose hands were also soiled by the dirty money of the slave trade.

CHAPTER THREE: NOTES

1. T. R. Robinson, *Seiges of Bristol During the Civil War* (Oxford, 1861) p.31
2. Richard Atkyns. *Military Memoirs of the Civil War* (ed. Peter Young) p. 28
3. P. McGrath, *Bristol and the Civil War* (1981) p.46
4. S. Seyer, *Memoirs of Bristol* (Bristol, 1822-1825) Vol 11, p.452
5. P. McGrath, op cit, p.42
6. S. Seyer, op cit, p.461
7. ibid p.458-459
8. A. Clifton-Taylor, *English Parish Churches as Works of Art*, p.160
9. S. Seyer, op cit, p.483-496
10. Russell Mortimer, *Early Bristol Quakers* (Bristol, 1967) p.4
11. S. Seyer, op cit, p.509
12. Samuel Pepys diary, August 1st, 1667.
13. J. Evans, *A Chronological Outline of the History of Bristol* (1824)
14. J.F. Nichols and J. Taylor, *Bristol Past and Present* (1881) Vol 3, p.112-113
15. C. M. MacInnes, *Bristol and the Slave Trade in Bristol in the 18th Century* (ed. P. McGrath, 1972) p.117
16. W. Barrett, *The History and the Antiquities of Bristol* (Bristol, 1789) p.655
17. J. Latimer *Annals of 18th Century Bristol* (Bristol, 1893) p.86
18. J. F. Nichols and J. Taylor, op cit, p.136
19. H. J. Wilkins, *Edward Colston* (Bristol, 1920) p.4

Selected Reading

P. Fryer *Staying Power, The History of Black People in Britain* (London, 1984)
R. Mortimer, *Minute Book of the Men's Meeting of the Society of Friends in Bristol 1686-1704* (Bristol Record Society, Bristol, 1977)
B. Little, *City and County of Bristol* (1954)
C. M. MacInnes, *Bristol: A Gateway to the Empire* (1968)
Bristol Broadsides, *Bristol's Other History* (1983)

View of South Bristol in 1717. 'The city itself' wrote Alexander Pope in 1739 'is very unpleasant with no civilised company in it'.

4—The Golden Age

The beginning of the eighteenth century saw Bristol entering its 'Golden Age', an exciting pioneering era when trade and industry expanded at an unprecedented rate.

Although domesticated animals still freely roamed the streets, the Southern Parishes had lost their spacious rural character. Daniel Defoe wrote of Bristol in 1723 'that there is hardly room to set another house in it'. Bristol was now a bustling, frontier town, the streets echoing with exciting news and rumour from the new colonies and other far off places.

Visiting Londoners, however, accustomed to the wide streets and the new styles of architecture that had grown out of the ashes of the Great Fire of 1666, were often surprised by Bristol's old fashioned and grimy appearance. As Bristol had been through no such cleansing process as the Fire the impression of the city, which was constructed in a half timbered style more befitting the fifteenth century, was distinctly provincial. To Londoners it all seemed very out of date. When Horace Walpole visited Bristol in 1766 he remained unimpressed by all the industriousness around him and merely remarked that Bristol was 'the dirtiest great shop I ever saw'.[1]

Daniel Defoe was equally scathing in *A Tour thro' the whole island of Great Britain*, the first comprehensive, and regularly updated, guide book of Britain. In his first edition, published in 1723, he was particularly unflattering about Bristol and its inhabitants:

> 'The greatest inconveniences of Bristol are its situation, its narrow streets and the narrowness of its river . . .'

Adding insult to injury Defoe continued:

> 'and we might mention also another narrow that is the mind of the generality of the people; for let me tell you, the merchants of Bristol, tho' very rich are not like the merchants of London . . .'

Defoe did, however, seem to approve of Bristol's puritanical streak:

> 'A great face of seriousness and religion appears in Bristol, and the magistrates are laudably strict in exacting the observation of the sabbath, considering the general dissoluteness that has broken out almost everywhere else.'

Alexander Pope on his visit in 1739 was also most unimpressed:

> 'The city itself is very unpleasant with no civilised company in it . . . the streets were as crowded as London, but the best image I can give you of it is 'Tis as if Wapping and Southwark were ten times as big; or all their people ran into London.'[2]

But despite these adverse comments, Bristol was nationally famous for its maritime trade, and the parishes of Redcliffe, Temple and St Thomas known for their industries. These ranged in size from small backroom enterprises to larger concerns of national repute. Many of the industries relied on coal from Kingswood in their production; consequently some made a considerable impact on the environment. Indeed, Alexander Pope commented that his first impression of Bristol was of a city overshadowed by 'twenty odd pyramids smoking over the town'.[3] These tall brick cones necessary for the production of glass and pottery were beginning to compete with the church towers and spires for the dominance of Bristol's skyline. The tall glass houses not only changed the skyline of Bristol but also, together with the fumes from the soap makers, the tallow chandlers and the sugar boilers, polluted with smoke and 'noxious effluvia' the atmosphere of the Avon valley—and especially so during calm anti-cyclonic weather. To make conditions even more unpleasant during the day, there was a constant barrage of noise from the numerous coopers, smiths and braziers in the parishes.

Of course, many people were employed in the Southern Parishes in the provision and maintenance of Bristol's expanding fleet. There were shipbuilders; sail, chain and rope makers; and numerous coopers providing the kegs and barrels that were indispensable for long journeys. And in conjunction with the unusual and exotic commodities arriving at the quayside there was a new breed of industry—tobacco rolling, tobacco cutting, pipe-making and sugar refining—that indicated a widening and changing world. All in all, the Southern Parishes of Bristol had become an area as industrialised as anywhere else in the country at the time. 'Commerce might be king in Bristol' wrote Patrick McGrath, 'but in industry it found a worthwhile consort'.[4]

Sugar

Of all the new enterprises, sugar refining was one of the most important. Whilst the wealth of Bristol's new up-and-coming rival, Liverpool was said to have derived from slaves and cotton, Bristol's eighteenth century riches have been attributed to slaves and sugar. The sugar refining industry which was carried out on a large scale, was, however, disliked by many parishioners because it created both fumes and a fire risk. The raw sugar, which was boiled in large copper vats, was heated to such a high temperature that it was prone to ignite—something not to be encouraged in a city whose dwellings were built mostly of wood and in an age when the most sophisticated piece of firefighting equipment was a bucket.

Indeed in 1661 there were so many complaints regarding John Hine's sugar house in Thomas Street that he was forced to close and move to less crowded quarters off Temple Street 'where he could give no further offense'.[5] However, in 1661, what had been feared for so long happened: a sugar house in Redcliffe caught fire one night and burnt to the ground causing £1,000 worth of damage. Worse was to come the following year when another refinery in the same street burst into flames on a dark and blustery night. The strong winds fanned the fire which soon threatened widespread destruction. At first, there was chaos. No buckets could be found for water and to make matters even more difficult those people hunting for water containers could not see, for their candles were blown out by the wind. Eventually when the buckets were located they were found to be riddled with holes. It was more by luck than anything else that the fire spread no further. The Corporation must have learnt one small lesson for not long afterwards it was proposed that they keep a store of torches for times when candles were unsuitable.

The refining of sugar obviously had its problems, but it was a lucrative business and was to remain a staple industry of the Southern Parishes for many years.

Crown, Flint and Bottle Glass

The rise of the glass industry in the city was remarkably rapid. In the earlier part of the seventeenth century the majority of glass makers in the country were located in the Weald of Sussex. The rapid demise of the Sussex industry was brought about by an acute shortage of fuel. The glass makers and iron founders of the Weald had denuded the landscape of timber to such an extent that legislation had to be passed in 1615 forbidding the use of 'Timber or Wood, or any Fewell made of Timber or Wood'[6] in their manufacturing processes. In effect the new ordinance put an end to the Sussex glass industry.

This scarcity of wood, and the ensuing legislation, together with the discovery of a method for making glass using coal, enabled Bristol to become a natural successor to the

Above: Tile picture, dated 1820, of the Bristol Pottery on Temple Back. *City of Bristol Museum and Art Gallery*

Below: Bill head for Henry Ricketts glass works. In the late eighteenth century the Southern Parishes became an important national centre for the production of glass. *City of Bristol Museum and Art Gallery*

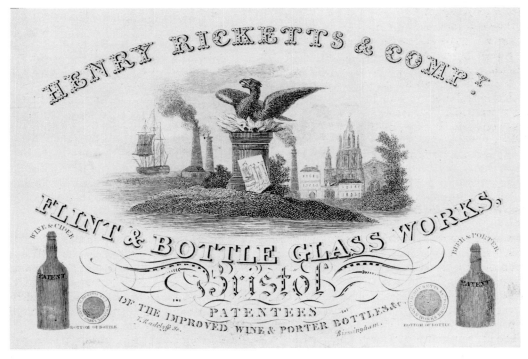

Weald. Bristol not only had coal deposits on its doorstep at Kingswood, it also had sand and limestone at hand. Redcliffe sand, tunnelled from the caves or dug straight from the ground was particularly suitable for thick bottle glass.

A whole range of glass was soon being produced—there were makers of decorative glass, window glass and most numerous of all, bottle makers. Bottles were particularly in demand for the storage of both imported wine and locally produced cider and perry, some of which went to the West Indies.

To enable coal to generate a temperature high enough to produce glass, towering brick cones were built to increase the draught needed to fire the furnaces. As contemporary views show, these cones were large structures, some being up to 90 feet high and 50 feet in diameter round the base. Millerd's map of Bristol in 1710 shows six glasshouses in the city, five of these being in the Southern Parishes. The cones were expensive to build and indeed were sometimes not constructed to the highest specifications. It was reported that:

> 'A large glass house belonging to Sir Abraham Elton Bart . . . suddenly fell down; happy it was for the glass-men that the fire was out . . .'[7]

Once the cone was built, however, the production of glass was inexpensive. The glass maker's art lay more in his skill than his tools, his equipment consisted merely of a blowing iron, a few wooden implements for shaping and sometimes a mould for blowing glass into.

The process was observed by a man who simply called himself the 'Irish Gentleman' and wrote:

> 'I saw many glass houses, with which this town vastly abounds, as the inhabitants reckon upwards of thirty. The generality of them are built of brick, toperwise to the top. Within side is the Chaldron wherein the metal is boiled, by means of a large constant fire with a chimney, by which the smoke is conveyed to the top . . . I saw several things blown, this is performed by a long iron tube, the end of which they dip into the metal, and after they have given it a blast or two they form or shape it on an anvil.'[8]

The Irish Gentleman was not alone in being fascinated by the production of glass. Many visitors to the city, along with day trippers from the spa town of Bath, made a specific detour to observe this fascinating industry. By the end of the eighteenth century it was such a popular sight that Mathews' *Bristol Directory* recommended that:

> 'They who are strangers to the working of window glass, and to the blowing of white or flint glass which is formed in such a variety of modes and forms, may gratify their curiosity of observing these curious operations by presenting a small gratuity to the workmen, who living in hot climates are very glad of some suction to moisten their clay.'

Although the demand for glass from the new colonies and home was usually stable, the market was sometimes upset by outside influences. The excise tax imposed in 1696 of one shilling on twelve bottles hit the industry particularly hard. As a consequence of the duty many people found it cheaper to put their liquour in casks. Between this date and 1710 it seems that three of the nine glass houses in the city closed down.

Nevertheless there were soon signs of the industry's recovery. In the next ten years four new glasshouses opened. Demand was further stimulated by the popularity of the Hotwell Spa. There was an extensive trade in bottles for the sale of Hotwell Water which was marketed in London for the exhorbitant price of six shillings for a dozen of the largest bottles.

Today, apart from the world famous antique Bristol Blue glass and other highly prized Bristol glass objects, little is left to remind us of this once thriving industry. Except, that is, the truncated remains of Bristol's last glass cone which has been incorporated into the buildings of the Dragonara Hotel on Redcliffe Way. The cone of Messrs H. & T. Proctor stayed intact until the 1930s when weaknesses in the upper brickwork of the glasshouse demanded that it be cut down to its present 25 feet height. Once more the chink of glass can be heard in this industrial monument—the chink of wine glasses for the cone is now used as the hotel's restaurant.

Sauceboats and Galleypots

The numerous brick cones that pierced Bristol's skyline were not exclusively associated with glassworks: some housed potteries. Around the middle of the eighteenth century great advances were made in ceramic technology. At a time when virtually everybody ate from pewter plates, or more usually wooden trenchers, it was every potter's dream to be able to produce the high quality porcelain that was so expensively imported from China. As no source in England was yet known for kaolin, a whole variety of pastes and glazes were used as experimental alternatives. In late sixteenth century Bristol the nearest the potters could get to producing a ceramic look-alike was delftware. The making of delftware, named after the Dutch town where the technique was perfected, involved dipping and sealing the already fired earthenware 'biscuit' into an opaque lead glaze.

The oldest pottery in the Bristol area to make delftware was the Galleypot Manufactory in the village of Brislington. In 1684 the Brislington Pottery moved to premises on Temple Back. What is remarkable about the Brislington Pottery is that it continued in production, under one name or another, until the 1960s. The Pountney Bristol Pottery, as it was then known, moved from its premises in Temple Back to St Philips in 1884 and then to its final site at Lodge Causeway in 1906; it closed down in 1968 when it was the last surviving link with a tradition of industrial pottery that extended back to the Middle Ages.

By the mid 1740s, experiments in England in the manufacture of something that resembled porcelain were more successful. Strange mixtures of bone ash, glass frit, soapstone and so on were being used in the creation of what was called 'Soft Paste' porcelain. The production of this most sought after white ware involved difficult, secret and expensive manufacturing processes. Even so, the partnership of two Quakers, Benjamin Lund and William Miller, who established a factory on Redcliffe Back in 1750, was able to advertise for sale 'Very beautiful white sauce boats'. The quality of these sauceboats so impressed a group of businessmen from the West Midlands that they approached Lund to help them with the difficulties they were experiencing in their own manufactory. In 1752 Lund left Redcliffe and transferred all his stocks, utensils and equipment to the establishment that was one day to become the famous Worcester Porcelain Company.

Eventually, in 1765, another Quaker, William Cooksworthy, discovered a source of kaolin in Cornwall allowing true hardpaste porcelain to be manufactured in England for the first time. Cooksworthy, a Plymouth chemist, moved his works to Castle Green in Bristol and by 1770, to the envy of his rivals, was producing true Bristol Porcelain.

Yet despite the quest for porcelain one must not forget that the bulk of Bristol's pottery output was of a less glamorous, more utilitarian nature. All the potteries also made ordinary household ware, demand for which was more stable and less dependent on the fashion of the day. The majority produced 'redware'—bricks, pantiles, chimney pots, drainpipes and sugar moulds—whilst Frank's Pottery on Redcliffe Back specialised in Stoneware, glaze on the inside only, which was particularly suitable for jars and pots, which they made in all shapes and sizes.

Soap

Any description of the industries of the Southern Parishes would be incomplete without mentioning the humble, and sometimes not so humble, soapmakers. Soap was initially introduced to serve the woollen industry. For many centuries Bristol had enjoyed a great reputation for its soap, and in the twelfth century was so famous for this industry that Richard of Devizes had satirically suggested that soapmaking was the mainstay of Bristol's wealth. Even though this was an exaggeration, soapmaking was carried out on a large scale and much money could be made from it. Such a fortune was acquired in the later years of Elizabeth's reign by Alderman Robert Rogers who lived in the Great House, just off Bristol Bridge at the top end of Redcliffe Street. This house was so sumptuous that when Samuel Pepys saw it he described it as 'if fit for a King's palace'.

In 1633, the Bristol Soapmakers felt it necessary to prove the superior quality of their product in comparison to that produced by the Society of Soapmakers of Westminster. Accordingly Captain Conningsby organised a demonstration where two women washed some napkins, one using Westminster soap, the other Bristol soap. The result was as hoped for . . .

> 'It did appear and it was soe confessed by the said captaine Conningsby that the said Bristoll sope was as good in all respects as the saide sope by him produced. And allthough the saide napkins washed with Bristoll soape weare alltogether, as white washed and sweet or rather sweter than the other yet in the washing of the saide napkins there was not alltogethersoe much soap expended of the saide Bristoll soape as there was of the other soape. Soe it appeared to all present, that the saide Bristoll soape was as good or rather better than the saide other soape.'[9]

A New Economic Force

If there is one group that stands out in the eighteenth century for their prodigious commercial and financial acumen it is the Quakers. A characteristic of Bristol's eighteenth century industries is the number of enterprises, particularly capital-intensive ones, that were run by Friends. At a time when no banks were available (the first Bristol bank was established in 1750—and then it was the only bank in the country outside London) the willingness of Quakers to join together in the sponsorship of enterprises created a new economic force in the city; for the first time the establishment of new ventures was not left solely in the hands of the very rich.

Although the Friends were hardworking and scrupulously honest they nevertheless had a long struggle to gain respectability within the establishment. And even though the Friends had lost the fiery fanaticism that so characterised the early days of Quakerism they were still viewed as targets for discrimination; even in 1711 The Merchants Society ruled that no member should be a Quaker.

Matters were made particularly difficult for the Quakers in the years after the Restoration of the monarchy. Because of their refusal to swear the compulsory oath of allegiance to the crown—Quakers would only obey God, not men—they were branded as traitors to the newly established King. In Bristol, this act of defiance was seized upon by the authorities as an excuse for the punishment of Friends in all manner of ways: they were fined, jailed, transported abroad and even threatened with execution.

The most persistent period of persecution was the 1680s. The meeting houses were vandalised and boarded up, sometimes with Friends still in them, and many Quakers were thrown into Newgate Gaol—a place so nasty and stinking that one alderman was heard to say that he wouldn't send his dog to it. In 1684, Robert Vickris, a successful business-man, was sentenced to death, as an example to others for failing to take the oath. Vickris appealed against the sentence, his case being taken to the King's Bench in London and presented to the notorious Judge Jeffreys. In a rare moment of compassion Jeffreys freed the Quaker.

Vickris was lucky; such was the severity of the persecution of Quakers that when the newly crowned James II issued in 1685 his Declaration of Indulgence freeing all dis-senters from prosecution over one hundred Quakers were subsequently released from Bristol's Newgate Prison.

Although the Act of Toleration of 1689 gave freedom of rights to dissenters it could not confer upon the Quakers immediate social acceptability. The hectoring of Quakers was to continue, albeit sporadically, for many years. In 1714 there was a degenerate attack on some Quakers during celebrations for George I's accession. A drunken mob attacked the Temple Street Meeting House as well as some private dwellings. In Tucker Street they broke into the house of a Quaker, Mr Stephens, and refused to leave. When Stephens tried to eject the drunks they became violent and began to ransack his house, forcing open boxes and drawers and plundering plate and other goods. A fellow Quaker who attempted to come to Stephen's rescue was beaten to the ground, kicked about and mortally wounded.

Afterwards the rioters made their way across the river and over to the Custom House causing the ladies, it is reported, to flee in terror from the Coronation Ball. It was not until midnight that the mob dispersed.[10]

The next day, although it was rumoured that the ringleaders had escaped, several of the drunks were rounded up and brought to trial. They were fined £7 together with a prison sentence of 3 months: a punishment considered by many to be unduly lenient.[11]

Turnpike Roads—The Spider's Web

Bristol's rapidly developing commercial and industrial importance depended on its position at the centre of a great regional and coastal trading area. As transport by road was scarcely any the less dirty, dangerous and unreliable than it had been in the Middle Ages most of Bristol's products were transported by sea or river. Nationally the rivers, particularly the Severn and the Mersey, which were reputed to carry more traffic than any other rivers in Europe, remained the arteries of the seventeenth century. River transport did have disadvantages though; safe navigation could frequently be hindered by tidal movements, silting-up and seasonal variations of water depth.

If new markets were to be opened up and trade expanded, those areas away from water transport had to be exploited. From 1706 private trusts were authorised to take on the work of improving roads as the cost was beyond the purse strings of most parishes. These trusts were then permitted to recoup the cost of their outlay by collecting tolls from the road users.

For long distance travellers the new turnpike roads brought about a considerable im-provement of conditions. Local people, however, were not always so keen on the changes. Turnpike tolls signified an erosion of an age old liberty—since time immemorial people had travelled the road for free; to many, the very independence of the English way of life was at stake. In fact tolls were to be a cause of riot and strife throughout the eighteenth century and the Southern Parishes were to witness more domestic bloodshed and anger through these impositions than anything else. The English have always disliked road tolls; even one hundred years after their introduction William Cobbett in his *Rural Rides* avoided the turnpikes, as they symbolised the forces that were sublimating the life of the country to that 'great wen', London, to which the turnpike roads ran like the web of a spider.

In 1749 a new Turnpike Act was introduced and Bristolians quickly found their city surrounded by toll gates. Many of the country people were incensed by the infringement of their rights and in 1749, in an outright act of defiance, several of the toll gates outside the city were destroyed. The Turnpike Commissioners were not to be that easily discouraged. While new gates were being built they put chains across the roads and continued to collect the hated tolls. This only served to increase the anger of the Somerset folk. An angry crowd of several hundred people chanting 'down with the turnpikes' marched on the city. Some 'naked with only trouzers on', others with their faces blacked for anonymity, presented a fearsome sight as they came over Redcliffe Hill and approached Redcliffe Gate. As both the southern gates of Redcliffe and Temple were closed the crowd turned their energies to demolishing the Totterdown toll gate. They were soon pursued by a retaliatory force of police officers and constables, several turnpike commissioners and a rough bunch of sailors armed with muskets, pistols and cutlasses. After a brief but violent skirmish at the Totterdown toll gate the protesters dispersed.

But this was not the end of the disturbances; a magistrate was accosted and, more ominously, several letters were sent to the Mayor threatening to burn down the city. The threats were taken so seriously that a state of alert was declared. Troops were called in, the city gates were closed at 10.00pm every night and notice was given to the citizens that they should be prepared to defend Bristol from further attack.[12]

In fact, the intimidation came to nothing and calm was soon restored. A couple of days later the *Bristol Journal* was pleased to report that 'all those wounded in the Totterdown Conflict are in a fair way of recovery except Farmer Barnes, and even of him there are hopes.'[13]

These localised protests went largely unheeded and the turnpike trusts slowly spread their web of roads across the country. The effect of the new road system was far-reaching and often unforeseen. The turnpikes necessitated not only a new approach to road making but also stimulated innovations in the design of vehicles.

In 1747 a slow moving wagon left Thomas Street every Friday completing its eighty mile trip to Exeter by the following Tuesday.[14] With the introduction of coaches, conditions improved so much that by 1765 the coach leaving in the morning from The George in Temple Street arrived in Exeter the following day.[15] The cost for this speedy trip was one guinea. As methods of long distance travel were revolutionised (to make the ride a little less bumpy, harsh metal springs were increasingly substituted by soft leather straps) excursions turned from uncomfortable adventures into experiences that could almost be pleasurable.

By 1784 communication with London had improved to such an extent that a novel sight, the Royal Mail coach, was to be seen crossing Bristol Bridge and making its way as briskly as possible down Temple Street to the Bath Road. These new speedy coaches, delivering letters to the capital in just one day, were protected by guards, the cost of which was defrayed by passengers who also wanted to benefit from the increased speed and security. Only four passengers were carried by the two horse coach and the fare for this exhilarating journey was £1 8s 0d.[16] There was one drawback, however, this being the common belief that the speed attained by these coaches was dangerous to health. Travellers were warned to take care on these journeys for people had been known to 'die of apoplexy from the rapidity of the motion'. In winter, hypothermia was a more likely hazard.

Above: West end of Redcliffe Parade—a speculative building project financed on the money made by privateering.

Below: the new Bristol Bridge. Inspired by Westminster Bridge, the bridge was opened for foot passengers in 1768, and traffic in 1769.

In Bristol, the increase in vehicles on the roads caused jams at bottlenecks created by the gateways and Bristol Bridge. Even before the coaching revolution, Daniel Defoe had complained about Bristol's narrow streets. Particularly hazardous to both pedestrians and passengers were the city gates and the overcrowded bridge. Both became quickly congested by the constant flow of 'seamen, women, children, loaded horses, asses and sledges'[17] and were a frequent source of frustration and complaint. Accidents such as a man having 'his leg broke on the Bridge by the Wheel of a waggon going over it' were common.[18]

The narrow bridge was made especially hazardous by its incline towards the centre which caused passing high loads to lock.[19] These problems, backed up by the occasional petition of complaint, indicated that matters would soon have to be rectified. And, besides, the bridge was distinctly unfashionable and hardly befitted the status of the Kingdom's second city. The medieval London Bridge had long been replaced by a new model of elegant simplicity.

Two options were available; either the original bridge could be retained and widened or it could be replaced by a totally new structure. Whatever course was taken the cost would be enormous; not only would it include the demolition of some thirty houses that were perched upon the old structure but also the consequent loss of revenue from this property. A committee of twenty-four members was set up, and decided that a new, one-arch bridge should be built, adjoined by a temporary structure whilst work was in progress. But when the committee's proposals were presented to the Council they were quickly rejected in preference of the cheaper solution of widening. To the chagrin of the city's merchants the committee also suggested that the cost of these improvements could be covered by a duty on coal, a rate on houses, a wharfage charge on imports and exports together with a toll on the bridge for five years. Such an uproar ensued between the bridge committee, the councillors and the merchants that the entire scheme was shelved.

An independent group of businessmen took the opportunity of the stalemate to present a private bill to Parliament authorising its promoters to carry out the proposed construction. The threat of a private venture taking over Bristol's one and only bridge across the Avon gave the Council the vital impetus to resume their proceedings. Even though the Council now backed the proposals for a new bridge rather than a widened one, further controversy raged over the design of the structure. After a phenomenal seventy-six meetings it was finally decided to build a bridge of three arches on the original piers designed by John Bridges (and inspired by Westminster Bridge—though it is difficult to recognise this now, due to Victorian widening).

The new bridge, eventually financed as suggested (but omitting the duty on coal), was opened for foot passengers in 1768 and for traffic in 1769.

It wasn't only the bridge that became congested with traffic; if there was to be a free flow of vehicles through Redcliffe, Temple and St Thomas further modifications were needed. The city gates were an obvious problem, yet many councillors were loathe to demolish them for security reasons. The city gates were important for regulating the flow of strangers into the city. In 1674 both Redcliffe and Temple Gates were manned at night by five watchmen who were to look out for foreigners. In 1730 a petition from the Temple parishioners claimed that the gates were 'incommodious and dangerous'. After further protests from Redcliffe residents £250 was spent on replacing the medieval gates with a new structure in a dubiously named 'rustic classic style'. In 1734 Temple Gate was also rebuilt.[20] Yet the new gates offered little improvement; for although side passages were now provided for pedestrians the width of the roadway for carriages was still restricted. Soon pleas for demolition were heard again.

By the end of the eighteenth century the City had outgrown its walls. Redcliffe Gate was demolished in 1771, Temple Gate in 1808.

The character of the city was changing rapidly. One only had to stand at Redcliffe Gate and look southward—where there had previously been countryside there were now houses. There were new buildings on Redcliffe Hill and along the Addercliffe, a new speculative building project—the construction of Redcliffe Parade—was being financed by the profits of Sydenham Teast's privateering ventures. There was no escaping the fact that Bristol, like London which in a symbolic and practical act had taken down its gates in 1761, had outgrown its walls. Indeed, even back in 1674 several doorways had been cut illegally into the Redcliffe and Temple walls to make access easier to the fields and gardens in the suburbs. The idea of a walled city in eighteenth century England was an outmoded concept.

The gates were used for defence so infrequently—the last time being for the Turnpike Riot of 1749—that there was little justification for their continued presence. Accordingly, the Corporation overcame its conservative instincts and in June 1771 ordered that the new Redcliffe Gate, which was barely 40 years old, be taken down. Temple Gate stayed a little longer. It was in 1808 that a local journal announced the auction of 'material of Temple Gate, now standing at the top of Temple Street'. The materials were bought for £107.

Nutritious Ale

As the population of Bristol doubled between 1700 and 1750, so the number of alehouses increased correspondingly. By 1754, with one house in ten in Bristol being an ale house, there were in all 625 in the city. Sketchley's *1775 Bristol Directory* lists numerous victuallers—the names of some of their hostelries still being with us today. Familiar establishments are The Ship in the Cathay, The Ostrich in Guinea Street and The (Blue) Bell in Prewitt Street.

Ale figured largely in everybody's diet. The general belief was that the drinking of water, apart from spa water, was to be avoided at all costs. Water, even uncontaminated water, was usually viewed as medically unsound 'being cold, slow and slack of digestion'. Not only was ale safer to drink than water, it was also more nutritious. It has been calculated that one fifth of the nation's dietary requirements were supplied merely through the consumption of ale. During this time a staggering 800 pints per head of population were consumed yearly. The importance of ale was graphically illustrated in Hogarth's engravings of Gin Lane and Beer Street. In the 1730s and 1740s the noticeable rise in the death rate is put down to the high consumption of cheap, nutritiously worthless gin. In 1750, the year before its sale was effectively outlawed, the annual consumption of gin was 8 pints per head.[21]

The day started early but then so did the drinking. By 7.00am business was in full swing. Soon, as Defoe found 'just as in London, the taverns and coffee houses were crowded with bargainers and "Bristol Milk", which is Spanish sherry, nowhere as good as here plentifully drunk'.

The finish of work at 6.00pm would normally be followed by drinking in the local tavern. As the only available artificial light was from smoky tallow candles, the fall of dusk signified the time for people to return home and retire to bed.

The consumption of ale was also an every day anaesthetic that made life bearable. Indeed, Dr Johnson (himself a 'hardened and shameless tea drinker . . . whose kettle has scarcely time to cool') asserted that all decent people of his home town Lichfield got drunk every night and were not thought the worse for it.

Very little excuse was needed for the copious consumption of alcohol. One rather bizarre cause of revelry was the annual perambulation of the city boundaries and the accompanying duck hunt. One day in autumn, members of the council, heralded by the bells of St Mary Redcliffe, would grandly proceed to Treen Mills where they would be greeted by the city's trumpeters. When everyone was assembled the ducks would be released onto the mill pond and then, to everybody's delight, trained dogs would be set upon them. In 1742, the last recorded Duck Hunt, nineteen birds were purchased for this brutal entertainment. Excessive drinking accompanied the event which culminated in a rowdy walk along the city's boundary with some of the more drunken spectators being tossed up and down on the marking stone. Despite the almost universal penchant for alcohol, there was still an influential class of puritans who looked upon such ribald occasions as sinful and campaigned for their prohibition.

Redcliffe's Most Famous Son

Thomas Chatterton, Redcliffe's most famous son, was born in the shadow of Redcliffe Church in 1752. He became 'the boy wonder' who wrote poetry that was to be admired for many generations. Today, his literary achievements are not to everybody's taste. By modern standards his work is often criticised as being too contrived, but even so there is still an honourable place for him in English literature. The story of his life is of frustrated talent ending in a tragedy truly in keeping with the tenor of his Gothic verse.

Thomas Chatterton was born the posthumous son of a school teacher who was also part-time lay clerk at St Mary Redcliffe. His father died three months before his birth. Within a short time Chatterton's mother moved from the school house into lodgings on Redcliffe Hill where she eked out a living from dressmaking. When her husband was alive she had apparently pilfered some old parchment manuscripts from St Mary Redcliffe for use as patterns. The story goes that the young Chatterton, who at the age of five had been dismissed from school for being too dull to be taught, saw some of these coloured manuscripts and became so engrossed in their beauty that they gave him the vital encouragement to learn to read.

At the age of seven, it was again decided that he should try a formal education and this time he was sent to Colston's School. But once again he found the methods of teaching uninspiring and soon became bored. Yet outside school his thirst for knowledge continued. Within a couple of years he was using the small amounts of pocket-money that his widowed mother could afford to borrow books from a circulating library.

Chatterton left school at fifteen and took up employment as a clerk to an attorney in Corn Street. He worked the usual long hours—8.00 am to 8.00 pm—and was required to 'live in'. He was so efficient at his job that he found he could often condense his day's work into just a couple of hours. This left him plenty of time to continue with his studies and writing. He read widely, researching into books on the classics, the sciences, music, medicine and history.

About this time a variety of historical manuscripts were discovered by Chatterton. The first of these historical discoveries to be published was an ancient account of the Mayor of Bristol crossing the original newly erected Bristol Bridge in 1248. Chatterton claimed that his report was taken from a medieval manuscript. It was a topical subject for the old bridge had just been demolished and replaced by John Bridges' new structure. Other manuscripts followed. By an incredible chance Chatterton was able to supply an acquaintance, Mr Bergum, with a document indicating the great and noble antiquity of his

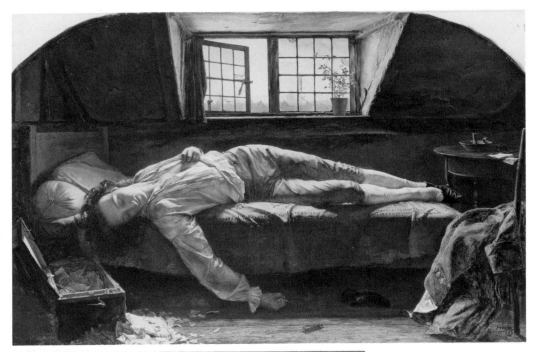

Above: The poet Thomas Chatterton was born in the shadow of St. Mary Redcliffe in 1752. He died at the age of 17—a phial of arsenic lay by his side. *Tate Gallery*

Left: Samuel Taylor Coleridge. The young poet was married in St. Mary Redcliffe in 1795. He later lived in 'pent up rooms' in Redcliffe Hill.

National Portrait Gallery

family's background. William Barrett was also glad to use some of Chatterton's manuscripts in his *History and Antiquities of the City of Bristol* which he was compiling at the time. Perhaps most remarkable of all was a marvellous series of poems that came to light that were written by Thomas Rowley, a chaplain, apparently, to the great William Canynges.

All these translations and manuscripts were outright fakes. They were simply a product of Chatterton's fertile imagination and extensive learning. What is surprising, however, is that they were accepted so credulously—it was only after Chatterton's death that suspicion was voiced about the majority of this work. Even the slightest critical inspection would have revealed Chatterton's manuscripts for what they were. Several years later, in 1776, Dr Johnson visited Bristol to inspect the Rowley Poems and was left in no doubt that they were written by Chatterton.

Boswell described how he and Dr Johnson visited Barrett and 'saw some of the originals as they were called, which were executed very artificially'. Upon careful inspection of the manuscripts they were quite 'satisfied of the imposture'. Regardless of the fakes Dr Johnson went on to say that 'This is the most incredible young man that has encountered my knowledge: it is wonderful how the whelp has written such things'.[22] Even after this authoritative judgement Barrett was not convinced of their fraudulence. He went ahead with the publication of his *History of Bristol* which included several of Chatterton's creations and became the laughing stock of the city. He was so humiliated that it is said the shame hastened his death in 1789, the same year as the publication of his book.

The limited success of Chatterton's manuscripts was not enough. He realised that if he was to succeed as a poet he would have to find himself a patron and to this end wrote to the famous dilettante Horace Walpole. Chatterton's letters were well received but his hopes of sponsorship came to nothing. Filled with despair at his apparently dead-end existence Chatterton let it be known that he was contemplating taking his own life. Barrett became so alarmed at Chatterton's despondency that he invited the young poet to his house for a paternal chat. Chatterton opened his heart to Barrett about his frustrations and after much tearful soul searching he promised to put all thoughts of suicide out of his mind.

Many of Chatterton's problems lay in the fact that Bristol was a literary backwater. The city was better known for its commercial achievements rather than its cultural refinements. Any interest in the arts was reserved at this time for the more effete residents along the Avon valley in Bath. Chatterton was to scornfully write of his home town:

'Lost of all learning, elegance and sense,
Long had the famous city told her pence.'[23]

It was obvious to Chatterton that if he was to make his mark on the literary scene he would have to move to London. Accordingly in April 1770 he took the bold step of leaving Redcliffe for a new life in the capital.

Although the letters Chatterton sent home to his mother boasted of his literary achievements and his admiring group of friends, his existence in London was in reality a turn for the worse. He was soon living the clichéd life of a poet wasting away in his garret. In four months he had written articles, mostly satirical, for eleven different journals. This brought in barely enough money to keep him from starving. When he did earn the fairly substantial sum of five guineas for a light hearted musical piece he spent most of the money on a box of presents which he sent to his family. His landlady in Holborn, Mrs Angel, noticed how weak he was becoming. On one occasion she offered him food but he proudly refused, saying that he was not hungry.

The young Chatterton was desperate for a landslide of fame and fortune; his adolescent impetuousness could not wait for it to trickle in. One morning he was found outstretched on his bed; a phial of arsenic was lying on the floor. The young poet had apparently not eaten for several days. Chatterton was given a pauper's burial in a communal grave. He was seventeen years old when he died.

Slaughter on Bristol Bridge

As we have already seen, nothing raised the heckles of Bristolians more than the imposition of tolls on roads and bridges. The expected abolition on September 17th, 1793 of the toll on Bristol Bridge was therefore contemplated with great pleasure. It was disliked on three counts. Not only had the toll been a burden to individuals but it was also reckoned to be detrimental to the commerce of the city as a whole. Furthermore the toll commissioners were suspected of making an unreasonable profit at everyone else's expense.

So on the day when the toll was due to cease the gates were joyfully pulled down and burnt. Two days later, however, new gates were erected. According to the commissioners the toll was to continue. The commissioners justified their decision by claiming, to the incredulity of many, that money was still owed for construction costs. For a few days general resentment of the toll quietly smouldered until the evening of Saturday, September 28th when a crowd, many of whom were drunk, gathered by the bridge and set about attacking the gates. The magistrates, after pleading vainly with the crowd to disperse, called in the military in order, they hoped, to avoid further trouble. In fact the presence of the Herefordshire Regiment did little to calm matters and after a prolonged period of physical and verbal harassment the troops were ordered to fire a volley into the air. It had its intended effect—and more. The crowd quickly dispersed leaving on the pavement one person dead from rifle fire and several others wounded.

Next morning a jeering group appeared at each end of the bridge. At noon, when men were posted to collect tolls there were scenes of angry protest. The mood was becoming increasingly violent. At the approach of dusk it was thought wise to allow free passage until the following day. On Monday, however, the commissioners resumed their attempts to collect the toll. But being constantly harassed and abused they had little success and many people fought their way across the bridge without paying. Several people were also arrested and taken to the Bridewell, an act which only served to increase the anger of the crowd. Eventually the Riot Act was read out three times but was met merely by hoots of derision. The magistrates, who so far had restrained themselves from recalling the military, at last felt compelled to summon further support and at midday warned that:

> 'Those who will not be advised must take the consequence, that if they receive any injury it must lay upon their own heads.'

On their arrival, the Herefordshire Regiment, under strict orders to show restraint, were pelted with stones and oyster shells. Again, as dusk approached the magistrates decided to close the bridge and shut up the toll house so as to avoid further confrontation. But as soon as the soldiers withdrew, the crowd went on the rampage; the toll house was broken into and its furniture was thrown onto a bonfire that was soon blazing on the bridge. One anonymous pamphlet writer later observed that the fire served to fuel the anger of the crowd:

> 'Every man of observation knows that there is such a natural connection between a bonfire and mobbing, to the common people of England, that it is, in general necessary only to form one in order to create the other.'[24]

The soldiers were hastily brought back to the bridge and ordered to fire on the crowd to disperse it. The first volley, directed towards the south side of the bridge, was into the air. It had little effect. The second volley was aimed low, and several bodies fell to the ground. No sooner had the troops discharged their weapons than they were attacked by a hail of stones and missiles from the north end of the bridge. The soldiers about turned and fired along the High Street. In all, eleven people were killed and another forty-five were injured.

Strangely, there was a rumour circulating that the soldiers could not legally fire at the mob; if they did it was thought that they must use only powder and not shot. Thus when the militia did at first fire into the air the belief that they were using blanks was further reinforced. The fatal consequence was that few of the crowd dispersed. This point of view was held by Bristol historian John Evans, who was an eye witness:

> 'The writer was at this instant between seven and eight in professional attendance at the theatre but so strongly was he possessed of the belief that only powder had been discharged, of which some of the flying mob, whom he first met near the Back Hall, repeatedly assured him that he passed one man lying prostrate, as if fallen in flight through inebriety, at the foot of St Nicholas church steps . . . and with unabated security, another man lying near the place of the watchbox in the church yard railing, from whom a stream issued down the pavement.'[25]

It would seem that either Evans was exceptionally shortsighted—which he was not— or he had the utmost faith in the placidity of the soldiers, for these were not drunken bodies that he was stepping over, but corpses. Oblivious that he was walking through a battlefield Evans calmly continued on his way home even though:

> 'A bonfire blazed on the bridge and the firing of musketry and the roll of drums had not ceased on the side of St Thomas Street.'[26]

The slaughter on Bristol Bridge is a bloody and shameful day in Bristol's history. Admittedly the soldiers had suffered prolonged harassment for several days but even this was little excuse for their indiscriminate firing. Prior to the massacre the Riot Act had not been read for several hours during which time a number of spectators had gathered to watch the mob's antics. Many innocent bystanders were injured during the discharge; three teenage girls from the parishes of Redcliffe and St Thomas were hurt whilst a visitor from Castle Cary who was merely passing through the city at the time was killed.

The inflammatory behaviour of the magistrates and the bridge commissioners caused a national outcry. In Bristol, the coroner's court expressed its extreme disapproval by passing a verdict of wilful murder by persons unknown on ten of the victims. Yet the situation was not straightforward. In the absence of an established police force, when large scale violence threatened there was no alternative but to call out the military. Such a decision was never easy to take, for subsequent events might prove that the problem did not justify military intervention. Also, the justices were notoriously keen to punish any soldier accused of using undue force against a civilian. Thus soldiers ordered to fire upon a crowd might well be accused of murder if they obeyed, or if they disobeyed, be shot themselves for mutiny. In this case the military were accused of murder but no particular soldier was singled out for punishment.

And of course, members of the crowd were not blameless. A demonstration always offers a chance for the more disruptive elements of society to take revenge against authority and doubtless this demonstration was no exception. Besides, across Europe the French Revolution of 1789 had roused a real feeling that the toppling of old inequalities was possible. In England, even though the common individual was powerless, the common mass was capable of a good deal of noise and sometimes violence. This violence, or threat of it, was sometimes the only way that the voice of the working person could be heard.

Despite claims by the Corporation that it was 'neither wise nor salutary' and 'was a dangerous concession to the populace'[27] the dispute over the tolls was finally settled when a number of citizens joined together to pay off the remaining debts. The Corporation, mindful of the guillotine that had recently been set up in the Place de la Revolution, Paris, warily dismissed the idea of any further enquiry into the massacre by denouncing the promoters of such an investigation as 'revolutionaries'.

Coleridge's Early Days in Bristol

In the 1770s Chatterton had found the cold wind of indifference to his talent too harsh and moved to London to seek fame and fortune. Times were changing, however. To the editors of Defoe's 1778 guide, the city had altered almost beyond recognition. 'Its gentry, merchants and capital traders are polite and superb in their town and country houses, equipages, servants and amusements as any in the Kingdom'. They added that there was now an element of culture to be found in the city: 'Literature and genteel education are much cultivated in Bristol; and it abounds with agreeable women whose modes of dress are universally approved'. Only one thing rankled though, for even behind all this finery the Bristol accent could not be disguised. Although Defoe's guide admitted that 'People of rank and education here, as everywhere else, pronounce with propriety' it had to be said that other members of the trading classes spoke in a 'broad dialect much worse than the common people in the metropolis'.[28]

If Chatterton had been born twenty years later he would have found that the presence in Bristol of the formidable Hannah More (a best selling writer in her time, but now considered unreadable) acted as a magnet to other literati. One such person was the young poet Samuel Taylor Coleridge.

Coleridge had been influenced to move to Bristol by the future Poet Laureate Robert Southey. Together they were advocates of the unfortunately named Pantisocratic scheme which involved a communal search for Utopia—it was all part of the idealism that was sweeping Europe after the French Revolution. Coleridge and his fellows proposed a plan where a dozen or so 'kindred spirits', along with their wives, would move to a settlement on the banks of the Susquehanna (they liked the sound of the name) in North America and establish a commune.

There they thought the good life would come easily. A mere three or four hours work a day would make the group self sufficient whilst the rest of the time would be spent in literary and artistic pursuits.

Whilst waiting for converts to the scheme, Coleridge busied himself by writing radical lectures which, for a small fee, he would present at the Pelican Inn in Thomas Street and various other inns in the city. Although his talk of revolution was rarely passively received he was well able to defend himself against hecklers with his acid wit. On one occasion a hostile audience expressed their disapproval by hissing. Coleridge quickly retorted:

> 'I am not at all surprised that when the red hot prejudices are plunged into cold water they should go off with a hiss.'

His audiences were also amused by his dragged-through-a-hedge-backwards appearance. A local journal wrote:

> 'His speech is a perfect monotonism, his person is slovenly . . .
> Mr Coleridge would do well to appear in cleaner stockings and if his hair were combed out every time he appeared in public it would not deprecate him in the esteem of his friends.'[29]

The Pantisocratists were all to be partnered in their Utopian world and to this end they descended upon the daughters of the widowed Mrs Fricker. Poor Mrs Fricker found that her daughters were every Pantisocratist's dream and they were duly courted.

Robert Lovell, a member of the group had already married one of the Frickers. Robert Southey became engaged to another, Burnet was engaged to a third (she eventually had second thoughts about it realising that he only wanted 'a wife in a hurry') and on September 4th, 1795 Coleridge and Sara Fricker were married in St Mary Redcliffe. After the wedding the young couple went on a protracted honeymoon to the seaside village of Clevedon.

After two months in sleepy Clevedon it comes as no surprise that Coleridge was straining to return to Bristol. He felt that he could no longer remain on his honeymoon whilst 'his unnumbered brethren toiled and bled'.

Coleridge's marriage to Sara could not be described as happy. They married in a blur of idealism; but with time the haze cleared, yet to Coleridge's dismay the marriage bonds remained. Coleridge was not an easy person to live with—even in these early days he was addicted to laudanum, the alcoholic tincture of opium, and consequently subject to unpredictable extremes of mood.[30] Sara was also the victim of malicious gossip amongst Coleridge's literary colleagues. As the poet Shelley was to observe of the Fricker sisters: 'Mrs Southey is stupid; Mrs Coleridge worse'.

They moved back to Bristol into pent up rooms with Mrs Fricker in Redcliffe Hill and from there Coleridge dabbled in journalism, publishing a political rag called the *Watchman*. The magazine, whose motto was 'All might know the truth and the truth might make them free' was intended to stimulate political discussion; in fact the immature and contradictory ramblings served more to muddle than to educate. This confusion was aggravated by the decision to publish every eighth day. Although this avoided stamp tax, the magazine confounded its readers by appearing on different days of the week. After ten issues the paper folded and Coleridge elegized—'O Watchman thou hast watched in vain'.

Undaunted by the lack of converts for the commune and the failure of the magazine, Coleridge turned his attention to something that was to be of more lasting value—the production of his first book of poems. Prior to his arrival in Bristol, Coleridge had offered works to various publishers in London. The best advance to be had was six guineas. Impoverished though he was, the poet was not willing to accept such a miserable fee.

In Bristol, however, the bookseller Joseph Cottle was able to promise a healthy advance of £30. Subsequently there were times when Cottle regretted his benevolence, for Coleridge's procrastination could try even the most patient. Cottle was repeatedly obliged to remind the poet of his commitment. In return Coleridge would send back notes to his publisher explaining his tardiness. His messages ranged from the optimistic: 'I have been composing in the fields this morning' to dramatic excuses: 'A devil, a very devil, has got possession of my left temple, eye, cheek, jaw and shoulder . . . I write in agony'.[31]

The Coleridges left Redcliffe Hill in March 1796 and moved to Oxford Street in Kingsdown.

After much delay the book was published in April 1797. It proved that Coleridge was not merely a hot headed hedonist but also a serious poet and was to pave the way for the works of genius that were to follow.

Overleaf: Neptune, Bristol's most travelled statue. Here, in 1823, standing by the conduit at the corner of Bear Lane.   *City of Bristol Museum and Art Gallery*

Mrs Watts' Dream

Apart from Chatterton and Coleridge, Redcliffe Hill also boasts the residence of another visionary, the plumber's wife, Mrs Watts.

In 1782, Mr Watts, a plumber of Redcliffe Hill, patented a new and startlingly simple process for the manufacture of lead shot. The lead that had been mined in the Mendips since Roman times had given rise to a small lead smelting industry in Bristol. Prior to Mr Watts' new process, lead shot had been laboriously cast in moulds. Like all great inventions the idea behind the new technique was simple. Basically it involved pouring molten lead through a sieve and into a vat of water below. The blobs of lead cooled by the water, formed perfectly spherical balls. Manufactured by this process Mr Watts' lead shot was of good quality and cheap to produce.

There are various tales as to who stumbled across this process, for both Mr Watts and his wife have been accredited with the original inspiration. Mr Watts was allegedly inspired by a dream in which molten lead was pouring from the roof of a burning St Mary Redcliffe. As the lead hit the wet ground it formed into lead shot. Mrs Watts, however, is also reputed to be the visionary. The story is told that in her dream she saw lead pouring from the top landing of her staircase into a container of water below. When she looked into the water she was surprised to find it contained lead shot. She awoke from her sleep and immediately roused her husband and excitedly told him about her dream. Mr Watts, who was unenthusiastic about his wife's wild rantings in the middle of the night, muttered something about 'the folly of dreams' and went straight back to sleep. Mrs Watts also fell asleep but her dreaming continued. Again she woke her husband who was so infuriated by this second interruption to his well earned sleep that he could not help expressing himself in 'somewhat strong saxon'. The next morning in the calm of the day, Mr Watts pondered his wife's dream and thought that there might well be something in it.[32]

Whoever had the dream doesn't matter—what is important is that the process worked. With experiment it was found that the size of lead shot produced depended on the length of the drop. The larger the shot, the longer the drop required. Mr Watts was so sure of the value of the invention he converted his house for production. First, he knocked out the floors and ceilings of his living accommodation and then above this, to gain a 60 ft drop, he built a tower. To make even larger shot, he doubled the drop by digging down below his house into Redcliffe Caves.

Soon Mr Watts' business was doing so well that he was able to make further plans for expansion. A newspaper announced that the inventor was about to enlarge his premises with the erection of a new 'gothic tower'. This structure, alongside the other tower, was to be designed in such an elegant manner that the view of the building was expected to remind the spectator of Westminster Abbey! The expectations were somewhat overstated for the original tower was exceedingly plain, if not ugly, its only embellishment being a castellated top.

But the tower was never built; Mr Watts turned his attention to the fad of speculative building that was raging in the city and Clifton at the time. Mr Watts unwisely invested £10,000 in the development of Windsor Terrace in Clifton. With its steeply sloping terrain it was a precarious building site and most of Mr Watts' money was spent on merely securing the foundations. By 1792 his funds were exhausted and he was forced to offer the building for sale in an unfinished state.

In 1794, the bankrupt Mr Watts, having sold his lead shot business to Philip George (the founder of George's Brewery) disappeared into obscurity. Nevertheless Mr Watts' invention lives on; the original shot tower continued in use till 1967. And even today,

Reputedly inspired by his wife's dream the plumber Mr. Watts built the world's first shot tower on Redcliffe Hill in 1782. Demolished 1967.

City of Bristol Museum and Art Gallery

Sheldon Bush's modern shot tower dominating the skyline of central Bristol is a constant reminder of a two hundred year old vision.

CHAPTER 4: NOTES

1. W.S. Lewis (ed.) *Horace Walpole's Correspondence*, (1941), Vol X, p.232
2. J.H. Bettey, *Bristol Observed*, (Redcliffe Press, 1986) p.67
3. S. Hutton, *Bristol and its Famous Associations* (1907) p.48
4. P. McGrath, 'Bristol since 1497' in *Bristol and its Adjoining Counties* (ed. MacInnes and Whittard, 1955) p.214
5. I.V. Hall, *Temple Street Sugar House under the first Partnership of Richard Lane and John Hine, 1662-1678* (B.G.A. 76.1957) p.1286
6. Cyril Weedon, 'The Bristol Bottlemakers' *Chemistry and Industry* (June 3rd, 1978) p.378
7. ibid. p.379
8. P.T. Marcy, '18th Century Views of Bristol and Bristolians' *Bristol in the 18th Century* (ed. P. McGrath, Newton Abbot, 1972) p.16
9. H.E. Mathews, *The Company of Soapmakers* (Bristol Record Society) p.196
10. P. Roger, *Defoe, John Oldmixon and the Bristol Riots of 1714* (B.G.A.S., 1973) p.145-146
11. J. Evans, *A Chronological Outline of the History of Bristol* (1824) p.256-257
12. *Sarah Farley's Journal* July 29th, 1749
13. *Bristol Journal*, August 12th, 1749
14. J. Latimer, *Annals of 18th Century Bristol* (1893) p.269
15. ibid, p.367
16. R.C. Tombs, *The Bristol Post* (1899) p.20
17. S. Hutton, op cit, p.48
18. *Felix Farley's Bristol Journal*, February 6th, 1947, p.48)
19. P.T. Marcy, *Bristol's Roads and Communications on the Eve of the Industrial Revolution* (B.G.A.S., 1968) Vol.87, p.152
20. J. Latimer, op cit, p.175
21. J.A. Spring and D.H. Buss, *Nature* (December 15th, 1977) Vol. 270
22. *Boswell's Life of Johnson* (Globe Edition) p.370
23. B. Cottle, 'Thomas Chatterton', in P. McGrath, *Bristol in the 18th Century* (1972) p.104
24. Anon. *An Impartial History of the Late Riots in Bristol*, p.9
25. J. Evans, op cit, p.300
26. ibid, p.300
27. Anon. *An Impartial History of the Late Riots in Bristol*, p.14
28. P.T. Marcy, 'Views of Bristol and Bristolians', *Bristol in the 18th Century*, p.36
29. M. Carpenter, *The Indifferent Horseman*, p.63
30. M. Lefevre, *The Bondage of Love* (London 1986) p.54
31. J. Cottle, *Reminiscences of Coleridge and Southey* (London, 1848) p.37
32. *Work in Bristol*, Bristol (1883) p.187

Other Sources

B. Cottle, 'Thomas Chatterton', in *Bristol in the 18th Century* (ed. McGrath)
John Dix, *Life of Chatterton* (London, 1837) W. Ison, *The Georgian Buildings of Bristol* (London)
P.T. Marcy, *Bristol's Roads and Communications on the Eve of the Industrial Revolution* (B.G.A.S., 1968) Vol 86, p.149-172
W.J. Pountney, *Old Bristol Potteries* (Bristol, 1920)
C. Witt, C. Weeden, A. Palmer Schwind, *Bristol Glass* (Redcliffe Press, 1984)
C. Witt, 'Good Cream Color Ware', in *The Connoisseur* (September, 1979)

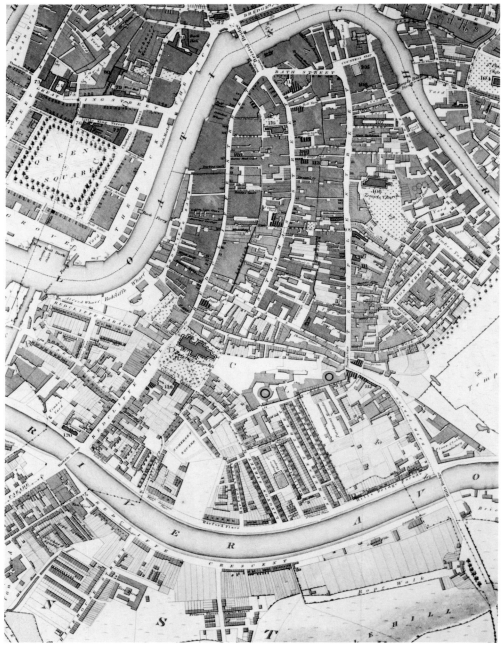

Part of Ashmead's Map of Bristol, 1828. Yards and gardens have been built over—landlords utilised every inch, cramming dwellings into any little space available.   *City of Bristol Museum and Art Gallery*

5—The Floating Harbour

The findings of the first official census of England in 1801 were a disappointment to Bristolians. It had always been believed that the city, with its self-estimated population of over 100,000, was second only to London in the number of its inhabitants. In fact, the national census judged Bristol's population—at a mere 65,645—to be much lower. The census only proved what many well travelled people had already guessed: that Bristol had slipped well behind its rival Liverpool as holder of the cherished position of second city in the nation. Despite the war with America, Liverpool had grown so rapidly after 1775 that Bristol was not able to compete. Liverpool's dynamic expansion was largely due to the success of the cotton trade in Lancashire which produced an increase in both imports and exports.

Meanwhile at the beginning of the nineteenth century the prospects for Bristol did not look good: its trade hinterland was shrinking; its merchants seemed drained of the dynamism that so characterised Bristol's Golden Age and its docks were antiquated.

A change in the national economy was affecting Bristol's local trading position. With the development of the canals, several industries that had traditionally depended on Bristol were able to use services nearer at hand. Bristol was now no longer the 'Welsh metropolis' for the Welsh were developing their own ports.

But in many ways Bristol's merchants had only themselves to blame. It was largely their own attitudes to trade that contributed to this stagnation. They were conservative and content to rest on the laurels of their past achievements. Having enjoyed a healthy and prosperous trade for so long Bristol's merchants no longer looked to expand. Bristol was moving at a slower pace than the hustling, bustling cities of the north that had become the workshop of the world.

Surprisingly, American Independence (1776) and the outlawing of the slave trade (1807) had less of an adverse effect on Bristol's trade than might have been expected. Bristol's involvement with the American War of Independence was only half hearted. In reality Bristolians were not interested in the matter of sovereignty—they wanted trade. With regards to slavery, Bristol's share in the trade had long been dwarfed by Liverpool's—indeed Bristolians and their parliamentary representative Edmund Burke played an active role in the anti-slavery campaign. Although the transportation of Africans was made illegal, Bristolians still benefited from the products of their enforced labour—as late as 1833 one prominent Bristol merchant was to say that without the West Indian trade in slaves and sugar Bristol would have been a mere fishing port.

Even so, the decline of Bristol's trading position was further hastened by the condition of the city's inadequate and old fashioned dock facilities. Only with great difficulty could they handle the large ocean-going ships that plied the Atlantic. For a long time efforts had been made to improve the shipping accommodation offered by the port—plans had first been drawn up in 1765—but it was not until the full implications of the census had sunk in that the matter was considered seriously.

On a local level, there was, at first, persistent opposition to any radical changes in the harbour. At a parish meeting held in Redcliffe in May 1803 the view that a new floating harbour 'would ultimately destroy the present Accommodation of the Port, and would be the ruin of our commerce and trade' was typical of the conservative argument. More to the point perhaps, was the indignation expressed when it was realised that a rise in house rates would accompany any such scheme. The Redcliffe meeting concluded that the advantages of a floating harbour 'must be very remote'.

Despite the opposition of local parishioners, the new harbour development went ahead.

Designed by William Jessop, one of the main objectives was to obviate the inconvenience caused by the ebb and flow of the tide. Jessop's plan was to dig a new channel for the Avon—The Cut—whilst converting, with the aid of locks and dams, the original course of the river into a two and a half mile floating harbour. The main entrance into the float was to be through the Cumberland Basin lock gates. Smaller vessels would be able to sail up The Cut and enter through a side entrance into the triangular Bathurst Basin (named after the MP for Bristol, 1796-1807) which covered the former site of the Treen Mills and Malago Brook.

Jessop's design was not original—in fact it suspiciously echoed a similar proposal put forward in 1791 by the vicar of Temple Church, the Reverend Mitton. The Dock Company was reluctant to admit this, and only very grudgingly did they acknowledge that their plan owed anything to Mitton's original inspiration. As a sop they did, however, award the Reverend with 'a piece of plate not exceeding the value of one hundred guineas'.[1]

On a scale that matched the medieval dock improvements, the building of the Floating Harbour was an undertaking that demanded a large labour force. Six hundred and four navvies started work in 1804 but by the end of the project their numbers had swollen to over a thousand. (Regardless of a long standing tradition that the Cut was dug by French prisoners, there are in fact no records to verify this.) Progress was slow and it soon became clear that the cost and length of the task had been seriously underestimated. In the end the works took over a year longer, and cost twice as much, as originally planned.

At last, precisely five years after its inauguration, the Docks Company were proud, and somewhat relieved, to announce that:

'after struggling through numberless unforeseen difficulties, both local and accidental . . . after having perhaps undertaken to perform in a given time more than it appears possible in the capacity of human art to execute, the directors of this concern have fulfilled their engagement.'[2]

The construction of the Floating Harbour had finally been completed.

To celebrate the event the directors of the Dock Company treated the labourers to a dinner.

'In the good old style of English hospitality,' *Felix Farley's Bristol Journal* cheerfully reported, 'two whole oxen, 6 cwt of plumb pudding, 1,000 gallons of stingo and other things in proportion had been provided'.

But as the stingo was consumed, emotions rose. The *Journal* carried on to report that 'the people indulged themselves of all the graceful eccentricities of liberty'. However, 'upon the arrival of a cart with a fresh supply of ale, some honest Hibernians proceeded rather unceremoniously to disburthen the vehicle of its contents'. The sight of the sack of the beer wagon was just too much for the patience of the 'John Bulls' and soon a full scale drunken brawl broke out. The dinner, now turned riot, was only 'terminated by the interference of the police and the press gang; but not without taking one party of combatants to Bridewell'.[3]

Though the Floating Harbour was completed in 1809 little economic benefit was derived from it for many years. The Dock Company insisted on a good return for its investment by the imposition of unrealistically high rates. A great deal of business must have been lost for the levies were extortionate: they exceeded those paid at Liverpool by 60% and London by 115%.

The Floating Harbour was a grand undertaking and even today it is an epic monument to the spirit of nineteenth century engineering. It is still virtually intact and now represents the very heart and character of the city of Bristol. But even so, this show of confidence was not enough to halt the downward turn in the city's trade—in reality the building of the Floating Harbour turned out to be the port's swansong.

Entrance to Bathurst Basin. Floating Harbour completed in 1809:smaller vessels were able to sail up The Cut and enter through a lock into the Bathurst Basin.

71

'An Extensive and Commodious Building'

'This is an extensive and commodious building,' wrote the editor of the 1825 *Mathew's Bristol, Clifton and Hotwell Guide*, 'which for health convenience and excellent arrangement is not to be equalled in England, commanding extensive views of the surrounding countryside . . . The boundary wall (20 feet high) is built in hewn variegated marble which has a beautiful appearance'. What was this handsome construction? An hotel in Clifton? Or perhaps a new commercial citadel? In fact, the writer of the guide was describing Bristol's latest contribution to progressive thinking—The New Gaol.

Prior to 1820 Bristol's two prisons—Bridewell and Newgate—were housed in buildings most unsuited to their use. Of the whitewashed Newgate, John Howard, the outspoken eighteenth century prison reformer wrote 'it is white without and foul within'.[4] It was largely due to the pressures exerted by such selfless agitators as Howard that attention focused towards the end of the century on the national scandal of the country's prisons. But it was a slow process: Howard visited Bristol in 1774, and in spite of his public protests very few improvements were made. The insalubrity of the Bridewell is emphasised by the fact that a cat had to be kept in the cells at night to stop rats and mice from gnawing the prisoners' feet.

However, in 1816, after a series of enquiries and reports the Corporation at last proposed that a new gaol should be built at a cost of £60,000. A piece of land away from the more crowded areas (just outside the Redcliffe Parish Boundary) and sandwiched between The Cut and the Floating Harbour was chosen for building on—the vicinity today is still known colloquially as Spike Island. The building of the gaol was finished in August 1820 when the first prisoners were transported by wagon from Newgate, the Bridewell continuing in use.

Unquestionably the New Gaol was a great advance on the buildings that it superseded and was held up as a model to be emulated across the country. It was designed to hold 197 prisoners, all to be kept in single cells measuring 6 feet by 9 feet. Facilities were such (and this was unusual) that the prisoners were expected to be able to wash their hands and faces and comb their hair daily—and even bath once a month.

The water for their ablutions was to come from an inexhaustible well one hundred feet deep, the water being raised by a treadmill. The treadmill, or cockchaffer as it was euphemistically called, was a familiar feature of nineteenth century penal institutions. The New Gaol was equipped with treadmills for twenty persons—besides drawing water the treadmills were also used for grinding corn.

Both sexes were catered for in the prison—but were to be strictly segregated. The female prisoners were supervised by a matron and no male warders were allowed to visit the female prisoners unless accompanied by the matron or another female officer.

The granite gatehouse with its mock portcullis was equipped with a flat roof and a trap door specifically designed for executions. Executions were, of course, public affairs—and good crowd pullers at that. This could cause a problem as space for spectators was limited by the New Cut which was just across the road from the gatehouse. At the first public execution in 1821 of a young lad sentenced for killing his girlfriend there was such a crush that notices had to be put up warning people to beware of being pushed into the unfenced Avon.[5]

As exemplary as the prison was, by 1840 conditions had, for a variety of reasons, declined. A report by the visiting magistrates published in 1841 is reminiscent of the bad old days; much of the damage from the 1831 Riots had never been rectified, conditions were overcrowded and unpleasant, and discipline was lax.

For a start, the magistrates found the so-called inexhaustible supply of water to be undrinkable whilst the much vaunted availability of baths was non existent. Many of the prisoners were poorly clothed against the winter cold and some even had no shoes or other footwear. Also, due to the smallness of the windows, the air-supply in the prison was static, the atmosphere consequently becoming stale and fetid. On the other hand many of the cells had unglazed iron windows with wooden shutters; in the winter the prisoners were compelled either to be shut in darkness or suffer the cold.

Additionally the magistrates noted that the supervision of the prison at night-time was difficult as, apart from times of a clear sky and a bright moon, the buildings were swathed in darkness. The installation of gas lamps was therefore recommended.

The magistrates had already ordered food allowances to be increased: 'five ounces of dressed meat to be given twice a week, soup twice a week, and larger portions of bread when meat was not allowed'. Lest the magistrates were thought of as soft or extravagant, they felt compelled to point out that they were only meeting the requirements laid down by the Secretary of State, adding that due to this new dietary regime 'far less sickness is to be found in the prison'.[6]

And finally, with regards to security, the Justices found the prison to be grossly understaffed. There was one clerk and just six warders, or turnkeys as they were called, for both day and night duty, and only one female officer to act as matron. Not surprisingly the segregation of the sexes had proved impossible. It was even claimed that two female prisoners had become pregnant by one of the warders—who had subsequently absconded. Security being of the utmost importance, even by the time the Justice's report had been published, the number of staff had been increased to twenty-three.

With more staff, the Justices were able to operate their 'new system' of discipline within the gaol. It had long been recognised that prison was not so much a place of correction but more a college of crime. 'To commit a fellow creature to jail in its present state,' wrote the magistrates in 1837, 'is to consign him to almost irretrievable infamy and ruin'. The 'new system', however consisted of minimising the contact of fellow prisoners so that they lived in virtual solitary confinement. According to an enthusiastic report of 1841 the new arrangements were so successful that 'we know of one hundred and one prisoners tried and convicted since this new system was enforced, who now honestly earn their bread by the sweat of their brow, and appear to be thoroughly reformed characters'. Indeed, no lesser an authority than the Deputy Lieutenant of the County of Cork backed up this claim by writing that 'having devoted many years to the improvement of my own county gaol, and for this purpose (having) closely examined many gaols in England and on the continent, I feel confident in stating that I have seen none equal to the Bristol gaol'.

Despite this glowing report, over the following years conditions yet again deteriorated. In 1872 the Home Office remonstrated with the Corporation that the prison was unfit for its purpose. The gaol was in such a state of decay that nothing could be done except to start building yet again. Accordingly the Corporation bought some land north of the city at Horfield Gardens but wisely procrastinated from doing anything further. Bristol was spared the expense of building another prison when, in 1878, the Home Office took over responsibility for penal institutions across the country.

All that remains of the New Gaol today—it was last used in 1883 and sold to the Great Western Railway in 1895—is the flat roofed grey gatehouse beside the Cumberland Road, and a few yards of wall that is incorporated into the buildings of a coal merchant.

Above: The New Gaol (opened 1820) 'an extensive and commodious building which for convenience and excellent arrangement is not to be equalled in England' was held up as a model to be emulated across the country. *City of Bristol Museum and Art Gallery*

Below: The gatehouse with its flat roof and 'drop' for public executions is all that remains of the prison today. *M. Manson.*

Anarchy and Anger

On the morning of Saturday, October 29th, 1831 Bristol's Recorder, Sir Charles Wetherall, arrived to open the Court's Quarter Sessions. Wetherall's presence in the city signalled the beginning of the Bristol Riots, a short period of rebellion that was to both shatter the city and stun the nation. In the days that followed, Bristol experienced a sustained riot that has since remained unequalled in England's history; for the next three days anarchy and anger were to rule the city.

What sparked off this explosion of lawlessness? The upset caused by Wetherall's arrival in Bristol must be viewed against a wider backdrop of both local and national discontent. The mob's targets over the next few days were to give an indication of where some of the local problems lay. As Lord Byron had said to the House of Lords: 'You may call the people a mob; but do not forget that the mob often speaks the sentiments of the people'. Thus attacks upon the Mansion House, the prisons and the Bishop's Palace were all expressions of long standing grievances. Unemployment was certainly one reason for discontent. Some believed that ever since the construction of the floating harbour wages had dropped and jobs had become scarce. During the riots the Luddite cry was frequently heard to 'cut down the lock gates'.

The greatest amount of hatred was, however, reserved for the Corporation. The Corporation had become so aloof and remote from the working classes that its workings were generally regarded with suspicion. Where was the rate money going? Whose interests were really being looked after? To many, the Corporation was seen merely as an openly wasteful clan, a self electing secretive clique, that indulged itself at the cost of the rate payers, in numerous official dinners, ceremonies and other extravagances. In the slowly deteriorating parishes of Redcliffe, Temple and St Thomas it was generally thought that the rates could be put to better use than these shows of pomp and civic pride.

There were also national problems. 1831 was the year of the controversial debate on Parliamentary Reform. Due to the rapid growth of population in some parts of the country large areas had found themselves without representation in Westminster. The House of Lords' eventual rejection of an electoral reform that would rectify, to a certain extent, this inequality had caused a national uproar. One person who had openly been opposed to reform was Wetherall.

Even at the best of times Wetherall was an unpopular man. Indeed, the London newspaper the *Morning Chronicle* had gone so far as to call him 'the most detested man in the Kingdom'.[8] To make matters worse, because he held the office of Recorder in Bristol, Wetherall had recently taken it upon himself to speak in Parliament on behalf of the city. According to a reformist writer he asserted himself in a most unusual manner. It was reported during the Reform debate that:

> 'The conduct of Sir Charles Wetherall, at all times eccentric, was during the discussion of the Reform Bill in the House of Commons the most extraordinary that has ever been witnessed, even in that place'.

Wetherall was jumping the mark here, for far from being Bristol's elected member he merely represented a small rural parish in Yorkshire, a rotten borough, that was due to disappear if the Reform Bill was passed.

So the riots were not entirely unexpected. Indeed, during the previous twelve months there had been numerous large and sometimes boisterous Sunday political meetings in Queen Square. A few days prior to the riots the Council, sensing that trouble was brewing, had taken steps to recruit special constables. Unfortunately their appeal for help from the more respectable members of society fell upon deaf ears (in itself a measure of the council's unpopularity) and eventually one hundred and seventeen less suitable 'bludgeon men' were recruited. It was Wetherall's presence in Bristol that was to act as a final catalyst to emotions that were already running high.

As Wetherall's coach pressed on down Temple Street it was almost hemmed in by a mud slinging, jeering crowd. Even though the Corn Street courts were heavily guarded it was felt that the opening of the assize would be unwise against such a volatile background.

The Judge therefore made his way hastily to an official luncheon with the Mayor in the Mansion House in Queen Square.

As a large and jostling crowd quickly gathered outside the Mansion House it was obvious that if the situation were to be contained a calming influence was required. Unfortunately, the special constables tended to inflame matters rather than soothe them. The last thing that was needed was a heavy handed bunch of ill disciplined special constables throwing their weight around. Consequently there were sporadic outbreaks of fighting as a group of 'specials' unwisely made some arrests.

The shouts of the crowd in Queen Square were soon punctuated by the sound of shattering glass as the windows of the Mansion House were broken and the iron railings torn down. The Mayor, Charles Pinney, a reformist, and therefore not unpopular with the crowd, attempted to address the throng. But they were in no mood to listen and eventually the Riot Act was read with no effect—the increasingly restless crowd merely responded with jeers and catcalls. Then, after the special constables had been brutally disarmed, a number of the mob broke into the ground floor of the Mansion House and looted furniture, food and drink. One of the ringleaders, Christopher Davis of The Counterslip, Temple Parish tucked into the banquet that had been prepared for the Mayor and Recorder saying 'what a shame it is that there should be so much waste when so many poor wretches are starving'.[9] Wetherall, meanwhile, realising that he was in great danger escaped by a back window over the rooftops to make a timely exit from the city.

Surprisingly, it was not until 6.00pm that the two troops of horse soldiers that had been stationed outside the city in preparation for trouble were brought onto the scene. The Alderman and the Town Clerk advocated the immediate use of force to clear the square but the Colonel-in-Charge, Colonel Brereton, strongly disapproved of the use of violence in this case, and ordered his troops to disperse the crowd by slowly and peacefully riding through them. It seemed to do the trick for after talking and handshaking with many of the crowd the Colonel reported that they were in good humour and that he was satisfied that they would soon be going home for the night.

By the next morning Brereton believed that the worst of the violence was over. After the breaches in the Mansion House had been boarded up he ordered the handful of troops left in the Square to be withdrawn. But Brereton had seriously underestimated the depth of discontent for by 8.00am a crowd had again gathered outside the Mansion House. Seizing their chance they stormed the unprotected building. It was now the Mayor's turn to flee for his life across the rooftops.

It was about this time that a most ill-advised and fateful decision was made; the two troops of the 14th Light Dragoons, 'the bloody blues', were ordered to leave the city at a trot. This surprising command was given because the troops were reported to be not only exhausted after a twenty hour period on standby but also it was believed that the Dragoons' reputation for violence was causing more harm than good. Doubtless it was a tactical blunder. The small force of the Third Dragoon—numbering only thirty-three cavalry men—that remained, were powerless by themselves to maintain order; they were left in the position of being merely helpless onlookers. The city was at the mercy of the looters. The withdrawal of the 14th Dragoons was a rioter's charter.

The news of the soldiers' departure spread quickly and soon several buildings were under attack. The gaols were the rioters' first target. The antiquated Bridewell was ransacked within minutes and all the prisoners were freed. Over at the New Gaol, Mr Humphries, the governor, fearing that his prison would be under attack at any moment hurried to the Guild Hall to receive instructions as to whether he should defend the gaol or release the inmates. But officials in the Guild Hall were in such a state of panic that he received no guidance and left announcing that he would use his discretion.

Within minutes of his return a crowd swarmed across Princes Street Bridge and besieged the Gaol. A gaoler who viewed the scene from the roof excitedly, and somewhat inaccurately, shouted down to his colleagues that the prison was surrounded by ten or twelve thousand people. In comparison with the gate of the Bridewell the metal gates of the New Gaol were strong: but not strong enough to resist the continued battering of the crowd. After three quarters of an hour of energetic hammering, accompanied by 'language of a most savage nature', a hole was beaten through the gate. After a couple of people had climbed through, the gates were opened to the mob. Three hundred people surged into the building to liberate the inmates; within minutes the gaol had lost its 170 prisoners.

The mob continued on its wave of violence with drunken gangs marauding through the city unopposed. The Bishop's Palace was raided and the Mansion House, along with other property in Queen Square, set alight.

In the evening a troop of yeomanry from Gloucestershire unexpectedly arrived in Bristol to offer their assistance. Captain Codrington spent two hours riding round the city trying to obtain the permission from various authorities for his troops to be engaged against the rioters. Eventually, he was so exasperated by the confusion that he shouted at Brereton 'This is too bad. I will not be humbugged in this manner any longer', and rode home.[10]

It was on Monday morning, the third day of the riot, that the troops of the 14th were called back and reinforcements arrived from Gloucester. Order was only restored after much bloodshed. The troops charged through the streets freely slashing with their sabres. In all it has been loosely estimated that between two hundred and fifty and five hundred people died in the disturbances from drunkeness, drowning, fire and the sword.

The riots were, of course, a national topic of discussion and the events added fuel to the already explosive debate over Reform. The anti-reformists saw the riots as a foretaste of the new democracy and claimed that the rioters were madmen bitten by the 'fiery serpent of the press'.[11] In an article on the troubles the anti-reformist *Blackwoods Advertiser* warned that 'there is not a city, town, village or hamlet . . . where if the restraints of law were removed the mob would not rise up above their superiors'. On a more positive side, however, a pamphlet *Thoughts on Education, Union of Classes and Cooperation suggested by the Late Riots of Bristol* noted that a vast proportion of rioters were unable to read and pressed for the extension of education to lift the working man from a life of 'ignorance, sensuality and vice' to a state of 'knowledge, intellect and virtue'.[12]

Back in Bristol, after the disturbances the Mayor was tried for neglect of duty and Colonel Brereton was court martialled. The Mayor was acquitted, though more on account of sympathy for his frail physique—he was unable to ride a horse—than for his management of the debacle.

At the end of the fourth day of Brereton's trial, the mild mannered Colonel could take the humiliation of his court martial no more. He went home, and without, as was his custom, saying goodnight to his children, shot himself through the head.[13]

A special commission was also set up to try the rioters—eventually four were hanged outside the New Goal and eighty were sentenced to transportation or lesser punishment. Although some of those convicted were hardened trouble makers, there were many who were hitherto honest family men who had unfortunately become carried away by the horrific dynamics of mob violence.

Whatever view is taken of the riot, the Corporation was utterly discredited. That even the law-abiding citizens felt a certain distance from the Corporation is exemplified by the lack of response at the height of the riot to pleas for help. The citizens not only refused to enroll as special constables before Wetherall's arrival but they also withheld their support for the duration of the troubles. In fact, thousands of 'well dressed' onlookers unintentionally protected the rioters by their presence on the street and did nothing to stop the looting that was so brazenly happening under their noses.

In short, a new age was dawning on local government yet the Corporation was still muddling through on an outmoded system of laissez-faire when it should have been offering positive guidelines for the improvement of a rapidly expanding city. The riots were part of the price to be paid by an alienated corporation that had neglected the working person and their changing environment.

(Afterword—The Reform Act was eventually passed in 1832; the King, who felt 'deepest affliction' due to the 'scenes of violence and outrage . . . which have occurred in the City of Bristol' recommended the establishment of municipal police forces throughout the Kingdom; and finally, in 1835, the Corporation of Bristol was re-organised under the auspices of the Municipal Corporations Reform Act.)

Brunel's Blunders

If the spirit of the Victorian age is symbolised by the railways, then Brunel's Temple Meads station must surely be the era's cathedral. The station's sheer scale and size dwarf any other previous secular buildings in Bristol; not for nothing has it been called 'one of the greatest industrial monuments to the city'.[14]

Temple Meads station was originally built as the terminus for the Great Western Railway, the seeds of which were sown at a meeting of Bristol businessmen in offices at Temple Back in 1833. The railway was established with a capital of £2½ million. By the time the line to London opened in July 1841, costs had exceeded £8 million. The chief engineer to oversee the work was Bristol's most famous adopted son, Isambard Kingdom Brunel. Brunel was at the height of his creative energy; his design for Clifton suspension bridge had been accepted in 1831, the ss *Great Western* had been launched in 1837, and the ss *Great Britain* in 1843. One could travel to Bristol in Brunel's railway, stay in Brunel's Great Western Hotel and sail to America on Brunel's boats. The 'little giant' was master of both the land and sea.

Brunel's station at Temple Meads—built on part of the site of the only recently established cattle market—was in two distinct parts. The front, in tudor castellated style, was built for large offices, the reception of passengers and living accommodation for the station master. Victorian arbiters of taste like Pugin and Ruskin ridiculed the GWR's tudor style as anachronistic and inappropriate; they certainly had a point, but in many ways, the design, rather than being backward looking is so confident—almost theatrical—that it seems a suitable reflection of Victorian ebullience.

Once the tickets had been bought travellers proceeded, surprisingly, upstairs to the railway which was raised up on an arched viaduct. It was all very exciting and dramatic.

City of Bristol Museum and Art Gallery

The Temple Meads terminus of the Great Western Railway was opened in July 1841.

The engine shed is enormous and even by today's standards the 72 feet span of the mock hammerbeam roof is impressive.

Despite the seemingly obvious advantages of railway transport there were those who objected to its introduction. The landed gentry formed the most vociferous opposition for it was mostly over their land that the railways ran. There were also some more bizarre objections; farmers feared that their sheep would be stained by smutty smoke, whilst in Buckinghamshire it was conjectured that the sight of a GWR train puffing past the playing fields of Eton would stir up thoughts of revolution in the minds of the impressionable pupils.

Nevertheless, these objections were overruled and the Great Western Railway built. Today Brunel's work is overwhelmingly remembered with respect and affection. But Brunel has not always been held in such reverence. Brunel may have been a man of exciting vision, but, in common with many geniuses, he was also arrogant and unwilling to compromise. His stubborness, and indeed the way that he would sometimes ignore the practicalities of the matter, did not endear him to everybody. The Mayor of Bristol was to declare that the city was 'waking from its trance' and he foresaw 'the light of better days approaching at railway speed'. This may have been so, but because of Brunel's unfortunate insistence on the use of broad gauge the speed was not so much of an express, but a goods train.

Even with the benefit of hindsight, John Latimer wrote 50 years later that Brunel was 'an inexperienced theorist, enamoured of novelty, prone to seek difficulties rather than evade them, and utterly indifferent to the outlay which his recklessness entailed upon his employers'.[15]

So why the discontent? Brunel had contentiously chosen the 7 feet broad gauge railway for the Great Western line rather than Stephenson's more widely accepted 4 feet 8½ inches narrow gauge. The broad gauge's advantage of providing a more comfortable ride in effect threw a barrier round the South West and handicapped Bristol in its competition with the northern ports. It was a remarkable blunder. Usually a man of vision, Brunel seemed unwilling to accept that the rail network would spread across the land, asserting that the GWR would never have any connection with other main lines. He was soon proved wrong. By 1844 it was possible to travel by rail from Bristol as far as Newcastle. The journey was interrupted, however, at Gloucester where it was necessary to change from broad to narrow gauge. Such a change, which was merely an inconvenience for passengers, entailed a good deal of extra labour for freight. The cheapness of railway transport came through its continuity; to lose this and incur the unnecessary loading and unloading of freight increased costs drastically. Because of Brunel's stubborness Bristol's port and industries were unable to take full advantage of the invention of the age.

There was another problem. 'God's Wonderful Railway' had come so far, yet it stopped a few hundred yards short of what should have been its most useful destination—the Docks. It seems almost inconceivable that it was not for another thirty years that a line connected Temple Meads with the port. Eventually, a tunnel was dug under Redcliffe Hill taking a line that ran across the mouth of the Bathurst Basin to Wapping Wharf. It was such an immediate success that ships were soon reluctant to moor anywhere except by the railway. It was consequently decided 'to connect also Bathurst Wharf with the General Railway System; where for want of such accommodation consignees refuse to have their vessels berthed, and sheds now lie idle'.[16]

Brunel's blunders aside, one hundred and fifty years later Bristol can only be grateful to the engineer; the Clifton Suspension Bridge, the ss *Great Britain* and the GWR Terminal epitomise Bristol to many visitors.

The Dark Secrets of Redcliffe Caves

Whilst building the docks railway in 1861, the navvies tunnelling through Redcliffe Hill uncovered an underground passage; once again, Redcliffe's best known secret had been 'discovered'. But for most people living in the vicinity, the unearthing of the passage came as no surprise. Any true Redclivian knew only too well about the caves and the tales of smugglers and slaves attached to them. The railway engineers, however, were keen to find out more and so, in true pioneering spirit, armed with candles and torches and clinging nervously to a rope lest they lost their way, they ventured into the darkness.

> 'After creeping through a low narrow passage, some twenty yards in length, the party came to a row of arches, each of which led in an opposite direction. Taking the centre one, the party had to crawl on their hands and knees for about ten yards under a great rock, and then they emerged into a spacious and lofty cavern, whence there were other branches. A journey of two or three hundred feet further, chiefly through low narrow corridors, brought them to what appeared to be the grand salon or chief cave. It is perfectly circular in form, the room sloping to a few feet off the ground . . . Although the party explored some six or seven branches most were walled up or filled with rubbish'.[17]

What had happened was that over the years the caves had been used as a rubbish tip. Numerous shafts had been dug from above and all sorts of detritus deposited down them. The Shot Tower had made use of such shafts for dumping ashes which were then carried away by wheelbarrow to far-off corners. Excavations in 1938 and 1939 also revealed great piles of pottery and glass. So, with all this spoil, and also because several of the chambers are walled up, the caves have retained some of their secrets and even today their true extent remains unsurveyed.

The caves are man-made; in some places there can still be seen the marks of the hatchets used in their excavation. But why was this network of caves dug? The answer is tantalisingly simple. Sand may be the world's most common mineral, but it is still highly prized, especially when the source is within a city. The uses of sand and sandstone are almost limitless and would have been used for building, repairing roads, glass industry—it was particularly suitable for the production of heavy bottle glass—and as a glaze for the local coarse pottery. And it also played an important part in Bristol's maritime trade—indeed Redcliffe's sandstone is said to be spread round the ports of the world because of its use as ballast. It was written in 1657, of one ship that the 'Ballist that was then on board was good clift Ballist and such Ballast as ships of this port of Bristoll doe usually carry to Virginia'.[18] As to the age of the caves, although the earliest written reference appears in the sixteenth century they must be much older—some parts of the excavations are probably as old as the Southern Parishes themselves.

Caves are invariably imbued with dark secrets and mysteries and this warren of chambers is no exception. Across the country stories of caves and smugglers seem to go hand in hand. What are caves for if not to be used as a warehouse for contraband? Unfortunately for storytellers any such tales about Redcliffe Caves are certainly spurious—so obvious an hiding place would have defeated its own purpose.

Local folklore also links Redcliffe Caves with Bristol's slave trade. Shackles are reputed to have been found in the caves, but are unlikely to be anything to do with slaves. The few slaves that did come to Bristol were far too valuable to be kept in such dark and dank surroundings.

Prisoners of war, however, were another matter—and this is the more likely origin of the shackles. From 1654, when Cromwell ordered that Bristol's Norman castle be demolished, the city had no secure place for the detention of foreign prisoners. In 1665 the situation became so desperate that fifty Dutch prisoners, captured by Admiral Blake and Vice Admiral Penn, were brought to Redcliffe and lodged, of all places, in the crypt of the church, where they stayed for over four months before being transported to more suitable accommodation at Chepstow Castle.[19]

When the difficulties of prison accommodation arose again a century later when wars raged on the continent, a Mr French offered his one-acre yard as a makeshift detention centre. Records of Mr French's prison—on a site at the rear of the present day General Hospital (a French's lane still runs off Guinea Street) are scant and disjointed but they do seem to indicate that his yard was connected by a passage to the caves. Spanish prisoners were kept in this passage in 1741 and it was again used for French prisoners in 1744.[20]

The security in French's yard was lax. It was bounded by a nine foot high wall, but even when prisoners escaped where were they to go? Apart from stowing away on a ship foreign prisoners were unlikely to get far. Nevertheless there were escapes. On one occasion a group of Spaniards who had been given leave to wash their linen failed to return[21] while in January 1745 it was reported that 'a number of men attempted to escape by scaling a wall in Guinea Street; one being shot dead by the sentinel, the others retreated to their prison in the rock'.[22] Despite this breach, in March of the same year another '175 men were landed at the Key, and from there conveyed to Redcliffe Hill where they were immediately put under proper confinement'.[23] The yard continued in occasional use, but after an outbreak of typhus in 1780 it was abandoned, and the prisoners transferred to a less crowded spot at Knowle.

Over the following years the caves gradually slipped out of public notice being used for the more mundane purposes of pottery store and, of course, rubbish tip. Until, that is, the railway navvies hacked their way through what was probably the very passage that led to French's Yard.

In the Second World War the caves were in the news again when they were used for air-raid shelters. How safe they were is open to conjecture for when bombs demolished Redcliffe Infants' School a crater penetrated right down into the caverns below.

And what of the Redcliffe caves today? At the time of writing the caves are closed to the public whilst the City Council ponders developments on Alfred's Wharf. Hopefully, in the not too distant future, the caves will once more be open for guided tours—they are certainly a fascinating and mysterious link with Bristol's past.

CHAPTER FIVE: NOTES

1. J. Lord & J. Southam, *The Floating Harbour* (Redcliffe Press, 1983) p.34
2. *Felix Farley's Bristol Journal* April 29th, 1809
3. *Felix Farley's Bristol Journal* May 13th, 1809
4. J. Latimer, *Annals of Bristol in the 18th Century* (Bristol, 1893) p.407
5. L. Vear, *South of the Avon* (Wotton-Under-Edge, 1978) p.120
6. *Report of the Visiting Justices into the Gaol and Bridewell of the City of Bristol* (1841) p.5
7. Ibid p.9
8. *Morning Chronicle* (London, January 4th, 1832)
9. W. H. Somerton, *Report of the Trials* (Bristol, 1832) p.77
10. G. Amey, *City Under Fire* (Guildford and London, 1979) p.78
11. Blackwoods Advertiser, *What Caused the Bristol Riots* (1832) p.474
12. *Thoughts on Education, Union of Classes and Cooperation suggested by the Late Riots of Bristol* (London, 1831) p.10
13. P. MacDonald, *Hotheads and Heroes* (Swansea, 1986) p.129
14. R. A. Buchanan, *Industrial Archaeology of Bristol* (1967) p.15
15. John Latimer, *Annals of Bristol in the 19th Century* (Bristol, 1887) p.191
16. J. Lord & J. Southam, op. cit, p.76
17. A. Birmingham newspaper dated October 24th, 1868
18. P. McGrath, *Merchants and Merchandise in 17th Century*, (Bristol, 1955) p.247
19. J. F. Nichols & J. Taylor, *Bristol Past and Present* (Bristol, 1881) Vol 2, p.22
20. J. C. Whitting, *Redcliffe Caves*, unpublished manuscript Bristol Central Reference Library B24381/p.26
21. Margaret Franklin, *Prisoners of War in Bristol*—extracts from Public Record Office Greenwich, unpublished manuscript, Bristol Central Reference Library B30152
22. J. C. Whitting, op cit, p.26
23. *Bristol Oracle and County Intelligencer* March 9th, 1745

Other Sources

R. A. Buchanan & M. Williams, *Brunel's Bristol*, (Redcliffe Press, 1982)
C. Crick, *Victorian Buildings in Bristol*, (Redcliffe Press, 1975)
F. Greenacre and S. Stoddard, *The Bristol Landscape* (Bristol, 1986)
A. Gomme, M. Jenner, B. Little, *Bristol, An Architectural History* (Bristol 1979)
R. Walters, *The Establishment of the Bristol Police Force* (1975)

6—Public Health

Indian Cholera first appeared in the northern coal ports and spread across England reaching Bristol in the summer of 1831. The disease mostly struck in those areas that were the least salubrious; in Bristol, the finger of death pointed first to the desperately overcrowded St Peter's Workhouse and then the parishes of Redcliffe, Temple and St Thomas. To many people, even in an age when the nature of disease was not understood, it came as no surprise. There was an innate feeling that the filthy, overcrowded condition of the parishes constituted a time bomb that would eventually claim many lives. By the beginning of the nineteenth century the golden age of the Southern Parishes had become severely tarnished.

Of course, the parishes had always had a boisterous feel about them. Sailors crammed into the inns, taverns and boarding houses spending their wages, or making the most of what Bristol could offer before they set off on voyages that could last months, or even years. When Revd. Thomas Clarkson gathered evidence in 1787 for Wilberforce on the evils of the slave trade he made straight for the low-life of the Southern Parishes. Clarkson's brief was to see how the trade corrupted those who took part in it. To this end, with a face blackened like a miner, he hung around such pubs as the Seven Stars just off St Thomas Street. He heard plenty of talk about atrocities. For many sailors, life was nasty, brutish and often short. This had always been so. Yet the difference now was that the very fabric of the Southern Parishes, the buildings, the sanitation and the roads, was overstretched and overburdened. Redcliffe, Temple and St Thomas were so teeming with life that they seemed to be bursting at the seams. The decline is evident as early as 1813 when a guide book to Bristol warned visitors of the perils that could be encountered on a visit to St Mary Redcliffe:

> 'The usual approach is by a long narrow street (Redcliffe Street) skirted by small shops and from its contracted nature and its peculiarity of position is generally dirty, black and perilous to the passenger, several manufactories, warehouses and workshops of not the most pleasant and odoriferous kind are distributed on the left and the right whilst the narrow thoroughfare is generally crowded by colliers, sandmen, sledges, sailors, asses and carts.'

The writer concluded by emphasising that: 'In such a situation personal safety is the first care.'

Mathews' Guide of 1815 also warned of something that was as much a concern to the residents as it was to genteel visitors: the 'most noxious pestilential filth' of the harbour:

> 'Every care is taken by the Dock-company to prevent all unwholesome exhalations; though in strict justice it must be acknowledged, that in opposition to all truly laudable exertions, in the summer season particularly, the water acquires a dark unpleasant surface; and where it is most subject to the reception of drains emits a rather offensive smell.'[1]

Simply, the foul smell of the floating harbour arose from the six miles of sewers draining into it. In the old days the odour had been bearable for the harbour had been cleaned twice daily by the tides. But now, with the slower circulation of the water because of the Float the nuisance was becoming intolerable. The float was not just unpleasant to smell, it was also a health risk.

Despite what the editor of *Mathews' Guide* had written, it was a problem that the Dock company resolutely ignored. Even though it was undoubtedly their responsibility, the directors felt under no obligation to help. Eventually in the hot summer of 1825 the company's stubborn refusal to cooperate led to a writ being issued against them. The dock company was at last ordered to make whatever alterations were necessary to clear the Float of sewage.

When the poor were ill or suffering poverty beyond endurance, they could as a last resort enter St Peter's Poorhouse. St Peter's which was across the water from our parishes, had been a poorhouse in one form or another since 1697 when the parishes of Bristol were grouped together to form a co-operative system of relief. Although the half timbered medieval building was maintained as well as conditions allowed, it was dreadfully crowded with up to six hundred inhabitants at any one time. So, not surprisingly, when the 1831 epidemic of cholera swept the country it was a primary target for the disease. Of two hundred and sixty-one cases reported in the city, one hundred and sixty-eight occurred in St Peter's.

On just one day at the peak of the epidemic, thirty-one victims of the disease were ferried across the river and buried in Temple churchyard. Because the numbers were so high a bizarre rumour spread that paupers were being buried alive just to get rid of them. There followed a macabre scene in the churchyard where members of a crowd exhumed some of the recently buried bodies so as to be sure that they were truly dead.

Even before the cholera outbreak it had been obvious that the medical facilities in Bristol were overstretched and that a new hospital was needed to supplement the work of the Bristol Infirmary (established 1737). With this in mind a group—many of whom were Quakers—got together to promote the establishment of the Bristol General Hospital. With the cholera outbreak, the Bristol riots and general state of national unrest because of the reform bill, 1831 was hardly an auspicious year for new ventures. Nevertheless, after a survey of sites in the city, suitable premises were found in Guinea Street, in accommodation already owned by Dr Kentish.

The situation, by Bathurst Basin and The Cut was described as airy and was well placed for the growing populations of South Bristol and Bedminster. There was one objection, however—its closeness to Acramans Anchor Works. Concern was expressed that the constant hammering and clattering from the forge,—as well as the fumes—would have a far from recuperative effect on the patients. A sub committee appointed to look into this reported that any such fears were unfounded and furthermore declared the site to be 'particularly salubrious and desirable'.[2]

After a slight delay over the appointment of staff due to 'the disturbed state of public affairs' the hospital was formally opened on November 1st, 1832. From the beginning the twenty beds were well used; indeed with up to 40 in-patients being looked after at any one time, beds frequently had to be shared. Even though there was still no understanding of bacteria or anaesthetics the patients were at least well fed. The meals provided were:

> Breakfast—6ozs. of bread. 1 pint of tea.
> Dinner—6ozs. of meat and potatoes, four days a week. 1 quart of broth, and 12 ozs. of
> boiled rice on other days.
> 1 Pint of beer.
> Supper—6ozs. of bread. 1 pint of gruel.[3]

Doctors were trained to as high a standard as medical knowledge would allow, but in the days before Florence Nightingale the quality of nursing was not high. The matron's job was said to be particularly demanding—so much so that she requested a supply of beer to steady her nerves: 'The matron finds it necessary for her health to use a little porter', the hospital committee were told. Accordingly they ordered three dozen pint bottles for the matron's use.[4]

Acramans was finally silenced in 1851 when the General Hospital bought the works for further development. In its early days the hospital led a hand-to-mouth existence but by the 1850s finances were on a sure enough footing for new purpose built premises to be planned. Two four-storey blocks were built—one facing the New Cut, the other the Bathurst Basin. Compared with the rudimentary Guinea Street premises the new

Above: View from Welsh Back looking towards Redcliffe Back and St. Mary Redcliffe. The Floating Harbour was not just unpleasant to smell but was a risk to health.

Below: 'Vermin Farm' in the shadow of Redcliffe Church—a warren of dirty rotten sheds rumoured to be a haven for criminals.

hospital was a showpiece. There was a bathroom with hot and cold water on each floor, a steam driven lift, speaking tubes and even heating in the passageways.[5] Another novel feature of the hospital was that the ground floor was designed and let out as a warehouse. It was hoped that the prime warehouse space so close to Bathurst Basin would generate extra income for the hospital.

Although the terrible mortality of 1831 caused some to wonder if cholera was connected to the unsanitary conditions of the large towns, Parliament did not consider the matter seriously until 1840. An enquiry in 1840, into the public health of towns was a pioneering initiative. For the first time it showed an awareness of the need for statutory control in planning the future of the nation's rapidly expanding towns and cities (though how seriously this was taken at a local level was another matter). The national commission of 1840 was followed in 1844 by local enquiries into public health and predictably the picture that was drawn of Bristol's dark and reeking streets was most unflattering.

Commissioner Sir Henry De La Beche found conditions so unpleasant during one of his tours of Bristol's slums that he hastily disappeared down an alley to vomit. Even the strong stomach of the Government was turned by what it saw.[6]

The report announced that the mortality rate in Bristol was scandalously high—at thirty-one in every thousand, it was exceeded only by two other areas in England. To the commissioners the cause of this high rate was obvious: the lack of sewerage in many parts of Bristol. They wrote:

'Viewed as a sanitary question there are few if any large towns in England in which the supply of water is so inadequate as Bristol'[7]

The Parishes of Redcliffe, Temple and St Thomas were singled out as having the worst conditions. The parishes not only had a growing population in an already over crowded area but moreover the water supply was insufficent and sometimes unreliable. Everybody depended on the communal taps and ancient conduits for their 'fresh water'. No house in any of the three parishes had its own water supply. Sometimes in the summer months even the minimal supplies would fail and parishioners had to buy water by the jar for the exorbitant price of a halfpenny or three-farthings. The opinion of the commisioners was that;

'As the climate is salubrious and poverty not particularly severe we can only look for the causes of the unhealthy state of the city in the neglect of the proper sanitary conditions. We have seen these to be bad drainage and sewerage, deficient supplies of water, bad structural arrangements of streets and dwellings and an overcrowded population.'[8]

The report optimistically concluded:

'These are in great measure removable causes and most of them are within the recognizable province of legislation.'[9]

At a time when the mere hint of guidance from central government gave rise to fears of 'centralisation' and 'interference', the commissioners' faith in legislation was unjustified. Little was done to remedy the unhealthy conditions.

With monotonous predictability yet another epidemic was soon to rage through Bristol. The outbreak of cholera in the city in 1849 claimed 444 lives in just four weeks. The outbreak even swept through the previously salubrious Redcliffe Parade, a row of houses on a high and airy situation overlooking the docks. It did, however, nudge a few councillors into action and another inquiry was initiated. Once more the conditions of the three Southern Parishes were brought to the forefront and described as shocking in every detail. Bristol's great historian John Latimer omitted the details from his *Annals of Bristol* explaining that:

Three Kings Inn, St. Thomas Street. The community had grown rotten with old age; the houses had decayed, as had the reputation of their inhabitants.   *City of Bristol Museum and Art Gallery*

'no conception of the actual facts could be given without employing terms repugnant to modern habits and good taste'.[10]

According to the police there were a hundred and thirty-two grimy, overcrowded courts in the parishes of Redcliffe, Temple and St Thomas some of which were never visited by the scavenger. With few restrictions on what owners could do with their property, landlords utilised every inch by cramming dwellings into any little space available. Yards and gardens were built over, passages and landings colonised and even windowless cabins constructed. Little consideration was given to sanitation. Typical was Nelson Place, a row of sixteen tiny hovels behind Redcliffe Parade, which was without drainage. The privies at the rear of the houses were emptied only every three or four years, the contents being dumped into a hole in the small front garden.

The Southern Parishes had turned into a human warren of dirty rotten sheds, and because of the anonymity that they offered it was rumoured to be a haven for criminals. In the crowded Queens Head Court, there was a slaughter-house: 'a very objectionable place with pig stye, stable and manure heap all under cover'. The Dean of the Cathedral described in the report a Dickensian underworld of 'squalid dwelling places 'which demoralised the population into a life of vice maddened with lust, drunkeness and violence'. The Dean saw the people as morally contaminated by their surroundings and asked:

'How can the inhabitants be decent and orderly when they are compelled to live by day and night in rooms crowded with persons, many of them of the most abandoned character, from the sight of whose disgusting habits and the hearing of whose blasphemous words they have no escape?'[11]

But the picture gets even worse for not only were the living crowded together but so also were the dead. Although the Arnos Vale cemetery had been opened in 1838 its use was only slowly adopted. The graveyards in the Southern Parishes were described as full yet in St Mary Redcliffe's churchyard, for example, there were still on average 146 internments a year. The churchyards of St Thomas was so full that there were bones strewn over the ground whilst at other churchyards the smell of decay invaded nearby houses.

Conditions were so undeniably bad that this time the Council took heed of the report and set up a Sanitary Authority. At last things began to happen: in the next fifteen years a most impressive drainage system was installed throughout the city and, moreover, by 1866 it was claimed that nearly every house was connected to the mains water supply. On a less dramatic scale an Inspector of Nuisances diligently went about his work closing down illegal slaughterhouses, isolating fever cases and providing an efficient scavenging service. The courts were now visited almost daily and large iron bins were provided for household refuse.

Although Bristol as a whole was becoming a cleaner and healthier place in which to live there was still little room for complacency. For the problems of Redcliffe, Temple and St Thomas these measures were merely a palliative—the over crowded slum dwellings, the winding, crooked passages of the Southern Parishes needed an altogether stronger medicine.

CHAPTER SIX: NOTES

1. *Mathew's Bristol Directory* (Bristol, 1815) p.5
2. J. Odery-Symes, *A Short History of the Bristol General Hospital* (Bristol, 1932) p.4
3. J. Odery-Symes, op cit, p.20
4. ibid, p.21
5. C. Crick, *Victorian Buildings in Bristol* (Redcliffe Press, 1975) p.35
6. D. Large & F. Round, *Public Health in Mid Victorian Bristol* (Bristol, 1974) p.3
7. *Royal Commission on the Health of Towns* (1845) 2nd Report, Appendix on Bristol p.71
8. ibid, p.75
9. ibid, p.75
10. J. Latimer, *Annals of Bristol in the Nineteenth Century* p.313
11. *Report to the General Board of Health on the City and County of Bristol* (1850) p.48

7—Hunger Haunted Homes

Like many other cities in the Victorian period, Bristol grew at a phenomenal rate. During Queen Victoria's reign, the city virtually quadrupled in area whilst the population which in 1869 amounted to 190,000 had by 1901 nearly doubled to 365,000. Villages such as Brislington, Bedminster and Knowle which not long before had been in the clean air of the countryside were swallowed up.

The physical growth of Bristol was due both to an expansion of population and to an exodus of middle and artisan classes from the older, central parishes. The middle classes moved into spacious suburban houses in the tree-lined streets of Clifton, Redland, Cotham, St Andrews and Knowle, whilst many artisans moved into new accommodation especially to the east and south of the city. Such moves were not always a change for the better and it was warned in 1908 that 'whole areas of the suburbs are arising which from lack of any definite policy will soon become little better than slums'.

With so much building going on around them, the older parishes of the city were left becalmed like the vortex of a hurricane. The parishes of Redcliffe, Temple and St Thomas soon found they housed a disproportionate number of sick, elderly and other generally disadvantaged people, in other words, all those who had little opportunity to move to the new Eden of the suburbs. This does not mean the parishes emptied. Far from it, for it was in this area that many of Bristol's biggest employers were based, so that accommodation for people working locally was at a premium. Between 1801 and 1841 the population of Redcliffe, Temple and St Thomas had increased by over fifty percent—from 9,042 to 14,617. Every house was crowded and because of high demand, accommodation was by no means cheap.

Some of the worst dwellings were squashed round the base of St Mary Redcliffe forming a notorious 'red light' area (being a port there was never a lack of demand for prostitutes) known to the police as Vermin Farm. Here, it was not unknown for eight to ten people to sleep in one room. And similar tales are told of Temple Parish where poverty and pauperism were said to be indigenous. Temple was reputed to be a haunt of thieves; the crowded alleys, the low cavernous courts and the narrow lanes were accredited with sheltering marauders who spent their nights plundering the city only to return at daybreak to catch a few hours' sleep before they 'hasten to get drunk— the business of the day'.

The shocking fact was that much of this slum dwelling belonged to the church. The St Mary Redcliffe Vestry had made the mistake of leasing houses to unscrupulous people who for years were entrusted with the control of the dwellings. Unfortunately, when many of these leases had expired the church found that their property had declined into slum dwellings.

There had been some improvements. One weekly event that had not helped the state of the streets was the Thomas Street market that had been initiated way back in 1570. By now it was largely for horses, cattle and pigs. In 1829 it was transferred to the less populous Temple Meads.

Ten years later another long standing tradition, the Temple Street Fair, came to an end. Held at the beginning of March it was an important trading event bringing together hawkers of produce from all over the country. For nine days Temple Street was crowded with colourful stalls; with hardware from Sheffield and Birmingham, lace from Nottingham, millinery, haberdashery and trinkets from London and a wide amount of local produce including everything to do with woollen manufacture—cloths, carpets, rugs, blankets, linen, and a remarkable selection of buck, doe and hog-skins for breeches.

There was also a great show of cattle and horses and a variety of sideshows, exhibitions and entertainments.

But as the years went by, it appeared that the places of trade were diminishing whilst the number of shows, entertainments and amount of general disorder increased. Amongst other things *Mathew's Bristol Guide* of 1815 listed: 'Exhibitions of Wild Beasts and Birds, Wax-works, Wire-dancing, Tumbling, Balancing, Puppets, Punch with his wife Joan, Seafights, Conjuration, Magic and Mummery of all sorts'. Alcohol was sold at a number of unlicensed premises and by the 1830s the fair was said to be a centre of corruption and demoralisation, attracting an increasing number of thieves, pickpockets and swindlers. A quick-eyed councillor reported that on one night he had counted no fewer than two hundred and twenty thieves and prostitutes loitering about. A committee consequently appointed to investigate the fair recommended its suppression, 'thereby preventing a re-occurrence of those disgusting scenes of profaneness, of drunkeness and debauchery which invariably and to an alarming extent prevailed'.[1]

The suppression of Temple Fair can be seen as a reflection of a new scale of values forming at the beginning of the Victorian era. The Bristol Tee-Total Society had been formed in 1836 and a year later boasted over 1,000 members. Previous social reformers had been content to denounce only alcoholic spirits, recognising beer as a cheap and wholesome drink greatly preferable to impure water. But to the new temperance movement even beer threatened the realization of the Victorian dream: the secure home, family life, sobriety, christianity and happiness. This fad for abstinence was all very well for the middle classes in their comfortable homes. For the down-trodden slum dwellers of the inner cities, alcohol was still an important escape. Indeed, in these quarters the drinking man was so respected that the tobacco manufacturer W.D. Wills is reported to have lost his seat in Parliament because of a dastardly last minute notice which circulated before election time amongst the ward's publicans that he was an unrepentant tee-totaler.

Improvements in the environment also came about through the benevolence of individuals. In 1829 a wealthy citizen, Mr Weare, had donated £10,000, subject to an annuity of £500, that made way for a widespread series of developments: in 1839 a plan was initiated to widen some of the narrow streets and create new ones where this would not suffice. Money was also set aside for something that today we take for granted: the naming of streets and the numbering of houses.

Priority was given to the plans to widen Redcliffe Street and lower the tortuous Redcliffe Hill which became impassable due to mud in the winter and wet weather. Nearby, a new street, Phippen Street, was to be built through part of the Vermin Farm locality. By the 1880s the renovations were such in this area that one man was quoted in the *Bristol Mercury* as saying:

'Pile Street, Sir; Why its the Mall—Clifton itself—compared to what it was in the old days before the worst courts were swept away'.[2]

And alongside these improvements the moral tenor of the area was to be improved. It was proposed that a maximum fine of £2 be imposed on anyone committing a nuisance—a term that included soliciting for prostitution.

Such positive plans reflected a refreshing change of attitude for a council renowned for its indifference to environmental problems. But such enlightenment was not widespread. When the council submitted its proposals for comment to the local parishes no replies were received. Pressure did, however, come from other areas, namely local business men.

The increase in the speed of travel offered by the change from stage coach to train was quite remarkable. Indeed by 1850 railways had reached a stage not seriously improved upon until the abandonment of steam in the the mid twentieth century. Although the railways opened up communications nationally, on the local roads they indirectly wrought havoc. Because of the concentration of industry to the north of Temple Meads station, and the consequent coming and going of carts, wagons and workers, the streets were becoming stiflingly crowded. It is interesting, and somewhat paradoxical, that the railways far from being the death knell of horse transport actually encouraged it. In contrast to the declining number of coach horses (prior to the railway there were twenty-two coaches daily between London and Bristol—within three months of its introduction they had all stopped) the number of dray and cab horses actually increased. One had only to look at the number of carts loading, unloading and waiting at a factory like Finzel's where 1,800 tons of sugar a week was produced, to realise this.

In the mostly medieval streets of Redcliffe, Temple and St Thomas such an upsurge in road use was a constant source of discontent. The route from Temple Meads Station to Bristol Bridge was circuitous, narrow, dangerous and more to the point, unprestigious—it did nothing to project the modern image the city fathers wanted of Brunel's metropolis. Consequently, in 1846, a report was issued strongly condemning the streets of Temple Parish and recommending that a new street, Victoria Street, should cut a swath through the area. As always, funding was a problem and the city had to wait until 1870 before its new commercial thoroughfare was built. Similarly, Redcliffe Street, Bristol's main artery for traffic to and from Somerset, was broadened from ten to twenty feet between 1875 and 1877. Likewise a scheme to widen Bristol Bridge was completed in 1873. A second bridge, the Half Penny bridge, had already been built across the Avon linking Temple Back with St Phillips in 1838. 'Everything in Redcliffe following the widening of the thoroughfare takes on a far bigger scale than in olden days' wrote the *Bristol Mercury* in 1884.[3] As we shall soon see, with the widening of the roads the full potential of the area's industries could now be unleashed. Yet again a revolution in communications was to enable widespread industrial change.

It should not be thought that these inner city problems were peculiar to Bristol. At a time when Britain was celebrating fifty glorious years of Victoria's reign it was becoming apparent that there was a reservoir of poverty, destitution and crime at the base of this so-called rich and civilised society. Although per capita income had increased substantially the rich benefitted more than the poor. These problems were soon to be given national publicity by such mild mannered men—not revolutionaries—as William Booth and Seebohm Rowntree. William Booth's survey in London, which was echoed by Rowntree's investigations in York, presented the unpalatable view that thirty per cent of the capital's population were living at a level below which they could adequately be fed, housed and clothed.

Remarkably enough, on a lesser scale, Bristol had its own social activist in the form of the campaigning journalist James Crosby, chief reporter of the *Bristol Mercury*. In 1883, five years before Booth's London portrayal, the *Bristol Mercury* launched a survey of the city's poor. The study was notable not only for its compassion but also its relative restraint—a rare feat for high-flown Victorian journalism. Crosby examined some of the rundown parishes of Bristol and talked to the inhabitants. The following report of a conversation with an old Redclivian is typical of what was published:

> 'We had an interesting conversation with an engine fitter of 60 years of age who was at the Avonside works seven years. He is out of work and has brought up a family of six and now has two children under the age of 14. He is a merry minded man who says he is able to work "in the shape of strength but not in the strength of eyes" as he is obliged to wear spectacles and his employers did not think he could do much with spectacles . . . He used to get 34 shillings to £2 a week and now receives nine shillings a week from his society but that is not enough to live on. He would not live in this dull hole if he could help it. He pays five shillings a week for his house including an old fashioned roomy low roofed kitchen with

many signs of comfort but he is "obliged to light the lamp sometimes to see if the fire is burning" and where there is no light there cannot be a lot of health as "light and fresh air are as essential as victuals". No one ought to be "stived up like this" and he thinks Sir—has a much better place for his horses.'[4]

For many of the older people the rapid growth of the city had been traumatic. The countryside was no longer a stone's throw away and the days when a young poet like Chatterton or Coleridge could disappear into the fields adjacent to our parishes were long gone.

'One of them complained that "she could not step into the fields like she used to in her younger days—a few hundred yards from her house". She only had to go out of the big gate and up Redcli' Mead Lane and there she was "in the fields at the top". She remembers the time when there was a large tree still growing in the middle of Avon Street, and when the larger houses were inhabited by wealthy traders and merchants. This old lady had lived 95 years and brought up a family of twelve children'.[5]

The *Mercury* took note of recent developments and concurred that there had been much improvement of late. Extended compulsory education and street improvements had done a great work in Redcliffe in the past two decades. The improvements of Redcliffe and Pile Streets had swept away some of the 'foulest dens in the city' whilst the church had done much with the slum property that had been returned to them. Indeed model houses were being built on Redcliffe Hill where they were sacrificing three of the old homes for just one of the new dwellings. However, the *Mercury* went on to say that although the parish of Temple benefitted greatly from the construction of Victoria Street many problems remained: 'the brand new thoroughfare of Victoria Street literally put a new face on Temple—but behind this mask are still the old tumbledown houses'. As they so graphically put it 'a large part of the parish seems to be faithfully following in the footsteps of the church and leaning too'.[6]

CHAPTER SEVEN: NOTES

1. G. Bush, *Bristol and its Municipal Government 1820-1851* (Bristol, 1976) p.162
2. 'Homes of the Bristol Poor', by the Special Commissioner of the *Bristol Mercury* (Bristol, 1884) p.70
3. ibid, p.67
4. ibid, p.67
5. ibid, p.58
6. ibid, p.58

Other Sources
J. H. Bettey, *Bristol Observed* (Redcliffe Press, 1986)

8—Victorian Industrial Enterprise

For many Bristol historians, the nineteenth century in comparison with previous times was a period of economic inertia. Certainly Bristol had its problems; it had long ago lost its cherished status of the realm's second city and it lagged behind the fantastic development of Liverpool, Manchester and Birmingham. But in real terms it was hardly stagnant. As we have seen, the population doubled between 1851 and 1901 and also there were some conspicuous examples of industrial success. Unfortunately Bristol's problems, which centred to a large extent on the decline of its docks, have detracted from its successes. One should realise, however, that by the 1870s companies like Frys, The Great Western Cotton Mills at Barton Hill and the Bristol Wagon Works at Lawrence Hill (also with a large and handsome showroom in Victoria Street) all employed upwards of 900 workers and there were many more firms with employees totalling over 500. Victorian industrial enterprise had not by-passed Bristol.

Despite Brunel's self-inflicted wounds on the Great Western Railway, the railway's development was the very keynote to much of the industrial expansion. Mass production depended on the railways—our local industries could not have done without them. It is therefore not a coincidence that within half a mile of the new Temple Meads Station several companies were growing at a rate undreamed of a few years before. Of the many firms clustered in the loop of the Avon that encompassed the parishes of Redcliffe, Temple and St Thomas perhaps Finzel's Sugar Refinery, Messrs ES & A Robinson and WD & HO Wills stand out as the industrial giants. Their products may have been dissimilar, but their style of management, their interest in technology and their commercial cunning ranked them amongst the best of Bristol's industry.

The Finzel Refinery, which by the 1870s was the largest of its kind in England, was based at the Counterslip, on part of the site now occupied by Courage's Brewery. It was founded in 1836 by Conrad Finzel, a German by birth who had been a refugee from Napolean's army. 'The Good Conrad Finzel', as he was called by many, was a benevolent man. He was reputed to give at least £10,000 a year to Muller's Orphanage at Ashley Down and was also generous to his workforce who were paid more than anyone else in the country doing a similar job. The social relations between Finzel and his workforce were described as 'liberality on the one hand and appreciation on the other'.[1]

Finzel's success came from his invention of the centrifugal process—a process that enabled him to be the first person to manufacture granulated white sugar. Prior to this all sugar had to be dried slowly in loaves, or baked, creating a somewhat inferior product. With Finzel's invention, however, treated sugar was put into a spin dryer and revolved at a remarkable 500 revolutions a minute, producing after two minutes sugar 'a pure and colourless appearance'.[2]

Although the factory suffered an almost disastrous setback in 1846 when it was entirely destroyed by fire, by 1873 the firm employed 700 people and had an output of 1,800 tons of sugar a week.[3] The amount of raw material consumed was staggering. Merely to provide power for the operation, 1,000 tons of coal were delivered weekly by barge to the factory.

'There is something stupendous,' wrote the *Practical Magazine* in 1873, 'about the appearance of the street area in front of the building, where drays constantly come and go, and along the tramways at the entrance a continuous stream of raw sugar in boxes, bags and hogsheads are going in, whilst an endless successsion of tierces, bags and packages coming out is like the double procession of bees in a mighty hive'.[4]

And once inside the factory the view was equally impressive.

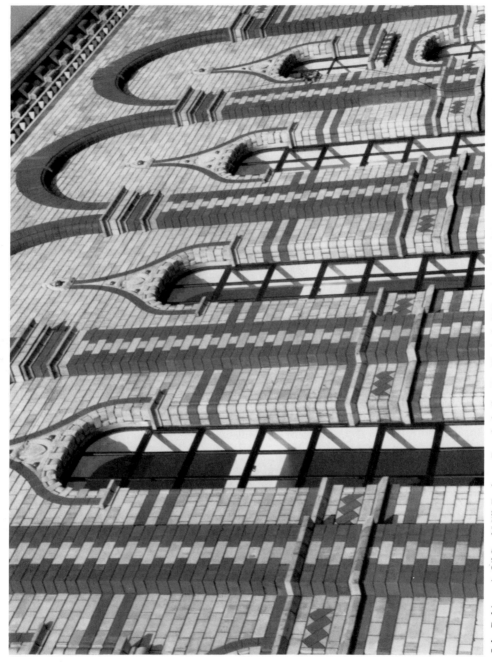

John Robinson's Oil Seed Mill, Bathurst Parade, built 1874. Typical of Victorian Bristol Byzantine architecture. Now restored and a facade for housing.

M. Manson.

'Some indication of the extent of the works is afforded to the visitor, who having passed through various general offices, cashiers departments, the sale rooms and the sampling room where raw sugars are inspected and purchased, is asked to inspect the engine house and the boiler house . . . In order to see it properly we must ascend a spiral staircase through the very core of the building, where amidst a prevailing sense of stickyness and a general impression that we are taking in saccharine through the pores, we peer through long dim vistas amidst beams and apertures where the immense series of filtering cylinders are reached only by devious galleries and footways'.[5]

Although the reporter was certainly inspired by what he saw there was one sour note amongst all this sweetness, for 'the recent enormous increase in the price of coal makes a very serious loss to the firm, who have not however raised their quotations for sugar'.[6] A recent reduction of duty on sugar had enabled Finzels to keep their prices stable—but only just.

Another of Bristol's staple imports was, and is, tobacco. The great family-run tobacco firm of Wills had moved from Castle Street in 1791 to a triple gabled, ramshackle building in Redcliffe Street. The firm puffed along at an unremarkable rate producing snuff and pipe tobacco until 1861, when with the introduction of a steam engine, business expanded so rapidly that by the end of the decade new premises were needed again.

It was in the 1870s that smoking cigarettes became popular and in the next few years Wills was to become a household name not only in Britain but throughout the empire.

The introduction of the cigarette allowed women to sample tobacco with somewhat less stigma being attached to what had previously been considered an unfeminine habit. In 1890 H. H. Wills contentiously announced that smoking is a matter that every English woman must settle in her own conscience, and if she is married she must settle it between herself and her husband.[7]

The fine new Wills factory built in Redcliffe Street in 1869 was not merely utilitarian—it was also an impressive monument to Victorian industriousness. Designed by the architects of Bristol's Grand Hotel, Foster and Wood, its facade was of a similar flamboyant renaissance style. Inside, the factory contained not only the most modern machinery but also, for the convenience of the management, a passenger lift. Every floor had toilets and washrooms and there was a library 'to which all have access'. Indeed, for some, conditions at work were probably healthier than those at home.

'Instead of having to mount stairs innumerable, the aid of a friendly lift is called. A bell is sounded, and almost in less than no time down comes the machinery with its attendant; the visitor takes his place alongside his guide and in a twinkling he finds himself at the top of the building . . . This part of the manufactory faces Redcliffe Backs, and here the trollies land the hogsheads, tierces and bales in which the leaves are packed. By means of a hoist they are hauled up to the top of the five storey building . . . '[8]

As with many other Bristol factories both men and women were employed, though departments were usually segregated by sex (sometimes boys would work alongside women). Thus, in Wills, the sorting of tobacco was done by women, the cutting by men and then it was the women again who did the packing into tins. An enthusiastic reporter from the *Bristol Times and Mercury* was most impressed by the quality of the Wills workforce—numbering about 500 in the Redcliffe Street factory in 1883—and wrote:

'Looking at these trim tidy girls with their smiling faces and nimble fingers, one somehow instinctively feels the system of work adopted must have a wonderful influence for they are far removed from Midland and Northern types of factory "hands" as can be imagined.'[9]

And it was not only the girls that took the reporter's fancy for on his tour of the factory he remarked on the men:

'that judging from their general physique there must be something decidedly invigorating in their work for a finer set of men it would be difficult to find.'[10]

The reporter's visit was concluded by noting that:

'In management there is an enormous amount of vigour and business capability that augurs well for future prosperity'.[11]

In that observation the reporter was certainly correct.

The third large firm of the area was Robinson's, a printing and stationery firm based at the top of Redcliffe Street, just a stone's throw from Bristol Bridge. The firm was founded on May 1st, 1844, a significant date also marking the opening of the Bristol and Exeter Railway.

Robinson's most important products were stationery and paper bags. The introduction of the penny post in 1840 had done much to encourage sales of envelopes and stationery. Robinson's Ancient Vellum boasted that it 'contained none of the colouring matter so common and objectionable in cheap writing paper'.[12] With regard to paper bags it may come as a surprise to find that they were a novelty in the 1840s. Until Robinson's rectified the matter, paper bags were rarely used; grocers would merely place loose produce on a sheet of wrapping paper and fold the edges. A grocer might occasionally make a few bags in his spare time but few bothered for there was really little or no money to be made in packaging. Or so it was thought. Elisha Robinson, however, saw the potential for manufactured paper bags and with clever marketing and hard sales work he soon generated a need for them.

In 1846 Robinsons moved to 2 Redcliffe Street and in the following years took over many of the adjacent properties. With the widening of Redcliffe Street between 1875 and 1877 the opportunity was taken to build, on the same site, smart new premises to the design of William Bruce Gingell the architect also responsible for the Bristol General Hospital. Like the rest of Victoria Street the building was in a robust style, built largely of brick with a corner tower topped by a cupola. It remained a landmark on the Bristol horizon for nearly 90 years and is still remembered by some for its frieze illustrating the various stages of paper making.

Robinson's, like Wills, were not afraid to be technologically innovative. A machine was devised that produced 100-200 bags a minute, the factory producing, in all, one and three quarter million bags a week in 1883. The more expensive bags, however, were still made by hand. 'The process', wrote the author of *Bristol at Work*, 'must be witnessed with a great amount of pleasure owing to the marvellous dexterity of the women'.[13] The women also worked with some of the machinery such as the ingenious envelope making machines. Printing, however, was the men's domain, Robinsons being involved in both letterpress and the finer art of lithography. Every year the firm would buy paintings, usually more sentimental or moralising than artistic, from the Royal Academy. The staff of ten artists would then assiduously translate them into lithographs to be used for Robinson's famous calendars and advertisements. Sometimes the lithographic plates, made from blocks of stone, could take up to seven weeks to prepare and in the more elaborate prints twelve such plates would be used.

It is recounted that at Christmas time Elisha Robinson, in agreeably Dickensian manner would 'walk round the warehouse greeting all those he could, seeing that those who lived at a distance were in time to catch their trains and often giving Christmas boxes'.[14] Indeed Elisha Robinson was quite a character—not only was he an astute and innovative businessman, he was also at times a man of few words. Whilst on a business trip, on being told that there was a fire in his warehouse he merely telegraphed the company 'Put it out. Robinson'.[15]

Robinson's suffered two serious fires at its Redcliffe Street factory. The first, on April 1st, 1903, necessitated the rebuilding of a large part of the premises including the famous corner tower; the second was started by bombs on the night of November 24th, 1940

Above: The corner of Redcliffe Street and St. Thomas Street prior to demolition making way for the building of Victoria Street in the 1870s.

Below: ES and A Robinson's original premises at 2 Redcliffe Street.

during one of the most intense air-raids experienced by Bristol during the Second World War.

What the writers from the *Practical Magazine* and *The Bristol Times and Mercury* omitted to mention in their glowing tales of industrial enterprise was just how hard the work was on the shop or factory floor. By today's standards the hours were long and exhausting. In the early 1870s the day at Robinson's commenced at 6.00am and continued until 7.00pm. Until 1857 it had been a six day working week, but from that date onwards a half day off on Saturday was allowed. There were no other days off, no summer holidays, except for public holidays. Even so, not all employers were ruthless exploiters. Smothering paternalism largely kept the labour movement at bay, though when employers did overstep the mark the unions were quick to get involved. A dispute arose in 1892 at Sanders chocolate factory in Redcliffe Street when the women workers, who were already doing a long day, were expected to work another hour until 7.00pm. The women quickly enlisted the aid of the Gas Workers Union who helped bring about a suspension of the extension of hours. The problem did not end there though, for any of Sanders women who joined the union were dismissed from their jobs. The whole affair culminated in what came to be known as the Black Friday March.[16]

So far we have looked at stories of industrial success, but as always there is another side to the coin. Although the railways were of benefit to the majority they did not help everybody. In the older Southern Parishes some of the traditional smaller industries were being elbowed out, whilst many of the retailers suffered from the loss of the Welsh trade. Until the coming of the railways Bristol's trade hinterland had spread over the River Severn to South Wales; with the railway's penetration into that area this trade was lost.

But these setbacks were minor compared with the failure of Finzel's. 1879 was a year of industrial slump nationally—this, combined with a series of other factors, had a calamitous effect on the firm's trading position. Finzel's profits were not high, and by the end of the decade they had deteriorated even further. Over-investment in new property and warehouses had already weakened the company; this, together with fierce product competition from Liverpool, where charges for sugar importation were half those at Bristol, and a committed policy of free trade by Disraeli's government had further contributed to the firm's downfall. Despite several rescue attempts by local businessmen the refinery was finally and disastrously closed in 1881.

With Finzel's closed, the once flourishing sugar trade of Bristol disappeared. Alongside a direct workforce of 800 there were many other related workers—coopers, draymen, warehousemen who were also laid off. Perhaps a thousand jobs were lost in all. Although other companies were thriving, such a large number could not directly be assimilated into their workforces. It hit the Southern Parishes hard; many houses, crowded a few years previously, became untenanted, large warehouses were left idle and property generally depreciated in value. 'It is difficult to imagine' wrote the *Times and Mercury* 'the poverty and scale of dire misery that followed'.[17]

Other companies did continue to prosper. Elisha Robinson, on completion of a new building at 1 Redcliffe Street, announced 'Gentlemen, I have the finest printing factory in the West of England and neither I or those who come after me will ever want to enlarge it'.[18] How wrong he was. For just eleven years later Robinsons were building further premises in less crowded Bedminster for the lithographic and colour printing department.

Likewise Wills, whose production rocketed from six and a half million cigarettes in 1884 to nearly 14 million in 1886, also looked southwards to Bedminster where they built their new factory, the commanding redbrick monolith, part of which still dominates East

Street today. Of Wills' many brand names, Woodbines which sold at five a penny in paper packets and Three Castles were the most famous. The name Three Castles came from Thackeray's novel 'The Virginian': 'There's no sweeter tobacco comes from Virginia, and no better brand than Three Castles.'

In Redcliffe Street, in Bedminster and further afield both Robinson's and Wills continued to thrive.

CHAPTER EIGHT: NOTES

1. *Practical Magazine*, 'Crystalised Sugar—Messrs Finzel's Sugar Refinery (Bristol, 1873) p.166
2. G. Meason *The Official Illustrated Guide to the Great Western Railway* (1860) p.819
3. *Bristol Times*, September 28th, 1872
4. *Practical Magazine*, op cit, p.163
5. ibid, p.163
6. ibid, p.163
7. *Bristol Times and Mirror* 'Work in Bristol' (1883) p.81-82
8. R. Till, *Wills of Bristol*, p.41
9. *Bristol Times and Mirror* 'Work in Bristol' (1883) p.84
10. ibid, p.83
11. ibid, p.89
12. ibid, p.64
13. ibid, p.64
14. B. Darwin *Robinsons of Bristol 1844-1944* (Bristol, 1945) p.23
15. ibid, p.21
16. E. Malos, *Bristol's Other History*, 'Bristol Women in Action 1839-1919', (1983) p.120
17. *Bristol Times and Mercury* 'Homes of the Bristol Poor', (1884) p.60
18. B. Darwin, op cit, p.22

Other Sources
B. Atkinson, *Trade Unions in Bristol* (1982)
R. A. Buchanan, *The Industrial Archaeology of Bristol* (1967)

9—Flickering into Darkness

With the introduction of both tramways and electricity, Bristol appeared to be purposefully heading towards the twentieth century. Horse drawn trams were first introduced into the city in 1875 whilst another novelty soon to be found on the streets was electric lighting. Initial trials of electric street lighting in 1881 had proved uneconomical but after pressure from several companies wishing to become involved, the Corporation, hoping to avoid any private monopoly, decided to go ahead with its own supplies. Various experiments were carried out; amongst several schemes one gentleman suggested the idea of harnessing the power that he believed could be generated by the ebb and flow of the Avon.

Eventually Bristol's first electricity generating station was opened in 1893 on Temple Back. Once a supply was established the City Council jealously guarded its monopoly of the production of electricity. When the Bristol Tramways and Carriage Company started to run electrically driven trams, the power had to be generated from a base just beyond the city boundaries at Beaconsfield Road, St George. The electrification of the trams brought improvements in service—they held more passengers, they travelled about half as fast again as the old horse drawn trams, and they were cheaper—with the result that it became vital that a generating station was established in a more central position.[1]

After a long battle the Bristol Tramways Company won through and built an impressive new power station at the Counterslip on land previously occupied by Finzel's Sugar Refinery. Tactlessly, it was directly across the road from the unprepossessing Temple Back generating station which it swaggeringly dominated. Today, apart from the absence of the two enormous 180 feet chimneys at Temple Back both buildings remain from the outside substantially the same.

Unfortunately the introduction of the electric light was unable to stop the community of Redcliffe, Temple and St Thomas flickering into darkness. A Board of Trade enquiry in 1908 into working class rents, housing and retail prices found the living conditions in the parish of Redcliffe to be still in the slum category. But in the Edwardian era working class poverty seemed to be no longer a matter of immediate concern. That the middle classes were content to disclaim any responsibility for them is exemplified by a series entitled 'Curious Living Places' published by the *Bristol Evening News* in 1908. Despite admitting that 'too often conditions which afford material for a picturesque drawing are the very reverse of attractive when invested with the squalor of slum life' the tone of the *Evening News'* articles was one of condescension.

> 'Looking down an alleyway one may detect with surprise a public lamp . . . and entering find a minute square surrounded by small houses or rows of little dwellings facing a narrow court. From one court there may in certain cases be passages leading to others . . .'

> 'How many thousands who hurry through Redcliffe Street have any idea what is implied by Warry's court or Golden Lion Passage; Warry's Court . . . is entered by a passage above which the Redcliffe Street frontage extends. The passage is narrow but leads to a wider one open to the sky. In this space have been built in a line four pairs of small dwellings with tiny yards between the pairs. The opposite side of the court is bounded by a wall, on the other side of which is a timber yard, so for airspace the inhabitants are better off than others. Golden Lion Passage is so curious that a visitor wonders how it came into being. It might be accounted for if it be supposed that some former Bristolian owning a home in Redcliffe Street decided to pack a number of residences into his back garden. It is another case of utilising every inch of the ground . . .'[2]

It is at the beginning of the twentieth century that the story of our parishes falters. The community was already dying; the introduction of the railways had started this decline as from that time the large scale industries began to stifle the smaller

After a long battle with the Corporation, Bristol Tramway Company completed its impressive new generating-station in 1900 (background). It was across the road from the Temple Back Power Station (foreground), which it swaggeringly dominated.

M. Manson.

entrepreneur who had given the community its life for so long. One of the final blows came with the widening of the notorious Redcliffe and Temple Streets. The personal businesses with their family accommodation above were destroyed only to be replaced by large soul-less warehouses and factories. The community of Redcliffe, Temple and St. Thomas had grown rotten with old age; the houses had decayed as had the reputation of their inhabitants. Any respectable person lived in the fresher air of the new suburbs and commuted to work by tram or train. Given the circumstances the only remedy to the malaise was to sweep away any residential premises and given the whole area over to industry. Redcliffe, Temple and St Thomas turned from a community teeming with life into an area populated by gaunt warehouses and faceless factories.

In the Thirties slum clearance meant moving many families from the Southern Parishes to new residential areas, like Knowle West. For some it was an unnerving change. The streets of Knowle were so quiet—there was no humming of factory noise. Many claimed that they had been banished 'to a strange, quiet, tree-less plateau on the outskirts of the city'.

On account of its out-of-fashion architecture Victoria Street was known as the 'ugliest street in Europe'. To many visitors to Bristol, arriving at Temple Meads station was a daunting introduction to the city. In 1933, J. B. Priestley wrote that all he ever knew of Bristol was 'Temple Meads Station in the dark hours, Victoria Street and the deserted smoke room of the hotel there. The natural result was that I carried with me the vague impression that this was an unpleasant city . . . '[3]

The slow process of the area's decline was unintentionally hastened by Hitler. The Luftwaffe had earmarked the factories and warehouses for their special attention. On Sunday November 24th, 1940, in one of Bristol's worst air-raids of the Second World War, Redcliffe, Temple and St Thomas, along with much of the city centre, were severely blitzed. Not only were commercial and industrial buildings destroyed but also many of the areas' historic landmarks. Temple Church, which had withstood the ravages of six hundred years, was completely gutted, though the famous leaning tower still stood as a monument to the skill of its medieval builders. (Sappers, not familiar with its alarming tilt viewed the tower as unsafe and were only just stopped from demolishing it). Nearby, Burton's Almshouses whose history was almost as long as the history of our area was gone forever. St Mary Redcliffe narrowly missed a similar fate; bombs fell on Redcliffe Hill demolishing the infants school and blasting pieces of tramline into the air, one piece plunging into the graveyard where it still remains as a graphic reminder of those perilous days.

In between the air-raids life carried on as normally as possible. To ease traffic congestion between Redcliffe Street and Bristol Bridge a long-planned new bridge was built linking Redcliffe Back with Welsh Back.

By the end of the war what was left of the community of the Southern Parishes had also been blown apart. Following the devastation of the land between Bristol Bridge and Temple Meads Station there was much debate about what to do with the area. Amongst others, proposals were put forward by the Rotary Club of Bristol recommending that the area be turned into an enormous civic centre. Under the Rotarians' plan, Victoria Street was to be widened to 120 feet (almost double its present width) and the rest of the area was to be given over to all the civic facilities that Bristol needed. The plan noted that 'it would make an attractive vista to meet the eyes of those coming into Bristol from Temple Meads or the airport'.[4]

Even though no such large scale schemes went ahead, under the pressure of post war development what little was left of the community slowly disintegrated. The original area—to the north of Portwall Lane—became uninhabited, given over entirely to commerce and industry. The few remaining residents were re-housed in tower blocks and flats that dwarf even St Mary Redcliffe. Development in the 1960s saw the introduction of dual carriageways ripping across the district; a busy ring road passes by Chatterton's doorstep whilst that historical industrial landmark, the shot-tower disappeared under tarmac. In a final insult the Corporation even took it upon themselves to alter the name of Redcliffe by dropping the last 'e'.[5]

CHAPTER NINE: NOTES

1. P. G. Lamb, *Electricity in Bristol*, (Bristol, 1981) p.15
2. G. F. Stone, *Bristol As It Was and Is*, (Bristol, 1909) p.258-260
3. J. B. Priestley, *English Journey*, (Penguin, 1977) p.29
4. *The Builder*, December 21st, 1945, p.500
5. City and County of Bristol, *Housing Nomenclature in Bristol*, (1969) p.45

Above: Merchants Landing, on the west side of Bathurst Basin: one of the first and probably most successful new housing developments breathing new life into the area.

Below: The pleasures of waterside workplaces. Warehouses and bombsites by Bristol Bridge have been replaced in the 1980s by offices. After many centuries industry has largely abandoned the parishes of Redcliffe, Temple and St. Thomas.   *M. Manson.*

10—New Life

By the early 1970s the waterfronts along Redcliffe and Temple Back were dreary and decaying. Large bomb sites from thirty years before were left undeveloped whilst many of the warehouses stood empty and rat infested. The aromatic smell of the tawny weed no longer wafted down Redcliffe Street. Wills' main factory was at Hartcliffe; its renaissance style building, after years of neglect, was finally demolished in 1976.

The Southern Parishes formed part of what a planning report was to define as a ring of dereliction surrounding the commercial core of the city. Bristol had to face the fact that the docks were an eyesore and that their decline was finally complete and irreversible. It was small consolation that the City was not alone in this decline. With the containerisation of ships both of Bristol's long term rivals—London and Liverpool—had suffered a similar fate.

By this time the immediate and urgent demands of post war development had been attended to and planners were able to stand back and take time to deliberate on how they wanted their city to look in the future. To this end, in 1971, Casson, Conder and Partners, an independent group of consultant planners, were commissioned to produce a redevelopment study. Although good in parts, the Casson plan was largely marred by the suggestion that a motorway should run east-west along the docks, bridging the floating harbour at St Augustine's Reach and also at Wapping Warf.

Happily, many of the suggestions put forward by the 1972 Docks Redevelopment Study were eventually abandoned, though due more to lack of finance than wisdom. The consultant planners did establish, however, two concepts that were to be of more lasting value—first, that widespread access to the docks should be made available to the citizens for recreational use and second, that new housing should be encouraged in the area.

These were novel ideas which took a while to become accepted. In the end it was left to a few far-sighted individuals, who saw the vast recreational potential of a large, sixty acre, city centre waterspace, to make the move. Once the Arnolfini had established itself at Bush House right in the heart of the dereliction, things started to happen.

In 1977 an overall plan, this time produced by the City Planning Department, superseded the 1972 report with more specific recommendations on recreation and housing. The 1977 plan was of marked contrast in its scale and tone to the hasty post war developments that in many cases had proved so disastrous.

New life was to be pumped into the docks. It has happened slowly and the saving grace of the Bristol planners' ideas has been that they have had little money. Development has been in a piecemeal, organic way. With no large scale plan there have been no large scale disasters.

The twentieth century dock pioneers were soon followed by others who began to see the pleasures of waterside workplaces. In the 1980s the gaps by Bristol Bridge and along part of Redcliffe Back have been filled by brickwork buildings echoing the elaborate and imposing Victorian architecture they replaced. The intricacies of the Victorian Byzantine architecture have recently begun to be reappraised and it has been realised that in its totality Victoria Street was really rather impressive. But unfortunately too late. At present the only buildings of the 1870s that remain in Victoria Street, numbers 2 to 22, are in a sorry state and if nothing is done to restore them they will surely not be with us for long. Opposite, at the angle of Redcliffe Street and Victoria Street, Robinson's are still very much in evidence. Bags are no longer made there, though the company, in the form of DRG, boasts Bristol's first tall office block—a stark 16 storeys and 250 feet high—as their administrative headquarters.

The DRG building overshadows another controversial development at Courage's brewery in Bath Street. Over the years, with Bath Street blocked off from public use and encompassed within the Brewery site, the fine Georgian terrace built by Thomas Paty in the 1790s had been largely forgotten. Despite informed opposition, this made it easy for Courage's to demolish half the row in 1986 to make way for a lorry park.

Courage's brewery is now the last working industry left in central Bristol. Employment is mainly in the commercial sector and in the age of the computer and electronic communications Bristol has proved popular with companies relocating from London. Industry has left—there are no sulphurous or other smells, no 24 hour clatter so that the area, especially along the waterfront, is becoming for the first time in many, many years an attractive place to live.

The first and probably most successful of the housing to be built in this area is along the western side of Bathurst Basin. Since the Second World War, when the lock connecting to The Cut was filled in to minimise the chances of bomb damage to the float, the Basin had become something of a backwater, apart from use by Holms Sand and Gravel Company. The new development incorporated long-derelict Georgian housing and a splendid Bristol Byzantine seed mill. The renamed Merchants Landing waterfront development is impressive—only one thing rankles, and that is the change of name itself and the renaming of the Bathurst Tavern as The Smugglers. Street and place names are important and to change them for purely marketing reasons is historical vandalism.

At Merchants Landing the large, architecturally bland Turner Edwards Warehouse was demolished to make way for housing. At Buchanan's Wharf, in what must be the boldest revitalization scheme yet, the two listed, 8-storey red brick mills are to be kept and converted into shops on the ground floor and flats above.

Although Victoria Street is still bland and Temple Street remains totally nondescript the ambitious development at Buchanan's Wharf should breathe real life back into Redcliffe. Perhaps, for the last eighty years the Southern Parishes have been not dead, but merely slumbering.

Selected Reading

Casson, Conder and Partners—*Redevelopment Study* (1972)
City Docks Joint Study Team, *Bristol City Docks Local Plan* (1977)
A. Gomme, M. Jenner, B. Little, *Bristol: An architectural history* (London, 1979)
J. Lord, J. Southam, *The Floating Harbour* (Redcliffe Press, 1983)
Reece Winstone's unique series of *As it Was* books contain an unrivalled photographic record of the city

Index

TRIC

PARTE OF S

Chilton
Sudbury · Newton
Li Cornard · Gr. Cornard
Henney
Buers
Wiston
Stoke
Higham
E. Bragholt
Tatingeton
Chempton
Tomlee
Wurmingford
Neyland
Stretford
Brantham
Sutton
Holbroke
Harkstede
Shotley
Yf of ende
Pedmersbe
Gr. Horsley
Langhm
Dedham
Catwade bridge
Amberton
Orwell haven
Whit colne
W. Bergholt
Myle end
Lawforde
Manytre
Mystley
Bradfelde
Ytray
Harwich
Chapel pyshe
Fordhm
Ardley
Li Brumley
Vhrabnes
Ramsey
Dover Court
Colne engane
Cohwake
Grinsted
Elmsted
Gr. Brumley
Li Bentley
Gr. Ookeley
Li. Ookeley
Erlescolne
LEXDEN HV
COLCHESTER
Wisenhoo
TENDERING
Gr. Tay
Aldhm
Lexden
E. dony land
Fratng
Wyley
Tindringe
Mose
Marke shall
Li. Tay
E. dony land
Gr. Bentley
Marke slay
Stanwey
Thurtyngten
Thorp
Beamont
Horsey Insul
Bladwater
Cogshall
Stanwey hall
Fingringhoo
Brickesley
Sot Ofsythe
L: Claokton
Kirkbay
The Nast
Li Cogshall
Fering
Copford
Langenho
Walton
Easterford
Gr. Birch
Li Birch
Layerdelahay
Peldon
Weybotough
Gr. Holland
Reucnall
Inworth
Messing
Easthorpe
Layet marney
WINSTRED
Layerbretton
The blockhowse
Li Wyborough
Gr. Claokton
Gr. Braxted
Toleshunt knyght
Saluet
Verley
Frynton
Li braxted
THVRSTABLE HV
Gr. Tothm
Li Tothm
Gr. Toleshunt
Toleshunt derfye
W. Marsey
E. Marsey
Li. Holland
Whitham
Goldhanger
Li Tothm
Toleshunt
Tolesbury
Vlting
HV
Lang ford
Hey bridge
OCEA NVS
Wodhm wa
Northey
Ofey
St Peters cha.
Maldon
Ramsey
Braduell
Mundon
Stansgate
DENGYE HV
Woodhm nurtinet
Lawlyng
Steple
St Lawrence
Tillingham
Purleygh
Lashindon
Ashuldon
Dengye
Norton
Woodhamferis
Altherne
Mayland
Southminster
Stow maries
N. Fambridge
Crikesey
Burnhm
amingfeld
Huff bridge
S. Fambridge
Crouch flu
endon
WALLOT INSVL
Rawreth
Canwidon
Foulnesse
Hoclye
Assington
Pachesbm
Hawkeswell
Li Stambridge
Barlinge
ickford
Raleghe
Rochesorde
Gr. Stambrige
Li Wakering
ell
E. Wood
Sutton
Gr. Wakering
Bemflete
ROCHEFORDE HV
Thundesley
Hadlighe caftle
Prittlewell
N. Shobutye
S. Bemflete
Lyghe
Shopland
S. Church
S. Shoburye
CANVE INSVL

1602
ESSEXIÆ
COMITATVS
descriptio Continens
Ni Se opida, marcatoria
20. pagos et Villas 414 Vna
Cum Singulis hundre
dis. 19. et fluminibus 7.
Pontes. 28. parkes 46.
In eodem.

Market Townes
Parishes
Hamlets
Castles
Howses of name

GRANE
Grate
INSVL

Clyffe
Alhalows
Colinge
St Maries
Stoke
Halsto

Quinboro Cas
Mynster
Warden

Medway flu

SHEPYE INSVL

Scala Miliarum

shell haven

ORIENS

ES

THE
SLEEPERS
AND THE
SHADOWS

For
all my friends

The county of Essex, c.1360, from the 'Gough' map of Great Britain.
Reproduced by courtesy of the Bodleian Library, Oxford.

THE
SLEEPERS
AND THE
SHADOWS

Chelmsford: a town,
its people and its past

BY HILDA GRIEVE

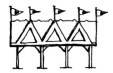

VOLUME 1
The Medieval and Tudor Story

MAPS AND PLANS DRAWN BY
JOHN FULBECK

Published by the Essex County Council, Chelmsford
in association with the Chelmsford Borough Council
ESSEX RECORD OFFICE PUBLICATION NO. 100
1988

Published by the
ESSEX RECORD OFFICE
County Hall, Chelmsford, Essex, CM1 1LX

British Library Cataloguing in Publication Data
The Sleepers and the Shadows: Chelmsford, a town,
its people and its past
Vol 1. The Medieval and Tudor Story
I. Title
942.6'752
ISBN 0-900360-71-2

Essex Record Office Publication No. 100

Mirams Design

Printed in Great Britain by
Witley Press, Hunstanton, Norfolk

CONTENTS

overleaf

CONTENTS

ILLUSTRATIONS

County of Essex *c*.1360, from the 'Gough' map of Great Britain. *Reproduced by courtesy of the Bodleian Library, Oxford* Frontispiece

Lawford Lane (Lollefordstrat) in Writtle, 1987 p.4

Late-15th-century porch of St Mary's parish church (now the Cathedral Church of St Mary the Virgin, St Peter and St Cedd) p.71

Initial portrait of Queen Elizabeth I on Crown grant of manor of Chelmsford to Thomas Mildmay of Moulsham, the queen's servant, 1563 p.109

Proceedings of the parish assembly of 7 June 1590 in the handwriting of Myles Blomefylde (with transcript) pp.124-7

North-east area of manor of Chelmsford on map drawn by John Walker in 1591, showing mill, Bishop's Hall, and rectory p.137

Monument to Thomas Mildmay (d.1566) and his wife Avice erected in the parish church in 1571 by their son, Sir Thomas Mildmay (d.1608) p.140

Chelmsford town area of map drawn by John Walker in 1591 p.149

North and central area of map of manor of Moulsham drawn by John Walker in 1591, showing mill, bridge, Baddow Lane, Moulsham Street, Moulsham Hall, and the hospital p.152

All photographs except the 'Gough' map by N. Hammond

MAPS AND PLANS

Topography of the site of the new town at Chelmersford, 1199-1201 pp.12-13

Town, Upland, Hamlet, mills, and bridges, 13th century p.16

Plans showing the locations of key medieval and Tudor sites, including major inns:

Upper Town	p.43
Middle Town	p.54
Lower Town	p.62

Manor of Chelmsford redrawn from John Walker's map of 1591:

West side	p.118
East side	p.121

Map of Chelmsford Town showing street numbers adopted in 1876 (with loose copy for quick reference) p.179

All the above maps and plans drawn by John Fulbeck

End papers Map of Essex, 1602, by Hans Woutneel

PREFACE

WHEN THE LAST war ended in 1945 I was still as ignorant of Chelmsford's Past as I had been when I first came here in 1939. It was the Chelmsford Planning Survey of 1944-5, sponsored by a Chelmsford Area Planning Group formed in 1935 and directed by Mr Anthony Minoprio, that drew my attention to it, by inviting me to contribute a brief historical chapter to the final Report published in 1945. I discovered then that a business review of the *Industries of the Eastern Counties* published in 1888-90 considered that Chelmsford was 'happy in possessing little in the way of history'; that Frederick Chancellor confessed to the Essex Archaeological Society in 1906 that 'the ancient history of Chelmsford has still to be written'; and that in 1921 J.H. Round dismissed this neglect with the judgement, 'There seems to be very little about which to write'. My superficial reconnaissance in 1945 convinced me that Round might be wrong. I will always be grateful to the impetus of the Minoprio survey and to Round's challenge, and to the forebearance of all those friends and former colleagues who have tolerated for so long my subsequent obsession with the county town of Essex.

It was an inestimable advantage to have the Essex Record Office and its resources close at hand. For over forty years its successive county archivists, Dr F.G. Emmison, the late Mr K.C. Newton, and Mr V.W. Gray, and their staff, upstairs and downstairs, have met my insatiable appetite for Chelmsford source material of every kind without complaint and with great kindness. It would be invidious to pick out individuals, but I hope I have never seemed to take any service for granted or failed to express my thanks. I have received the same courtesy and support in other repositories, most notably in the Public Record Office, the British Library, and the Greater London Record Office. In my search for local material I have had occasion to appeal to members of the town's business community, and have never been rebuffed. The older title deeds of town sites were made available to me by Barclays Bank, the Westminster (now National Westminster) Bank, the Norwich Union, the late Mr Ralph Arnold, the late Mr D. Bellamy, the late Mr A.S. Cutts, the late Mr Raymond Gray, the late Mr Basil Harrison, Mr A.S. Raven, and the late Mr A.H. Woolford; some of those documents have since been deposited in the Essex Record Office. A question concerning the Burgess Well water supply was resolved by the Essex Water Company and, through the good offices of Mr D.H. Gibson, the current files of the Borough Council. For generous guidance on particular historical problems, or for drawing my attention to useful sources or out-of-the-way references, I am grateful to Mrs Nancy Edwards, Dr F.G. Emmison, Dr W.H. Liddell, Dr Alan Macfarlane, Mr E.L.C. Mullins, Dr A. Prescott, Mr Arthur Searle, Mrs E. Sellers, and Mr R.G. Wood.

Thanks are quite inadequate for the late Dr Gladys Ward's years of encouragement, and for the support of Muriel Eakins, Judy Cowan, and John Fulbeck. For many years Muriel has disentangled my tortuous first drafts, with their tiresome but vital accompanying source references, and returned them to me in perfect order, immaculately typed. More recently Judy's lively comment, skill with modern technology, and infectious enjoyment of hard work under pressure, have revived my flagging spirits, and seen me through the grind of transforming revised, re-revised, checked, and re-checked, drafts, into copy fit to present to a printer. The patience, care, and understanding that John has brought to the preparation of accurate maps and plans, has produced the indispensable visual keys to bring the narrative to life on the ground. All shortcomings are mine, and no one else's.

It has been a great happiness to me that the Essex County Council and Chelmsford Borough Council have decided jointly to publish this first volume of a history of the county town of Essex, not only in the Borough's centenary year of 1988, but also timely for the County Council's centenary of 1989. I am deeply grateful to Vic Gray for negotiating this arrangement, reading the manuscript, and shouldering the burden of publication, and to Keith Mirams for the sympathetic book design and Nelson Hammond for the skilled photography.

Hilda Grieve
1988

The Past — the dark unfathom'd retrospect!
The teeming gulf — the sleepers and the shadows!
The past — the infinite greatness of the past!
For what is the present after all but a growth out of the past?
(As a projectile form'd, impell'd, passing a certain line, still keeps on,
So the present, utterly form'd, impell'd by the past).
WALT WHITMAN (PASSAGE TO INDIA) 1871

We shall not cease from exploration
And the end of our exploring
Will be to arrive where we started
And know the place for the first time.
T.S. ELIOT, LITTLE GIDDING (FOUR QUARTETS)

Explanatory notes to the reader

NAMES

The spelling of medieval and Tudor names was seldom consistent. The form under which each individual most often appeared in contemporary sources has been adopted, and the choice of variant concentrated on distinguishing (particularly in the index) between individuals of the same name. Some variants are shown in the index.

MEDIEVAL COINAGE AND ITS DECIMAL EQUIVALENTS

Medieval and Tudor			*Decimal*		
Pound (£)	=	20s	Pound (£)	=	100p
Mark	=	13s 4d			
Angel	=	10s			50p
½ Mark	=	6s 8d			
Crown	=	5s			
Shilling	=	12d			5p
Groat	=	4d			

From 1971 the pound(£), which had been divided into 20 shillings or 240 old pennies, was divided into 100 new pence.

SITE IDENTIFICATIONS

All site identifications are to the house numbers adopted in the town for the first time in 1876, and hardly altered since.

PLACES

All places mentioned are in Essex unless otherwise stated, or obviously not, e.g. York.

DATES

All dates are in the New Style adopted in 1752.

CHAPTER ONE

The Site

CEOLMAER'S FORD

This is the story of Ceolmaer's ford in Essex, and the town that a Norman bishop planted there. After the Romans withdrew from Britain in the early 5th century, new invaders, the English (Angles, Saxons, and Jutes from Germany) landed and settled in south-east Britain. One of them called Ceolmaer gave his name to a fording-place across a river in the heart of the wooded region which became the kingdom of the East Saxons. A succession of perilous river crossings lay before those who ventured through the East Saxons' territory travelling between London and Colchester. There was the 'street' ford across the river Lea at Old Ford, Stratford; the ford across the river Hile (the ancient name of the Roding) at Ilford; the wide (*rum*) ford at Romford; Ceolmaer's ford; then the crossings of the river Brain at Wulvesford in Witham and the river Pant at Easterford, now called Kelvedon, and so to Colchester. Ceolmaer's ford became so well known, even notorious, that by the 11th century the whole district in which it lay was called the 'Hundred of Celmeresforda'. The name stuck, shortening over the centuries from Chelmersford to Chelmesford, even Chemsford, until Chelmsford, its form today, won general acceptance.

The river of Ceolmaer's ford flows from the north of Essex southward, through Dunmow, Felsted, and Great Waltham, to the site of the Saxon crossing in modern Chelmsford. There it veers away eastward to the sea. In the middle ages it was known as the 'water of Shelmereford' (1238) or 'Chelmersford river' (1485); by 1576 it had become, simply, the Chelmer. In the 16th century and later it was often called the 'auncient ryver', or, more casually, 'oulde Chelmer flu'.

Not far below the site of the ford the Chelmer is joined by another river flowing into it from the west, from Writtle. By 1607 some people were calling that river, as now, the Can. But earlier it was known locally as the 'Great River' (1413, 1560), or 'Writtle River' (1591), and in Saxon times, according to tradition, travellers made a detour by way of Writtle to avoid it.

Between the two converging river valleys the land rises gently to 100 feet, to a broad expanse of higher ground which was known in the middle ages as 'Le Upland'. This upland, formed of London clay deposited on chalk and capped with gravel, tapers to a narrow tongue where it falls away south-eastward downhill to the site of the ford and the flood plain where the rivers meet.

A BISHOP'S MANOR

In the time of King Edward the Confessor (1042-66) the two rivers formed the east and south boundaries of a small rural manor of some 600 acres held by William, bishop of London from 1051 to 1075. It is not known how or when it came into the bishop's possession, but there is no evidence that it had belonged to any of his predecessors. Much of the manor was woodland, waste, and watermeadow, but sufficient land was cleared to keep seven plough-teams at work. The bishop kept the manor in his own hands. It was cultivated for him by his men, five villeins who, with their households, comprised the population. Two plough-teams worked the bishop's fields, while his men's five plough-teams cultivated their own holdings. Whatever degree of freedom those peasants and their families may have enjoyed before 1066 was lost after the Norman Conquest, when their status for some 300 years became that of 'neufes', 'natives', or 'lordes bondmen of bloud'. Unfree by birth and bound to the manor, in theory they and all they had belonged to their lord, the bishop, at whose will they occupied their holdings and scraped their livings, and to whom they owed their labour and service. The bishop's hall, watermill, and manor buildings, the cultivated fields, and the dwellings and 'hamstalls' (home fields) of the villeins, all lay upland, half a mile or more from the ford. The vicinity of the ford itself was an uninhabited marshy waste, dangerous, if not impassable, at times of flood, a no man's land parting the bishop's manor of Chelmsford (or Bishop's Hall) from the lands of the Peverels, lords of Springfield.

Sparsely populated, and hemmed in by the two rivers, the bishop's manor was surrounded in 1066 by the more populous lands of other lords. East of the ford in Springfield 30 households were counted; to the north of the manor in Broomfield, 36; to the west in Writtle, a royal manor, 194; and to the south, across the Great River, in the abbot of Westminster's manor of Moulsham, 12. Archaeological evidence has identified the Moulsham side of the Great River as the site of the former Roman settlement of Caesaromagus, or 'Caesar's Plain'. But since those days it had become 'Mulsham', the 'ham' or home farm of Mul, a Saxon like Ceolmaer.

The bishop's manor did not change hands in 1066 after William of Normandy's victory at Hastings over Harold, the last Saxon king. Bishop William was not an Englishman. He was a Norman, who had come over to England with Emma, the Norman wife of King Ethelred the Unready, and been rewarded with the bishopric of London by their son, King Edward the Confessor. At the time of the Conquest William was, in fact, the only Norman bishop in England. He kept his see and most of his lands until his death in 1075, when he was succeeded as bishop by another Norman, Hugh D'Orival.

In the twenty years between the Norman Conquest and the compilation of the Domesday Book in 1086 changes took place on the manor. More land was brought under cultivation for the bishop, requiring a third plough-team. But the number of villein families fell from five to four, and their lot deteriorated. The land they held to cultivate on their own behalf had become reduced by 1086 to the capability of one shared plough-team.

According to the Domesday survey in 1086 there were thirty acres of meadow on the manor and enough woodland to feed 300 pigs. The meadows lay in the flood plain bordering the rivers. The woodland spread over the north-west of the upland; there a map drawn by John Walker in 1591 showed fields called Great, Lower, and Little Okeley, containing 120 acres by then cleared of trees, but with 17 acres of timber still standing on the fringes of those fields and in Great Okeley Spring on the north boundary of Great Okeley.

The stock on the manor in 1086 comprised, besides the plough-teams, a flock of 100 sheep, 27 pigs, and two other 'animals'. With the bishop's watermill, the manor was said to be worth £8 a year. Writtle, its royal neighbour, was worth over £100. As for Moulsham, the abbot of Westminster's manor on the other side of the Great River, in the two decades since the Conquest its annual value had increased from £9 to £12 and its population had more than doubled.

The thinly-populated rural manor at the ford was, however, fortunate in the standing of its medieval lords. The bishops of London held the manor until the 16th century, and after it passed out of their hands it continued to be known as the 'manor of Bishop's Hall *alias* Chelmsford in Chelmsford'. The bishops of London were among the most powerful magnates in the kingdom. In the hierarchy of the province of Canterbury they came to rank second only to the archbishop. Their diocese embraced the City of London, two whole counties, Middlesex and Essex, and part of a third, Hertfordshire. They had been reasonably endowed with lands by successive Saxon kings. Indeed, the manor at Ceolmaer's ford may have originated as a royal gift, carved out of the vast royal demesnes of Writtle. After the Conquest the Norman kings, too, favoured the bishops of London, employing them in the royal household and appointing them to the highest secular offices in the kingdom.

After the death of Bishop Hugh in 1085, Maurice, William the Conqueror's chaplain, and for a time his chancellor, was consecrated bishop. Maurice held the see under three kings, under William I, and under two of his sons, William II (Rufus), and Henry I. William I recognised Maurice's right to all the lands and privileges of his predecessor; so did William II, 'not wishing that he should hold of me in worse state than under my father'; and Henry, when he succeeded his brother in 1100, followed suit.

THE BRIDGES

According to local tradition, it was Bishop Maurice who bridged the Great River, thereby diverting from Writtle the main through traffic of Essex. Sir John Bramston (d.1700) of Skreens in Roxwell, near Chelmsford, wrote in his autobiography:

> 'It was commonly beleived and tradition had delivered it for truth ... that the bridge was built by a Bishop of London ... before which tyme the roade to London lay through Writtle, as is traditionally told and beleived.'

William Camden (d.1623) named the bishop. In 1610 the translation of his *Britannia* from Latin into English by Philemon Holland (who was born and educated in Chelmsford) stated:

> 'Maurice, Bishop of London ... built the Bridges heere in the Raigne of Henry the First, and turned the London way thither ...'

There is more than folk-memory to support Camden's statement. A main London way did formerly pass through Writtle. In the early 13th century the road between Writtle and Margaretting was called the 'king's highway (*cheminus regalis*) to London'; its continuation between Writtle and Chelmsford survives today as a broad but often overgrown bridle-path called Lawford Lane. The lane runs north from St John's Green, Writtle, alongside the river Wid, to cross the Can where it is little more than a brook. Below the crossing, now bridged but once a ford, the tributary waters of the Wid flow into the Can, which widens, to become the 'great river' that daunted Saxon travellers. The lane was described

Lawford Lane (Lollefordstrat) in Writtle, 1987

in 1292 as 'the king's highway running from the market in Writtle to Chelmerisford'; in 1376 as Lollefordstrat; and in 1423/4 as 'the king's highway (*regia via*) in Lollefordstret'. As late as 1739 it was still referred to as a 'high road'; only in 1871, after long disuse, was it officially downgraded to a bridle-path.

There is also evidence that a bridge over the Great River existed by the late 12th century. In 1200 William de Lanvalei paid King John 200 marks for the custody of the Forest of Essex 'as far as the bridge of Chelmaresford, as he had it in the time of King Richard'. By John's reign the shorter route to north-east Essex by way of the bridge was in regular use, for in 1205 a site in Chelmsford 'next to the bridge' was identified as lying on the left 'as the way goes towards Colchester coming from London'.

Tradition placed the building of the bridge between the accession of Henry I in 1100 and the death of Bishop Maurice in 1107. Maurice was renowned as a builder, as the 'magnificent founder' of St Paul's cathedral, which he began to rebuild on a vast scale after a disastrous fire in the City in 1087. He was the kind of man likely to order the building of a bridge to shorten the journey to one of his rural estates and the far north-eastern parts of his diocese. Bridge-building was, moreover, in the middle ages, an act of piety befitting bishops and other great people; about the same time, between 1100 and 1118, Henry I's queen, Maud, was building the first Bow and Channelsea bridges at Stratford, to improve the main road from London into Essex.

Finally, in 1960-2 the Essex River Board, engaged on a flood prevention scheme, drained a section of the river Can, half the width of the channel at a time. This exposed in both north and south banks, at river bed level alongside the present bridge, small areas of revetment of Norman construction, such as could only in that position have once formed part of the abutments of a bridge.

With the Great River bridged there remained the problem of Ceolmaer's river and the dangerous passage of the ford. Two bridges had been built to assist that passage by 1238. In that year, Simon de la Feld and his wife Sabina granted to John de Barham half an acre of land 'between the two bridges of Springefeud', together with an acre of pasture by the 'water of Shelmereford'. The half acre of land was the small island on the Springfield road formerly encircled by two arms of the Chelmer, and known in 1665 as Tyrell's Marsh, and in the 19th century as Mesopotamia Island. Whether Maurice was responsible for those two bridges also, as Camden seemed to suggest when he wrote that Maurice built, not 'a bridge' but 'bridges (*pontes*)', remains, in the absence of other evidence, an open question.

In the Bodleian Library in Oxford there is a curious 14th century doggerel written in Old French. It lists in rhyme the famed attributes of over a hundred places in England. Thus Salisbury had its 'Pleynes', Bath its 'Bayn', and Stonehenge its 'Merveille' (marvel); Yarmouth had its 'Haraung' (herring), and Dover its 'Chastel'. Among nine claims to fame in Essex, including Thaxted's 'Cotels' (knives), Tilbury's 'Passage' (ferry), and Colchester's 'Russet' (russet cloth), the 'Trespas de Chelmeresford' — in Old French its 'passing across' — must surely refer to the phenomenon of the three bridges built to assist the passage of the Great River and Ceolmaer's ford.

VILL AND PARISH

The diversion from Writtle of the main stream of Essex traffic was not the only consequence of bridging the Great River. Sir John Bramston noted another:

'... This bridge being built joyned Moulsham and Chelmsford togeather'.

In 1086 Chelmsford and Moulsham, divided by the Great River, were two separate hamlets. By 1199, although they remained two manors held by different lords, they had become in the eyes of the law, in the medieval local government hierarchy of vill, hundred, and shire, one 'vill' — Chelmsford. Thus in 1214 a fine of 10 marks for unlawful hunting in Moulsham was laid on the whole vill, on 'the men of Chelmereford', but the fine was shared by the king and the abbot of Westminster in whose manor the offence was committed. But Moulsham never lost its separate identity. Both manors were often loosely referred to as individual vills, and sometimes they were even assessed as separate vills for taxes.

The two manors, once they were joined by the bridge, also became for ecclesiastical purposes one parish. Parishes were formed around existing churches. There was a church on the bishop's manor by the early 13th century. It stood at the top of the hill leading down to the bridges and ford for over two hundred years. In 1983 a limited excavation was carried out during the restoration of its late-medieval successor, now (since 1914) Chelmsford Cathedral, on the same site. When the floor was taken up to install a new underfloor heating system, remains of the flint rubble walls and foundations of the original church were exposed beneath the present building. The excavations suggested that the earlier church consisted of chancel, aisled nave, and west tower, of similar dimensions to the 15th-century replacement, apart from the south aisle, which was narrower. In 1908 J.C. Cox claimed that in the outer masonry of the great 15th-century tower there was evidence 'to the trained eye' of the re-use during rebuilding of squared stones trimmed with axes in the Norman manner, and also of moulded stones of the Early English period of King Henry III, including the circular base of a slender shaft.

Which of the energetic 12th-century bishops of London as lord of the manor began the building of that Norman church dedicated to St Mary, is not known. Maurice, perhaps; or his successor, Richard de Belmeis (d.1127), who lavished the whole revenues of his see on buildings; or Gilbert Foliot (d.1187), King Henry II's counsellor and supporter against Thomas Becket; or Richard FitzNeal (d.1198), King Richard I's treasurer and author of the *Dialogue of the Exchequer*; or his successor, William of Sainte-Mère-Église. Whichever one it was, the living, a rectory, remained in the gift of the bishops of London until the 16th century, endowed with glebe from the manorial demesne near the bishop's hall. Today the juxtaposition of Rectory Lane, Glebe Road, and Bishop's Hall Lane are reminders of that original relationship between bishop, manor, and church. The first rectors of the parish are not known. Roger, 'dean of Chelmsford', who is named in 1220, 1226, and 1228, may have been the rector; Richard de Gorges, presented to the living when it fell vacant in 1242, is the earliest authenticated incumbent.

The abbots of Westminster owned a chapel in Moulsham in 1157, but they never built a church there. By 1200 most places with no church of their own had become associated for ecclesiastical purposes with one nearby. This was how Moulsham came to be a hamlet in the parish of Chelmsford. The ecclesiastical parish of Chelmsford and the civil vill became, in fact, coterminous, a situation expressed in such phrases as '... *in villa et parochia de Chelmsford alias dicta Chelmersford* ...' (1434). Moulsham was separately identified as '*Mulsham in Chelmersford*' (1339) or 'the hamlet of Moulsham in the parish of Chelmsford' (1334).

CHAPTER TWO
The Town

A NEW TOWN

King Richard I died in France on 6 April 1199, and on 27 May his brother John was crowned king. Among the bishops present at John's coronation was a new bishop of London, William of Sainte-Mère-Église, who had been consecrated four days earlier. William, another Norman, and a trusted servant of both Richard I and his father, Henry II, was bishop from 1199 to 1221. It was William who planted a town at Ceolmaer's ford.

Three weeks after his coronation, on 16 June 1199, King John recognised by charter the new bishop's claim to all the possessions of his predecessors, their liberties, and their free customs. No doubt Bishop William paid the king well for this, for fees for the inspection and confirmation of charters were a well-exploited source of royal revenue. Indeed, in the autumn of 1200 King John, in pressing need of money, instructed the justices of the bench to disregard any charters which he had not confirmed.

The charter guaranteed to the bishop and his successors, and to their lands and men, exemption from certain royal taxes and demands for money from royal officials such as sheriffs or foresters, and their underlings; it spared them the burden of attending the shire and hundred courts, and released them from liability for fines laid on the hundred for unsolved murders and robberies. The charter allowed the bishop wide jurisdiction over his own lands and men, with the right to hang thieves, and to hold the view of frankpledge in his own courts, though the royal serjeant was to be present. That last concession saved the bishop's tenants the inconvenience of attending the sheriff's twice-yearly tourn in the hundred court, when tithings were checked and minor criminal offences judged.

Further, the charter gave the bishops of London 'and all their men' highly valued trading privileges, with exemption throughout the king's dominions from tolls, bridge dues, and stallage, and from customs duties on goods passing by land or sea. 'Let none', warned King John's charter, 'vex or disturb them, their realty, possessions, lands, or men, contrary to the liberty of our charter ...'

But for all their privileged status and their influence on the counsels of the realm, the bishops of London were not as wealthy as many of their brother bishops. The expenses of their household and diocese were heavy, and the fabric of the great cathedral church of St Paul, begun by Maurice and still unfinished, was a constant drain on their finances. The uncompleted building had been damaged by fire in King Stephen's reign, and although in King Richard's reign Bishop FitzNeal had been 'at vast charge and great care to restore it', there was still much to do. Indeed, the work was not completed until 1240 or formally dedicated until 1241. So it was necessary for the estates of the see to be made as profitable as possible.

Chelmsford, an episcopal manor farm populated mainly by peasants, had little to contribute to diocesan resources but farm produce, wool, and timber, and perhaps simple lodging for the bishop when his pastoral duties brought him into those parts of Essex. Small rural estates yielded few, if any, money rents or court fines. The manor was well situated, in the centre of the shire, at a crossing-place with a steady flow of traffic passing through. But to enjoy a regular money income from it the bishop required conditions favourable to trade, and a freeborn rent-paying tenantry.

It was not long before Bishop William secured those conditions. On 7 September 1199, less than three months after confirmation of his general charter of liberties, he won from King John, and doubtless paid for, the right to hold a weekly market on Fridays 'at Chelmersford in Essex, in that part of the vill which belongs to his manor of Chelmersford'. The wording of the charter saw to it that the market franchise did not extend across the Great River into Moulsham, but applied to the bishop's side of the bridge only. It was no part of the bishop's purpose to advance the interests of the abbot of Westminster. This discrimination between two manors in the same vill and parish no doubt contributed to the uneasy, even hostile, relationship between their tenants which prevailed for centuries.

Encouragement to freeborn men to become tenants in the bishop's new market followed seven months later. Many new market-based towns were planted in England after the Norman conquest, to the profit alike of the kings and their great subjects who created them, and the merchants, tradesmen, and property speculators who developed and settled them. A few years before, in 1194, King Richard I had founded Portsmouth. It was there, on 25 April 1200, that King John on behalf of Bishop William, granted the right of freeholding to all men who accepted from the bishop houses (*messuag'*) or plots to build upon (*placeas ad edificandum*) on his demesne at Chelmsford, with such liberties and free customs as the bishop chose to assign to them.

From that date the bishop, who held the manor as a tenant-in-chief directly from the king, could alienate, sell, or give away as freeholds, such parcels of the manor as he pleased, on his own terms. He may, indeed, have been seeking to regularise development which had already begun. The charter of 1200 refers to 'houses' as well as 'plots to build upon', and the original grant of one of the 'new plots in the new market', dated 1205, described it as 'that which was Robert de Marigny's together with the buildings that were Robert's'. Certainly wine merchants were established in Chelmsford by 1198, when William Vinitor, Henry Basket, and Henry de Tony were fined for over-charging for the wine which they sold there.

A year later, in March 1201, the bishop won a third concession. King John had been on a progress to the north of his kingdom, accompanied by his new young queen, Isabella. Returning south from York by stages, they reached Bury St Edmunds on 19 March, Sudbury on the 20th, and Chelmsford on the 21st. There the king granted the bishop the right to hold an annual fair at Chelmsford, on the Feast of St Philip and St James (1 May) and three days following. The bishop paid the king two palfreys for the privilege.

The new market was sited on the short hill leading down to the crossing, in the extreme south-east corner of the manor. From the narrow entrance to the manor across the bridge from Moulsham, the highway broadened out as it led up the hill about a quarter of a mile, to a wide open space in front of the churchyard. The elongated triangle so formed between bridge and churchyard became at the same time market-place (*forum*) and high street (*alta strata*). The whole area may at an early stage have been marked out in plots, which were then taken up over a period of years. In 1972-3 Nos.63-6 High Street were demolished for redevelopment. The cleared site was excavated and found to form

'... much of two ancient plots, which it appears were originally demarcated by ditches. The ditch within the excavated area had silted up naturally before the site was occupied ... a gap of perhaps 15-20 years occurring between demarcation and development. The two plots were eventually taken up as one, an aisled hall of three bays ... being erected early in the 13th century'.

When this hall house and its later additions were demolished in the early 14th century

'... the large plot (was) again divided into two along the line of the original division'.

Each of the two plots had a frontage of about 2½ rods (about 41 feet, or 12.57 m). Partial excavation in 1982 of the site of Nos.37-8, on the opposite side of the High Street, revealed a similar boundary ditch dating from the early 13th century. Plots fronting the street were developed on both sides of the hill. Their long narrow 'backsides', curving outward like ribs from a central spine, sloped gently down towards the watermeadows of 'Chelmersford river' on the east side of the street, and towards the 'Great River' on the west side. The situation was such that the surface waters of the market plots drained naturally into one river or the other.

Details exist of three of the original grants of plots. One grant, dated 1205, survives among the muniments of the dean and chapter of Saint Paul's; copies of two more, undated, but from the names of the witnesses of about the same date, were engrossed in 1416 on the Chelmsford manor court roll, when they were produced in court as evidence of title. The plots were conveyed as freeholds, subject to fixed annual manorial rents. The rent for one of these sites was two shillings, for the other two, one shilling (twelve old pence) apiece. On the oldest surviving rent roll of the manor (1428) free rents of twelve pence or of multiples of a shilling predominated in the town. The size of two of the plots was not stated, but the third had a frontage of 4 rods (about 66 feet or 20.11 m).

Besides the fixed rent, the free tenants owed the bishop certain feudal duties as a condition of their tenure, in particular an oath of fealty to him as lord, and attendance at his court; the penalty for defaulting in these duties was a fine. The bishop had not created an independent town; this was a controlled investment, in the words of the charter of 1200 and of the three original grants of freehold plots: '... for the profit and betterment of our church and our successors as bishops of London'.

Even without independence, the town's advantages were enough to stimulate the competitive dealing in real estate which has flourished to this day. Once the freehold plots of former demesne land passed out of the bishop's hands, they could be bought and sold, devised by will, mortgaged or leased, subject only to the fixed manorial rent and feudal obligations reserved to the bishop. While some purchasers were content with a single plot, others bought two or more. The 1972 excavation exposed the site of an early 13th century aisled hall built over two adjoining plots. Richard le Lolymer acquired no less than six plots, which in 1261 were providing an enviable inheritance for the heirs of his daughters Amicia and Albreda.

Among the first plot-owners were two of the bishop's officials. John of Witham and William Glunde, both described as *serviens episcopi*, the bishop's serjeant or bailiff, acquired in *c.*1205 two of the best sites in the town, close to the bridge over the Great River. Some of the new inhabitants were Frenchmen: Peter Peytevin (1225) came from Poitou; Robert, who had a plot before 1205, came from Marigny in Normandy. Most of the people personally identified in contemporary records between 1200 and 1250 as, 'of Chelmsford', bore continental names introduced into England after the coming of the Normans. They were called Mauger, Joce, or Richard; Henry, William, Peter, or Walter. Their wives and daughters were also named in continental fashion, Juliana or Alice, or Amphilise, a name not found in England before *c.*1190.

The new free tenants in time became collectively 'the townsmen'. By 1261 the watermeadow alongside the Chelmer to the north-east of the market was called 'Tunemanemedue' — the townsmen's meadow.

Within the manor the free townsmen of the market were a community apart from the native villeins, the 'tenants in bondage' who lived in the upland and laboured in their lord's fields. A 'common fine' of ten shillings was owed twice a year to the lord of the manor to recompense his purchase of the right to hold the view of frankpledge in his own court. The fine was gathered separately from town and upland: six shillings from those who dwelt *infra burgum huius ville*, and four shillings from those who dwelt *infra le upland huius ville*. With the latinising of 'town' as 'burgus' it was natural to style the townsmen *burgenses* (burgesses). It was the *burgenses* of Chelmsford who were credited with a feudal payment to the king in 1262. This was how the English survey of Chelmsford compiled in 1591, by Edward Moryson, esquire, surveyor, and John Lathum, gentleman, steward, '... upon the searche of the Courte rolls, rentalls, and other materiall escriptes' of the manor (written in Latin), came to state that the town was 'sometime written the Burrowe of Chelmesforde'.

TOWN AND COUNTY

The 1591 survey picked out the town's situation as 'a greate thorowefare' as one of its distinctive features. Its location at a convenient stage on the road from London to Colchester, Harwich, and Ipswich opened up from the beginning opportunities to cooks and vintners, brewers, bakers, and hostelers, to offer food, drink, and lodging to travellers, and stabling and fodder for horses; to shoemakers to ease the passage of footsore wayfarers who arrived ill-shod; to smiths and horse-doctors to practise their skills on draught, pack, and riding animals; to saddlers to refurbish harness and horse furniture; and to wheelwrights and carpenters to repair carters' and waggoners' wains and drays broken by the rigours of the rutted roads they travelled laden with merchants' goods and countrymen's produce.

Before long, in addition to the daily travellers passing through, and the villagers gathering weekly to buy and sell in the market, the town became host from time to time to greater concourses of people, summoned to attend when the king's representatives sat there to deal with his judicial and financial business in Essex.

No evidence has been found of the presence in Chelmsford of the king's court (*curia regis*) in the earlier years of the 12th century. The greater importance at that date of nearby Writtle is evident. In 1099-1100 Bishop Maurice had to produce his charters to royal justices sitting at Writtle to obtain confirmation of his privileges. In King Stephen's reign (1135-54) royal documents were dated at Writtle on at least two occasions.

But in 1184 an entry in the Great Roll of the Exchequer, or 'pipe roll', may imply that a royal court had sat at Chelmsford, for 37s 7d was charged for the keep of one William Tusard, 'approver', and escorting him in custody from London to Chelmsford and back again. An 'approver' was a felon who offered to give evidence against an accomplice in order to secure a pardon for himself. In 1198 royal justices sat at Stratford to hear pleas of the crown in Essex. But in 1201 the king's court was at Chelmsford, where the grant of the town's fair was dated, and witnessed by four of King John's regular counsellors, John de Gray, bishop of Norwich, William Brewer, Hugh Bardolph, the justiciar, and Fulk de Cantelupe.

In 1202-3 the king's justices sat at Chelmsford. Judgement in one case which came up that year, however, involving Richard, son of Gilbert of Colchester, was deferred 'until the coming of the justices to Colchester', because 'the burgesses have their liberties that they may not be impleaded outside their city'. In 1206 the justices sat at Stratford and Colchester. In the years which followed no justices were sent on circuit in Essex, but in 1214 the justiciar, Peter des Roches, settled various cases at Chelmsford as he passed through travelling on the king's business.

In 1218 the government of King John's successor, the boy-king Henry III, renewed the practice begun in the 12th century but abandoned during the troubled later years of John's reign, of despatching 'justisis errauntz' (itinerant justices) to go on 'eyre', that is, to ride the circuit holding the king's court in the counties. The writ of 1218 instructed Geoffrey de Bocland and seven other justices to ride together through Essex, Suffolk, Norfolk, and Hertfordshire, and ordered them to meet first at Chelmsford. It was the only centre where they sat in Essex before moving on. From that date Chelmsford was the normal place of session of the Essex eyre. Additional sessions sometimes held at Colchester and Rayleigh were necessitated by the special liberties claimed by the burgesses of Colchester, and by the tenants of the Honor of Rayleigh in the Rochford hundred.

The eyre was held at intervals of several years, but other official visitations drew people into the town between the eyres. In 1219 the town was the place of assembly for the sheriff, jurors, verderers, and foresters summoned to set out on a forest inquest throughout Essex. In 1221, 1236, and 1256 forest courts were held there. In 1225 justices appointed to hold possessory assizes (settle land disputes) and deliver gaols (try prisoners detained in gaol) in all the counties were instructed in Essex to sit at Chelmsford, and in the same year royal commissioners sat there to assess and collect from Essex a tax of a fifteenth on movables.

The circuit justices sat from day to day, week to week, until their business was done. During that time people from all over Essex (and beyond) swarmed into the town: litigants, attorneys, juries, witnesses, compurgators or oath-helpers, pledges summoned as sureties for the appearance of the accused, bailiffs and tithingmen. Every hundred, every vill, in the county, had to be represented before the justices. When John de Nevill, chief justice of the forest, sat to hear

11

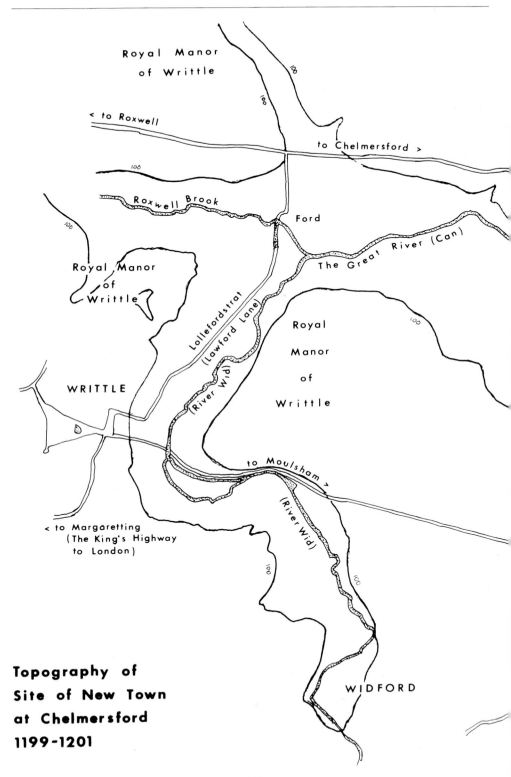

Royal Manor
of Writtle

< to Roxwell

to Chelmersford >

100

100

Roxwell Brook

Ford

The Great River (Can)

100

Royal Manor
of
Writtle

Lollefordstrat
(Lawford Lane)

(River Wid)

Royal
Manor
of
Writtle

100

WRITTLE

to Moulsham >

(River Wid)

< to Margaretting
(The King's Highway
to London)

100

100

WIDFORD

**Topography of
Site of New Town
at Chelmersford
1199-1201**

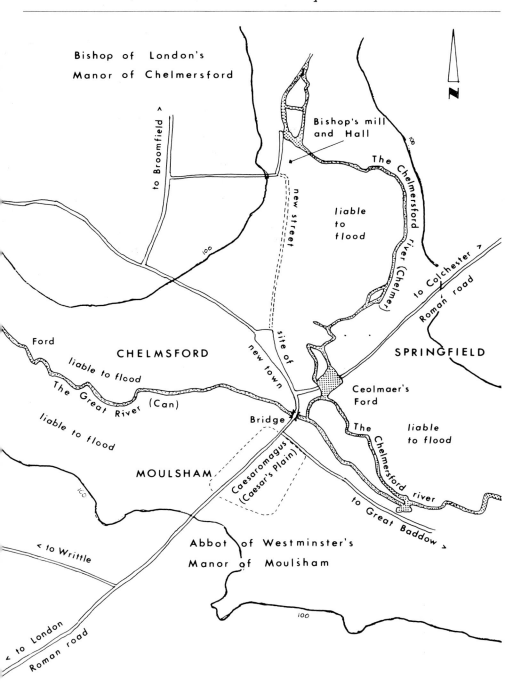

Bishop of London's
Manor of Chelmersford

to Broomfield >

Bishop's mill
and Hall

The Chelmersford river (Chelmer)

liable
to
flood

100

to Colchester >
Roman road

Ford

CHELMSFORD

liable to flood

The Great River (Can)

liable to flood

site of
new town

new street

SPRINGFIELD

Ceolmaer's
Ford

Bridge

The
Chelmersford river

liable
to
flood

MOULSHAM

Caesaromagus
(Caesar's Plain)

to Great Baddow >

< to Writtle

Abbot of Westminster's
Manor of Moulsham

< to London
Roman road

100

100

13

pleas of the forest at Chelmsford in 1236, the sheriff of Essex summoned to appear before him not only all archbishops, bishops, abbots, priors, earls, barons, knights, and free tenants, who held lands or tenements within the bounds of the royal forest in Essex, but also four men and the reeve from each village, and the royal foresters and verderers. Attendance at such sessions from remote villages was a memorable event. When John atte Clyve gave evidence in 1300 of the age of Katherine, daughter of James of Langdon Hills, he particularly remembered her birth sixteen years before, because it was the year 'he was at Chelmsford in the company of James of Langdon her father at the eyre of the justices ... at Michaelmas'; and ten other men of the little village of Langdon Hills could swear to the year for the same reason.

The Church, too, found Chelmsford convenient for large gatherings. In 1223 the bishop of London held an ordination service there, an occasion memorable for a mighty tempest of wind and rain which arose during the ceremony, striking terror in the assembled company. This was interpreted by the chronicler, Ralph of Coggeshall, as a sign of Almighty God's displeasure at the unworthy motives of many of those who presented themselves for ordination, seeking to live well off their stipends and the offerings of the faithful, in feasting, tippling, and lechery.

The status in Essex achieved by the bishop's new town within half a century of its creation was startling. By the 1250s, with its central position in the shire, it had become the place usually appointed for the transaction of 'the king's business' in the county. It had become, in short, the county town. J.H. Round pointed out in 1903 that

> '... of all the towns to which Domesday applies the term *civitas* Colchester and Rochester are the only ones which are not now the capitals of their counties; and Rochester of course was the capital of West Kent ...'

Geography, shrewdly exploited by a Norman bishop, denied Colchester, in the far north-east of Essex, the status that its size, wealth, and antiquity might have seemed to warrant.

The emergence of Chelmsford as the main seat of royal justice and administration in Essex no doubt explains the existence of a 'king's gaol' or 'king's prison' there, mentioned in 1253-4, 1256, 1260, 1262, and from time to time later. The county gaol in the middle ages was in Colchester Castle, but a place of custody was needed in Chelmsford to hold the prisoners brought there for trial from Colchester, and to hold local suspects until they could be carried to Colchester. When Walter, son of Walter and Amphilise Trygg who lived at the top of the high street (site of 2 High Street), was accused of murder in 1256, he was held in the king's prison at Chelmsford.

The success of the new town slowly eroded nearby Writtle's standing, although Writtle remained more populous than Chelmsford for several hundred years. Writtle was indeed the venue chosen for an official gathering in 1237, when the sheriff summoned earls, barons, knights, and free men, with four men and the reeve from every vill, to assemble there before the king's representatives. But the purpose of the summons was to consider how the king's peace could be preserved from 'many wandering evil-doers in Essex openly gathering in the king's woods', harboured and succoured by the neighbourhood, with no one raising the hue and cry against them. The dense royal woodland in the south and south-west of Writtle may itself have been paramount in that particular enquiry. The ancient county court presided over by the sheriff was still in the 13th century 'wont to be held' (*teneri solet*) in the 'green place' in Writtle known as 'Greneberi' (Greenbury). But by 1326 that court was also being held in Chelmsford.

Writtle's market, too, could not survive the establishment of Chelmsford's. In *c.*1258 a survey made of tenancies on the Knights Templars' estates in Cressing and Witham shows the Chelmsford market by then a customary outlet for the Templars' produce. The heir of Walter the Gardener at Cressing owed the Templars a 'work' which obliged him to come to their barns at Witham and Cressing on Saturdays when summoned to perform a 'carrying service', the transport of half a load of corn or the weight of half a load of corn, to Colchester, Maldon, or Chelmsford. In 1185 the Templars had demanded Saturday carrying services to Maldon only. Those unwelcome market visitors, the purveyors who procured corn and victuals for the king's use, were descending on Chelmsford by 1274, when the men of High Easter complained that the purveyors took 13 quarters of corn from them there, paid only 2*s* the quarter for it, though it could have fetched 5*s*, and kept the sacks. The men of Little Waltham were even more aggrieved, because a purveyor took half a load of wheat worth 5*s* from them at Chelmsford, without even paying for it. The purveyors were not the only un-popular participants in the Chelmsford market. 'Forestallers' were soon at work, buying up whole stocks of goods before they reached the market, to re-sell there at a higher price; nine men were fined for this offence in 1292, among them William, the miller.

As Chelmsford's market grew, Writtle's died. Although Chelmsford and Writtle were barely two miles apart, Chelmsford's market charter in 1199 had contained no clause to protect the interests of any neighbouring market, as became usual from 1200. In 1230 Writtle market showed an annual profit of 4 marks (£2 13*s* 4*d*). By 1304 the market profits were being farmed for only 20*s*, and in 1361 and 1377 for 6*s* 8*d*. In 1419 a survey of Writtle noted: 'There was there in ancient times a market every Monday which is not now held'.

TOWN GOVERNMENT

The affairs of the new town were run by two officials of the bishop, his steward and his Chelmsford bailiff, and by the inhabitants themselves. The steward rode down from London to preside over the manor courts; his presence was only occasional, but as the official in charge of the bishop's secular interests he was directly responsible to the bishop for the manor. The bailiff lived on the manor, in a day-to-day neighbourly relationship with the inhabitants. He was in fact one of themselves. He carried out the steward's and court's orders, collected tenants' rents and fines, made distraint on defaulters, and had to account to the bishop's steward and auditors for the money rents, bond 'works' owed, court profits and market tolls, and for the expenses and income of the demesne farm, its crops, stock, implements, and buildings. He represented duly appointed authority in the daily life of the inhabitants; when an honest couple in 1274 found some money lying about on the manor they handed it over to Laurence, the bishop's bailiff. Laurence is the earliest identified bailiff, for it is not clear whether Ralph the

Clerk, described as *serviens* or bailiff of Chelmsford in 1220, was the manor bailiff, or the Hundred bailiff answerable to the sheriff. An officer similar to the bailiff, but answerable to him, as well as to the steward, was the reeve, whose responsibilities lay entirely in the upland. But whereas the bailiff was appointed by the bishop as lord of the manor, the reeve was the joint choice of the upland villein tenants and the lord. In the 14th century the leading upland villeins submitted three names for the lord's final choice. When John of Thorpe was bailiff (*serviens*) in 1339, Thomas atte Wall was reeve (*prepositus*)

The excessive zeal of one Chelmsford bailiff to further his master's interests led in 1280 to a confrontation with the archbishop of Canterbury. The archbishop, John Pecham, like the bishop, claimed for his men freedom from tolls throughout the kingdom. He protested to Bishop Richard Gravesend that the Chelmsford bailiff demanded tolls from tenants of Canterbury travelling through the town or trading there, and confiscated their goods when payment was refused. The arch-

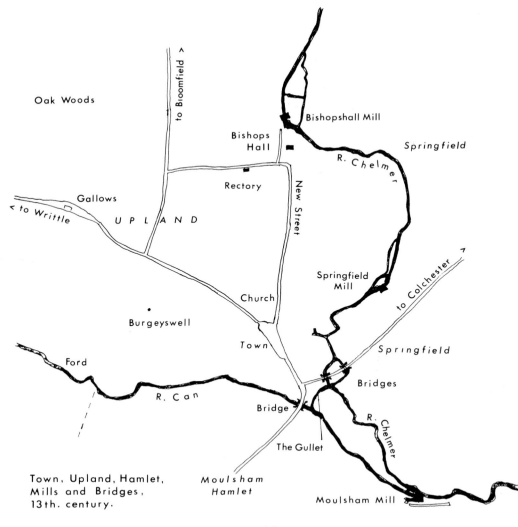

Town, Upland, Hamlet,
Mills and Bridges,
13th. century.

bishop required the bishop 'forthwith' to restrain his bailiff and order restitution of the goods seized.

Toll franchises often caused friction. Chelmsford's own traders were challenged early in the 14th century by the Colchester bailiffs, who demanded tolls from them when they took their goods and merchandize to Colchester. Bishop Ralph Baldock came to the rescue of his tenants; in 1311 he obtained a writ prohibiting the Colchester bailiffs from doing this, claiming freedom from toll for his men under his charter of 1199. The Colchester burgesses appealed to the courts, but prepared themselves in the event of defeat to 'abstain from such demand ... in as cautious a manner as they could'. They lost their appeal; their bailiffs were forbidden to exact toll from the bishop of London or his men, and ordered to release the bishop's men at once from any distraint put upon them for payment.

The inhabitants of both town and upland were involved in the running of the manor through the ancient institution of frankpledge. This required all males over twelve years of age, bond or free, to be 'in frankpledge', grouped in tithings of ten or twelve members, each under a head man, known in Chelmsford as the 'chief pledge'. Each tithing was responsible for the behaviour of its own members, for bringing its wrongdoers to justice, for seeing that they paid any penalties imposed, and for meeting the fines of defaulters. Twice a year the sheriff held special hundred courts (known as 'tourns'), minor police courts, at which he also 'viewed' the frankpledges, that is, inspected the state of the hundred tithings. Those manors whose lords had won from the Crown the privilege of holding the 'view' themselves escaped the sheriff's tourns. The Chelmsford view was held in the bishop's own manor court, with his steward sitting as judge. There the chief pledges of town and upland separately reported on their tithings, and presented their accusations of local petty crime, dishonesty, and unneighbourly behaviour.

No records of the Chelmsford court in action in the 13th century have survived. But when King Edward I in 1285 set on foot an enquiry into royal jurisdictions in private hands, the bishop of London was summoned before the itinerant justices sitting at Chelmsford to say by what right (*Quo warranto*) he claimed for his Chelmsford manor view of frankpledge, gallows, tumbrel, pillory, and the assize of bread and ale. These questions tell something of how the town and upland were governed. The bishop's manor court supervised the tithings and punished social misdemeanors; it enforced the assize of bread and ale enacted to protect the public from short-weight loaves and flat ale; 'hand-having' thieves taken with the goods were hanged on the bishop's gallows; scolds and 'unquiet women', cheats, and troublemakers, were set on the stool or chair called the tumbrel or cucking-stool, or stood in the pillory, exposed to the jeers of passersby and volleys of rubbish and filth. The fines imposed by the court belonged to the bishop. Dishonest bakers were an unfailing source of revenue. As early as 1214 King John's justiciar, Peter des Roches, when he was at Chelmsford, fined William Folke 'and his fellows' ten marks (£6 13s 4d) for breaking the regulations for the sale of bread laid down by the king in 1202.

In reply to the *Quo warranto* enquiry of 1285 the bishop's attorney produced King John's charter of 1199 granting the view of frankpledge to the bishops of London for ever. As the justices read it through they noticed the stipulation '... so that the said view be made in the bishop's court in the presence of the king's serjeant'. Questioned about the serjeant's presence, the bishop's attorney hedged, suggesting that the bishop had already 'made sufficient answer' to the question, 'By what right?'. The justices promptly took the 'view' back into the king's hands. Who held the courts, if any, in the next five years, is not known. But the bishop successfully appealed against the decision, and in 1290 King Edward ruled that the franchise had been 'unadvisedly and in error seized', and 'wishing to show the bishop grace' restored it to him. The bishops' right to the franchise was never seriously challenged again, though vigilance was always necessary to preserve their liberties from infringement by the sheriff of Essex and his officers. Bishop Ralph Baldock had to write sharply to the sheriff in 1306 to remind him that 'we and our men' were freed by royal charter from suit at the courts of the shire and hundred. The view of frankpledge (or manor court leet) was to have no rival in the civil government of the town until the mid-16th century.

The bishop's officers and court had, of course, no jurisdiction at all in Moulsham. There the abbot of Westminster, under a charter of King Henry III, held his own view of frankpledge, appointed his own officers, set up his own gallows, and enforced the assize of bread and ale. Only in spiritual matters did the bishop, as diocesan and patron of the parish of Chelmsford, hold any authority in the hamlet.

CHAPTER THREE

The Settlers

THE TOWNSPEOPLE

As no 13th-century records of the townspeople's own making have survived, their names are only to be found in random references in official sources. Inevitably it is the names of those who made their mark in some field, or entered into formal business or property transactions, or became entangled in the processes of the law, as plaintiff or defendant, victim or villain, witness or surety, which have been preserved. The name of the earliest known schoolmaster of the town, Walter, 'Master of the scholars of Chelmsford', has survived because he was fined 40*d* at a Forest court in 1292, for cutting down and carrying off fourteen young oaks. A fatal quarrel in 1231 between two Chelmsford wine merchants, Ralph Vinetar and Robert Hardel, has handed down not only their names but also those of relatives and friends who became involved. When Ralph died, Juliana his wife and Alice his mother accused Robert of murder, saying that Robert had struck Ralph with a knife on the left side of his body, inflicting such a wound that he died the next day. But Robert's friend, Aylwin of Chelmsford, stood by him, and when Robert appeared in court the two women admitted that he had not been to blame.

Henry of Chelmsford, called 'the Norman', was one of those who did well for himself. He secured a position of trust in Henry III's household as one of the king's messengers, entitled to a letter pouch bearing the king's arms to hang at his belt, and a free pair of spurs; but he had to provide his own horse. He was sent across the channel in 1243 to King Henry in Gascony, with 20*s* for the expenses of the journey. In 1246 the barons of the exchequer were ordered to pay him an allowance of 1½*d* a day for life. In 1255 he carried King Henry's letter about a truce to the king of France in Gascony, and in the same year he and other messengers were sent to all the sheriffs of England with letters about money to be collected for the king. In 1259 he was given, by the king's order, a russet robe, but 'without fur', a subtle distinction of household rank. A more menial and less reliable member of the royal household was John of Chelmsford, who absconded in 1251 while travelling with the king's white baggage-horse, taking the horse with him.

Stephen of Chelmsford was a wine merchant and became a London citizen. Since the Conquest French wines had been in much demand; the chronicler, Roger of Hoveden, who died about 1201, wrote that '... the whole land was filled with drink and drinkers'. Vintners were conspicuous from the first among traders active in the bishop's new town. About 1205 Roger Vinitor held land near the bridge. Philip Vinetar stood surety for Ralph the Clerk when Ralph was held responsible for the escape of a captured robber in 1220. In 1225 three merchants, William Hardel, Robert Hardel, and Peter Peytevin had to give security for payment to the king of the duty due, a fifteenth share, on their stock of wine stored at Chelmsford; a great deal of the wine imported into England came from Peter's native district, Poitou. The same Robert Hardel was fined three marks (£2) in 1230 for infringing at Chelmsford the regulations for the sale of wine, and a year later was on trial, though acquitted, for killing a rival, Ralph Vinetar, in a brawl.

Stephen of Chelmsford was one of the top rank of wine merchants who supplied the royal household. Like all wine importers he was liable for the wine prise; this was the king's entitlement to buy below the market price two casks in twenty from every cargo landed, one cask from 'before the mast', where the inferior wine was carried, and one cask from 'behind the mast' where the better wine had more protection from the sea. In 1256 Henry III's chamberlain paid Stephen 20s a cask for prisage casks, but 33s 3d a cask for those bought at the market price. Stephen's trade was two-way; in 1254 he was licensed to sail a ship called *La Helop of Winchelese* laden with oats for Gascony, to Bordeaux, provided he gave security for his return with the first favourable wind to Portsmouth, presumably with a cargo of wine. In January 1261 the king's steward confirmed that Stephen, with the chamberlain and another London merchant, was owed 350 marks (£233 6s 8d); this was to settle accounts with other wine merchants to whom they had guaranteed payment for 100 casks of wine sold to the king 'against last Christmas'. In the same year Stephen with his partner Henry the Welshman sold 165 casks to the king for £380, besides prisage wine. He supplied Queen Eleanor too; nine casks were bought for her by her butler in 1258 for £22 10s, and three casks of expensive 'old wine' costing £3 8s 4d a cask by the chamberlain in 1261.

Stephen of Chelmsford's loyalty to Henry III cost him his life. During the Barons' War between Simon de Montfort's followers and the king, Stephen, by then an old man, with three other London citizens tried in December 1263 to prevent the rebels from entering London from Southwark by locking the gates of London Bridge and throwing the keys into the Thames. But other Londoners who favoured the rebels let them in. Stephen and his friends were taken prisoner by the rebels and carried with them on the march to the battle of Lewes on 12 May 1264. There de Montfort tricked the royal forces by stationing his personal litter conspicuously on a hill, with his standard and pennons flying, to draw the main attack. The prisoners, Stephen and the other loyal citizens, were secured inside the litter, which became the target of the strongest royalist assault led by Prince Edward. When the litter was taken, its occupants were killed unrecognised by their own friends, while de Montfort was launching his own successful attack against the weaker forces led by the king himself.

The Barons' War ended with the defeat and death of de Montfort at Evesham in 1265, leaving many personal wrongs to be righted, lands unlawfully seized to be restored, and looted goods to be recovered. Justices appointed to determine such matters sat in 1268 at Chelmsford from 28 February to 16 March, hearing not only the cases presented by the Essex hundred juries, but also cases referred by the sheriffs of Hertfordshire, Kent, and Suffolk. Places which were independent of the hundred jurisdiction, such as Chelmsford, made their own reports. Chelmsford had escaped spoliation; its jurors said that they knew nothing of lands given away or seized in the town. But Peter the Priest of Chelmsford was accused by William de Ferigges (? Feering) at Colchester of buying goods worth 10 marks (£6 13s 4d) which had been plundered from him during the late disturbances.

THE BLACK FRIARS

In the middle years of the 13th century a new group of settlers, the Black preaching friars, followers of St Dominic, arrived in the parish. Camden records a 16th-century tradition that their Chelmsford house was founded by Malcolm, King of Scots, but this is not possible; the last Scottish king of that name, Malcolm IV, died in 1165, and the first Dominicans did not come to England until 1221. The Chelmsford house was founded at some date between then and 1277, when the presence of the friars in the parish is authenticated.

The donor of the original priory site is not known. It was in Moulsham, west of the London road, by the meadow land alongside the great river; it was close to the hamlet habitations but not amongst them. The meadow became known as Fryers Meade. The site was of the kind often sought out by the friars. Instead of shutting themselves away from the world, as some of the older religious orders did, they chose to work among people, settling on the outskirts of great cities or growing market towns, where, as their contemporary Matthew Paris wrote, 'They busied themselves in preaching, hearing confessions, the recital of divine service, in teaching and study'. They cared too for the sick and lepers, taught the poor, and relied almost entirely on charity for their subsistence and housing.

Their presence could be particularly effective in parishes where the local parson was non-resident or inadequate. Very little is known of the early rectors of Chelmsford. One of them, Thomas de Broncille, who was illegitimate, already had two other livings when he became rector some time before 1305, with a papal dispensation to hold them though he had not even been ordained priest. When he resigned the other two livings in 1305, he received another dispensation to continue holding Chelmsford, then in 1306 obtained a royal protection for three years as he was going overseas. While a parson like Thomas de Broncille enjoyed the fruits of the living, responsibility for the cure of the inhabitants' souls was apt to fall on more humble chaplains, and no doubt such pastoral care as the friars could offer was gladly received. Certainly they were welcomed locally. In 1281 John Burgeys and his wife Margaret, with the consent of King Edward I, gave the prior of the house, Brother Adam of Malmesbury, as free alms, a plot of land measuring 30 feet by 20 feet; in return the benefactors were to be remembered in the friars' prayers forever. The goodwill of the king had already been shown in 1277, when he sent an alms of 10s from Havering, by the hand of Brother Ralph, to the friars preachers of Chelmsford, to provide them with a days' food; this sum suggests a community of about thirty brothers by that date, allowing 4d a day for each brother. In 1289 the same king sent them from Rayleigh an alms for three days' food; and his queen, Eleanor, two weeks later sent them 40s. In 1291 Eleanor's executors paid over to them no less than 100s under her will. The friars, better educated than many of the clergy, were of course useful to the Crown: in 1289 Brother Robert of Chelmsford went to Guyenne in the king's service, as companion to his confessor; there he was detailed to care for a sick squire of the king's, was repaid his expenses, given a new pair of boots, and a tailor was paid to make him a summer garment. When he was injured on the way back to England, he made the day's journey from Dover to Canterbury to join the king carried on a cart for which the king paid fifteen pence.

The cordial relations between the Crown and the Chelmsford friars continued after Edward II succeeded his father as king in 1307. When Edward II stayed at Coggeshall abbey in 1325 the friars sent him a present of 243 apples; the king reciprocated the next day, when he came to Chelmsford, with an alms of 8*s* to provide one day's food for 24 brothers.

TOWN GROWTH

Two documents of the early 14th century, a *compotus* or bailiff's account of 1318, and a tax assessment of 1327, begin to bring the manor and town into better focus. Bishop Richard Newport died in August 1318. His successor Stephen Gravesend was elected in September and took possession of his estates in November. Two bailiffs in turn, Richard Jordan up to Michaelmas (29 September), and Ralph atte Wall from Michaelmas to 15 November, managed the manors of 'Chelmereford and Suthwode' in the interim. The account submitted by Ralph has survived.

'Suthwode' was Southwood, a hamlet in Writtle, which was described in 1335 as being in the parishes of Writtle and Chelmsford. A connection between Chelmsford and Southwood, which had no common boundary, can be traced back to the early years of the 13th century, when Robert de Marigny, a sub-tenant of the bishop of London in Essex, held land and buildings in Chelmsford before 1205, and also thirty acres of land in 'Suwod'. Bishop Fulk Basset (1241-59) certainly owned land in 'Suthwode', where he was said to have illegally cleared six acres 'of his own fee and soil' for cultivation. In the 1280s three acres of land 'in the parish of Chelmsford' were said to lie 'at Suthwode', and in 1292 Bishop Richard Gravesend (1280-1303) was holding the six acres there cleared by Fulk, with another eight acres of his own. The 1318 *compotus* confirms that by then the bishops of London were lords of Southwood as well as of Chelmsford, and that Southwood, though termed a 'manor', was farmed with Chelmsford. Its identity as a separate manor is supported by a lease made by Bishop Robert Braybrooke in 1399 to Thomas Wyllyngale of his lands and tenements called 'Southwode', with the demesne, the grange, and the house called 'Le Hewenhous', but excluding the rents and services of the tenants, bond and free, and various feudal services. When the relationship between Southwood and Chelmsford was examined in 1539, Southwood, no longer termed a manor, was explained as being 'in the lordship of Chemysford but not of the same'. This detached part of the parish of Chelmsford in Writtle existed until 1889, when a revision of parish boundaries added Southwood to Writtle parish, rectifying a feudal topographical anomaly which had long lost any meaning.

Ralph's account covered both town and upland. He answered for the money rents which he had collected for the Michaelmas quarter. They totalled 79*s* 3¾*d*; thus rents, almost entirely from the 'new places' in the town, were by then yielding £15 17*s* 3*d* a year. The bond tenants upland still owed services or 'works' for their holdings. In the six weeks and five days since Michaelmas, manor court customary payments yielded 29*s* 3*d*, market tolls 19*d*, and court fines 18*s* (to which Ralph added 29*s* 1*d* for fines collected by his predecessor Richard before Michaelmas). Comparison with some of the demesne management costs lends more meaning to these figures: a new ploughshare had cost 12*d* and a new coulter the same; the demesne farm's twelve 'stotts' or plough-beasts had been shod for a whole quarter year for 4*s*, and eight oxen for 2*s*; half a bushel of salt had cost 4*d*;

and at Southwood 110 perches of water furrows had been made for 5½*d*, that is 20 perches (about 110 yards or 100 m) for 1*d.*

During October and early November wheat and oats had been threshed and winnowed, 59a. of wheat had been sown in the lord's fields called Melnedenn, Cherchfeld, and Schapelefeld, and 14a. of rye in Cherchfeld. Ralph accounted for corn ground at the watermill, for allowances of mixed corn or maslin given to the lord's servants, and for fodder provided for the horses and oxen. Finally he accounted for 87 customary 'works' owed by bond tenants over the six weeks and five days of his charge, 13 works being owed each week. He had allocated 20 works for digging water furrows at Chelmsford to drain land for new crops; 39 works had been used to fence in the corn sown at Chelmsford, works which included cutting, carting, and binding the brushwood and stakes to form the enclosure, and helping to set it up; four works were used to carry two letters to Braintree, four for two letters to Wickham Bishops, two for a letter to Laindon, and three for a letter to Stortford, the bishop of London having other estates in those places. Ralph himself was credited with 13 works. Two works were left over, which he had sold for 1*d*. The normal value of a 'work', usually a day's labour unless allocated to a special task, was thus ½*d*.

'Schapelefeld' took its name from the 'chapel by the manor', first mentioned in 1321, when a priest called Thomas Isoude was presented to be its chaplain, and, significantly, required to swear an oath to be resident. This was a free chapel in the gift of the bishop of London, and dedicated to St Margaret the Virgin. Sixteen of its chaplains are named between 1336 and 1371; one of them, in 1362, was Thomas Thebaud *alias* Sudbury, who was a nephew of Simon Sudbury, bishop of London, and later became rector of Chelmsford. No mention of the chapel has been found after 1371; it had certainly ceased to exist by 1535. John Walker's map of 1591 shows the site of the chapel near the manor buildings, at the north-west corner of the field still at that date called 'Chapell fyelde', where the 'oulde church yearde' is named. In 1723 William Holman wrote that the ruins had 'been long ploughed up'. It is said that skeletons were unearthed in that vicinity when the foundations of Hoffman's ballbearing factory were being laid in 1898. No doubt this chapel was convenient for the bishop when he lodged at the hall. Bishop Simon Sudbury (1362-75) in particular celebrated ordinations eleven times in Chelmsford and usually visited the town at least once or twice a year; his presence there is recorded no less than seven times in 1362. The chapel may indeed have been the original place of worship for the small Saxon community of the Upland before the church was built near the site chosen for the new market.

The other two fields named in the bailiff's account were near the manor buildings. Melnedenn, or Mellefeld (1382), lay west of the bishop's mill. Cherchfeld, lying south of the rectory, and divided from Chapel Field by the lane leading from the town to the mill, later became known as Townefyelde (1591), the name perpetuated today in Townfield Street.

The 1327 subsidy list reveals a little more about the manor and growing town. The subsidy was a tax of one-twentieth on the personal wealth of heads of households, men and women, not on real estate, but on movable property worth ten shillings or more. None were exempt, whatever the liberties claimed under ancient charters, except most churchmen, and the poor with goods worth less than 10s. The fifteen-year-old king, Edward III, needed the money only a few months after the death of his father, Edward II, to meet the threat of a Scottish invasion led by Robert Bruce. Movables might include stock, grain, household possessions, merchandize, and 'treasure', though in practice household necessities, food, and tools, were not assessed. In towns a few items were specifically excused: a garment each for a man and his wife, and a bed; a ring, a buckle of silver or gold, a silk girdle in daily use, and a drinking cup of silver or mazer.

Chelmsford was probably the collecting point in 1327 to which the Essex sub-collectors brought the money gathered in the county, for delivery by the chief collectors to Westminster. This was certainly so in 1296 and 1306. Juries of neighbours drew up separate assessments for Chelmsford and Moulsham. In Chelmsford 38 men and 5 women were taxed on goods worth 10s or more; the minimum tax paid was 6d on goods valued at exactly 10s. John the Dyer, with goods worth £13 8s 4d, contributed most to the total sum of £3 10s 9¼d raised in the town. In Moulsham, where 29 men and one woman had goods worth 10s or more, the amount raised, £3 2s 0¾d, was disproportionately high because of the wealth of two individuals, Francis Bacheme and Nicholas of Moulsham, whose goods were valued respectively at £14 15s 5d and £10 7s 1d. Francis Bacheme was a Genoese merchant who held the so-called 'manor' of Bekeswell (later Bexfields) in Moulsham.

1327 SUBSIDY VALUATION

Valuation of goods	*Chelmsford*		*Moulsham*	
	Men	*Women*	*Men*	*Women*
Over £10	1	—	2	—
Over £5-£10	—	—	—	—
Over £2-£5	10	—	4	—
10s-£2	27	5	23	1
	38	5	29	1

These tax assessments are no guide to the number of inhabitants in 1327, or householders, omitting as they do, churchmen, those whose wealth was in land and buildings, and those, possibly the majority, whose worldly goods did not amount to 10s, which was no mean sum at that date. After all, when one 'work' could be sold for a halfpenny, 240 days' labour could be hired for 10s.

But the assessments can suggest the relative distribution of movable wealth in Essex. In the whole vill and parish of Chelmsford 73 people paid £6 12s 10d. There were three higher assessments in the Chelmsford hundred: in Great Waltham, 125 people paid £8 11s 8¼d; in the three Hanningfields, which were grouped together, 68 people paid £9 17s 3¼d; and in Writtle 158 people paid £14 0s 3½d. But besides those three, in the whole of Essex there were only nine other places assessed higher than the county town, including, notably, Colchester, which paid £14 0s 8d, Waltham Holy Cross, which paid £14 3s 8½d, and Barking, which paid £17 17s 6½d. In a county with over 400 parishes, this is some measure of the economic standing of the town and adjoining hamlet a century and a quarter after Bishop William of Sainte-Mère-Église created his 'new market'.

The assessment reveals something else: that by 1327 the bond tenants of the

24

Upland were not necessarily poor. Four of the bishop's villeins, Walter and William Southwood, Geoffrey Gibbe, and John Hasyl, were taxed, John on movables worth £3 3s 4d.

The assessments may identify some of the town taxpayers' trades. There were Hugh the Cook and John the Cook, William the Vintner and John the Taverner; Nicholas the Spicer, John the Spicer, and Elias the Chandler; Matthew the Skinner and John the Dyer; Alice the Painter and Alice the Wheeler. William the Vintner and John the Dyer were also taxed for goods in Moulsham. Other sources yield the names of butchers, bakers, smiths, tailors, tanners, an arrow-smith and a wool merchant, known to have been in business in the town in the early 14th century. There was a 'scolemayster', too, John Fadlet, accused in 1327 of stealing goods worth 40s from one of the most important freeholders in the town, John of Thorpe. John of Thorpe, owner of two large properties in the high street (sites of 37-8, 72-5 High Street), with goods in 1327 worth over £3, and perhaps a kinsman of Thomas of Thorpe, rector of Chelmsford, *c*.1318-32, was the manor bailiff in 1339.

John of Thorpe's two town properties were still known as 'Thorpes' in the 16th century. Indeed, by the early 14th century real estate was a sure means to wealth and prominence in the town. The freehold 'new places' were changing hands briskly, whether by inheritance, marriage, or sale. The sources begin to distinguish 'shops' among the conventional 'messuages' changing hands. John the Cook bought two shops, one in 1323 from William the Arrowsmith, and another from John of Dunmow in 1336. In 1324 the tailor, Peter Campe, sold a shop to Henry of Felsted and his son Robert. Londoners were investing in property in the town: Roger Torold, a taverner, and William Andrew, a butcher, both of London, in 1341 sold two shops and a dwelling in the town. Conversely, in 1300, Beatrice, the daughter of Thomas, a Chelmsford vintner, inherited a shop in London. By the 1350s one of that most valuable class of property for investment, an inn (*hospitium*) in the middle of the high street (site of 72-5 High Street), formerly Thorpe's, owned and let by John de Benenton, was yielding him a commercial rent of £3 a year, whereas the fixed rent he owed the bishop for it, as a freehold tenant of the manor, was only 10s 8d.

It was not only merchants and tradesmen who were interested in property in the town. Humphrey de Bohun, earl of Hereford and Essex (d.1361) had a house there, which was broken into by rioters led by Sir Robert de Marney in 1342. But the most remarkable accumulation of real estate was assembled between the 1260s and 1340s by the Wendovers, a family described in the 14th century as 'of good condition'.

The first of the Wendovers known to have invested in property in the town was John of Wendover, who may have been a kinsman of Richard of Wendover, a canon of St Paul's who died in 1252. In 1261 John bought from Roger Curteys's widow, Avice, the valuable corner site (its free manor rent was 6s) on the south side of Tunemanemedue Way (site of 1 High Street), facing the market. The house on the site became known as Wendovershall. Then Henry of Wendover in 1284 bought the property of Gilbert the Taverner from his widow, Quenilda. This comprised most of both sides of the lane leading out of the high street towards Springfield, including both corner sites, and much of the frontage property on the east side of the high street between the lane and Moulsham bridge, including the site where Gilbert had carried on his business. That site (now 40-1 High Street) was to develop into one of the largest medieval inns in the town, known by 1469 as the 'Boreshed' and from *c*.1633 as the King's Head.

The Wendovers also acquired property in Springfield, where Peter Wendover, and his son, Peter the younger, were both taxed in 1327. One of the four most important men in Chelmsford in the 1330s was another Wendover, William. The whole Wendover estate came eventually into the hands of Peter Wendover (no doubt the younger), who also inherited in 1341, on the death of his cousin William de Pervill (Peverel), a quarter share of the manor of Springfield. When Peter died, before 1361, each of his three daughters inherited a third share in 8 houses, 6 shops, 245a. of land, meadow, and pasture, and 16*s* worth of rents in Chelmsford, Springfield, Writtle, and Broomfield; Peter's widow, Elizabeth, enjoyed for life his quarter share of the manor of Springfield. The three daughters were all married: Joan to William Nafferton, and after his death to a London vintner, Simon Bodenham; Margaret married Richard Duk (Deuk, Duke); and Elizabeth married John Southam. When the widowed Elizabeth Wendover died in 1361 her daughter Margaret Duk inherited the Springfield manor share; this was the origin of the 'Dukes' estate in the manor of Springfield. The Dukes, an acquisitive family, independently came by other property in the town, most notably in the street leading from the town to the Upland (sometimes called Brocholestrate or Braintree Way, but known to this day as Duke Street), but also in New Street and the Fishmarket. Then in 1371 Margaret's husband, Richard Duk, bought from the Southams his sister-in-law Elizabeth's share in the Wendover inheritance. This was the first in a series of family dispositions involving Joan and her two husbands (William Nafferton and Simon Bodenham), Thomas and Guy, the sons of Margaret and Richard Duk, and Thomas, the son of John and Elizabeth Southam, whereby the three sisters' inheritance in the town passed by the 1420s from Peter Wendover's descendants to the Tyrells of East Horndon, later also lords of Springfield. The final transaction was completed in 1425 when Thomas Southam released to Sir John Tyrell (d.1437) any remaining claim he might have in ten messuages, six shops, nine butchers' shambles, rents worth 40*s*, and a large quantity of land, in Springfield, Chelmsford, Writtle, Little Waltham, and Broomfield.

From this concentration of certain Chelmsford town properties in the hands of the lords of the manor of Springfield arose a complicated manorial tenure whereby the lord of Springfield owed a large free rent, fealty, and suit of court, for the whole complex, to the lord of Bishop's Hall in Chelmsford, while the separate tenancies into which it became divided were held of the manor of Springfield with Dukes, the tenants owing rent, fealty, and suit of court to Springfield's lord.

If real estate was one early source of local wealth, the buying and selling of wool was another. The scale of the business of John of Chelmsford, wool merchant, is suggested by mention of the large sums of money owed to him, £80 in 1327 from a Kentish man, and £160 in 1331 from a London skinner. John was one of the many creditors of the young King Edward III, who borrowed £7 3*s* 7*d* from him in 1327, which the collectors of customs at the port of Ipswich were ordered to allow John on the next cargo of wool, hides, and woolfells which he exported 'to parts beyond the seas'.

CHAPTER FOUR

War, Pestilence, Piety, and Public Works

THE HUNDRED YEARS' WAR

King Edward needed something more substantial than a loan of petty cash when he became committed in 1337 to war with King Philip VI of France. This war, to defend the Gascon lands which the kings of England had ruled since Henry II married Eleanor of Aquitaine in 1152, and to pursue Edward's own claim to the French throne through his mother, Isabella of France, was to become known as the Hundred Years' War. Edward began to raise money for it in 1337 by borrowing vast sums from English and Florentine bankers, by deals with English wool merchants, and after the formal start of the war in May 1337 by direct taxation. A plan was made to raise money from the counties. In Essex in late August the 'men of the county', including merchants and 'other rich people', were summoned to meet at Chelmsford early in September to hear from royal officials the king's 'intentions in regard to the safety of the realm'. At that meeting the men of Essex offered an unknown sum as a contribution and John of Thorpe, 'the king's clerk', was commissioned on 16 September to receive the money from them at Chelmsford on the 21st. This well-documented treasury official, who was appointed to the office of writer of tallies of the receipt at the Exchequer in 1339, may have been another kinsman of John of Thorpe of Chelmsford. The scheme for the county contributions was, however, abandoned. Instead, a 'Great Council' was held at Westminster on 26 September with an unusually wide composition. The prelates, lay magnates, elected knights of the shires, and burgesses, who were usually summoned to attend the king's 'parliaments' — 'to deal with the great business of his realm and foreign lands' — were reinforced. To this September assembly were also called 120 notable people, and representatives from 90 towns, separately ordered on 2 September to send to Westminster three or four townsmen each. One of the towns was Chelmsford, which sent William the Butcher (le Maskal), John the Horse-leech (le Mareschal), William of Wendover, and John of Thorpe. John the Horse-leech was from Moulsham, the other three from the town.

The Great Council, joined by the unaccustomed townsmen, voted the king a tax on movables for three years. Only the poor with goods worth less than 5s were exempt. The well-to-do in market towns like Chelmsford enjoyed the usual personal allowance of a suit of clothes, a bed, a few personal ornaments, and a drinking vessel.

Many such taxes had been imposed before, and many more would be voted in the future. But in 1337 King Edward, in debt already to his bankers for between £90,000 and £100,000 borrowed since August 1336, and committed to pay his allies on the continent £124,000 before the end of 1337, was in desperate need. The representatives from Chelmsford and the other 89 towns were summoned to broaden the basis of assent to the costly undertaking of invading France. The assembly, alternatively styled a 'Council' and a 'Parliament', was unique. It was the only occasion when Chelmsford sent representatives to a 'Parliament'.

The war was a foreign war fought in Flanders and France, but no place could escape its burdens. There were the endless demands for money to pay for it, with the attendant problems of assessment and collection. When a tax of a 'ninth' was granted by Parliament to the king for 1340 and 1341, to pay for both Scottish and French wars, 'to travail to keep his realm and maintain his wars and to purchase his rights', six local assessors were appointed for the parish. Two of them represented Moulsham, John the Horse-leech who had gone to Westminster in 1337, and Walter the Dyer; the town's assessors were John the Cook, Elias the Chandler, John of Stanway, and William de Poley. They empanelled a jury of twelve parishioners, who swore that the true value of Chelmsford's ninth was £9; Writtle (£20), Great Waltham (£13 0s 4d) and Mountnessing (£12) were all assessed higher in the Chelmsford hundred.

The war made military demands too. For the invasion of France and the Creçy campaign in 1346 two hundred archers were demanded from Essex county, and five Essex towns had to recruit and equip thirty-eight armed foot-soldiers, twenty from Colchester, six from Saffron Walden, and four each from Chelmsford, Braintree, and Waltham Holy Cross. Chelmsford won a reduction of its quota, and permission to commute it for a money payment; the bailiff of Chelmsford was ordered to cease demand on the townsmen to find men for the campaign, because they had 'paid 10 marks (£6 13s 4d) for the expense of 2 armed men to go with the king at his next crossing of the seas'. But the order stipulated that the concession should not create a precedent. One of those who went to France with the army in 1346 was John the Porter of Chelmsford, who did good service in the earl of Lancaster's company. During the long winter siege of Calais in 1346, when men entrenched in bleak conditions outside the town began to melt away from the army, to stop the rot royal pardons were freely issued for offences of all kinds, even murder, to those who remained. One pardon was in favour of John the Porter, on condition 'that he do not withdraw from the king's service so long as he shall stay this time on this side of the seas'. A prudent man, perhaps with something on his conscience, John later in 1350 secured an attested copy under the current great seal of his pardon granted at Calais.

Edward's early invasion fleets sailed from the Orwell in Suffolk to Flanders. Much war traffic, knights, archers, and men-at-arms, mounted and on foot, with baggage-horses, supply waggons, and cumbersome military engines, must have passed through Chelmsford on the way to Ipswich to join the mustering armies and ships. Edward sailed from the Orwell with the fleet on the *Christopher* in July 1338. When he returned from the campaign eighteen months later in February 1340 he crossed from Sluys to the Orwell. In June 1340 Edward's fleet of 200 ships again assembled in the Orwell. The archbishop of Canterbury, John Stratford, had to make his way there to resign his office of chancellor, and hand over the great seal to the king on board his ship, *La Cogge Thomas*, two days before he sailed. After witnessing the breaking of the seal the archbishop returned to an inn in Chelmsford, to wait there until the king sent him the new seal, rolled in a piece of linen cloth, for delivery to his successor.

Chelmsford was the natural halting place in journeys between London, the coast of Essex, and East Anglia, whether for great personages like the archbishop of Canterbury engaged on the king's business, or for travellers like the two men 'de outre mer' — coming from beyond the sea — one on foot, the other on horseback, who stopped there in 1274 to bargain for a second horse to continue their journey. The earliest map of England to name the town was appropriately a road map — the so-called 'Gough' map of *c*.1360, which is preserved in the Bodleian Library in Oxford. The map shows the route from London to Ipswich, setting down in their proper order: 'Brendwod', 'Chelmesford', Witham, Colchester, and 'Yepeswych'. By the size and combinations of the symbols employed to indicate towns, the maps seems to suggest their comparative status. The scale of the vignette of 'Chelmesford', a combination of buildings and church spire, indicated to the traveller the most notable town to be met between the capital and the ancient walled town of Colchester.

The additional traffic generated by the early years of the war was too much for the 'bridge of Chelmaresford'. In 1351 the bridge, by then some 250 years old, was reported to the justices to be partly broken down and in ruins. While everyone agreed that, time out of mind, liability for its repair had lain jointly with the abbot of Westminster and the bishop of London, each responsible from their own bank to midstream, both parties protested that their half was in good condition. The court decided that the bridge was broken on the Moulsham side. The abbot carried out minor repairs in 1350-1, but they cost no more than 8*d* for the work of two carpenters. This patching up was clearly inadequate, for in 1360-1 the bridge cost the abbot £6 9*s* 6*d*, including a fine of 3*s* 4*d*, presumably for not having repaired it properly before. The work done in 1360-1 suggests that the bridge was basically a timber structure and that it was the carriage way which was collapsing. The contractor employed to restore it was a carpenter, hired for £3 6*s* 8*d*. Two sawyers, each paid 5*d* a day, were hired for 18 days to saw timber and planks. Eight men on a daily wage of 3*d* each were hired for 8 days to lift old timbers from the bridge and lay new ones. Carters were hired at a shilling a day: five of them fetched timber from Feering; one spent five days carrying timber cut in Moulsham to the bridge; another spent three days carrying hurdles to the bridge, and another two days carrying gravel. Two ropes were bought for 2*s* to haul timber to the bridge; food and drink bought for the workmen at various times cost 2*s* 6*d*. The miller of the earl of Hereford's mill at Writtle was paid 4*s* to turn and hold back the water at the mill to lower the water level until the bridge was finished. As the mill stood at the junction of the Can, the Wid, and the Roxwell Brook, the flow could easily be controlled there.

THE BLACK DEATH

The cost to the abbot of hired labour for repairing the bridge in 1360-1, to pay sawyers, carters, and labourers, for tasks which might well have been demanded as villein 'works', may well reflect the aftermath in Moulsham of the Black Death. The pestilence had reached the west of England from the continent in 1348, spreading eastward to appear in Essex in the spring of 1349. In that year the abbot's bailiff in Moulsham recorded that there were no rents from thirty-one tenements because the tenants were dead, and that such necessary 'works' as hoeing had had to be abandoned for lack of labour (*propter caritatem hominum*). There is no comparable record for the town-dwellers in Chelmsford, but Lynches, an upland villein holding, 'in decay for want of a tenant with buildings falling in' in 1383, had been vacant and in the lord's hands 'since the first pestilence'. The reference to the 'first pestilence' suggests that the locality did not escape the later outbreaks of 1361-2 and 1369.

The high mortality in England in 1349 disrupted patterns of work. Employers were ready to pay inflated wages to pre-empt the limited labour left. Villeins fled their lords' demesnes to seek the paid employment so easily to be had elsewhere. To counter this Edward III's parliament passed a Statute of Labourers in 1351, '… against the malice of servants which were idle and not willing to serve after the pestilence without taking excessive wages …'. The act aimed to freeze wages at the rates which had prevailed before the Black Death, with heavy fines on those who offered more. In 1351 no less than 77 employers in Chelmsford and Moulsham were fined for contravening the act. The list does not distinguish between the town and hamlet, but most of those who can be identified came from the town. One of them was John of Thorpe who had attended the Great Council in 1337. The identifiable trades penalised included chapman, chandler, fishmonger, miller, cook, innkeeper, mason, smith, ropemaker, shoemaker, spicer, butcher, baker, skinner, tailor, and carpenter. Most of the fines ranged between 2s and 1 mark (13s 4d). Two men more heavily fined, at 19s and 20s, were wool merchants, Thomas Thrower and Adam atte Ponde; these two men were charged in the same year with conspiring annually with fifteen other wool merchants, from such places as Maldon, Kelvedon, Benfleet, and Fobbing, to fix the maximum price they proposed to pay for a sack of wool, and also for using false weights in order to cheat sellers of wool of one pound in ten. One Chelmsford employer, William of Birchanger, whose business has not been identified, was fined 100s, a sum unequalled in Essex.

In the immediate locality, when it came to paying excessive wages, Chelmsford (with Moulsham) was in a class by itself. Fines there totalled £25 7s 4d, compared with Writtle (£8 2s 4d), Great Baddow (£5 11s), Springfield (30s), and Broomfield (21s 8d). This surely reflects the growing concentration of urban trades and means of employment in the town.

While seeking to steady the effects of the high mortality on the labour market, the government could not ignore the real distress it had caused. 'Labour money' totalling £675 11s, from the fines imposed in Essex in 1351, was distributed at the discretion of the justices of the peace to certain vills, '… because of poverty and destitution arising after the pestilence', to ease the burden of war taxation due from them. Chelmsford and Moulsham were allowed £9 13s, Writtle (still far more populous than Chelmsford) £13 8s, and Springfield, Great Baddow, Broomfield, and Sandon much smaller sums.

The enforcement of the labour laws brought into greater prominence a rising local arm of government, the keeper (justice) of the peace. The keepers, usually appointed from the local landed gentry, had no power at first to determine cases and impose punishment, only to enquire into felonies and trespasses and arrest suspects for trial in due course before the royal justices. They were concerned in particular with enforcement of the Statute of Winchester passed in 1285. 'Forasmuch as from Day to Day', declared the Statute, 'Robberies, Murthers, Burnings, and Theft, be more often used than they have been heretofore …', malefactors must be relentlessly pursued from town to town by hue and cry, 'concealers' and 'receivers' must be punished, watch must be kept in every town from sunset to sunrise, and strangers passing in the night arrested for examination in the morning. The highways between market towns were to be widened, and the undergrowth cut back two hundred feet on either side of the way, 'so that there be neither Dyke, Tree, nor Bush whereby a man may lurk to do hurt', excluding only 'great trees', provided their lower branches offered no concealment. In 1350 the 'keepers of the peace' had won the power to determine and punish, and become 'justices'. In 1361 weights and measures were added to their jurisdiction, and in 1364 the marketing offences of forestalling and regrating. At least one of the 1351 sessions of the Essex justices of the peace was held in Chelmsford; their sessions were to become a regular quarterly feature of the town's calendar, a new source of enlivenment, bustle, and profit for the townspeople, and one which was to continue for over six hundred years.

One of the early Essex justices of the peace was Sir John Mounteney, who was on the commission in 1376 and 1377; he was a member of the family which gave its name to Mountnessing and to the 'manor' or farm of Mountneys in Writtle. Sir John's name is associated with the earliest recorded chantry foundation in Chelmsford.

CHANTRIES, CHURCH, FRIARS, AND LEPER HOSPITAL

Chantries were founded by well-to-do people, usually to provide for a priest to sing mass for ever for the souls of the founder, his ancestors, family or friends. A less costly memorial was an 'obit', a mass to be said on the anniversary of the founder's death, or the endowment of a light, to burn before the Holy Rood, or the image of Our Lady, or one of the Saints, in the church. The 'Mounteney' chantry was a chapel built in the churchyard and dedicated to the Virgin Mary. The chapel is first mentioned in Sir John Mounteney's lifetime; two of its chaplains were named in 1365 and 1369 in the bishop of London's register, and the chapel is well documented thereafter. Sir John (d.*post* 1379) was buried beside it, for in 1406 John de Sheryngton, chaplain, asked in his will to be buried 'in the chapel of Blessed Mary in the churchyard of Chelmsford church, situated by the tomb of John Mounteney, knight, once my master'. In 1497 a dyer, Richard Corall, left 13s 4d in his will to the 'chapel of Blessed Mary in the churchyard', for its repair and the upkeep of a light. Sir John and his wife Cicely owned property in both Writtle and Chelmsford, and the endowment to support the chapel priest comprised the rents from the small manor of Benedict Otes in Writtle, and from a little house in Duke Street (site of 83 Duke Street) in Chelmsford. Sir John also owned a larger house, with a garden and yard, in the town, on the east side of the high street; this property, inherited by Isabel, probably his granddaughter, and mother of Thomas Colman, became known as 'Colmans' (site of 27 High Street).

The mid-14th-century rectors of Chelmsford feature little in records of the local scene. They may have been preoccupied with more prestigious preferments. John of Newport Pagnell, rector 1361-74, had property in London and held the office of Keeper of the 'Old Work' at St Paul's Cathedral. As Keeper he was responsible for the fabric of the older part of St Paul's, completed in 1240. He built a new house over the north gate of the cathedral, which the bishop allowed him to hold rent-free for life. Clearly his office as Keeper required his presence in London. It is during the years when John of Newport was rector that a Chelmsford 'parish chaplain' is first mentioned, in 1365. He was always carefully

31

distinguished from the chaplains of the free chapel of St Margaret by the manor, and of Mounteney's chapel in the churchyard, either as the 'parish chaplain', or 'the chaplain of the parish church of Chelmsford'. No 'vicarage' was ever formally ordained in Chelmsford, but a small cottage on the west side of the churchyard was described in 1417 as the 'house of the rector ... called the presteshows', when the bishop granted to John Wolrych, chaplain, and to the rector, Peter Henewyk, and local trustees, a small rectangular plot of ground by the churchyard, abutting on Duke Street, to enclose the cottage. This cottage, known in 1591 as the 'Vicarage or priest's House', with its garden wall known as the 'Vicarage Wall', was no doubt the parish chaplain's house. A particular duty which fell on him from time to time was the induction of new chaplains of the free chapel of St Margaret or the Mounteney chantry chapel in the churchyard; in 1375 the mandate to induct a new rector, Thomas Baketon, was directed to 'Master Hugh, parish chaplain there'.

The reaction of some parishioners to the rectors' failure to serve the cure personally may have prompted the foundation 'by divers and sundry persons' (unnamed), some time before 1392, of two fraternities or guilds, each to provide a priest for ever to sing mass in the church, at the altars respectively of Corpus Christi and Blessed Mary, and 'to help serve the cure there'.

Throughout the middle years of the 14th century the preaching friars continued to receive local support. In 1341 they were granted royal licence to keep two plots of land next to their property, given to them earlier without permission, 'to enlarge their dwelling place;' the donors were William the Vintner and his wife Joan, and Emma and Christine, the daughters and heirs of Arthur atte Grene of Moulsham. In the same year, after William the Vintner's death, his widow Joan and son John, the chandler John Baldewyne the younger, and John the Smith, each gave to the prior and brothers one acre of land, all three acres lying in Moulsham. Also in 1341 the friars were licensed to make an aqueduct from a spring 'in the field of Chelmsford', to carry water to their dwelling place. The field, named in 1385 as 'Burgeysfelde', lay on the opposite side of the river, in the bishop's manor. A local inquiry was held on the oath of twelve 'honest men', including John the Horse-leech who had attended the Westminster Council, and Elias the Chandler. It was agreed that the scheme would harm no one, because the water pipes were to run underground from the spring, some 385 yards through the bishop of London's manor lands down to the Great River, across the river to Moulsham, and for 165 yards under the manor lands of John de L'Isle, the abbot of Westminster's tenant, to the priory. The spring was known by 1428 as 'Burgeyswell'. The tile and stone walls of the culvert leading the water into the priory, through a small arch faced in Caen stone and floored with Purbeck marble slabs, were uncovered in 1973 during excavation of the priory site. Stone foundations of some of the priory buildings had been uncovered before, in 1937, when the Chelmsford Rural District Council Office was being built on the west side of New London Road. Excavations carried out in 1968-70, during preparations for the construction of the nearby dual-carriage ring road (Parkway), had established the site of the nave, choir, and cloister of the priory church. The 1973 excavation, during re-development of sites opposite the R.D.C. offices, on the east side of New London Road, added not only the course of the medieval water supply, but also the location of the friars' dorter or dormitory, and the reredorter or latrines served by the water conduit. The side road which linked New London Road with Moulsham Street, and was swallowed up with the remnants of the priory by Parkway, had long been known as The Friars.

The friars' reputation was high, and the house had no lack of novices. In the decade 1362-71 Bishop Simon Sudbury ordained thirty-three candidates from the priory. The brothers enjoyed the patronage of the great. When Edward III visited Chelmsford in 1342 the friars met him in procession and received from his own hand an alms of 3s 4d. His heir, Edward the Black Prince, in 1361 sent £5 to a London glazier to make a window for their church. The dedication of their church is uncertain. It has usually been assumed that like most Dominican houses it was dedicated to St Dominic, but John Brewer in his will dated 1423 asked to be buried 'in the church of Blessed Mary of the order of friars preachers'. The friars received bequests from Elizabeth de Bohun, countess of Northampton (£20 in 1356), and from her kinsman, Humphrey de Bohun, earl of Hereford and Essex (£10 in 1361) in return for their prayers. They had their smaller benefactors too: Gilbert Koo, a Londoner, left them 20s in 1369, and William, rector of Springfield, half a mark in 1371.

William also left half a mark in 1371 to 'the lazars of Chelmsford'. This hospital for lepers was founded some time before 1293; in that year John of Sandwich, rector of Dengie, left two shillings to it in his will. The hospital was not in the town, but in the hamlet: the 'prior of the lepers of Moulsham' and 'the spetellgardyn' are mentioned in 1413. The 'hospitalle', standing by the roadside on the outskirts of the village, is shown on John Walker's Moulsham map of 1591, on the site of the present almshouses. Its dedication, sometimes quoted as to St Thomas or St Nicholas, is usually given as to St John. The appointment of many of its 15th-century keepers, and their admission to the two-acre garden and croft adjoining the hospital, are entered in the Moulsham court rolls. There is some evidence that they were appointed for life.

The Black Friars were not the only socio-religious group in the parish in the mid-14th century. About 1368 a mutually benevolent fraternity of the Holy Trinity, open to men and women, was founded in the church by the gifts of 'certain faithful Christian people of the town and neighbourhood'. New members took an oath of loyalty to the fraternity. The brothers and sisters met in the church to hear mass on Trinity Sunday, when they made voluntary offerings. The fraternity's sole possession was a money-box, into which each member once a year put 20d, to pay for wax candles to burn before the image of the Holy Trinity on feast days, and for a chaplain to celebrate mass and pray for their well-being and for the souls of all the faithful departed. They wore special hoods when they met, and after mass enjoyed a pleasant meal together at a 'certain place' in the town, after which they chose two masters from the members to govern the fraternity for a year. Each brother or sister who lived within ten leagues (about thirty miles) of a member who died, attended the funeral, and every member gave 1½d to the poor to pray for the soul of the deceased. An enquiry made in 1388-9 into the origin of the fraternity noted that the money-box then contained 100s 8d.

BUILDING THE GREAT BRIDGE

By the 1370s the bridge between Chelmsford and Moulsham needed more than patching up, and when Simon Sudbury was bishop of London (1362-75) it had to be rebuilt. It was, however, the abbot of Westminster who called in the master mason of the king's works, Henry Yevele, to examine its condition, at a cost of 12*d* for his labour, his counsel, and his breakfast. As a result of the survey the abbot contracted Yevele to rebuild the bridge for £73 6*s* 8*d*; drawing up the contract cost two shillings, and a robe given to Yevele as agreed in the contract cost 17*s* 3*d*. The contract was apparently completed in 1372. The rebuilt bridge consisted of three gothic arches, the central arch much higher than the two side ones. It was built of stone; repairs done on the abbot's behalf in 1391 mention cartloads of stone, bushels of lime, and the wages of a mason and his servants. From the time of its building it was usually distinguished as the 'Stone Bridge' or the 'Great Bridge'. It was to stand for four hundred years.

How far Bishop Sudbury was involved in Yevele's contract is not revealed, but the Chelmsford manor court records attribute the rebuilding to the bishop, adding that he had the bridge 'made greater in width than it had been of ancient time'. Whatever the arrangement between bishop and abbot, the undertaking precipitated a long dispute with one of the bishop's freeholders. The workmen who laid the stones for the widened bridge appear to have damaged or even demolished a small building on the bishop's side of the river, standing next to the bridge on the west side of the high street (site of 51 High Street). The owners of the building, whose permission to lay the stones had not been sought, were Thomas Osteler, who kept the adjoining inn (site of 52-4 High Street), and his wife Nichola (familiarly known as Colletta), neither of whom was likely to accept such an outrage meekly. They were among the most obstinate offenders to be presented at the manor court, usually for overcharging for their victuals, breaking the regulations for the sale of ale and wine, or throwing filth into the river, and were particularly tenacious of their rights of property. Some time later, therefore, they pulled down the ruinous remains and built a new house on the site, aligned to the original frontage on the street. In 1403 Colletta, by then widowed, was charged in the manor court with making

> '... an encroachment on the highway on the lord's soil at the end of the great bridge of Chelmsford one foot wide, there placing and building a new house so that the highway was narrowed'.

The case, initiated when Bishop Braybrooke (1382-1404) was lord, dragged on through the successive episcopates of Roger Walden (1404-6) and Nicholas Bubwith (1406-7), and into that of Richard Clifford (1407-21). Finally, in 1416 an inquisition of twelve townsmen was empanelled to advise the steward of the truth of the matter on oath. The jury found unanimously in favour of Robert, son of Thomas and Colletta, and his right to that one foot wide strip of soil. Satisfactory widening of the high street approach to the bridge had therefore to wait for another four hundred years, until 1787.

It seems that the bishop's steward was displeased with the jury's verdict. The record of it, engrossed on the manor court roll, was struck through, and a note in the margin reads:

'Cancelled by Thomas Rolf steward, with his own hand'.

But there is no evidence that the steward was able to set the verdict aside; the building stayed.

CHAPTER FIVE

The Great Revolt, 1381

THE TIME OF THE RUMOUR

King Edward III died in June 1377. He was succeeded by his ten-year-old son Richard, as King Richard II. Six months before his death, to meet yet another crisis in the long war with France, his last Parliament in December 1376 had granted the old king a new kind of tax. This was a poll tax of a groat, fourpence per head, to be paid by every lay man and woman over the age of fourteen years, exempting only those who begged for their living. The proceeds of this tax offer a clue to the growth of the town since its creation. The bishop's manor, both town and upland, yielded £4, representing 240 adult inhabitants. The figure may reflect a population diminished by the Black Death, but nonetheless it emphasises how small a community the county town still was. The bishop's manor had, however, by then overtaken the abbot's manor in terms of numbers; Moulsham hamlet had only 180 taxpayers. Writtle was still more populous than Chelmsford, with 600 taxpayers, but they were spread over a much greater area, and with Writtle's original superiority in numbers — 194 households in 1086 compared with Chelmsford's five and Moulsham's twelve, Writtle had had a long start. It is important, too, to recall how small a portion of the bishop's manor, no more than the short hill leading down to the river crossings, had been made available to settlers. The broad upland, with its valuable timber and cultivated fields, remained in the bishop's hands, its only dwellers manorial servants and the villein families who provided most of the labour in the bishop's fields.

Even in the small area available to freeholders, some plots were not taken up for more than 150 years. There was at least one vacant plot (*una vacua placea*) on the high street frontage still in the lord's hands in 1396. The plots disposed of since the early 13th century were not densely built over by 1377. Hall houses and shops, cottages, and smithies, were spaced out on the frontage, divided one from the other by yards and gardens, with wide cartways or narrow lanes leading out of the high street through to the 'backsides' with their workshops and stables, pig styes and henhouses, privies and dungpits, and open ditches draining down to the rivers and watermeadows.

The small scale of the community revealed by the tax receipt of 1377 is a salutary reminder of F.W. Maitland's warning how easy it is to 'hurry the history both of our villages and our towns because we fill them too full'; and, as he adds, 'there are some thoughts which will not come to men who are not tightly packed'. Chelmsford in 1377 was not yet tightly packed.

In 1379 a second poll tax was levied, on lay men and women over sixteen years, but graduated to charge the rich more than the poor. Thus, while a duke paid 10 marks (£6 13s 4d), a justice of the bench £5, or a great merchant £1, lesser merchants and artificers only paid from 6d to 13s 4d, and those too inferior to be classified but not quite reduced to beggary, 4d.

The yield from this tax was poor. The French war, going badly, grew ever more costly, and in November 1380 Parliament granted the third poll tax in three

35

years. It was the most burdensome yet. Three groats (one shilling) were charged on all lay people over the age of fifteen except beggars, with no graduation, only a pious hope that 'the strong might aid the weak' to raise the amount assessed on the adult population of each town or village. But no one was to pay less than one groat (4*d*). On 7 December assessors were commissioned 'to go with speed from place to place', summoning before them two men and the constable 'from among the best and most discreet men' in each place, to supply the 'number, names, estate, and rank' of everyone dwelling there, house by house, and collect the sum due. One of the five Essex assessors was the Chelmsford wool merchant, Adam atte Ponde. A month later, when Adam had failed to join his fellow assessors, they were ordered on 9 January 1381 to carry out their commission without him, the king having discharged him, 'as he is too aged'.

This tax of 1380-1 antagonised rich and poor alike, and provoked almost universal evasion. If the lists returned early in 1381 were to be believed, every county had suffered an extraordinary decrease in adult population since 1377, far greater than could be attributed to the raising of the qualifying age from fourteen years to fifteen. The adult population of Essex seemed to have shrunk in three years from 47,962 to 30,748, that of Colchester from 2,955 to 1,609. The discrepancy in Chelmsford was glaring: the number of taxpayers recorded in the town and upland had fallen since 1377 from 240 to 122, and in Moulsham hamlet from 180 to 64. Fraud was obvious.

Analysis of the Chelmsford and Moulsham returns, which purported to name all taxable inhabitants, house by house, shows the nature of the fraud. The list for the town and upland is mutilated in places; ten of its 122 names are missing. The remaining 112 names comprise forty-four married couples, seventeen unattached men, bachelors, or widowers, four unattached women, and three 'servants': Cecilia, maid to the maltster, John Babbe; John Grene, the servant of Thomas and Nichola Osteler; and an unnamed servant of the innkeeper William Prentys. Three of the four unattached women, if not all four, were widows, carrying on their late husbands' businesses: Margaret Lightfoot and Matilda Baker were fishmongers, Mabel Wymond was an innkeeper. The list is almost entirely a roll of householders and their wives. It conceals the existence of any dependent members of each household, except in the three households which name a single servant. Not one householder admitted to supporting a widowed parent, an aged relative, a sister or brother, son or daughter, nephew or niece, of taxable age; or to housing as master any apprentice, craftsman, journeyman, or hired man or woman employed in his trade. There was a conspicuous absence of marriageable young women. Concealment was just as blatant in the hamlet, where twenty-six couples were named, nine unattached men, two unattached women, and one son, John, living with his parents, John and Matilda Baud.

Such consistent concealment of dependants and employees could only have been achieved if the whole community was united in conniving at it, including the two 'best and most discreet' men and constable responsible for collecting the money. The names of the 1381 local collectors have not survived, but no doubt they were men of the same standing as the four men who collected the town's groats in 1377. Those four were John Totham, a victualler, who was the lord's bailiff in 1388; John Goldsmith, who owned property in both town and hamlet, including market stalls; and two of the town's four leading innkeepers, John

Gybon, and William Prentys, who was one of the county collectors appointed in 1383 to raise another subsidy throughout Essex. If anyone knew the truth about the tax due from the town in 1381 those four men did, and indeed one or other of them may well have served again as local collector in 1381; but their own households were as fraudulently returned as those of their neighbours.

By 16 March 1381 the government had '... trustworthy and notable evidence that the taxers and collectors ... have spared many persons ... omitting some of them at random, and others through negligence and favour, so that a great part of the subsidy is concealed and detained from the king ...'. So commissions were set up in each county to check the returns. They were '... to go from town to town and from place to place ...', and to '... search out and examine the number of lay persons ...' who ought to pay. The six Essex commissioners were headed by Sir John Gildesborough of Wennington, an Essex justice of the peace. Hostility to the tax itself was now to be intensified by the prying questions of the commission and the demand for more money.

The first serious violence broke out in Essex on Thursday, 30 May, at Brentwood. Men of the Barstable hundred, which included the Thames-side village of Fobbing, had been summoned to appear there before Sir John Gildesborough, who was accompanied by John Bampton and other Essex justices of the peace. The Fobbing men, led by their tax collector, protested that the commissioner 'did come for a new tax', and refused to pay a penny more. Threatened with arrest, but reinforced by their neighbours and supporters from as far as Bocking, they attacked the commissioner and his company with bows and arrows, and drove them from the town. Prominent among their supporters was a Chelmsford barber, John Stalworth. After this heady triumph the protesters hestitated to commit themselves further, fearful of the consequences. But the Fobbing collector, Thomas Baker, 'so called from his trade ... putting on a bolder front began to urge others of his village to join him, and more and more did so, and one and all sent to their friends and kinsmen and so on from village to village and neighbourhood to neighbourhood ... seeking without delay for advice and aid in these matters of such grave urgency to them all'.

The tax had set alight the smouldering popular discontent kindled by the cost of the long, inconclusive French war, by the restrictions and obligations of villein birth and tenure, by labour laws which interfered with wage covenants, and by the market monopolies enjoyed by such favoured places as Chelmsford. Revolt swept through the county and beyond. It was called 'the time of the Rumour', and news of it travelled fast. In the charge later laid against the Brentwood protesters it was denounced as a time when 'men rode about armed in a land of peace and did many evil deeds'.

On Whit Sunday, 2 June, Sir Robert Belknap, justice of common pleas, arrived at Brentwood to restore order. Sent without an armed escort, and confronted by a riotous mob, he prudently withdrew, after agreeing to swear on the Bible to hold no more such sessions. But the mob burned his documents, and cut off the heads of some unfortunate local jurors who had been summoned to name and present charges against the men of Fobbing and their supporters.

By then the infection had spread. On that same Whit Sunday, while rebels in south Essex outfaced Sir Robert Belknap at Brentwood, farther north malcontents from Bocking, Braintree, Coggeshall, Stisted, and Dunmow, were assembling at Bocking, where they were said to have sworn an oath to kill the king's subjects and to acknowledge no law in England but that ordained by themselves. Their first target was the unfortunate sheriff of Essex, the Crown's principal agent in the county in financial matters. Sheriff John Sewale lived near Bocking at Coggeshall. He also owned a house in Chelmsford, convenient for his attendance there on county business, such as justices' sessions or the assizes. On Thursday 6 June the Bocking band made an attack on the sheriff and on an exchequer clerk who was with him at his house in Coggeshall, so that, in the conventional phrase, 'their lives were despaired of'. A rebel leader who emerged in Chipping Ongar on Sunday 9 June joined forces with this Bocking band.

On Monday 10 June a concerted rebel attack was made on the estate of the king's treasurer, Sir Robert Hales, prior of the Order of St John of Jerusalem, at Cressing Temple near Coggeshall. Among the attackers were the dissidents from south Essex, including the Fobbing baker, whose assault on the Essex justices on 30 May had precipitated the rising. With them were the men from Ongar, the Bocking band, a band from Benfleet, Hadleigh, and Leigh, in south-east Essex, another band from the three Hanningfields led by the bailiff of East Hanningfield, John Geffrey, and supporters from places as far apart as Barking on Thames-side, Felsted north of Chelmsford, and Goldhanger and Maldon on the east Essex coast. The Chelmsford barber was there, and so was a fellow townsman, another baker called Thomas. The massed attackers were said to have been incited and led by a Londoner, Thomas Faringdon. After looting and setting fire to the treasurer's buildings at Cressing, the whole body of rebels moved on, the same day, to Coggeshall, where a band from Manningtree in north-east Essex joined them. Sheriff Sewale was not found in Coggeshall, but another officer of the Crown, the king's eschaetor in Essex, John Ewell, was captured and killed there. The rebels broke into the sheriff's house, seized (but did not destroy) all the king's writs and exchequer accounts found there, recognisable by the exchequer's seals of green wax, then burned down the house. The Fobbing baker and the barber and baker from Chelmsford were still with them in this attack, in which another Chelmsford man, Roger Fuller, and William Saresson from Moulsham, were also identified.

The seizure of the sheriff's exchequer documents was a calculated act. From Coggeshall the rebels, carrying the documents with them, set out for Chelmsford. There, the next day, Tuesday 11 June, they found the sheriff. He was again assaulted, and his clothes torn, probably resisting demands for the surrender of any remaining exchequer warrants in his custody in Chelmsford. The insurgents, who may well have outnumbered the town's inhabitants, then built a bonfire of the exchequer documents and set it alight. The public burning in the county town of Essex of the king's exchequer writs could not have been bettered as a taxpayers' demonstration of protest. About forty writs were saved from destruction, to be displayed stuck up on long poles 'en commune chemin' — along the highway — probably along the London road as the rebels moved on from Chelmsford towards the capital.

While the main body of the rebels successfully sabotaged the machinery of tax gathering in Essex by destroying the sheriff's exchequer writs, other rebels picked on the records of manor courts for burning. They did this, the chronicler Thomas of Walsingham explained, 'so that all memorial of ancient matters being destroyed, their lords thereafter could claim no rights in them'. Chelmsford's villein population was small: the 1381 poll tax only listed six families living in the Upland as 'natives', the Helders, Frydays, Tylers, Mundes, Paulyns, and Gibbes. In fact, no members of those families have been found named as having taken any part in the uprising. But the manor court rolls of Chelmsford were certainly destroyed. In 1393 John Heyward and his wife could not prove how they had acquired a tenement and land in Chelmsford called Paulyns from Ralph Paulyn about thirty years before, 'because in the time of the rumour the rolls of the court of former years were burned'. As late as 1408 Joan, widow of Roger atte Noke, had to pay a fine to have her own copy of the original court entry re-enrolled on the Bishop's Hall manor record, 'because the rolls of the court of that copy were burned at the time of the rumour'. The surviving series of Chelmsford court rolls dates only from the late autumn of 1381.

The Moulsham court rolls were also destroyed. The abbot of Westminster's subsequent complaint of the attack on his Moulsham buildings and burning of his writings, charters, and muniments, named the alleged perpetrators. Five of them were Moulsham men: William Chypenham, a well-to-do brewer, Geoffrey Andrew, tailor, John Baldwin, cobbler, Stephen Pays, whose family were fishmongers, and John Fletcher. With them were three outsiders from villages a few miles away, two from Boreham and one from Hatfield Peverel.

Other Chelmsford men were later accused of isolated acts of violence. Simon Skynner and Henry Taillour were involved in affrays at the Princess of Wales's manor of North Weald; Simon's father, William Skynner, a pelter, owned some of the most valuable property in Chelmsford high street. John Brid, who joined in the destruction of lawyer Richard Stacey's charters at Broomfield, was a chandler and minor alehouse-keeper. The most surprising local man to be identified later as a ringleader in the revolt was the Moulsham 'franklin', Richard Baud, a free man of good family, and the wealthiest man in the hamlet with holdings worth 100s a year and movables worth 40s. Yet no evidence of the part played by him has been found in any contemporary source.

Meanwhile the revolt had taken hold in Kent, under the leadership of Wat Tyler and John Ball, and by the 11th, the day of the Chelmsford demonstration, the Kentish men were marching on London, intent on killing 'traitors' and speaking to their king. The Essex bands, too, were moving in that direction. By the eve of Corpus Christi, Wednesday the 12th, the Essex rebels were encamped at Mile End, 'on the other side of the water' from the Kentish men assembled at Blackheath. Among the seven Chelmsford men later identified as rebels in London were three of the town's senior tradesmen and householders: the baker Robert Baker, a member of the town's ruling élite, and two of the town's four most prominent innholders, William Prentys, collector of the 1377 poll tax, and the aggressive Thomas Osteler, owner of the inn by the Great Bridge. Three Moulsham men, William Saresson, William Chypenham, and Stephen Pays, were also identified there. Robert Baker's next-door neighbour, John Spicer, was another townsman who arrived in London. He had travelled far as a rebel, having originally joined a band from Ware and Thaxted in an attack on John of Gaunt's castle at Hertford, and ridden with them down the Lea to London.

On Thursday, 13 June, while negotiations went on for a parley with the king, the Chelmsford rebels joined in wanton attacks on property in London. John

Spicer's band played a prominent part in the sacking of John of Gaunt's palace of the Savoy, in which John Berham of Chelmsford was also said to have been involved. The under-sheriff of Middlesex, John Butterwick, named eight men from Chelmsford and Moulsham among those he accused later of attacking his houses at Westminster and Knightsbridge. They were William Prentys, Thomas Osteler, Robert Baker, William Skote, and John Lokyere from Chelmsford, and from Moulsham William Chypenham and Stephen Pays, who had helped to destroy the Moulsham manorial records, and William Saresson who had been with the mob who burned down the sheriff's house at Coggeshall.

On Friday, 14 June, the rebels met the fourteen-year-old King Richard at Mile End. He promised them the liberties they sought, the abolition of villeinage, freedom to buy and sell anywhere, and pardon for their rebellion. Froissart tells how on the same day the king employed more than thirty clerks 'to write with all diligence letters patents sealed with the king's seal' confirming his promises, for the insurgents to take away with them to their villages. Satisfied, most of the Essex rebels went home, but the Kentish men, led by Wat Tyler and other extremists, representing what Froissart called 'the great venom', remained behind. On Friday, the same day as the Mile End settlement, the extremists had already dragged the chancellor (Simon Sudbury, formerly bishop of London and lord of Chelmsford, but since 1375 archbishop of Canterbury), and the treasurer, Sir Robert Hales, from the Tower, beheaded them, and set their heads on London Bridge. On Friday, too, the chief justice, Sir John Cavendish, was murdered in Suffolk and his head carried to Bury on a pike. On Saturday, 15 June, the rebels who had stayed in London, with Tyler at their head, confronted the king at Smithfield with bolder demands. Tyler, growing insolent, was killed, struck down by one of the king's company at the king's feet. When the mob, leaderless and confused, began 'to murmur among themselves', the young king, in the well-known account, rode forward alone to face them, crying out: 'Ye shall have no captain but me: I am your king: be all in rest and peace.' Reassured, they began to disperse homewards, carrying their charters of enfranchisement with them. Reinforcements were belatedly mustering to the government's support. The immediate crisis was over.

After the Smithfield encounter the government, by then without chancellor, treasurer, or chief justice, at last began to act decisively. The mayor of London, William Walworth, and others were appointed at once 'to take order for the safety of the city and suburbs'; commissions of *oyer and terminer* were issued to them to try the perpertrators of the worst excesses. The next day, 16th, the great seal was handed over to Sir Hugh Segrave, as temporary keeper 'until the lord king could conveniently provide himself with another chancellor'. On the 18th letters were despatched throughout the kingdom enjoining resistance to all rebels, and denying rumours that they had acted with the king's approval. On 22nd the king and his council moved out of London into Essex, accompanied by a force estimated as 40,000 men; they established the government at Waltham Holy Cross, and there appointed Sir Robert Tresilian to replace the murdered chief justice, Sir John Cavendish.

On the next day, Sunday 23rd, the king received at Waltham messengers from Essex rebels who had regrouped at Billericay. Their demand for confirmation of their letters of manumission and pardon was refused, and they were told bluntly:

'Villeins ye are still and villeins ye shall remain'. They were allowed to depart unharmed; but on that day and the next the government despatched from Waltham about a hundred copies of a proclamation, addressed to officials and individuals in fifteen counties from Northumberland to Cornwall, and in nine important cities and towns, including York and Bristol, warning them against rumours that the rebels had the king's support, forbidding unlawful assemblies, and assigning powers to resist and punish insurgents. On the same day a commission of *oyer and terminer* was issued to Sir Robert Tresilian and William Morrers, to deal with treasons, felonies, and trespasses committed in Essex and Hertfordshire.

The king and his council remained at Waltham until the 25th, then moved deeper into Essex to Havering, where they stayed from the 26th to the 30th. There a general proclamation was drafted on behalf of lords of manorial estates, warning 'that all tenants free and neif shall without gainsaying, murmuring, or resistance, perform the works, customs, and services due to their lords as they used to do before the disturbance now arisen ...'. The first copies of this proclamation, dated at Havering on the 30th, were despatched to Lincolnshire, and to the constables of certain south-west Essex parishes, including East and West Ham, where the abbot of Stratford had manorial interests.

Meanwhile the Essex rebels' last serious stand, near Billericay, had been routed on the 28th, leaving only isolated pockets of resistance in the county. By the 30th it was safe for the king to advance from Havering into the heart of the county, to Chelmsford, the county town.

For nearly a week, from Monday 1 July to Saturday 6 July, Chelmsford became the seat of government. In those six days the government's policy on the issues which had stirred up so much trouble, and its determination to restore order, were made abundantly plain. The king probably lodged at his nearby manor house at Writtle. He was attended by his council, headed by the temporary chancellor, Sir Hugh Segrave, the steward of his household; by the new chief justice, Sir Robert Tresilian, and his fellow William Morrers, marshal of the household; and by the king's secretariat, the royal chancery. The senior chancery officials, the 'Spigurnel' or 'sealer', the 'Chaffwax', who tempered the wax, and the 'Portejoye', who kept the chancery rolls, were accompanied by the boy in charge of the sumpter horse (which carried the chancery hampers, packed with rolls, parchment, ink, and wax), and by the clerks of chancery, first and second rank. Their formidable task in Chelmsford was to draft, engross, date, seal, and despatch by messengers riding to the farthest corners of the realm, the daily batches of commissions, mandates, letters, orders, and proclamations issued by the government, not only to speed the process of pacification of the kingdom, but to conduct much ordinary day to day business of the Crown and Government.

On Monday, Tuesday, and Thursday some thirty-two more copies were dated of the proclamation of 30 June reaffirming the services due to their lords from tenants 'free and neif'; these were despatched in favour of individual lords in Essex, Suffolk, Norfolk, Sussex, Huntingdon, and Northampton, who had asked for them. On Wednesday, Friday, and Saturday some sixty-seven more copies were dated of the orders of 23 June, to suppress unlawful assemblies and punish insurgents, for despatch to various personages in eight midland and southern counties. On Tuesday the king, on the advice of the council, settled the awkward

41

matter of the promises he had made at Mile End on 14 June, and the charters given to the rebels. Letters dated that day, 2 July, sent to every county in England for general proclamation, revoked all the letters patent 'lately issued in haste to insurgents in divers counties'. The decision to revoke the charters, 'made under compulsion', was later, in November, explained to Parliament by Sir Hugh Segrave and readily endorsed by the members.

On Wednesday, 3 July, orders were dated for the constable of Dover castle and warden of the Cinque Ports to forbid any man but well-known merchants and their servants to pass to foreign parts from any of those ports except Dover without the king's command. But on Friday, after the government had learned (probably from Sir Robert Tresilian's investigations) that many rebels guilty of crimes committed in the rising were, '... purposing not to be justified by law but to pass over sea', stricter orders were dated for the keepers of Dover, Sandwich, and nineteen other ports,

> '... to suffer no man of whatsoever estate or condition ... for any cause or upon any pretence to pass to foreign parts ... without the king's command under great or privy seal'.

Wednesday, 3 July, was a particularly busy day. Commissions were dated to punish rebels in Cambridge, and to investigate disorders in Cornwall; proclamations were dated for despatch to every sheriff in England forbidding unlawful assemblies and risings and ordering that all those

> '... who peradventure move the king's lieges, secretly or openly, to make or support the same, shall be taken and dealt with as rebels and traitors; as certain lieges of Essex and Kent, who lately rose in rebellion, willing craftily to draw other lieges to them, are resorting to divers counties to stir up the lieges to make like assemblies'.

Other letters dated that day commanded the obedience of all ministers and subjects to the king's uncle, John of Gaunt, who had been in the north negotiating with the Scots, and was now hurrying south with an armed force to reinforce the king. As his departure left the North unprotected, another letter dated on Thursday ordered the archbishop of York to put all fencible men of the clergy of the diocese between the ages of sixteen and sixty under arms, ready to march with the archbishop to repel invaders or put down rebellion.

During the week, too, victims of the rebels came to Chelmsford to lay before the king petitions for restitution of plundered goods. One of those was Sir John Gildesborough of Wennington, the Essex poll tax commissioner, who was licensed on Friday, 5th,

> '... to claim all goods he can prove to be his, in whosesoever hands they are, recently seized in Essex by insurgents, and recover them, howsoever he pleases, from those who detain them, without hindrance from the king or his ministers'.

While the king and his council were reasserting government control, the new chief justice, Sir Robert Tresilian, was in session with William Morrers in the town to see that the guilty were 'justified by law'. There were in Chelmsford at the time 'two houses where the courts are held', both of them the property of the bishop of London as lord of the manor, and used for court business. One of them

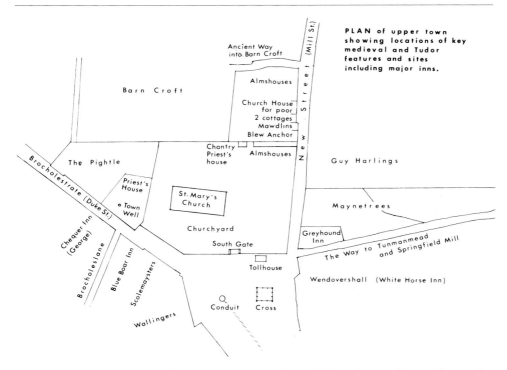

PLAN of upper town showing locations of key medieval and Tudor features and sites including major inns.

stood against the south side of the churchyard, and the other in front of it in the open street, at the upper end of the market. Both buildings were then known as 'Le Tolhouse'. The building in the street, which was only a house (*domus*) in the sense that it was a roofed space, open on all sides, was used weekly by the corn-men as a market house, and was often referred to as the 'Cornemarkete', 'Markett Cross', or 'the Cross of Chelmersford'. It was also occupied as a court-house by the assize judges on circuit and justices of the peace holding sessions.

According to Thomas of Walsingham a crowd of frightened Essex rebels, estimated as five hundred, made their way to Chelmsford that week, probably on Monday, 1 July, barefoot, with heads uncovered, to beg the king's mercy. They might well fear, Essex being judged the county whence 'the whole madness first sprang'. Mercy was granted to them on condition that they handed over their leaders to justice. Not only Essex suppliants came. The brother of the imprisoned Hertfordshire rebel leader, William Grindcob, travelled to Chelmsford that week, 'to intercede for him with the king's court'. Learning there that the earl of Warwick and Sir Thomas Percy were advancing towards Hertfordshire with a thousand armed men to aid the abbot of St Albans against the insurgents, he was able to send his brother warning of their approach.

On Tuesday and Wednesday, 2 and 3 July, sworn juries presented before Tresilian the names of some 145 rebels as ringleaders in Essex. Thomas, the Fobb-ing baker, headed the lists, and no fewer than 27 of the other men named were identified as 'of Fobbing'. The Chelmsford barber, John Stalworth, was one of the accused. Execution of those found guilty of treason followed swiftly on Tresilian's sentence. As traitors they were condemned to be 'drawn' — dragged along the road bound on a hurdle tied to a horse — to the gallows, and hanged.

The Chelmsford gallows stood about half a mile outside the town in the Upland, on open space by the Writtle road (site today of Primrose Hill). The nearby fields were still called Gallows Fields in 1843. Thomas of Walsingham estimated that about a dozen men suffered a traitor's death at Chelmsford. He may well be right, for the names of at least eight of them are known. Thomas Baker of Fobbing, picked out in the Knighton chronicle as 'the first mover and after a principal leader', was charged on 2 and 3 July and executed with three other Fobbing men on Thursday 4 July, the day after their trial. The Moulsham franklin Richard Baud died on Saturday 6 July. A fifth Fobbing man, and two men from East Hanningfield, John Geffrey and the miller John Fillol, were executed on dates unknown during the same week. Five more rebels condemned as traitors that week, three of them from Fobbing, either died with the rest, or fled away in time. The Chelmsford barber, John Stalworth (who was named on the same charge list as the Fobbing baker on Tuesday 2 July) and two other Fobbing men, all three condemned for treason, escaped death by flight. The lands and chattels of dead or fugitive traitors were forfeited to the Crown. John Stalworth's possessions were meagre: a basin, ewer, and towel; bedclothes and a tablecloth; a platter, a brass pot, three shovels, and two iron andirons; all worth 40s. Richard Baud's more valuable lands and tenements in Moulsham were granted in 1382 for life to one of the king's servants. Besides the traitors drawn and hanged, Walsingham claimed that nineteen rebels, whose names are not known, but whose participation must have fallen short of treason, were hanged that week in Chelmsford on one gallows.

On Saturday 6 July, after settling a few final matters, including the appointment of an official to inquire into the insurrection in Southampton and Wiltshire, the king and his train left Chelmsford. They stayed for a couple of days at Havering, then returned to London, before moving on to St Albans to mete out punishment to the Hertfordshire rebels.

In London the king and his council on 10 July appointed a commission, headed by the earl of Buckingham, to carry on the search in Essex for any insurgents who had been charged but escaped. But the fugitive Chelmsford barber, John Stalworth, managed to evade capture. After parliament declared a general amnesty on 14 December 1381 he obtained a special pardon on 26 January 1382, and returned home to his wife Agnes and his barbering. He became a respectable householder and chief pledge in the town, occupying the little high street corner house (part of the site of 38 High Street) on the north side of Springfield Lane. An annual offering of 2s, which he was said in 1392 to be paying towards the upkeep of a light before the Holy Cross as a charge on his shop, may well have been a thank-offering for deliverance.

None of the Chelmsford and Moulsham rebels who went to London, and were later named in complaints made of attacks on private property there, are known to have met with any retribution. William Prentys, Thomas Osteler, and Robert Baker, returned to the high street to prosper in their trades for many years to come. The Moulsham men went home to the hamlet. John Spicer left London after the meeting at Mile End on 14 June to complete some unfinished business of his own. He headed north into Hertfordshire, where on 15 June he extorted from the parson of Thorley, under threat of decapitation, the transfer to him of the lease of some property in Chelmsford which he claimed. He then returned to

Chelmsford where, on 18 June, with William Berham, a Chelmsford spicer who later became an innkeeper, he attacked the house of Henry de Grey of Wilton at Sandon, just outside Chelmsford. Outrages such as Spicer's, suggestive of personal grievance or malice, were a common feature of the rebellion, but they did not constitute treason. John Spicer survived, and gave his name to one of the most valuable sites in the high street — 'Spicerestenement', later the Saracen's Head inn (site of 3 High Street).

AFTER THE REVOLT

With the departure of the king and chief justice and their retinue, life in Chelmsford returned to normal. The manor's surviving court rolls date from November 1381, when the usual late autumn or winter manor court was held. Bishop William Courteney (1375-81) had been translated from London to Canterbury in September, so in November twenty-nine tenants, bond and free, swore fealty to the dean and chapter of St Paul's, temporarily in charge of the manor while the see was vacant. The bond tenants also acknowledged the lordship of the dean and chapter by a customary payment of 6s 8d, called palfrey money, and submitted the names of three of their members as reeve, for the dean and chapter 'to choose whichever of them they will'. There was little other business at that court, or at a court held early in 1382 when the new bishop, Robert Braybrooke, was acknowledged.

In Moulsham, all the abbot of Westminster's customary tenants were required by his steward to come to court after the rebellion to take up new titles to their holdings. Two Chelmsford townspeople who owned property in the hamlet as well as in the town, Margaret Lightfoot and John Stalworth, cook (not to be confused with the barber of the same name) had their holdings seized by the abbot in 1382, 'because they have not come after the burning of the rolls to receive new title', until they complied and paid the customary fines for admission. But there is no evidence that this precaution was taken by the bishop's steward in Chelmsford, an omission which manorial officers were to regret later. In 1618 a surveyor investigating the descent of holdings in the manor complained that the date of John Gybon's admission to two acres of land called Waces, next to New Street, was unknown, 'for lack of rolls beyond the 5th year of Richard II'.

By June 1382 manorial administration had recovered its full vigour when the annual court with view of frankpledge, or court leet, met on the Thursday of Whitsuntide, as was the custom. Briskly the court fined thirteen tenants for non-attendance (3d each) and eleven chief pledges for not coming to present offenders (12d each). Twenty-two men and women were fined for breaking regulations governing the brewing and selling of ale (2d or 3d each), and six men and women for 'regrating' ale, that is buying it from others to resell at an inflated price (2d or 3d each). Thirteen men and women, bakers of white and horse bread (bread made mainly of beans and peas) were fined for bakery offences (2d or 3d), among them seven innkeepers. Four women were fined 2d each for regrating bread, and making too much profit. One innkeeper, Thomas Osteler, was fined, not only as a negligent chief pledge and unsatisfactory baker and brewer, but also as a dishonest retailer of wine. Five butchers were fined 2d each for selling bad meat and overcharging for it, and two cooks, Nicholas Cook (3d) and John Stalworth

(2*d*), for selling bad victuals and meat and charging too much for them. A tanner, William Hood, was fined 2*d* for poor workmanship. Three women, including Margaret Lightfoot, were fined 3*d* each for forestalling fish, buying it up early for re-sale later at a profit; four 'foreign' fishmongers from outside the manor were more heavily fined at 4*d* each. Finally, both the aletasters were fined 6*d* for neglecting their duties, and fourteen youths and men were fined 2*d* each for being resident in the manor without being sworn into a tithing.

The lord's court with view of frankpledge may at some earlier date have been held twice a year, but by 1382 it was being held only once, at Whitsun. The lord's court without the view, or court baron, usually met once or twice in late autumn or winter, or if business required, three times. The court records kept after 1381 show the continuing distinction in the manor between the town and the rural upland. On the court rolls upland matters, such as straying stock, trespass, uncleansed ditches, digging pits in the highway for clay or gravel, illegal felling of timber, occupancy of villein holdings and performance of villein services, were presented by the upland's own chief pledges and juries, and entered separately on the rolls. But changes were taking place in the late 14th century in the social and economic structure of the manor which in time would diminish the distinction between town and upland.

The town continued to benefit from its ties with the see of London. Robert Braybrooke, bishop and lord of the manor for over twenty years until his death in 1404, was granted by Richard II in 1395 the privilege of the return of the king's writs. This grant strengthened his town's independence of the county sheriff, for, as explained in the manor survey of 1591, it empowered the lord of the manor to execute and serve

> '... all processe, soe as not the Sheriffe of Essex nor any of his bayliffes or mynisters, or any other person or persons ought to serve anie proces within the said Libertyes, but the Lordes Bayliffe of the said Libertyes only ...'

In future, if an under-sheriff 'broke into the Liberty', as occurred in 1469, when William Lopham, a townsman, was arrested and mishandled, and in 1472, when a fish stall of William Fayrer's was seized, the officer faced a fine in the Chelmsford manor court.

By the 1380s the bishop's steward had abandoned the practice of direct cultivation of the demesne lands of the manor on the bishop's behalf, in favour of farming them out for rent. Shortage of labour after the Black Death may have encouraged this decision, as may a recent disaster: the bishop's hall or manor house, which is mentioned in 1274 and 1321, was said in 1591 to have been 'brent and wasted by fire' in the reign of Edward III. In 1382 the demesne lands were leased out by the bailiff in eighteen parcels to thirteen different tenants, most of them townsmen, for rents totalling £20 14*s* 8*d*; no manor house was listed among the parcels. John Scolemayster, John Totham, and the butcher, Adam atte Wall, jointly leased the two great fields called Okeley and Westfeld, and the schoolmaster also leased the lord's little barn; Simon the chaplain leased the great barn. Thomas Chopyn, the miller, had a house on the Mellehille, probably the millhouse, Thomas Wyllyngale the demesne lands at Southwood, and John Sadeler the lord's fishing in the river of Chelmsford. The other great demesne fields, Berefeld, Mellefeld, Chapelfeld, and 'the lord's field below the rectory' (i.e. Churchfield *alias* Townfield) were also leased, with a number of smaller parcels including the two court houses in the town. In 1384 a marginal note against the grant of space for a market stall — 'New rent 4*d* which belongs to the farmer of the market' — suggests that the market profits were also being farmed out. In 1391 the bishop's watermill was leased for three years at a rent of £6 13*s* 4*d*. Leasing of the demesne in many parcels did not continue long. In 1394 the whole demesne was let to farm in two parcels only, for a fixed rent of £40, to two townsmen, Thomas Wyllyngale (£17) and Nicholas Waleys (£23). The rent varied little thereafter. In 1399 Thomas Wyllyngale had a separate lease of the lands at Southwood for sixteen years, while Nicholas Waleys seems to have secured the farm of the whole Chelmsford demesne, which he certainly held in 1404 and 1408-9.

Nicholas Waleys (*alias* Nicholas Bayly) was not only the farmer of the manor; he was also the manor bailiff from about 1393 until his death in 1414. The practice of leasing the manor house and demesne lands to the bishop's bailiff at a fixed rent of £40 continued unchanged for nearly 150 years: in 1539 it was officially reported that 'John Taylor bayly ther having the hole lordship in ferme payth to the lord by the yere xl^li (£40)'. According to a statement of account in 1438 the farmer, then Thomas Mille, was also entitled to the manor rents of all kinds, and the profits of courts, market, and fairs, while the bishop reserved to himself the advowson of the church, the fishing rights, all woods and timber on the manor, and such ancient feudal perquisites as wardship and marriage of minors, profits from waifs and strays, and the forfeited goods of felons and fugitives worth more than 20*s*. In 1458-9 when Robert Lyston was farmer the lease included the watermill.

THE END OF VILLEINAGE

It was not only the management of the demesne that was changing. As upland villein or customary holdings were abandoned or fell into the lord's hands for lack of heirs, free men, whether townsmen or 'foreigners', secured possession of them. The bond holding called Lynches (site of the modern Tower Avenue development), unoccupied since the Black Death, was derelict in 1383, when the steward ordered the bailiff to restore it and show some profit from it; he leased it in 1384 to Adam atte Wall for 7*s* a year. Another townsman, the roper Adam Gynes, built up a large upland holding of customary lands, including Quyntescroft, Frydayescroft, Hosecroft, and Byrlecroft, which he held, like Crouchecroft, acquired in 1405, 'by the rod, at will, by the service and custom due'. Though personally free he was still expected to provide any labour services anciently attached to the holdings; in 1411 the steward authorised the bailiff to distrain on Adam to make him pay for three years' failure to send three men to help to gather in the hay.

With the demesne farmed out to the bailiff, and free men taking over villein holdings, the ancient office of reeve became redundant. When William Munde, John Helder, and William Paulyn were chosen by the bond tenants in 1386 for the steward to pick one of them as reeve, no one was sworn 'for the present, because the lord has a bailiff of his own choice'. In October 1404 the court agreed not to elect a reeve, because Nicholas Waleys (then bailiff) had been confirmed as farmer of the manor by the dean and chapter of St Paul's, acting during the vacancy of the see after the death of Bishop Braybrooke. The customary process of electing the reeve was also undermined by the reluctance of free townsmen-tenants of villein holdings to accept the office. In 1396 the chandler John Wright, who had some land which had once belonged to the native Helder family, paid a fine of 13s 4d when he was chosen as reeve by his 'equals' (fellow holders of villein lands), to be excused from serving the office for six years. In the same year Adam Gynes also paid a fine after election to be excused.

The suppression of the revolt and the restrictive proclamations of 1381 may have temporarily dampened any restlessness among Chelmsford's upland 'native' population, but within a decade there were signs of the collapse of villeinage. The bondman's livelihood need no longer depend on his lord. He could sell his labour to others, and claim his wages, if unjustly withheld, in the manor court, together with the customary 6d damages. When the bondman Adam Fryday claimed 20d and damages from the miller, Thomas Chopyn in 1384, the court agreed that the miller owed him wages, though only 11d, and the miller was fined 2d for detention. Some bondmen had individual skills and trades to offer for hire. The lord's rights in family matters were also being questioned: in 1391 William Smyth *alias* Arwesmyth was accused of marrying Joan, Adam Fryday's daughter, without paying the customary fine for the lord's consent to marry one of his villeins; only under pressure did he pay his 12d in 1393. Customary works owed by bondmen became neglected; in 1399 William Southwood admitted in court that the year before he had not come when summoned by the bailiff to do the work that he owed at haymaking.

Villeins who prospered tried to move into the free property market in the town. This was resisted by the lord of the manor. When a bondman, John Martin, acquired by charter from another bondman, William Hasyl, a freehold high street site, the bishop seized the property 'as his own, being purchased by his villein'. It was then regranted to John Martin to hold 'by the rod in villeinage according to custom'. John died some time before 1384, possibly at the time of the Black Death with all his family, for no heir ever came to claim the property, which William Prentys took possession of. His right to it was challenged by the bishop, who repossessed it, and in 1387 leased it for fifty years to his cook, Geoffrey Yve. Thereafter the tenure of the property became confused. It was investigated in 1401, when a sworn jury of twelve men remembered that John Martin, his forbears and kin, had all been the lord's bondmen, that the site was originally freehold, but that the lord had required John to hold it in villeinage. The site became divided, with one half (site of 59 High Street), described in 1591 as a 'tenement called 'Sharpes, ... sometime Martynes', reverting to freehold. But the other half called Felsteds (site of 58 High Street) remained copyhold, the solitary copyhold site among all the original freeholds fronting the high street, until the extinction of manorial incidents in the present century.

The bishop's officers tried to conserve the system of villeinage, but after the burning of the rolls and other written evidence of local custom, as the years passed old men died, memories faded, and it became increasingly difficult to determine which men were bondmen by birth, or on what terms ancient upland holdings were occupied. In 1399 a jury of twelve of the most senior inhabitants had to be sworn in to establish whether William Paulyn was one of the lord's bondmen or not; in 1381 everyone knew that he was. In 1404 John Fyssh, when he was charged with owing two works lifting hay in the lord's meadow and withholding one of them, claimed only to owe one; he appealed to the manor 'extent' or survey for confirmation of this, no doubt hoping that it had been destroyed in 1381. The court took the precaution of ordering that if the extent could not be found the matter should be decided by the usual jury of twelve inhabitants.

The most effective demonstration by Chelmsford's 'natives' of their rejection of their status was simply their departure from the manor. When all efforts to recover them failed villeinage on the manor was dead. It was the younger men who went. The older men, heads of families, such as Adam Fryday, John Helder senior, and William Southwood, lived out their lives on the manor. William Southwood, indeed, had been such a trusted manorial servant that he served as the lord's bailiff, *c.*1377-81. But by 1392 one of Adam Fryday's younger sons, William, a weaver, was 'staying away' in Moulsham; Robert, his eldest son, a dyer, had also gone away, as had John Helder's son, John the younger, a carpenter. The bailiff was ordered to find all three of them, and distrain on their goods to make them either return to serve the lord where he pleased, or pay a fine or 'chevage' for licence to stay away.

John Helder senior died early in 1393; his widow Agnes held his land for life, and John, the son and heir, still stayed away. Adam Fryday died in 1394. His sons Robert and William were both being sought that year, but in December the heir, Robert, attended the manor court to be admitted to his inheritance, and acknowledged that he was the lord's bondman. But he left again immediately afterwards. A third brother, John Fryday, early in 1394 paid 3*s* 4*d* as chevage for permission to stay away until the next court leet was held. He had acquired by charter some freehold property in Leighs, a few miles north of Chelmsford; when the next leet was held in May 1394 the bailiff was ordered to seize it for the bishop. In 1395 and 1396 Robert Fryday duly paid his chevage of 6*d* to remain outside the manor, but later in 1396 he disposed of the family holding, Frydayeslond, forever, to Richard Paulyn and his heirs, Richard paying 5*s* for the transfer to be enrolled in the court roll.

Meanwhile Robert Fryday's brother William was obstinately staying away, as was young John Helder. In 1399 the court issued an order, 'now as many times before', to seize the bodies, goods, and chattels of Robert, William, John, and William 'the dyer' Fryday, and John Helder, the lord's bondmen, wherever they might be found, and to hold them in safe custody until they paid chevage. Court by court the order was repeated. In November 1405 old William Southwood was the only bondman on the manor who came to court to swear fealty to the new bishop, Roger Walden, acknowledging himself to be *nativus ex sanguine* — bondman of the blood — and taking the oath of servitude.

In 1408, after John Helder's widow died, his son John did attend the court to take up his inheritance, but two years later he disposed of it; in 1411 he was reported to be staying with Sir William Marney at Layer Marney, and he was still there in 1416. As for the Frydays, in 1409 the court was told that Robert was at Writtle, one of the two Williams at Great Baddow and John at Sudbury. The bailiff, Nicholas Waleys, did, however, agree that since he, Nicholas, took over the farm of the manor, about 1393, he had received 6*d* from Robert each year at

Christmas as chevage; nothing was said about any payments made by the other two, who were fined 2*d* each in their absence. Year by year orders were given to arrest the absconders, and the fines imposed on them increased, first to 6*d*, then to 12*d*. It is doubtful whether the fines were ever collected. Robert Fryday remained at Writtle; his brother William had moved to Little Waltham by 1412, and to Broomfield by 1416, when his brother John was said to be at Colchester. Again and again the bailiff was ordered to arrest them, and produce them at the next court with their goods, chattels, and offspring, but the order may well have become a formality to protect the bishop's claim on them. In 1421 the fines imposed were raised from 12*d* to 40*d*. The last recorded order to bring them back was enrolled in 1422. Between 1422 and 1461 no record of the court's proceedings has survived. By 1461, when the record resumes, the futile attempts to recover the absconders had ceased. There is no further mention of them, or indeed of any individual classified as 'native', 'villein', or 'bondman of blood', whether living on the manor or an escaper from it.

The memory of villeinage lived on for many years in the ancient names of former villein holdings in the upland and at Southwood, such as Frydays, Helders, Gibbes, Paulyns, and Mundes, and in the terms 'customary and heriotable', still applied to those holdings after they came into the hands of free men. The heriot of the best beast or its cash equivalent was still demanded from the new tenants, not only after the holder's death, but every time a customary holding changed hands by surrender. Though personal servitude as an element in tenure had died out on the manor by 1461, tenure by the rod at will of the lord by copy of court roll, or 'copyhold', survived, and was increasingly applied to 'new rents' created by grants of small parcels of the bishop's demesne and manor waste soil. Another reminder of villeinage which survived was the levy of palfrey money, 'at every Lordes first courte keeping', which was still being demanded from the manor's copyholders in the 16th century.

CHAPTER SIX
The Town Grows, 1381-1422

THE LATE 14TH-CENTURY TOWN

From November 1381 the record of the proceedings of Chelmsford's manor court, renewed after the burning of the earlier rolls in the revolt, reveals the medieval town and its inhabitants in more intimate detail. By the 1380s the town had begun to spread outwards from the market-place in the only direction it could, northwards towards the upland. The lord of the manor was granting a few freehold plots alongside the road leading out of the town west of the church-yard. This road had many names. At first it was usually 'the way to Braintree' or 'Branketrewey'. Sometimes it was Church Street, or Brocholestrate, from Walter Brochole, who owned a freehold corner plot about 1344, where the little lane called Brocholeslane (Threadneedle Street) led off Brocholestrate down towards the river. But the name which outlasted them all was the present one, Duke Street. At the beginning of the 15th century Guy Duke owned a field on the west side of the way to Braintree which became, like the rest of his property in the town, part of the manor of Springfield Dukes. Just as the family name was sometimes written Duk, so the street sometimes became Duck Street. To simplify the narrative, the 'way to Braintree' will be referred to as Duke Street, though that name did not entirely supersede the alternatives until the 18th century. Indeed, in the 17th century 'Duck Street' was also an alternative for New Street, where Thomas Duke had owned a large built-on plot in the early 15th century (site of 2 New Street), which also became attached to the manor of Springfield Dukes.

But development west of the churchyard was very slow. It did not spread much farther up Duke Street than the site of the present Essex county hall before the 18th century, and took place mainly on the west side of the street, opposite the half-acre enclosure next to the churchyard, called The Pightle. The Pightle itself (site of 10-20 Duke Street), apart from the small plot assigned to the little Priest's House or Vicarage by the churchyard in 1417, remained virtually undeveloped until 1741. Most of the early buildings opposite the Pightle were cottages. Stephen the Sacristan had one of them in 1344. A whole block of sites towards the high street (sites of 85-91 Duke Street) belonged in the 1380s to Master John Scolemayster; the site of 85 was still identified as 'Schoolmaster's' in the 19th century. In 1392 the owner of Walter Brochole's former house, John Sponer, who brewed and sold ale, was granted some extra ground in front of it, 38 feet by 9 feet, to enlarge it, for an extra penny on his manor rent.

A few freehold plots had also been granted before 1381 east of the churchyard in 'Le Newestret', so-called by 1386. New Street has kept that name to this day. One of those plots, facing the churchyard (site of 54-9 New Street), was owned by John Manytre, whose sister Margaret, wife of John Taillour, inherited it about 1381. The present main house on the site is still called Maynetrees. The new street led from the town to the bishop's hall and mill. In 1566 local jurors ruled that the way leading on to the mill from 'Le Newstret' was 'not common for all purposes, but for access to the mill only.' The new street probably came

51

into existence in the 13th century, as the way to the mill from the new market. The built-up part of New Street was still sometimes called 'Milstrete' in the 1560s. Tounemanmedlane (Waterloo Lane) led off the new street to Tunmanmead and Springfield mill.

Near the bottom of the high street a narrow lane turned off eastward towards the wooden bridge which divided Chelmsford from Springfield. This was the 'highway leading from Chelmsford to Colchester', also known as Springfield Lane or Colchester Lane.

The late 14th-century high street presented an irregular façade of timber-framed buildings: hall houses, inns, cottages, shops, workshops, stables, and forges. When it became the practice to let the manor to farm, the bishop judiciously reserved to himself the timber rights, so that tenants in need of building material had to seek it from their lord, as John Fyssh did in 1404, when he was granted two oaks from Okeley to build the groundsill of his house. Tenants unwise enough to ignore the bishop's monopoly were fined by the manor court: in 1394 Thomas Hasyl was fined for felling a great oak and two little ones, and William Paulyn for cutting down and selling fourteen oak spars without licence. Roofs were steeply pitched and thatched. Some roofs may already have been tiled; William Tyler, a bondman, was named in the 1381 poll tax. Certainly roofs were being tiled by 1437, when 2,000 plain tiles were bought for 8s 4d (including carriage) to roof the Tollhouse by the churchyard, in the market. The many low single-storey buildings attracted the 'listener under the roofs' (*obauditor sub tectos*) or eavesdropper, a compulsion perceived as harmful to neighbours and punishable in the manor court. A growing desire for greater family privacy and comfort was being met by the addition of 'parlours', and 'solars' built over shops; living in the shop was being replaced by living over the shop, a life-style which was to predominate in the town for centuries.

There were few vacant plots left on the high street frontage by the end of the 14th century. One small 'empty place' on the west side of the street (part of site of 76 High Street) was granted to John Assheldham and his wife Margaret in 1396. A more valuable piece of undeveloped frontage on the east side, measuring 36 feet by 22 feet, remained in the lord's hands until 1413. It lay next to the stone bridge, alongside the great river, and backed on to the channel, probably man-made, called 'Le Gullet', which linked the Chelmersford river and the great river. The risk of flooding on this low-lying site may have made it unattractive while safer sites were available farther up the hill. But in 1413 the bishop granted it to a trio of businessmen, John Warwick, the Chelmsford spicer, and two Londoners, Thomas Rolf (the bishop's steward), and John Beaumond, a chandler. With its situation close to the bridge it became an inn, known by 1470 as the Cock (site of 49-50 High Street).

But some plots owned by freeholders were not yet built upon, or only partially so. In 1391 John Chever, a shoemaker, bought from his next door neighbours, Henry and Margaret Hunt, an enclosed plot measuring about 16 feet by 14½ feet between his house and theirs. He was careful to agree with them covenants concerning the gutters of any domestic buildings he or his heirs might choose to erect on it, to avoid future disputes. For as new building began to close the gaps on the street frontage, and upper storeys began to overlook or overhang adjoining single-storey shops or cottages, rainwater gutters and 'drippings from the eaves' became matters of concern between neighbours. When the baker Roger Springfield, with the consent of his neighbour, the widow Katherine Couper, built a house in Duke Street in 1415 partly joined on to her's (sites of 78-80 Duke Street), on ground where she had always enjoyed 'lawful drippings from the eaves', he agreed to put up a lead gutter to receive the rainwater falling between their two houses, 'and to empty the same in a fitting manner'. He undertook, too, not only to repair the gutter whenever Katherine warned him to do so, on pain of forfeiting a bond of 6s 8d, but also, because part of his new house stood so close to Katherine's ground that his drippings would fall on her soil, to pay her ½d a year for the privilege.

As the gaps were closed, too, it became necessary to protect time-honoured rights of way between sites, leading out of the high street to the backsides and rivers. When Emma, widow of Geoffrey Priour, in 1383 sold her property facing the fishmarket (site of New London Road gap), the conveyance included a right of way at all times to drive cattle through the gateway of her neighbour, the chandler John Wright, and to pass and repass with horses and carts. While some of these ways remained broad cartways, others were reduced to narrow alleys as the frontage closed, with no more room to pass than the width of a door.

As less and less space was left to build on the street frontage, development began in the market-place itself. The soil of the high street was manor waste ground, owned by the bishop as lord, including the upper part of the high street and the wide triangular space near the market cross, where the corn merchants gathered weekly. By the 1380s parcels of the street itself were being disposed of by the bishop or by his stewards on his behalf, notably down the middle of the street. There an island, or 'Middle Row', of buildings was springing up, creating a new lane at the back, and adding 'new rents' to the manor rent roll. By 1384 the island was called the Shoprow. The growth of the Shoprow no doubt originated in the grant of 'stall-places' to set up movable market stalls which, according to a town by-law, recorded in 1382 but probably older, had to be removed after the market closed. It was a short step from ownership of those precisely located and measured pitches to the erection on them of 'standing', 'roofed', and 'built' stalls, followed by the amalgamation of adjoining stall-places and stalls, and their enlargement into shops and dwellings.

The Shoprow grew piecemeal, a few feet at a time. When the two ropers, Thomas Roper and Adam Gynes, were granted eleven extra feet of waste in 1381 at the north end of buildings which they already owned 'at the end of the corn-market', to hold by copy of court roll for 2d a year extra rent, they built a kitchen on it. This expanding copyhold property (site of 97-8 High Street) became known as 'The Head', because until the 17th century it stood at the head of the Shoprow. Next to The Head, down the street, stood a freehold cottage called Rammes (site of 95-6 High Street). John Ramme was alive in 1351 and died before 1375, so this island growth had begun by then. Adam Gynes acquired Rammes too, and also the freehold shop with a solar built over it next to Rammes, which he sold to John Skyle in 1384; it was noted then as a 'new rent' of 4d. In 1398 Adam was granted vacant ground, on the west side of Shoprow, seven feet wide in a circuit eighty feet long around his house. When he died in 1423 he left to his widow Alice two shops with two solars built over and a parlour, joined on to the freehold house (Rammes) he lived in, with a parcel of

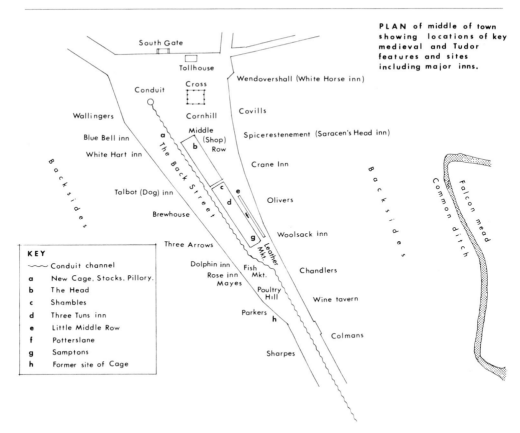

PLAN of middle of town showing locations of key medieval and Tudor features and sites including major inns.

KEY

~~~ Conduit channel
a   New Cage, Stocks, Pillory.
b   The Head
c   Shambles
d   Three Tuns inn
e   Little Middle Row
f   Potterslane
g   Samptons
h   Former site of Cage

land next to it and 'le workinghowse', all lying together in Shoprow. The 'parcel of land', described in 1428 as 'a piece of waste before the doorway of Rammes marked off by two posts', was probably a little forecourt. Title deeds of 96 High Street still identified the site as 'Rammestenement otherwise Ginns' in the present century. In 1400 William Fyssher was granted a piece of ground twenty feet long by two feet wide on the south part of his house in Shoprow, for a 'new rent' of ½d. Sometimes ground was granted for a particular purpose: in 1404 Ralph Watyer, a cook, and his wife Christine, were granted waste ground measuring thirteen feet by eight feet in front of their house in the Shoprow, for a copyhold rent of 4d, to build a 'Rostynghous'.

At the top of the high street, near the market cross and not far from the south gate of the churchyard, was a conduit from which fresh water flowed. The water came from the spring called Burgeyswell in Burgeysfield about half a mile upland of the town. From the spring the water was led underground in pipes made of elm into Duke Street, and down the street to the conduit-head where it surfaced, a constantly-running public source of spring water. From the conduit-head it flowed through the town as a watercourse (*via aquatica*) or open drain, down the back lane behind the Shoprow and the high street, into Springfield Lane; there it turned off into the Gullet at the back of the buildings on the east side of the lower high street. In 1384 John Gybon was fined for stopping up the watercourse at the end of the Shoprow by setting up a stall there. Filth and rubbish in the high street were swept into this open sewer and carried away into the Gullet and great river.

The origin of the conduit is not recorded. It was said in 1669 to have been provided 'many years before' by the inhabitants, 'at their own expense'. In 1782 much weight was given in legal opinion to the implications of the contemporary forms of the names, 'Burgess Well' and 'Burgess's Land', with a presumption (though no proof could be found) that the land where the spring rose was 'anciently common waste land'. As the earliest known form of the name (1385-1483) is consistently Burgeyswell and Burgeysfield, it is just as likely that the spring and the fields around it once belonged to John Burgeys, benefactor of the friars in 1281, and his family, landowners in the late-13th and early-14th centuries, whose name is not linked with any fields elsewhere in the parish. It may be that when the friars in 1341 laid pipes from that same spring to lead water underground down to the river and across it to their house in Moulsham, they also assisted the inhabitants to lead the water into the town. The friars were known in England for their skill in constructing conduits. Southampton (1310) and Gloucester (1438) both owed their public water supplies to the Franciscans, and in 1365 the Shrewsbury Dominicans were licensed to buy a spring to lead water to their house by pipes laid (as in Chelmsford) under a river. Whatever its origin, the Chelmsford conduit and conduit-stream were an established feature of the town before 1384. The spring which fed them, Burgess Well, sited behind the present Borough Council Offices by Burgess Well Road, was to contribute to the town's water supply for over six hundred years, until 1973. Burgess Well Road survived until 1987, when it was engulfed by the extension of the town's ring road — Parkway.

At the lower end of the town, on the east side of the high street between Springfield Lane and the stone bridge, was the Smythesrow, where the smiths and farriers worked in open wooden sheds. One forge stood alone, out in the middle of the street on the approach to the bridge.

Every Friday the market took over the town. At the top of the hill by the Cross was the Corn Market on Le Cornhill. Lower down the street, below the Shoprow in Le Fysshestrett, was Le Fysshmarket or Fisshrow. Nearby was the 'Ledermarket where leather is sold' (also called the 'Barkeresrow' or Tanners' row), and the Glover Row, between the fishermarket and the east side of the high street; this was where shoes were sold. In 1416 the glover John Yon paid a fine of 4*d* to be allowed a piece of ground 3½ feet by 2 feet 11 inches on which to add another stall to his stalls in Glover Row, for a rent of 2*d* a year, and also for a licence to put up a 'building called Le Pentys' [penthouse], standing on four posts with groundsill, over all his four stalls in Glover Row, for a further 2*d* a year rent, and there to sell his merchandise. Just below the fishmarket was 'Le Puktrygt', or 'market where poultry is sold', on 'Pultry Hyll'. By 1428 building had begun on Poultry Hill (site of 79-80 High Street). Traffic congestion, already created at the bottom of the high street by a forge standing in the middle of it, was aggravated on Fridays towards the bridge entrance by six butchers' stalls, which John Gybon used to set up outside his inn there, and four stalls before the doorway of his neighbour, the innkeeper Thomas Osteler, next to the bridge.

Some householders had the right to space in front of their own houses or shops to set up movable stalls on market day. In 1409 the chandler John Holewell and his wife Joan were granted stall-space twelve foot deep along the whole forty-foot frontage of the house they lived in, for a 2*s* rent. In 1420 Adam Gynes and the spicer John Warwick for the same rent secured a long pitch, fifty-seven by four feet, in the leather-market opposite John Warwick's house.

After the 1381 uprising, the destruction of the manor records seems to have tempted some traders to take advantage of the lack of record to set up unauthorised stalls in the market. In 1384 the lord of the manor granted Thomas Chopyn a vacant place in the market for one stall, between the cordwainer John atte Melle's stall and William Taillour's; the annual rent to pay for it was fourpence. This was the legitimate way to secure a pitch, and fourpence the usual rate for a 'new rent'. But later in the same year the manor court ordered the removal of 'certain stalls' newly set up in the market 'by butchers and others'. The first stallholder to be challenged by name was the innkeeper John Gybon, who was ordered in 1387 to show his title to his stalls. In 1388 six others were called to account: John Goldsmith, William Prentys, John Ditton, Michael Chapman, Thomas Wyllyngale, and Simon Heygate. The doubtful stalls were supposed to be confiscated until the owners' titles were established to the steward's satisfaction; but with the court meeting at such long intervals, and the bailiff no doubt reluctant to antagonise his neighbours, it is not surprising that it took some years to clear these matters up. Indeed, the traders who were challenged were among the most prominent inhabitants of the town; three of them were chief pledges. In 1390 John Ditton, and in 1391 Simon Heygate, were formally granted stall-space in front of their houses, and taken off the list of suspects. But in 1392 Richard Duke was added to the list, and the enquiry extended to include all holders of fishstalls. By then thirty-nine stalls were under review, and the bailiff was ordered to take legal steps to compel the ten townsmen who claimed them to produce their evidence of title. Stephen Spylleman had to account for five fishstalls; Geoffrey Colvyle (of the family that gave its name to Coval Hall) for four stalls; William Prentys for two spicers' stalls, one salter's, and two tanners'; Richard Duke for four fishstalls; John Goldsmith for six tanners' stalls; John Gybon for six butchers' stalls, one tanner's, one fish, and one turner's; Henry Flexere for a movable stall which he had already been fined for and told to pull down; Robert Glover for a glover's stall; John Nafferton for three stalls; and John Horner for another 'flexeres' (arrowmaker's) stall.

This enquiry seems to have ended in 1392, except for John Gybon's stalls, which were disputed until 1401. A fresh enquiry, begun in 1394 into the rent due from four stalls in front of Thomas and Colletta Osteler's inn by the stone bridge, was not settled until 1416, after their death. Their son and heir Robert Chelmsford [sic] then produced in court two charters of c.1205, the original grants of the 'new places' in the 'new market' on which the inn was built, and apparently established his right to set up stalls in front of the inn. Another check was made in 1411-13, when the bailiff was ordered to seize the movable stalls of all occupiers who could not prove to hold them by grant of Bishop Richard Clifford (1407-21) or his predecessors, or other just title.

In 1428 a definitive rental of 'Le Stalles', their owners, and fixed rents, was drawn up. Fifteen legitimate stallholders were listed, holding thirty stalls, and two standings for an unspecified number of movable stalls. Seven of the stalls were in the fishmarket, nine in the leathermarket. Some were fixed stalls, some movable, several were before the owners' doors, and one in Shoprow was roofed.

A few stalls were of recent origin, including John Waleys's 'new rent' of fourpence a year for an empty place in Barkeresrow measuring twelve by four feet, granted to him in 1417 to build one stall. Three of the fish stalls were part of the endowment of the Corpus Christi Guild, given to the guild about 1392 by the fishmonger Margaret Lightfoot. In 1428 'Le Stalles' were contributing about ten shillings a year to the rental income of the manor, payable after the manor was farmed out to the farmer of the market.

No reference has been found in 14th- and 15th-century records to the sale of cattle in the weekly market, except as butcher's meat, driven live into the town for slaughter in the Shambles (site of 91 High Street). Cattle were probably mainly sold on the four fair days in May. Laurence Isbrond was fined in 1392 for placing a pinfold or pound for stray cattle on the lord's land on fair day without licence. In the Upland, at the junction of the ways into the town from Roxwell and Braintree, stood a cross called 'Le Fayrecross', mentioned in 1418 and 1485, and later corrupted to Fairy Cross; the roadside croft on the south corner of the Broomfield and Braintree turning was known in 1416 (and later) as Cross Croft. When the fair took over the town watchfulness over trading practices was just as necessary as in the weekly market; in 1422 John Mawger, John Roper, and John Gynes, were all arrested by the bailiff and later fined for selling salt by false measures.

TOWN GOVERNMENT

Periodically the bishop's steward, receiver, and auditor, rode into the town to hold the manor courts and view of frankpledge, and to settle the manorial accounts. The cost of these visits was charged to those accounts, including the shoeing of the horses on the way. In 1437 their expenses amounted to 5s 8d on the journey to Chelmsford from Clacton, where the bishop had another estate, and 10s more in the town.

The manor courts were held in the Tollhouse, and reasonably decorous behaviour was expected of those present. William Tyler was fined a shilling in 1384, 'because he spoke falsely to the manor bailiff in full court in the presence of the steward, in contempt of court'. In 1417, a chandler, John Holewell, was fined 3s 4d for disrupting the court by arguing, and 'contradicting the evidence of the lord in full court'.

Assisting the steward in court proceedings were the 'sworn' men or jurors. At the court baron, a court for the tenants of land on the lord's manor who owed him services or rent for it and their homage, the jurors were called 'homagers'. At the annual view of frankpledge or court leet (a royal jurisdiction privately held) the jurors were the heads of the tithings, or 'chief pledges'. It was their duty, as the court roll of 1404 explained, 'to present for the king as chief pledges ought'; they drew the court's attention to those inhabitants who misdemeaned themselves and were a nuisance to their neighbours, so that they could be cautioned or punished. It was the court leet and the chief pledges who carried the responsibility for good order in the town.

The chief pledges were usually referred to collectively: 'The chief pledges present that ...', or 'The chief pledges say ...'. Occasionally they were listed in the court rolls, or individually named and fined for not attending court or otherwise

57

failing in their duty. On rare occasions the election of a new chief pledge was recorded. A 'roll of chief pledges' was kept, but none have survived. Analysis of the court rolls suggests that between 1381 and 1422 there were at any one time between 25 and 38 chief pledges on the town roll; that once elected they held that position until they died or left the town; and that they were chosen from the most well-to-do residents, the father often being succeeded by the son. These were the people who had everything to gain economically if the town had a good name as a reputable market, and as a clean place with honest inns for travellers, good food at a fair price, and protection from robbery and assault. Such was the standing of the chief pledges in the administration of the manor that, in the absence of the steward and bailiff, a copyhold tenant on his death-bed could surrender his holding to the use of his will out of court, before witnesses, by the hands of one of the chief pledges, as William Melle did in 1417, to chief pledge William Fyssher.

The tithings for which the chief pledges were responsible were checked annually at the view of frankpledge, to identify and swear in any male residents who had slipped through the frankpledge net. Boys who had recently reached the age of twelve years had to be sworn in, like young John Pye, son of the mason John Pye, found to be 'out of tithing' in 1384. The shifting population of servants employed by householders produced many offenders, either evading inclusion in a tithing, or failing to attend the annual view, like Thomas Byglond, John Scolemayster's servant, in 1383, and Pax, John Gybon's servant, in 1386. Newcomers, too, lately settled in the town, had to be sworn in: the two Harlings, Thomas and John, were found to be resident in the town but out of tithing in 1407.

The executive officer of the courts was the lord's bailiff. Distraint (seizure of goods) was the usual sanction employed to persuade people to pay their rent or court fines, or to comply with some order of the court or custom of the manor. In 1414 a pair of fuller's shears (for trimming the nap) was taken from William Wright, to be held until he swore fealty to the lord as required after the death of his father, the chandler, John Wright, and paid the usual 'relief', or feudal inheritance tax, due to the lord for succeeding to his father's property. Distraint was often resisted: in 1401 John Fyssh and his wife recovered their goods by force from the bailiff's man, who was distraining for unpaid rent; and in 1421 John Newport was fined 12*d* for using force to snatch back from the bailiff himself goods taken to the value of the rent owed. The bailiff could be punished for neglecting his duty; in 1391 he was fined 2*d* for not distraining as ordered on William Arwesmyth, to make him answer for marrying a bondman's daughter without licence. When the steward told the bailiff in 1415 to buy new weights and balances for weighing bread, he warned him that failure to do so would cost him a fine of 3*s* 4*d*.

Unlike the bailiff, who was directly appointed by his lord, the bishop, the other manorial officers, constables, 'affeerers', ale, meat, and fish tasters, and leather searchers, were chosen annually in the court leet. They all faced fines if their duties, unpaid, were not done well. Inferior people were not chosen to these offices, which were shared among the more substantial residents of the town. The town officers' authority ceased at the stone bridge, for Moulsham hamlet had its own officers, elected in the abbot's court. How the town's officers were chosen is never made clear, and their choice was not always recorded on the court rolls. But twice, in 1406 and 1410, the rolls state that the constables and aletasters were chosen 'by the chief pledges'. However much influence the chief pledges may have had on the election of officers, one thing is clear, that the choice of the most important of them, the constables and the 'affeerers', was shared between the inhabitants and the lord of the manor.

Four men were nominated as constables at the court, from whom the lord chose two, who were then sworn in to serve for one year. Often one of them was sworn again the next year, to serve a second year with a new partner: in 1397 Fulk Everard and Ralph Spamvyle served together, then in 1398 Richard Barber was sworn 'in place of Fulk Everard', while Ralph Spamvyle was sworn again, 'as he was before', to be his fellow. So far as the incomplete record of elections can show, the constables were chosen from among the chief pledges, including the most senior and distinguished of them: Adam Gynes, who became a chief pledge by 1391, was chosen as constable in 1421, not long before his death. Some constables held the office many times; Richard Marchall was constable four times in five years in 1406-10, and the shoemaker Robert Chever, who served four times in 1404-12, and again in 1421, may have been chosen in the intervening years as well, for no constables' elections are recorded between 1413 and 1420.

The other chief pledges were expected to support the constables in upholding the law. In 1385 the constables and the chief pledges were presented to the court for not arresting a stranger who came into the town and drew blood in a brawl, and the constables were fined 2*d*. Any inhabitant who was witness to a felony was supposed to raise the hue and cry on the wrongdoer, turning out the whole neighbourhood in pursuit with any weapons to hand; it was an offence not to do so. But it was equally an offence to raise the hue mistakenly or maliciously. When Stephen Baker attacked William Tyler in 1384, drawing blood, William 'justly' raised the hue on Stephen, who was fined not only for a breach of the peace, but for the nuisance he had caused by running away. The hue was justly raised, too, by Joan Cok in 1391, against poor John Cryket, who was 'out of his mind', and disturbed the neighbours roaming around at night beneath their windows, no doubt peeping in. But Richard Feversham was twice fined in 1385 for raising the hue 'unjustly'.

The other officers whose appointment was shared between lord and inhabitants were the 'affeerers', who assessed the fines imposed on delinquents. As with the constables, four names were put forward, 'that the lord may choose two of them'. At the court of 1405 four chief pledges, the spicer, John Warwick, the peltmonger, William Skynner, and two drapers, John Smyth and John Clerk, were chosen,

> '... to affeer the defaults of the court and leet, as by ancient custom they are used to choosing, as they say, so that the lord of the manor may choose two of them whom he wishes to choose; and the lord's bailiff chooses in the name of the lord John Warwick and John Smyth, and they are sworn'.

The affeerers were chosen from among the most senior and experienced of the chief pledges; between 1384 and 1390 William Skynner served as affeerer seven times, and Thomas Roper and John Sponer five times each.

Two aletasters were chosen each year, not from those who brewed ale, but from those who drank or retailed it. The office, like that of constable or affeerer, was often held repeatedly by the same man: John Sponer, who served as aletaster every year between 1386 and 1391, was a retailer of ale, regularly penalised for 'regrating' offences; the shoemaker John Gotier served as aletaster five times in 1403-10. It was not a popular office; in 1410 when Andrew Sadeler and John Couper were chosen, John Couper was sworn in, but Andrew Sadeler 'paid a fine not to be put in that office this year as elected by the chief pledges'. So only one of the old aletasters, John Ferrour, was removed 'and John Gotier stayed on in that office with John Couper'. The aletasters were often fined for doing their office badly. But they had their problems. In the 1380s there were never less than twenty-two men and women regularly brewing ale for sale, sometimes as many as thirty, and some evaded the tasting if they could. In 1406 six people were fined 2*d* each because after they had brewed they had not sent for the aletasters to sample the brew, and because they sold their ale 'in cups and dishes' and not by the statutory sealed measures. In 1421 Alice Fyssh was fined 12*d* and Joan Mawger 4*d*, 'because several times this year they rebelled against the aletasters doing their office as tasters of ale, and would not send for them to taste'.

The election, also in pairs, of fish and meat tasters and leather searchers, is first recorded in 1414. In 1417 the fish and meat tasters were fined for neglecting their duties, but in 1422 William Mason and Thomas Poucher, who had been elected in 1420, were congratulated on having done their office 'faithfully and well'. The court and chief pledges were clearly determined about that time to improve the quality of food sold in the town, for in 1419 four senior chief pledges, Adam Gynes, Thomas Prentys, Robert Chelmsford (Thomas and Nichola Osteler's son), and John Brewer, were chosen to supervise all victuals sold in the market. Adam had by then been a chief pledge for at least twenty-eight years, and Thomas was to become one of the nine 'trustworthy men of Essex' appointed in 1428 to collect in Essex a tax on movables granted by Parliament, an office he filled again in 1431.

Andrew Sadeler and Thomas Saykoc were the two leather searchers elected in 1414. Thereafter at least one of the two leather searchers chosen was always a leather-worker, such as a saddler or cordwainer (shoemaker), who could be expected to know good leather when he saw it. Poor workmanship in tanning and dressing leather had indeed been penalised by the court before 1414; William Hood, the sole offender named between 1382 and 1389, was fined regularly for tanning badly 'in deception of the people'. But by the 1390s other tanners were moving into the town. Three of them, including Hood, were fined in 1390-1, and by the mid-15th century there were about a dozen tanners offering their wares in the market, many of them 'foreigners' from outside the town. The time had come by 1414 for more formal supervision of their trade.

Women were never chosen to any of the manor offices, but many of them were active in business, mainly in the retailing of bread, ale, and victuals; some, like Rose Meller, wife of the miller, brewed and baked. It was usual for a widow to take over her late husband's business. One of these was Mabel Wymond, widow of the innkeeper John Wymond; the site of their inn (site of 63-4 High Street) was identified as Wymonds up to the present century. The formidable Nichola (Colletta) Osteler not only ran her late husband's inn and stalls by the bridge, but continued his quarrel with the bishop over the damage done to their property (site of 51 High Street) when the bridge was rebuilt, and their right to the stalls in front of the inn, until their son Robert was old enough to bring the cases to a satisfactory conclusion. Just as independent was the fishmonger, Margaret Lightfoot, widow of Richard; she had property in both town and hamlet, dealt in fish and general merchandise, employed female hucksters to serve in her shops (site of 56-7 High Street, subsequently known as Lightfoots), owned fish stalls in the Fishrow, and pursued her debtors relentlessly in the manor court.

The manor court's authority was reinforced by by-laws passed 'by the common assent of all the burgesses of the town'. Sometimes these echoed statutory enactments. The two earliest recorded by-laws are entered on the court roll of 1382, which may not be the date of their original enactment, but a re-statement of them after the destruction of the older rolls by the rebels in 1381. These by-laws provided that every Friday the market stalls must be removed from the highway after closure of the market, on pain of a fine of 12*d*; and that all dungheaps on the highway, including those at the townspeople's front doors, must be carried away within one month after they were heaped up, on pain of a fine of 3*s* 4*d*. It was the bailiff's duty to warn the tenants about the by-laws. The by-law relating to the removal of dungheaps was widely ignored, in spite of its restatement almost annually in court, and repeated orders to the bailiff to warn the townsmen of the penalties. Those who heeded court warnings escaped a fine, but those who delayed too long to comply were penalised. Adam Gynes was fined in 1404 for not removing a dungheap piled up close to the Cross. In 1415 the maximum penalty was increased to 6*s* 8*d* and a renewed warning given to the whole town. Yet in 1417 Adam Gynes and eleven others had to be warned again to remove their heaps before Lady Day. In 1420 twelve householders (including four of those warned in 1417) were each fined 3*s* 4*d* at one court. The disposal of the accumulating heaps of stable muck, and domestic and trade filth and refuse of every kind, created a problem which became steadily more acute as the town's population grew and its open space diminished.

Dungheaps were not the only obstructions to passage along the high street. Timber and firewood were often stacked before men's doors. In 1386 the 'stokkes' and 'logges' laid down in the highway opposite Roger Baker's house were 'dangerous to passersby at night'. Many townsmen kept pigs in the backsides of their tenements — one desirable property in the high street was con-veyed in 1384 as 'a messuage and four shops, with a garden, yard, and house for pigs' (site of 28-30 High Street); there was a pigsty by the stone bridge in 1410. Pigs scavenging in the street added to the traffic hazards; the butcher, Adam atte Wall, was fined in 1394 for allowing his pigs to wander in the market-place. Pigs contributed to the squalor of the street, which was also fouled by the droppings of horses, cattle, poultry, and dogs, and littered with garbage of every kind. Butchers, fishmongers, poulterers, cooks, and innkeepers, were only too ready to rid themselves of the refuse of their trades by casting it out into the street. Thomas Matthew and Richard Barber were fined in 1389 for throwing blood and animals' entrails and carcasses into the highway; but John Purchas, who in 1392 threw out carcasses 'by his neighbours' doorways', was fined 'nothing, because he is poor'.

The alternative dumping-place was the river. In 1386 four innkeepers, William and John Prentys, John Gybon, and Thomas Osteler, and two cooks, Nicholas

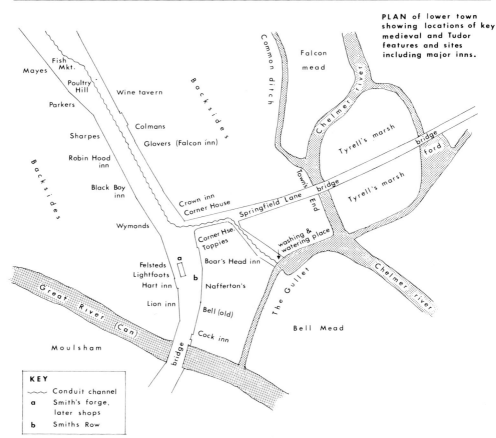

PLAN of lower town showing locations of key medieval and Tudor features and sites including major inns.

KEY
~~~ Conduit channel
a   Smith's forge, later shops
b   Smiths Row

Cook, and John Stalworth, were warned to stop throwing their dung into the river at the bridge; but the practice continued. The first sanitary Act of Parliament in England, which was passed two years later, in 1388, included measures against river pollution. Proclamation was to be made in towns throughout England, 'as well in franchises [such as the 'liberty' of the bishop of London] as without', that 'none of what condition soever he be, cause to be cast or thrown from henceforth any such annoyance, garbage, dung, intrails, nor any such ordure' into ditches or rivers, whereby 'the air there is greatly corrupted and infect, and many maladies and other intolerable diseases do daily happen as well to the inhabitants ... as to other[s] repairing and travelling thither'. In response to the Act, a third by-law was enacted in Chelmsford that year, against throwing filth in the river, carrying a maximum penalty of 6s 8d. But this did not deter the offenders and the fines imposed were paltry. In 1392 John Stalworth and Ralph Hukham were fined 2d for throwing stinking fish in the river. In 1410 fines of only a few pence were imposed on Laurence Reynold and John Cook who 'regularly' polluted the water with entrails and guts, on John Burgelon who cast in dung, and on Robert Doune who threw in a dead horse. In 1407, when Andrew Sadeler, John Gotier, and Robert Osteler, were fined 1d each for throwing filth into the river (in the Gullet), it was said that horses led to water there would not drink, and they were warned that a further offence would cost them 2s.

A fourth by-law of 1407 was aimed at butchers, some of whom were being regularly fined for bad and overpriced meat. Many of them travelled to Chelmsford from outlying parishes such as Baddow, Boreham, the Hanning-fields, Sandon, and Witham. The new by-law forbade them in future to ride to market on the backs of the beasts they were bringing to the shambles for slaughter, because this made the flesh 'hot, abominable, and sooner putrid'; a maximum penalty of 2*s* was set. This by-law was enacted in the same court in which eleven butchers were charged with this practice. The following year twelve butchers defied the by-law; each was fined 3*d* as a warning. When all twelve of them ignored the warning in 1409 they were fined the full 2*s* and the penalty for a further offence raised to 2*s* 6*d*; a solitary first offender that year was warned but not fined. No more breaches of the by-law were recorded until 1413, when three butchers, perhaps newcomers to the market, were fined a few pence for arriving riding on the backs of the beasts they brought to be butchered. The by-law seems thereafter to have proved effective in controlling the practice. Bad meat, however, continued to be offered in the market; in 1414 Richard Davy was fined 3*d* for selling putrid lamb's meat.

PRICES

The court leet kept an eye on the price of goods sold in the town as well as the quality. With monotonous regularity fines were imposed for 'excessive price' and 'excessive profit'. The same offenders appear on the rolls again and again. The fines of a few pence, never more than 6*d*, often 1*d*, were no deterrent, and may well have been accepted as a calculated risk in view of the profits to be made. Indeed, in a court dominated by tradesmen the fines may have been little more than a formality. In only one commodity (the most widely sold, other than bread) is the degree of overcharging in the 1380s known: ale, almost universally drunk in place of water. Ale was being widely sold in the town at fourpence a gallon, four times the usual price. But contemporary prices are seldom quoted in the court rolls, except in the context of dishonesty, debt, or goods distrained. Agnes Huxter was accused in 1384 of pocketing 2*s* 6*d* which she should have handed over to her master and mistress, William and Joan Bygood, the price of two boys' tunics which she had sold for them to Christina and Stephen Baker. In 1385 Margaret Lightfoot claimed that William Colvyle and his wife Beatrice had not paid her for purchases they had made from her, fourpence for an earthenware jar, 2*s* for a brewing tub, and 2*s* for four ells (about five yards) of linen cloth. A mattress and a worsted coverlet seized from William Southwood for distraint in 1388 were valued at 3*s*, and a brass pan taken from a felon and impounded by the constable in 1391, at 12*s*. Two sheets suspected of being stolen in 1387 were valued at 3*s*, and a blue worsted coverlet at 1*s* 6*d*.

In the battle to hold down prices medieval laws condemned the activities of middlemen who tried to create monopolies, buying cheap to sell dear. 'Forestallers' intercepted goods before they reached the market, buying them up 'by the way' from the country people bringing them to the town; the goods were then sold in the market at an enhanced price. 'Regrators' operated similarly within the market, buying up stocks early in the day to resell later at an inflated price when stocks ran out. Regrators and forestallers of ale, bread, fish, 'and other victuals', were fined nearly every time the manor court met. Isabella Bole was accused in 1404 of cornering butter, buying it up, not only 'by the way', but within the market as well. Robert Pulter was fined 6*d* in 1407 for forestalling capons, cocks, and hens, by the way, and warned to do so no more on pain of a heavier fine of 3*s* 4*d*. Peter Couper of Stock and John Fuller were fined 2*s* each in 1400 for regrating wheat and other grain in the market.

At a higher level than the manor court, allegations of excessive prices and dishonest trading practices were heard by the royal justices. An Essex inquiry held before the justices of the King's Bench at Brentwood in 1389, into infringements of the Statute of Cambridge of 1388 regulating wages and prices, produced startling revelations about some of Chelmsford's traders, on the information of their own neighbours. The shoemakers John Fermory and John Chever accused the tanner William Hood of buying raw oxhides and wool-fells (sheepskins) for the last six years, as many as a hundred skins a year, for 6*d*, 18*d*, and 20*d* each, and selling them tanned for 4*s* and 5*s* apiece, making as much as two marks a year excess profit. The two shoemakers were themselves accused by Thomas Osteler and Walter Bowyer of selling their shoes 'at most excessive prices', and for the last six years making as much as 20*s* a year excess profit. Thomas Osteler, John Glover, and others, said that two blanket-makers, John Hull and John Heyward, for the last seven years had made as much as 20*s* a year too much on their blankets. Thomas Osteler, ever the first to complain, with his fellow innkeeper William Prentys, and others, said that Nicholas Cook had been overcharging them for victuals for the last eight years (wine, ale, fish, flesh, biscuits, roast meats, batches of loaves, hay, oats, and horse bread), making as much as 40*s* excess profit each year; Thomas Osteler added that John Stalworth, cook, had also overcharged him, but only to the tune of 2*s* a year excess profit.

The turn of the victuallers to answer came when some of their customers, William Roberd, Thomas Pyebaker, and others, complained that on their visits to Chelmsford over the last six years Thomas Osteler, William and John Prentys, and Joan, wife of John Gybon, had made as much as 20*s* a year excess profit out of them on wine, ale, bread, meat, fish, hay, oats, and horsebread, 'and other victuals appropriate to an inn'. All these innkeepers had been regularly fined in the manor court for overcharging for their victuals. Thomas Osteler was fined 20*s* by the justices at Brentwood for these offences, which he freely admitted. The bakers and brewers did not escape. Thomas Osteler and William Prentys accused Thomas Baker, Robert Baker, and John Balle, of making bread by false weights for the last seven years, making 10*s* a year excess profit. William Hood and John Stalworth led the complaints against nine women (one of them Hood's own wife Alice), and two men, brewers of ale, for selling it in cups and dishes instead of sealed measures, and for charging 4*d* a gallon for it for seven years past, when the usual price was 1*d*, so that each of them made as much as 10*s* a year excess profit.

Chelmsford woolmongers showed up very badly in the 1389 inquiry. Wool and woollen cloth were perhaps the most profitable commodities in which any Chelmsford traders dealt in the 14th century. John of Chelmsford in the 1320s had been one of the wealthy wool merchants who lent money to the king. Thomas Thrower and Adam atte Ponde had belonged to the ring of Essex wool merchants charged with price fixing in 1351, and in the same year were among the highest fined traders in the town and hamlet for paying inflated wages to their employees. Two Chelmsford men, Geoffrey atte Wode and William Boneyr, baker, in 1368 were the Essex sub-collectors of the 'alnage' or duty on woollen cloth sold in the county. In 1376 when Geoffrey Taillour, William Webbe, and William Hosiere complained that a London sub-collector had illegally seized three packs of woollen cloth from them at Ilford, those packs were valued at a hundred marks (£66 13s 4d). In the 1389 inquiry Adam atte Ponde (an old man but still in business), Robert Glover, and Robert Savage, were accused of buying wool for the last six years at Chelmsford and elsewhere, not by the official weights, but by false balances. Adam had bought forty sacks, Robert Glover twenty sacks, and Robert Savage ten sacks, all at the price of four marks a sack, and, by means of their false balances, each stone of wool in their sacks contained sixteen pounds instead of fourteen. Another Chelmsford woolmonger, Geoffrey Glover, also using false balances, had been able to buy eleven pounds of wool for the price of nine, but had only been doing so for three years, and had only bought three sacks.

The King's Bench justices were just as determined to clamp down on excessive wages as on high prices. The 1388 statute against 'outragious and excessive hire' quoted 10s as the approved rate for a carter's 'hire by the year'. In 1389 the justices at Brentwood found that in Chelmsford John Pyttock had been employed as a carter by the bailiff, John Totham, from Michaelmas 1388 to Michaelmas 1389 at an agreed annual wage of £1 6s 8d and his dinner.

SOCIETY

In the late 14th century Chelmsford's innkeepers and cooks, traders and craftsmen, could supply most of the basic needs of travellers, and of the inhabitants and neighbourhood. Corn, salt, meat, fish, and bread, malt, ale, and wine, poultry, butter, spices, and candles, silk, woollen, and linen cloth, were sold. The miller at the bishop's mill, John Osemond (*alias* Meller) ground the inhabitants' corn for them, taking his toll for it. Tailor, hosier, glover, and shoemaker, made coats, tunics, hose, gloves, and shoes. There were carpenters and joiners, a tiler and a mason. Farriers, smiths, and saddlers, attended to horses and harness. A town bounded on both sides by running water attracted skinners and tanners, fullers and dyers. Dyers in particular were prospering, as were the rising élite of the town's traders, drapers and mercers. Ropes were made by Thomas Roper and Adam Gynes; Matthew Parchemynmaker prepared parchment; Walter Joynour, the bowyer, made bows for archery, and John Horner, the fletcher, arrows. The leech dosed the sick with physic, and the barber John Stalworth trimmed hair, pulled teeth, and let blood. Education was provided by Master John Scolemayster, 'teacher of the little ones in this town', whose name occurs between 1381 and 1405, a man of property and considerable standing. He may indeed be the John Rothyngg, 'scolmaister', mentioned in the town as early as 1373; both the men named had a wife called Margery. He may also be the same as John Chapman, 'scolmayster', named in 1389 and 1403. But whether there was one schoolmaster, 'Master John Chapman of Roothing, schoolmaster', or two, or three, it is not possible to say with certainty.

The erratic use of surnames at this period lays many traps. Surnames may be personal or inherited, recent or ancient, derived from the family's or the individual's place of origin, trade, office held (like William Sexteyn in 1392) or even from personal attributes, like Thomas Redhed (1397) and John Longelyfe (1382). Thomas Osteler's son and heir Robert, and all Thomas's five grand-children, bore the surname 'Chelmsford', but Thomas himself never bore any surname but 'Osteler' or 'Hosteler' in public or in local records. John 'Cor-yngham', who swore fealty to the new bishop after the revolt in 1381, John Draper of Corringham (1383), and John Corringham, draper (1385) are one and the same man, and are probably also the John Taillour of Corringham who in 1409 held the tenement called Corringhams (site of Victorian Corn Exchange, demolished in 1969). He may even be the otherwise unidentified John Taillour named in the 1381 poll tax list, in which neither John Draper nor John Corringham appear, as they should.

The inhabitants of late 14th-century Chelmsford were contemporaries of Chaucer. His world was their world, and the town's records reveal characters as colourful as any in his tales: Hugh Pluckrose and William Mustarder, Margery Shorthose and Alice Wardrober, and poor Thomasina, the chaplain's concubine. Thomasina was accused in 1387 of having come dishonestly by her two coverlets (one of them of blue worsted), a mattress, two sheets, a woman's coat, a lining of lamb's-wool, two cushions, and a little box of spice. The courtly elegance of the names bestowed on some of the town's daughters at baptism — Clarissa, Eunice, Nichola, and Beatrice, Letitia, Isabella, and Denise — presents a curious contrast to the lack of comfort, and squalor, of the times they were born into. They grew up accustomed to brutal public spectacles: the beasts openly butchered weekly in the town shambles, the convicted felons, men and women, led to the gallows or, as in 1381, dragged there at the horse's tail; the death of a heretic at the stake. This was William Caleys, a Lollard priest active in 1430 in Norfolk, where he kept schools of heresy, ate meat as often as he 'had lust to' on feast days, had many followers 'right hoomly and prive' with him, and as their leader was degraded from the priesthood, and sent to Chelmsford to be burned alive.

Chelmsford was host to every kind of traveller. In 1398 a pilgrim, John Bataill, halted there, 'en passant en pelerinage devers Jerusalem', to make his will, and persuaded Robert Chelmsford and Geoffrey Colvyle to act as its trustees. One of the town's own chaplains, William Eremyt, had set off in 1390 to travel to foreign parts, and been allowed to take 40s out of the country for his expenses, with letters of exchange to Italian bankers of Lucca for five marks more.

A careful eye was kept on leisure activities in the town, to prevent trouble. Hawise Swety, whose favoured pastimes included scolding her neighbours, steal-ing their poultry, and eavesdropping on their conversations, was reported in 1399 to the manor court and fined for it. When the baker William Bygood took in, day and night and particularly at night, customers so rowdy that nearby residents had no peace for their 'hubbub and chatter', proceedings were taken against him in 1389 before the court of the King's Bench. But this did not reform him. The next year it was the manor court which reprimanded and fined him, for permitting play at checkers (chess) in his house at night, leading to noisy disagreements which disturbed the neighbours. In 1392 his fine was increased, not only for nightly play at chess and tables (backgammon) in his house, but for allowing the neighbours' apprentices to join in; this time a warning that a further offence would cost him a fine of 20s seems to have put an end to his activities.

Not only were chess and backgammon frowned upon; so was a childish game popular in the 1390s — 'playing at ball over the houses of the lord called Le Tolhous and over the church'. In 1394 eleven people were presented at the manor court for indulging in this pastime. Three of them were chaplains and the case against them withdrawn, because they had been summoned to appear before the bishop to answer for their behaviour in a church court. The other culprits were fined from 2*d* to 6*d* each. Their identities show a surprising lack of sophistication among adults who might be supposed to represent the more mature and responsible inhabitants of the town. They included the draper, John Clerk, Laurence Isbrond, a retired citizen and tailor of London, who had travelled on the king's business in Picardy and later settled in Chelmsford as a victualler and wine merchant, Fulk Everard, another tailor (and his servant Martin), and Master John Scolemayster. John Clerk, Fulk Everard, and Laurence Isbrond, were chief pledges. John Fyssh, who was fined 2*d* in 1409 for playing at ball over the 'courthouse', became the manor bailiff a few years later in succession to Nicholas Waleys.

CHAPTER SEVEN

The Fifteenth Century

REBUILDING THE PARISH CHURCH

The choice of the church as a target for the ball-game suggests that it was of modest height, tall enough to present a challenge, but not so tall as to discourage the attempt. By the 15th century the building was perhaps large enough for the regular congregation, but of too unassuming proportions and appearance for the county town of Essex, and for the diocesan business conducted in it from time to time. It was for example the place where the local church courts sat; in 1306 the archdeacon of Essex was inhibited from proceeding with Roysia of Tollesbury's claim that John of Kent was her husband, because the bishop's official or commissary had taken over the case, and cited Roysia to appear before him in the parish church of Chelmsford. By the late 14th century candidates attending Bishop Sudbury's ordination services in the church numbered as many in a single day as 121 in 1368, 165 in 1370, and 126 in 1373.

The church was rebuilt in the 15th and early 16th centuries in the Perpendicular style, but the stages of its rebuilding cannot be precisely dated. John Weever wrote in 1631:

> 'This Church was reedified about some hundred thirtie and seven yeares since, as appeareth by a broken inscription on the out side of the South Wall
> Prey for the good estat of the Townshyp of Chelmsford that hath bin willying and prompt of helpys to [   ] this Chirch and for all them that be
> [   ] MCCCCLXXXIX [1489]'

This inscription, below the battlements of the nave, in raised Gothic letters about nine inches tall, was already 'broken' by 1631, and was completely destroyed in 1800 when the roof of the nave collapsed. In the interval Richard Newcourt (or his printer) in 1710 introduced confusion about the date by misquoting Weever's date as MCCCLXXXIX (1389). William Holman in 1723 accurately recorded Weever's date, but in 1747 the 'ingenious Mr John Booth' (as Morant called him) chose to investigate the inscription for himself. An ancient inhabitant of the town, William Humphreys, whom Booth consulted, claimed to have copied the inscription carefully 'some years ago', and to have read the date as 1424. Booth, dissatisfied, 'gott upon the leads of the South Isle very near this Inscription above', and examined it. After pointing out that 'severall of the Lettrs have been cutt away to putt Leaden Spouts to carry the water from the top of the church', Booth concluded that Humphrey's version of the wording was correct in general sense but not in detail, and that in spite of the damage most of the wording could be read, most of it, that is, 'except the latter part of the date'. He inserted the result of his investigation neatly in Holman's manuscript, where Morant found it. Morant published Booth's reading of the inscription, but unfortunately ignored his warning about the date, and adopted the ancient inhabitant's dubious '1424'. Later authorities have usually followed Morant, a notable exception being the researchers of the *Royal Commission on Historical Monuments* in 1921, who preferred the later date of 1489 recorded by Weever in 1631.

From the position of the inscription, just below the nave battlements on the south side of the church, and above the clerestory windows, the date on it must have marked completion of the nave and clerestory. The inscription's prayer for the good estate of the township of Chelmsford and, according to Booth, the 'willers and procorers of helpers to thys werke', also embraced, in Booth's reading, '... them that first began and longest shall contenewe ...'. Such contemporary written evidence as there is, and the oldest surviving features of the church, support a rebuilding begun some years before 1489, and continued for many years afterwards.

The work must have begun later than 1406. In that year John de Sheryngton, once Sir John Mounteney's chaplain, wrote his will. He left sums of money to the high altar of the parish church, to three named chaplains and 'other' unnamed chaplains, to a clerk, and to two minor clergy serving the church. The rest of his estate was to be distributed in alms and works of charity for the good of his soul and the souls of Sir John Mounteney and his wife Cicely and all the faithful departed. It seems unlikely that a will of this kind, consisting entirely of provision for the parish church, local clergy, and works of piety, would have made no contribution to the fabric of the church if any repair or rebuilding were then in progress or even contemplated.

The oldest surviving features of the church are the west arch of the north chapel, the graceful 'Fan Arch' which divides it from the chancel, the west arch of the south chapel, the arcade in the south side of the chancel opening into the south chapel, and the south chapel itself; they date from the first half of the 15th century. This suggests that rebuilding may have begun with the north and south chapels associated with the two religious guilds established before 1392, the Corpus Christi guild, and the guild of Our Lady. In the late-16th century these two chapels were usually referred to (for example in connection with burials) as the south or north 'gylde', 'gilde', 'yielde', or 'yelde'. One of them was mentioned in the 1560s as the 'Corpus Christi yelde'; Mr Ayliffe's wife was buried in Corpus Christi 'gylde' in 1574, and John Bridges in Corpus Christi 'gilde' in 1575. This was the south chapel. The chapel in which from 1550 the Mildmay family chose to be buried, the Lady Chapel, was the north chapel. In the south wall of the south chapel is a 15th-century 'piscina', near the altar, and a doorway, known in 1585 as the 'yelde door', leads out of the chapel into the churchyard. The limited 1983 excavation was not able to determine whether the north and south guild chapels were built on the site of earlier ones.

Weever's inscription date of 1489 is compatible with the oldest features of the north and south arcades of the lofty nave, the clerestory, and north and south aisles. The earliest written evidence of rebuilding occurs eight years later, in the will made in 1497 by a wealthy dyer, Richard Corall. Besides 6s 8d for the repair of the church, he left 13s 4d to the 'new building and making of the chancel', and ordered that the house which he lived in, with all the utensils and materials of his trade, be sold by his executors 'at the best price possible', and 40s from the sum raised given to the churchwardens towards 'the making and rebuilding of the bell-tower'. This conforms to the late 15th-century date usually attributed to the chancel arch and massive square west tower of three stages. Other bequests towards building the 'new steeple' followed, in 1503 (twice), 1504, 1506, and 1517. Some stone material from the old church was incorporated in the walling of the new tower. Henry Halsted, the parish clerk, left 3s 4d in 1522 to 'the making of Chelmsford porch'. The ambiguity of words makes it difficult to interpret work mentioned between 1529 and 1536. 'Yeld' is a variant of 'guild', but it is also an obsolete contemporary form of 'aisle'. In 1529 the wealthy draper Richard Humfrey gave four marks to the 'byldynge of the yle of the south side of the church'; in 1534 Robert Pese provided 40s 'to the buyldying of the new yeldes to be made to my parish churche ... that ys to saye at suche tyme when the parish do go in hande with them, 20s, and at the endying of the same worke, other 20s'; and in 1536 Thomas Stamer gave 6s 8d towards the 'building' of the church. The work undertaken at that time may have been the lengthening westwards of the aisles to flank the new tower. But it may equally, in view of Robert Pese's caution, have been work contemplated but never carried out.

The new church was built of flint rubble intermixed with blocks of stone. The roof was covered with lead. The church comprised chancel, north and south chapels, nave with clerestory, north and south aisles, porch, and west tower. A door in the north wall of the chancel led into a small low vestry next to the north chapel, with a little room over it; this room, which had a window in it looking into the church, was being used in 1557 to store the parish 'harness' or armour. The nave and aisle walls were embattled. The decorative south porch, of stone and flint in an elaborate inlay pattern, also had a room over it. The porch was topped by a panneled and pinnacled parapet. The parapet of the west tower was also embattled and pinnacled, and its west door carried the armorial motifs of the Bourchier and de Vere families. The Bourchiers owned the Patchinghall estate in Chelmsford and Broomfield. The de Veres owned no property in Chelmsford, but in 1464 Sir William Bourchier, son of Henry Bourchier, earl of Essex, married as his first wife Isabel, daughter of John de Vere, earl of Oxford. Surmounting the tower was a lantern supporting a slender spire; in 1576 a carpenter was employed to work on a frame in the 'lantrone of the steple' to hang the 'sance'. or *Sanctus* bell. Both lantern and flèche are shown on John Walker's map of 1591.

When Holman visited Chelmsford church in 1723 he described 'a sort of chappel' on the north aisle of the church. It seemed to him to be

'... as old as the church, but for what purpose founded I know not, unlesse for some of the chanteries that formerly belonged to the church.'

Peter Muilman added in 1771 that a doorway in the north aisle led into it. The 1983 excavation uncovered, beneath the outer north aisle built in 1873, the flint rubble and medieval brick foundations of this little building, which had been attached to the north wall of the north aisle. This may have been the chantry of St John, founded to provide a priest to sing mass at the altar of St John the Baptist, and, like the other two guild chaplains, to help to serve the cure. The chantry was one of the beneficiaries of Richard Corall's will of 1497.

The interior of the church was elaborately decorated and furnished. A 17th-century former inhabitant, describing the nave, wrote

'... the roof of the body of the church, which is very high, seemed to rest on the heads of divers Angels resemblances, which resemblances were solid wood as large as the body of a man, and plac'd on the sides of the church just beneath the roof at distances from one end thereof to the other. The inside of the roof

The late-15th-century porch of St Mary's parish church, now the cathedral church of St Mary the Virgin, St Peter, and St Cedd

was adorned with a great number of angels displayed, as if all on the wing overhead, and large bodies'.

The aisle roofs were more simple, but they too rested on the heads of small wooden figures and the timbers were carved with running foliage. The twelve apostles were 'curiously painted' upon the side of a gallery at the west end of the church; their date, on an inscription 'imperfect' by the 18th century, was read

71

then as, '1535'. The gallery may have housed the 'great organs' which needed a stopper mending in 1558. Richard Corall asked in 1497 to be buried on the north side of the church before 'Le Rodeloft', and made bequests towards the upkeep of the Corpus Christi and Our Lady guilds and the lights of St John the Baptist, to the lights before an image of St Ursula, and to 'necessary repairs' to the Mounteney Lady Chapel in the churchyard.

Perhaps the greatest glory of the new church was the four-light east window. This was described in 1643 as,

> '... a goodly fair window ... in which was painted the History of Christ from his Conception to his Ascension; and to perpetuate the memory of the benefactors, in the vacant places there were the Eschochions and Arms of the Ancient Nobility and Gentry who had contributed to the building and Beautifying that fair structure'.

Holman quoted a Visitation of 1634 as recording other escutcheons displayed in the timber ceiling of the nave, alongside the angels. They included the arms of the City of London, whose citizens had invested eagerly in the bishop's new town from the first, and the arms of the Drapers Company, the trade which by the late-14th century ranked foremost in the business hierarchy of the town. Among the families represented were the Warners of Great Waltham, the Bourchiers, earls of Essex and lords of Patchinghall, the Mounteneys of Mountnessing, the Beachamps of Sandon and the Hanningfields, and their kinsmen, the Nevilles and Mowbrays.

THE LATE MEDIEVAL TOWN, 1461-1509

While the church was being rebuilt the town continued to grow. With competition for space on the high street frontage, every vacant piece of ground, however small, was built upon, and cartways leading between buildings to the backsides behind them were bridged by gatehouses. The frontage was becoming fused into a solid block of buildings. Upper storeys were added, often jettied out over the street, and wings built on at right angles to the street, running down the backsides. The proportions of some buildings were becoming such that in 1464 Walter Hale could refer in his will to 'my great tenement'. At the same time, some larger frontage properties were being divided into smaller units. The inn which John de Benenton had owned in the 1350s, paying the unusually high fixed manor rent of 10s 8d, had been broken up into three parts as early as 1402-3, and the rent divided: 8s for the inn, known by 1467 as the Robin Hood (site of 73 High Street); 8d for a garden, soon built upon, on one side of the inn (site of 72 High Street); and 2s for a house, garden and yard, on the other side of it, given by 1428 to the Corpus Christi guild (site of 74-5 High Street).

The manor court could only control new building in the town if the work went beyond permission given, or if it encroached on the lord's waste ground, which was being steadily whittled away by the granting of 'new rents'. When William Aleyn, who had a leather stall next to Potterslane on the corner of the leather stalls, built a penthouse over it in 1471, 'where of old nothing so roofed used to be', he was ordered to take it down. The shoemaker, Richard Biggemore, had to make his peace with the lord in 1481, after building an enclosed stall on open ground under the eaves of his inn (site of 1 High Street); what he had done in effect was add on to the front of his inn a little shop built on a strip of the lord's waste.

By the end of the 15th century the Shoprow formed a complex group of buildings also known as 'Le Medyllrow', and it was still growing. At the head of it by the cornmarket the mercer John Munde, for an extra rent of 1*d*, was allowed in 1480 to take up another 48 by 16 feet of waste on the north and west sides of his house. A small garden nearby was fenced in by 1499. On the east side of the fishmarket Robert Lyston was granted 40 by 14 feet in 1455 to put up movable stalls on market and fair days. The smallest space was worth paying rent for: in 1492 the butcher, John Biglon, was willing to pay an annual rent of 2*d* for a pitch measuring 8 by 4 feet in the Fleshmarket. Between the Shoprow and the Leathermarket a new quarter of the market had come into being by the 1460s, Potterslane.

Inevitably development spread to the churchyard. By 1428 cottages were springing up on the south side of the churchyard on both sides of the south gate, next to the Tollhouse, and facing the Cross and conduit. By the end of the century there were at least five cottages and small houses there. In 1504 the owners, including the wardens of the Corpus Christi guild, were ordered to remove their back doors leading into the churchyard and stop up the doorways; household refuse and slops thrown out into the churchyard, and gossiping neighbours on the doorstep, could hardly have been acceptable to the churchwardens.

No doubt many petty trespasses on the waste escaped notice. But Humphrey Tyrell was caught out in 1498. He had not only put up a stall on a narrow strip of waste beside his house, a foot wide and ten feet long, 'to the prejudice of the lord and detriment of the cathedral church of St Paul's, London', but had also set up a free-standing sign on the waste in the street outside his inn, the Lion (site of 51-4 High Street), to advertise it. In 1490 the landlord of the Boar's Head had been in trouble for setting up a similar sign. This practice may have begun about the 1420s, when several requests were made for permission to erect two posts 'in the way' outside men's houses, for unspecified purposes, and fines imposed for posts put up without permission. Inn signs standing out in the street were to impede the traffic and passers-by for three hundred years before steps were taken to remove them. The only minor alleviation of the growing clutter of the street was the demolition by Sir Thomas Tyrell (d.1510) about 1479 of the smith's forge standing in the middle of the street towards the stone bridge, opposite the Boar's Head; but space being at a premium the site was inevitably built on again within a century.

The pressure on space in the town was a symptom of its economic success. In 1494 it was designated by act of parliament the Essex town to be 'limited for the safe custody of weights and measures according to the king's standard'. This reform of King Henry VII aimed to establish common standards throughout the realm. The king's standards of weight and measure, made of brass, were delivered in each shire to the town designated by the act, to remain there in the custody of the mayor or (as in Chelmsford) the bailiff. All weights and measures were to be copied from those standards, marked with the crowned letter H, examined and signed by the custodian, inspected twice a year, and supervised by the justices of the peace. The act also established uniformity of quantities: for corn, 8 bushels to a quarter; for wool, 14 lb to a stone and 26 stone to the sack.

Property in the town was sought after by London citizens, often purely as an investment. Henry Somer, citizen and merchant haberdasher of London, in the late 15th century owned no less than four adjoining properties in the back lane behind the Shoprow (the equivalent of most of the west side of Tindal Street, formerly nos. 14-23). Henry Somer had no personal or family interest in the town, did not attend court as a tenant of the manor or serve any local office, and had no business interest in the town other than the rents from his properties and anticipation of their rising value. When he died his will, proved in 1502, listed extensive charitable, religious, and personal bequests, none of which benefited Chelmsford, its church, its poor, or any of its inhabitants; the Chelmsford property was all devised to the mayor of London, Sir John Shaa, in return for his help to Somers's executors in carrying out the provisions of the will.

In New Street, too, building increased in the 15th century, particularly opposite the churchyard. About 1396 the large Maynetrees property (site of 54-9 New Street) was divided between the two daughters of John and Margaret Taillour, Joan, who married one of the chief pledges, Clement Warynger (*alias* Wallinger), and Isabel, who married John Sparew. The Wallingers were to be a leading family in the town for three hundred years. After Isabel's daughter Agnes, who married William Skinner, died childless in 1475, and her husband three years later, most of the Maynetrees property (sites of 54-7 New Street) reverted to Joan and Clement's son, Stephen Wallinger. The rest of it (site of 58-9 New Street) on the corner became detached from the Manytre inheritance. North of Maynetrees at the beginning of the 15th century lay a number of small separate holdings, a few houses, a croft, some gardens, and meadow. John Harling, who first appeared in Chelmsford in 1407, and was elected a chief pledge in 1422, was living in New Street by 1421; over the years he acquired and united all the former holdings there of Robert Dyer (Deigher), and of the Romayne, Sadeler, and Mason families. His son Guy inherited them all in 1453. Guy, who was to give his name to what became one of the most prestigious properties in the town, Guy Harlings, is a rather obscure figure, for no manor court records have survived between 1428 and 1461, and he died in 1470. He is mentioned once as a tailor, but his principal business was that of a brewer. Twice a year regularly from 1461 to 1470 he was fined for breaches of the regulations for brewers, and his fines were often double those of the other brewers. His widow Joan continued the business after his death, ignoring the regulations as consistently as her late husband had. She also grew saffron, and was penalised in 1473 for making a rubbish heap of the saffron 'paringes' in the churchyard opposite. Guy Harling also owned the house called Mayes opposite the fishmarket (site of New London Road gap), and the manor of Glamvyles and farm called Enfeldys in Felsted. But he lived in his house in New Street, next to his maltinghouse with a chamber built over it, his yard, croft with ponds and pits, and four new houses with gardens. His daughter Joan married one of the town's senior chief pledges, the mercer John Cornish the elder.

Holman stated in 1723 that the house called 'Gay Harlands' in Chelmsford was built by Thomas Wiseman, second son of John Wiseman (fl. *c.*1434) of Great Waltham. No other reference to a connection between the Wiseman family and the New Street house has been found, but one is possible. When John Harling, Guy's son, died in 1485, John's young nephew, John Cornish junior, inherited

Guy Harlings. The Cornishes lived in Mayes, which Guy's widow had given to her son-in-law in 1485, but they did not sell Guy Harlings until 1516, when Roger Alford bought it from them. Before 1516 the house could have been leased to Thomas Wiseman. Certainly he was living in Chelmsford in 1502, in business as a tallow-chandler, and was elected a chief pledge in that year. He may have rebuilt or altered the house while occupying it as John Cornish's tenant.

On the west side of New Street, north of the churchyard, lay two crofts of land of about two acres each, Waces, and Barn Croft. These had become enclosed from the lord's field called Churchfield in the 14th century, in the course of the progressive fragmentation and alienation of those parts of the lord's demesne which lay closest to the town. Waces was described in 1382 as, 'Two acres of land once Wacye lying in Cherchefeld'. On the fringe of these two crofts, alongside New Street, cottages, or 'two cottages under one roof', with little gardens, were appearing, some of them identified as having been 'sometime parcel of Waces'. One of these cottages was given by William Skinner (d.1478) as an almshouse for the poor.

By the end of the 15th century many properties in the town had assumed the identities which, in contrast to the anonymous 'messuages' and 'tenements', 'shops' and 'inns', of earlier years, were to distinguish them one from another until street numbers were adopted in 1876. Usually it was the name of some owner which became permanently attached, such as Chandlers, Glovers, Wymonds, Thorpes, Mayes, Maynetrees, and Guy Harlings. Inns were identified by their signs, among them the original (White) Hart, first recorded as the 'Hert' in 1416 (site of 55 High Street), and the Lion (1455; site of 51-4 High Street); the Robin Hood (1467; site of 73 High Street), Boar's Head (1469; site of 40-1 High Street), Crane (1470; site of 4-6 High Street), and Cock (1470; site of 49-50 High Street); the 'Wulsak' (1478; site of 15-17 High Street), Blue Boar (1491; site of 84 Duke Street), and Saracen's Head (1539; site of 3 High Street).

RELIGIOUS PROPERTY

A great deal of property in the town belonged to religious foundations by the end of the 15th century. The most ancient endowment comprised a group of adjoining sites at the upper end of the east side of the high street, facing the corn-market (sites of 4-6 and 7-8 High Street), together with a meadow in Tunman-mead behind them. In 1347-8 Philip de Aungre and his wife Alice gave to the college of Thele or Stanstead St Margaret's in Hertfordshire three messuages and some land in Chelmsford and Broomfield, to support a chaplain to pray for them daily at the college. In 1385 the warden and chaplains at Thele leased part of this property, 'two messuages and two gardens, side by side', to John Spicer of Chelmsford for 200 years; a garden next to them had already been leased by the college to John Wright, carpenter. In 1431 all the endowments of the college were transferred to the prior of the hospital of St Mary, Elsyngspitell, in London. By 1470 part of the hospital's property had become the Crane inn (site of 4-6 High Street); the name Crane Court survived on the site until it was redeveloped in 1967.

The rest of the religious property in the town was mainly owned by the three guilds in the parish church dedicated to Our Lady, Corpus Christi, and St John the Baptist, by the chantry of Our Lady in Mounteney's chapel in the church-yard, and by the guild of St John the Baptist in Writtle. The social guild of the Holy Trinity, founded in the 14th century, had no property, and seems to have lapsed, for it is not mentioned after 1392. The guilds' property was given to support chaplains to say masses for ever for the souls of their founders and benefactors, and to assist in serving the cure in the parish church. The Corpus Christi and Our Lady chapels in the church were sometimes chosen for burial: Roger Alford, who died in 1517 soon after buying Guy Harlings from John Cornish, asked to be buried in 'the chapell before Our Lady of Petye in Chelmesford church'. The butcher, John Biglon (d.1521) asked to be buried in Corpus Christi guild, next to his wife Florence, who had died in 1509.

The Corpus Christi guild, or 'Petytgeld' (1414), owned three fish stalls and the sites in the high street of numbers 13, 14, and 74-6. For some years before 1428 the guild owned the sites of numbers 56 and 57 and a shop in the Poultry on the sites of numbers 79-80 High Street; but these sites were confiscated by the bishop, because they had been given to the guild without his permission. The Corpus Christi guild also had property at the upper end of the west side of the town, once Master John Scolemayster's (sites of 86-90 Duke Street), and two little houses by the south gate of the churchyard (part of the present Shire Hall site). The guild of Our Lady in the parish church had the equivalent of the site numbers 67-8, 71 and 72 in the High Street, another house once John Scole-mayster's (site of 85 Duke Street), the Priest's House by the churchyard (site behind 10 Duke Street), a house on the south side of the churchyard (site of 4-5 Tindal Square), and two small sites on the north side of Springfield Lane. As the Priest's House by the churchyard was also known as the 'Vicarage', the chaplain of the guild of Our Lady may have served, not only as chantry priest, but also as the rector's vicar, or 'chaplain of the parish church', an office which still existed in the 1470s. Mounteney's chantry chapel of Our Lady in the churchyard was en-dowed with a little priest's house opposite the churchyard (site of 83 Duke Street), and property in Writtle. The guild of St John the Baptist owned a little house and garden for the priest on the north side of the churchyard (site of the National Boys School built in 1886 in Church Street). The chapel of St John the Baptist in Writtle owned a house (site of 79 Duke Street, part of the present County Hall site) opposite the Pightle. The pious donors of all this guild property are unknown, with the exception of the fishmonger Margaret Lightfoot, who was a benefactress in 1392 of the Corpus Christi and Our Lady guilds, and Nicholas Wollebergh, a fishmonger of Old Fish Street in London, who by his will dated 1407 and proved in 1420 ordered all his property (not named) in Chelmsford to be sold after his death and two-thirds of the proceeds devoted to the maintenance of a chantry in Chelmsford church.

The guilds, managed by their wardens and trustees, met a real need in the town, where there was a rapid turnover of rectors. In the sixty years between the institution of John Arundell in 1443 and the resignation of John Denby in 1502 no less than ten rectors held the living. Most of them held other livings elsewhere, particularly in London. One of them, John Arundell, for reasons unknown was deprived of the living in 1456. William Poteman in 1466 resigned simultaneously as rector of Chelmsford, canon of St Paul's Cathedral, and warden of All Souls' College, Oxford. So brief was the average incumbency, often non-resident, that no late 15th-century rector can have had much influence on the long-drawn-out rebuilding of the church, or on the spiritual life of the town. Without the chaplains supported by the guilds the parish church would have been ill served. The guilds may also have been associated with the 'players of Chelmsford', whose performance in 1490, probably at the Howard family seat at Stoke by Nayland on the Suffolk border, was rewarded by Thomas Howard, earl of Surrey, with 6s 8d. In 1539 the Dunmow churchwardens hired players' garments from Chelmsford, to costume their own players for performances on the feast of Corpus Christi.

In addition to the guild holdings, many properties in the town were charged with the cost of keeping up obits or anniversaries, sometimes for ever. An obit for Thomas Burre, who died at a date unknown after 1428, and his wife Joan, charged on a cottage in Duke Street by the churchyard (site of 10 Duke Street), provided for a requiem mass to be sung for their souls, and the bells to be rung, every year for ever on the Feast of Saints Crispin and Chrispinian, the patron saints of shoemakers. As this feast was also the anniversary of Agincourt in 1415, if Thomas was not a shoemaker, perhaps he was a veteran of the battle. After several changes of ownership the anniversary was still a charge on the cottage when it was sold to Richard Pratt in 1505. In the centre of the high street, 'Glovers Obits', charged since 1411 on three adjoining properties (sites of 28-30 High Street), paid for prayers for ever for Robert Glover, the fraudulent woolmonger of the 1380s; a little higher up the street Nycolles (site of 23 High Street) was forever charged with an obit for the souls of the draper Thomas Chalke, who died in 1498, and his wife Alice. Richard Corall the dyer, on the other hand, in his will of 1497, provided, not a perpetual rent, but a once-for-all sum of ten marks to pay a suitable priest to celebrate mass daily in the parish church for one whole year after his death, for the benefit of his soul, the souls of his three former wives, Joan, Joan, and Joan, and the souls of all their parents and friends. Ten marks a year seems to have been the standard rate for daily prayers. Roger Alford of Guy Harlings in 1517 provided ten marks a year for three years for a good honest priest to sing for his soul, the soul of Elizabeth his wife, who survived him, and the souls of all Christian people. As additional insurance against the frightening uncertainties of the after life, Roger also provided money to be disposed in deeds of charity, including 12d apiece to twenty honest maidens of the parish, 'for the health' of all their souls, and arranged for the reversion of Guy Harlings after his wife's death to be sold, and part of the proceeds used to buy a piece of land or meadow worth 10s a year to pay for an annual obit for him forever.

Many anniversaries coupled prayers for the dead with provision for the living poor. Almshouses, mentioned in 1478 on the west side of New Street ('Lez Almeshows'), and in 1527 next to the Blue Boar in Duke Street ('Le Almishowse'; site of 84 Duke Street) were connected respectively with the obits of William Skinner and William Heyward. Other obits contributed annual sums of money for distribution in alms. The fishmonger Robert Daysy, one of the most senior chief pledges, who died in 1481, sought indulgence in the next life for his shortcomings in this one by the gift of two little houses on Poultry Hill in the Shoprow (site of 79-80 High Street), confiscated from the Corpus Christi guild some years before, as almshouses for poor people.

SOCIETY

No realistic estimate of the total population of town by the end of the 15th century can be made. But the 420 adults over the age of fourteen years in the whole parish (240 in the town and upland, and 180 in Moulsham hamlet), who paid the poll tax in 1377, may be compared with estimates made by the chantry commissioners appointed in 1547, of eight hundred 'or more' communicants in the parish, later amended to 'a thousand at the least'. Subsidy returns excluded children and all the adults who did not pay tax. But it is worth noting that whereas in 1327 there were 73 taxpayers in the parish (43 in Chelmsford, owing £3 10s 9¼d, and 30 in Moulsham, owing £3 2s 0¾d), by 1523 there were 138 taxpayers (97 in Chelmsford, owing £32 4s 8d; 41 in Moulsham, owing £8 1s 10d). The gap between the town and hamlet in both numbers and wealth had significantly widened.

The town was constantly absorbing newcomers, like the Harlings in 1407. Richard Corall's roots were in Warwickshire, where his brother William still lived in 1497, and Richard remembered his brother's daughter and a church in the Forest of Arden in his will. In 1426 John Sexteyn, born in Holland, was living in his own house in the high street (site of part of 76 High Street), protected by royal letters permitting him to 'inhabit the realm peaceably and enjoy his goods'. A similar royal mandate was issued in 1481 on behalf of Thomas Orygge *alias* Rygge, born in Scotland, and dwelling in Chelmsford. The free market in real estate in the town was conducive to constant changes of ownership by purchase, marriage, and inheritance, and with many absentee or multiple owners there were ample openings for leaseholders. Richard Corall, who owned two properties, lived at his works, alongside the leaden vats, cisterns, and furnace of the dyer's trade, all conveniently situated next to the river and wooden bridge in Springfield Lane (site of 5, later 11, then 38 Springfield Road); but his valuable property in the high street, Olivers (site of 9-12 High Street) he leased to a pewterer, John Gogge.

Noblemen and knights were numbered among the bishop's tenants, such as Henry Bourchier, earl of Essex, and Sir Thomas Tyrell (d.1510); and 'gentlemen', a new term current in the town by 1479, when John Darsey, 'gentleman', was the victim of assault by John Fayrer, fishmonger. Wills testify to the widening range of domestic goods and personal possessions. Townsmen (and the more well-to-do in the hamlet) whose standard of living had risen by the end of their lives distributed their possessions with care. For his son Thomas, William Copildik (a chief pledge who lived on the north side of Springfield Lane, served as constable in 1492, and died in 1502) reserved his best flat piece of silver, a brass pot, his second-best maser (wooden bowl), four pewter platters, and a russet gown lined with blue; and for his daughter Ellen, a featherbed and bolster, a pair of blankets, a blue coverlet, his best maser and second best flat piece of silver, a little brass pot, four pewter dishes, and two salt-cellars. The rest of his goods he left to his wife Agnes. In 1504 a Moulsham plumber, John Tomson, set aside in his will an ample portion for his young daughter Anne on the day of her marriage: the house next door to her mother's, a featherbed, bolster, and pillows, six silver spoons, a 'garnish' (set) of pewter vessels, three brass pots, two brass pans, a chafing dish, two kettles, a dripping pan, a spit and andirons (spit support), a salt-cellar, a gridiron, and a frying pan, a cupboard, a 'banker' (tapestry covering), six cushions, six pairs of sheets, two 'borde' (table) cloths, two towels, a double table, a form, a latten basin and ewer, two bell candlesticks, and two plain candlesticks. The plumber may have done well for himself working on the lead roof of the new church; indeed, he left 40s towards building the new steeple, provided the churchwardens would 'goo or ryde as them please' to collect the money from Sir Thomas Tyrell, who owed it to him. His wife's house was charged with 8s to provide a requiem mass for his soul for ever. Richard Corall's three wives having predeceased him, he disposed of their best gowns carefully: to his niece Joan, who kept house for him, a mustard-coloured gown and a crimson gown harnessed (ornamented) with silver, and to another kinswoman a green gown harnessed with silver.

Roger Alford of Guy Harlings had an elegant gentleman's wardrobe to dispose of in 1517: harnessed silver girdles; doublets of black velvet, red leather, and green sarsenet; coats and gowns of camlet; a fox fur; one russet gown furred with white and another furred with black and guarded (trimmed) with red; a tawny gown furred with black and matching tawny hose; gaberdines and a chamber coat. These were shared out between his sons, his stepchildren, and his friends, including Richard Pratt, together with his coverlet of tapestry work, silver goblets, embossed piece of silver, silver spoons, sword and buckler, 'flight bows' and crossbow, colts and gelding, saddles, bridles and harness. His silver and gilt crown was reserved as a gift to Our Lady of Walsingham.

TOWN GOVERNMENT

Apart from the steward's conduct of manor court proceedings, and general vigilance over the bishop's interests in the town, and the lord's right to appoint the bailiff and share in the choice of constables and affeerers, the town was governed in the late 15th century by the bailiff and the chief pledges. Although the bailiff was the bishop's man, his local ties were strong. The family of Robert Lyston, bailiff from c.1458, had held property and been in business in the town since at least the 1380s. Robert himself was married to Albreda (Aubrey), a granddaughter of Thomas and Colletta Osteler, and daughter of Robert and Beatrice Chelmsford, the innkeepers at the Lion; he was therefore brother-in-law to Richard Chelmsford, a vintner, Robert junior, a draper, William and Juliana. Robert Lyston, moreover, was not only the bailiff and farmer of the manor and demesne, he was also landlord of the inn in the high street later known as the Saracen's Head. Robert's successor, Thomas Tendring, bailiff from c.1465 until some time after 1505, had been connected with the town for at least twenty years before he became bailiff, and he, too, ran the Saracen's Head inn. Indeed, he seems to have experienced some difficulty in reconciling his duties as bailiff and his interests as a victualler, for in 1473 he was fined 8d for obstructing the meat and fish taster and refusing to allow him to carry out his office. By the time Thomas became bailiff the office was becoming so onerous that in 1486 he required a deputy.

In the 1460s it was usual for two courts a year to be held. An autumn 'general' court, at the beginning of November, was mainly concerned with estate business, such as admissions and surrenders, and manorial rents, reliefs, and heriots. The annual Whitsun court leet was the town's governmental assembly. The steward presided over it, the bailiff carried out its orders, and the chief pledges initiated its business and endorsed its decisions. The roll of the 1490 court records:

'All the chief pledges there, that is, Richard Pratt (*and 23 others named*) present that all that is written above and below is agreed and approved by them; and they choose Thomas Broun and Nicholas Heyward to be aletasters, Richard Kele and Robert Downham to be meat and fish tasters, John Biggemore and John Banys to be leather searchers, and Richard Maryon and John Elys to be constables.'

Earlier rolls of 1478-9 make it clear that the chief pledges, when more of their number were required, chose them too. The chief pledges constituted, in fact, a self-perpetuating oligarchy.

The rural Upland still had its own half a dozen or so chief pledges, concerned only with Upland matters. The number of the town's chief pledges varied from year to year, but averaged about thirty-two. When the court leet was held, only about twenty of them were picked to be sworn in to make the presentments, and to take part in the choice of officers and other business, including the enactment of by-laws. By the 1480s a small group of up to a dozen of the chief pledges were being sworn in regularly, year after year, unless their names were marked in draft lists as 'sick', 'excused', 'absent' with no reason given, or, finally, 'dead'. These few may be identified as the effective governors of the town. The other chief pledges who made up the numbers of those sworn at the annual court were only occasionally sworn, though they might become, in time, members of the regular group. The characteristics which distinquished the dominant group were seniority as chief pledges, property-holding, business prominence, and experience of local office. Typical of them was the draper Thomas Chalke. He owned property, in the town (site of 23 High Street), in New Street (site of 29 New Street), and in the Upland. He was elected a chief pledge in 1467, served as aletaster in 1467, constable in 1471, meat and fish taster in 1472, and affeerer at least seven times from 1473; he became one of the dominant group about 1484, continuing until his death in 1498. He was also a man of recognised standing in the county, appointed in 1492 one of the Essex collectors of a parliamentary subsidy.

By contrast, the shoemaker John Biggemore never became one of the ruling group, although he had been a chief pledge since before 1472. He was only occasionally sworn in, and was several times fined for default as a chief pledge. He served as constable twice, as leather searcher eight times, and as meat and fish taster twice, and in 1486 he was deputy bailiff. In 1498 he was one of those sworn, but in 1499 his name was struck off the list of chief pledges, with the terse comment, 'pauper'. A townsman who for whatever reason suddenly became destitute had no place among the chief pledges, much less among their élite.

For many years one man, Richard Pratt, was the leader of the ruling group. His name headed the list of those sworn every year between 1486 and 1508 except 1487, 1492, and 1493. In 1487 the old dyer, John Bolle senior, who had been absent in 1486, headed the list above Pratt, who was also sworn; but Bolle died the next year. In 1492 and 1493 Pratt was absent, and Thomas Chalke headed the lists. Pratt may have continued to predominate after 1508, for he was still alive in

1517; but the court rolls for the years between have not survived. In the final years of the 15th century and early years of the 16th the members of the ruling group are easily identifiable. Besides Richard Pratt, old John Bolle, and Thomas Chalke, they were men like Richard Maryon, until his death in 1504, and Bolle's son John, until his death in 1507; the mercer John Cornish, butcher John Biglon, waxchandler William Browning, and shoemaker Richard Biggemore; John Wallinger and John Colvyle; and the shearman, William Davey, son-in-law and executor of Richard Corall, and father of Richard, Agnes, and Katherine, who inherited their grandfather's property in the high street in 1498.

The holdings of these men in the town, quite apart from their business interests and experience of local office, were notable. On the east side of the town, all the major sites close to the Cross and cornmarket at the top of the street, from the corner of Tunmanmead Lane (Waterloo Lane) downwards, were in the hands of Richard Biggemore at Wendovershall (site of 1 High Street), his neighbour John Colvyle (site of 2 High Street), the bailiff Thomas Tendring (site of 3 High Street), and Richard Pratt at the Crane (site of 4-6 High Street). Pratt, who married a wealthy widow, Katherine, former wife of the fishmonger Robert Daysy, also controlled in her right other properties in the town and in New Street (which were hers for life as Robert's widow), and paid an annual rent of £4 6s 8d to St Osyth's priory for the lease of the tithes of Moulsham.

Farther down the east side of the street the butcher John Biglon had his house (site of 31-2 High Street); he had, too, a stall in the shambles in the Middle Row, two acres of meadow in Tunmanmead, and land in the Upland. First elected a chief pledge in 1471, he served as constable in 1479, 1482, and 1483, and had become one of the ruling group by 1490. His first wife Florence was buried in 1509 in Corpus Christi guild in the parish church, where he erected a marble monument 'faire inlaid with brasse', intending to be buried there beside her when he died. Inscribed in Latin on the monument was a prayer for their souls, while brass 'labells', or scrolls, issuing from the mouths of their two brass figures, bore their separate pleas for mercy and salvation. He died about 1521, but the date of his death, as Weever noted in 1631, was never completed. Weever criticised the monument as 'befitting the corps of a more eminent man than a Butcher'. But Weever was not to know that in the town of Biglon's day there was no greater social eminence than to be numbered among its governing élite. Nothing remains of the monument today.

One of John Biglon's executors, his fellow chief pledge William Browning, lived opposite to him, on the west side of the street (site of 69-70 High Street). Browning was one of the inner group by 1489, and as a member of it by 1507 had served as constable four times, affeerer four times, aletaster once, and meat and fish taster three times. A little farther up the west side of the street the dyer, old John Bolle, and his son John after him, had Parkers, facing the fish market (site of former 10-11 Tindal Street and part of New London Road gap), with a large backside plot running down to the river. Old Bolle, a chief pledge by 1463, was constable twice and affeerer four times. His neighbour, also facing the fishmarket, was John Cornish of Mayes (New London Road gap), Guy Harling's son-in-law. Cornish also owned two shops in the Middle Row, and his son John as a child inherited the New Street property of his grandfather, Guy Harling. Still farther up the west side of the town Richard Maryon, a chief pledge by 1484 and one of the seniors by 1493, by the time of his death had served once as constable, once as meat and fish taster, and six times as affeerer. He held two large adjoining properties in the back lane (sites of former 25-6 Tindal Street). A few doors farther up was John Wallinger, whose father Stephen (d.1481), and grandfather Clement, had been chief pledges before him. Wallinger not only owned and lived in one of the finest properties in the town (site of former Victorian Corn Exchange demolished in 1969), a hall house with a frontage of thirty-seven feet, but also owned the Maynetrees property in New Street.

The members of the ruling group did not necessarily always agree among themselves. A serious dispute, described as 'dyvers varyaunces, debatis, sutez, and stryves', came to a head in 1486 between John Bolle of Parkers, and his neighbour, John Cornish of Mayes. Their difference centred on Cornish's claim to 'a carteway to be had to carie and recarie att all tymes', from the fishmarket to the ground at the back of Mayes, through the gate and passage between their houses, which belonged to Parkers. It was the kind of neighbourly problem which arose as the frontage of the town closed up, and this particular way out of the street had been the subject of covenants as early as 1383. By the mediation of their neighbours, both parties agreed to submit their quarrel to arbitrators, and entered into mutual bonds of £20 to accept their award. The arbitrators, all of standing comparable to the disputants, were headed by Richard Pratt, supported by the bailiff, Thomas Tendring, the mercer John Munde, the draper Thomas Chalke, and Robert Downham. Seeking 'contenuall unite, reste, and peas', the arbitrators awarded to John Cornish the right to use the gate and cartway, and 20d damages, but required him to repair the backside fence between his ground and John Bolle's, all the way down to the river. The sealed award required that all other disputes be 'forgeve and forgete betwyx them, and that thei owe eche to other good wille and be lovers as thei owghte to be'. The arbitrators could be well pleased; in a small town, enmity between two of its leaders could breed much social mischief.

URBAN PROBLEMS

Keeping the peace was one of the responsibilities of the bailiff and chief pledges in the second half of the 15th century. Disorderly behaviour and violence feature in the town's records of those years to a degree not found in the earlier years of the century, with assault and affray among the most common offences presented in the manor court. The prevalence of violence shows the darker face of the town which was at the same time so devotedly rebuilding its church. But these were violent times. After the Hundred Years War ended and the army's disbanded soldiers returned from France, a brutal domestic conflict, the Wars of the Roses, broke out between two factions of the nobility. The king, Henry VI, of the house of Lancaster, a grandson of the mad French king Charles VI, had succeeded his father Henry V as a nine-months-old child in 1422. He grew up unworldly, incapable of controlling the ambitious lords of his kingdom, and intermittently deranged. In 1461 his kinsman, Edward, earl of March, of the rival house of York, took over the government by force and was accepted as king; Henry was lodged in the Tower. The Chelmsford autumn court roll in 1461 dated its proceedings in the first year of the reign of King Edward IV. Nine years later in 1470

the Lancastrians, led by Henry's French queen and the earl of Warwick, and reinforced by French mercenaries, returned. Edward fled the country on 29
September, Henry was released from the Tower on 3 October and re-crowned on
13 October; the November court at Chelmsford was duly dated 'in the 49th year
from the commencement of the reign of King Henry VI and in the first year of
his recovery of royal power'. But in March 1471 Edward came back with
German mercenaries. On 11 April Henry, recaptured, was returned to the
Tower. On 4 May Edward defeated the Lancastrians in a decisive battle at
Tewksbury, where Henry's only son, Edward, Prince of Wales, was killed. On
21 May the Yorkist Edward entered London in triumph, on the same day that
the body of King Henry was exhibited to the people at St Paul's; Henry had
'died' in the Tower the night before. Thus the Chelmsford Whitsun court on 6
June was dated as 11 Edward IV. But the throne was not yet secure. Edward died
on 9 April 1483. The accession of his twelve-year-old son Edward was
acknowledged in the dating of that year's Chelmsford Whitsun court as Thursday, 22 May, 1 Edward V. But Edward V was never crowned; his uncle and protector, Richard of Gloucester, successfully intrigued for his nephew's removal
and his own 'election' as king. Richard was crowned in July, and Edward and his
young brother were murdered in the Tower. The Chelmsford autumn court in
1483 was dated in the first year of the reign of King Richard III, a brief reign
marked by yet more bloodshed and civil war, until, with the death of Richard at
the battle of Bosworth in 1485, and the coronation as King Henry VII of Henry
Tudor, son of Edmund Tudor, half-brother of Henry VI, and Margaret Beaufort,
a descendant of King Edward III, strong government was restored.

In a busy, bustling town like Chelmsford, overcrowded, and thronged by
strangers and travellers passing through, brawling with fists and staves was
common. More serious was the readiness to draw the lethal personal weapons
that were generally carried, knives of every kind, swords, poniards, daggers, and
short swords worn hung at the belt. Thomas Rede, a clerk, who was struck in
the breast with a poniard by a Kentish hosier in 1472, died of the thrust. William
Pacy, who attacked Richard Sadler in 1470 with drawn sword, was fined 3s 4d
for it; yet only ten days later Pacy and a companion attacked Sadler again with
sword and dagger, and when the constable John Bowyer tried to arrest them
both to keep the peace, they turned on the constable. Between 1461 and 1476 a
year seldom passed without attacks on the constables being reported to the manor
court. In 1462 Robert Colvyle, tenant of the bishop's mill, was fined 5s for hir-
ing 'certain persons unknown' to attack the two constables, Thomas Gawge and
John Aspenden, which they did on market day, with drawn swords, spill-
ing blood. The constable William Fayrer had his head broken in 1468, and in
1475, when John Myngey as constable tried to collect the latest tax granted by
parliament from John Biggemore (a fellow chief pledge), the shoemaker attacked
and wounded him with an iron 'fyreforke'. The nightly watchmen suffered too;
the two men on duty one night in 1472 were attacked in the middle of the night
by three men, who were each fined 8d for it.

The constables could not necessarily count on public support for their authority.
When Thomas Woderove arrested William Aleyn in 1467, the two Yelvertons,
father and son, attacked him and released Aleyn by force. In 1471 two brothers
were arrested and put in the stocks after they had broken open William Tyler's

window with a long poniard, and dragged him out of the house to beat him up. When two sureties secured the release of one brother, he immediately broke up the stocks to let the other out. Wilful damage of this kind doubtless accounts for the court's need in 1474 of a new pair of stocks and a pillory. Like all matters which were the direct responsibility of the lord of the manor, including provision of the town's penal equipment, and maintenance of its bridges, the request was passed on to bishop's council in London.

None but chief pledges served as constables; some served for two years in succession; John Cornish, John Biglon, and William Browning, served the office at least four times. But facing such risks it is not surprising that a few pledges became reluctant to serve. In 1472 the shopkeeper William Breton, the mercer William Munde the younger, the dyer Richard Corall, and Henry Sampton, were each fined 20s for absenting themselves from the Whitsun court to avoid being chosen as constables. In 1489 William Turnour and Richard Pake, having actually been elected to the office, 'wilfully absented themselves in contempt and derision of the court', to avoid being sworn in; they too were fined 20s. The heavy fine of 20s inflicted by a court which assessed all but the worst offences at a few pence shows how seriously evasion of this most important office was regarded.

A distinction should be made between impulsive acts of violence and pre-meditated villainy. Many attacks arose from sudden loss of temper, when any handy object was snatched up as a weapon. An innkeeper Thomas Sweteman in 1478 struck his victim such a blow on the head with a pair of pincers that he died. In 1477 Margaret Noreys, a procuress known to have attacked the constable, and on several occasions maliciously raised the hue and cry in the middle of the night, gave the chief pledge Henry Sampton a bloody head with a 'clustyr of keyes'; other weapons mentioned in the court rolls include a butcher's gambrel, a scythe, a candlestick, and a 'wasshyng beetyll'. But other attacks were deliberate. In 1463 the fishmonger Thomas Woderove 'took aside a certain servant of William Lopham' and gave him 6d to beat up Thomas Trott in the highway at Brentwood.

Margaret Noreys was not the only inveterate troublemaker in the town. Robert Colvyle, in 1462 (the same year that he hired men to attack the con-stables) was fined for being a 'nightwalker', for striking William Skinner, for breaking into the house of John Clamtree in company with five others and attacking his wife Alice and two servants, and for cheating his neighbours by using a 'toldysh which is far too big' at his mill. It was also discovered that two labourers who broke into the house of another miller, Thomas Chartesey, in the middle of the night, beat him up, and stole 40s from him, had been incited to do so by Colvyle. The labourers were well-known bad characters, having been charged the year before with receiving £5 11s 4d and six gold rings worth 40s stolen from Thomas Woderove. Robert Colvyle, was still causing trouble in the town in 1471 when he attacked and spilled the blood of a stranger.

Another bad character was Alexander Shoemaker, who broke into John Thressher's house in 1477 and raped his wife Joan. In the same year with a little knife and staff he broke into the house of a rival shoemaker, John Biggemore, and enticed away Biggemore's apprentice William from his master's service, wearing the clothes provided by his master, a long red robe worth 5s, two pairs of shoes worth 1s, and a shirt worth 1s.

Much of the unruly behaviour was probably a symptom of the dwindling efficacy of the tithing system. The later 15th-century court rolls recorded lengthening lists of tithing offences, of residents 'out of tithing', or 'deciners' (tithingmen) neglecting to attend the annual view of frankpledge. In 1469 John Aspenden, who twice served as constable, refused to allow his servant to appear in court to be sworn into a tithing.

At the same time as the tithing system was disintegrating, shady lodging houses were mushrooming in the town, the haunts of thieves and prostitutes. In 1474 the smith John Aldham, who kept company with thieves, was suspected of harbouring procuresses and prostitutes in his lodging house. By the 1490s the court was adopting drastic measures to control this problem. At Whitsun in 1498 Thomas Bere, charged with keeping ill rule in his house and annoying his neighbours, was given the choice of putting his house in order, or quitting the town. In October his wife was fined 40s for housing a 'certain unknown woman', and ordered to send her packing. In 1500 John Crompe, who kept ill rule in his house, disturbing the neighbours late at night, was ordered to be out of the town before 6 December, and warned that if he were found in the town after that date the constable would put him in the stocks, 'and he shall have no dwelling in the town nor coming or going in the town'; Crompe had already had one spell in the stocks, from which he was rescued, against the constable's orders, by one of his cronies. When John Clerk, weaver, and John Richardson and his wife, were charged in 1501 with ill rule, entertaining beggars and vagabonds and suspect persons in their houses, they too were threatened that if they did not mend their ways they must quit the town. Cecilia Sparkwell seems to have run a more elegant establishment, where she was said to 'live luxuriously'; but she, too, was charged with keeping ill rule in her house and receiving suspect persons, and ordered in 1504 to quit the lord's domain, and offered no alternative.

The ultimate sanction against keeping disorderly lodgings and bawdy houses, exclusion from the town, shows what a serious threat to good order the court judged them, and the same warning was given to any inhabitant whose behaviour was socially disruptive. In 1493 three married couples were each fined 12d and warned to curb their scolding tongues, or leave town; in 1503 Agnes Young, whose abuse 'disturbed the peace between her neighbours', was given no option, but fined 20s and given two months to quit the town. In the 1460s 'nightwalkers' like Robert Colvyle had escaped with a fine; but in 1493 five men, habitually found abroad at night disturbing the townsmen, were ordered to cease their 'gallivanting', or quit the lord's domain. Two nightwalkers caught eavesdropping in 1494 were similarly warned. John Crompe, banished in 1500 but discovered in the town again in 1504, living suspiciously and on the prowl at night, was immediately ordered out again, under the heavy penalty of 40s.

In the 1460s fear of disturbances arising from competitive games played a part in the fining, not only of the rector of Springfield and others for gambling with dice at the Cock inn, encouraged by the landlord, Robert Snell, but also of the glover, Robert Wolston, a chief pledge, John Yelverton and his two sons, John and John, the aletaster Thomas Rygdon, and five others, for playing tennis. Tennis and dice, with other idle games, had been discouraged by a statute of 1388-9 in favour of the more useful sport of archery. But a sterner statute of 1477-8 recognised that those games were not only unprofitable, but led to murders, robberies, and other 'heinous offences, to the great unquieting and trouble of many good and well-disposed persons'.

At the autumn court of 1503 an order to quit the town was made in different circumstances. The chief pledges presented that 'Richard Burton, dwelling in this lordship, is leprous of body, to the common harm of all the tenants and others'. The leper was ordered to be gone from the bishop's domain within three days, on pain of forfeiting 40s. But he had only to cross the bridge into the abbot's manor to reach the leper hospital in Moulsham.

With the increasingly packed state of the town the by-law against keeping dungheaps in the street in front of the house was broadened in 1475 to include stacks of firewood and logs, on pain of their forfeiture. By the 1470s even the small garden where the maypole used to stand was heaped with dung. People who threw the sweepings of their houses out of the front door into the street faced penalties, as did those who cast their domestic refuse and sweepings into the watercourse which ran down the street from the conduit. Cases multiplied before the court of nuisances arising from broken, blocked, or ill-directed rainwater and domestic gutters, which discharged into the street or bred discord between neighbours; the court first warned, then fined, those who offended. In 1478 Thomas Vyncent was ordered to alter his gutter, which discharged the water from his household washing of linen and other 'necessaries' into the street, 'and some falls on the heads of the people'; when he neglected to do so he forfeited the penalty of 12d. In 1479 action was taken against the fishmonger William Fayrer, who had 'a gutter running out of his house into the highway by which the water from his household washing and fish cleaning runs into the highway making a great stench'. In 1495 the court made a general order that before the next court all householders in the high street, on both sides, should mend their gutters, 'so that the water may have its right course'. In 1498 the court took up the cases of a widow, Alice Haselok, whose house was being damaged by her neighbour's broken gutter, and of Geoffrey Scott, whose blocked gutter made trouble for his neighbours.

The 'Chanell', the common gutter or watercourse which ran from the conduit down the back street behind the Middle Row, became increasingly polluted. The conduit water from Burgess Well was pure spring water, but orders had to be made in 1499 and 1504 to stop women washing their linen and garments where it surfaced. Three street wells in the town, including one in New Street, were misused in the same way. The channel itself was exploited by William Breton, who had a house in the Middle Row (site of 92-3 High Street) next to Shamble Lane (Crown Passage). In 1474 his privy was reported to be leaking into the channel and overflowing into the street, creating a great stench. He was fined, but far from remedying the defect he elaborated it. By 1479 he had taken over a piece of highway waste behind his house, in the back street where the channel flowed, and built upon it an extension to the back of his house, with a privy above the channel, draining into it. In 1484 his widow Alice was ordered to cease this unsavoury arrangement, but never did so. In due course Breton's ingenious method of domestic sewage disposal was adopted by other householders of the Middle Row who lived conveniently alongside the channel. Indeed, Breton initiated a new stage of the town's growth, whereby the houses and shops of the Middle Row expanded over the waste ground at the back of the Row, gradually encasing the channel within them. The highway behind the Middle Row was to be reduced in time to a narrow lane called Back Street or Conduit Street, while the channel emerged from the end house of the Row, Samptons or the 'Cornerhows' (site of 84-5 High Street), as a foul open sewer. Thence it flowed across the fishmarket into the high street, and down to Springfield Lane, where it discharged into the Gullet.

Market day rubbish was a constant problem, the fishmongers being the worst culprits. It was not enough to enforce the by-law requiring removal of all stalls immediately after the market closed, for in 1473 William Fayrer, Thomas Woderove, and five other fishmongers, obediently took down and removed their stalls, but they left behind in the fishmarket a stinking heap of fish guts and underfoot straw. On that occasion they were fined only a few pence each, but by 1498 stern warning had been given to all fishmongers (repeated in 1504) that those who threw straw under their stalls and 'Lez Guttez, Gorez, et Garbagez' of fish, without clearing them away before they departed, would be fined 6s 8d.

The town's pigs, however, relished the garbage. On the subject of pigs let loose on the street to scavenge, the 15th-century court rolls are eloquent. In 1463 the butcher John Biglon and four other householders were said to 'have and keep their pigs roaming abroad in the king's highway, rooting up the ground abominable to behold'. Even the churchyard was invaded, and the nuisance caused was worse when the pigs were not ringed to prevent their snouts turning up the soil. In 1475 the manor court made a by-law to control the pigs, forbidding those who kept them in the town to put them out, or allow them to wander and scavenge at will, with a penalty of up to 20d for each offence. This had little effect; the bailiff himself, Thomas Tendring, was twice fined the maximum 20d, and in 1486 William Styward was fined for no fewer then thirty pigs found at large, and Richard Pratt, the most senior of the chief pledges, for half a dozen. In 1488 the by-law was strengthened. The bailiff was empowered to seize and impound wandering pigs, other than those 'being driven by the way', and to value them in consultation with two or three tenants, sell them, and divide the proceeds between the lord of the manor and the churchwardens (for the good of the church). This may have met local resistance, for in 1490 the by-law was modified to provide a forfeit calculated at 2d a foot for each pig found in the highway or churchyard, of which sum one penny was to go to whoever took the strays to the pound, and one penny to the church. This may have helped to reduce the nuisance in the churchyard and high street, but pigs continued to be troublesome in Springfield Lane and Brocholeslane (Threadneedle Street). In 1496 in Springfield Lane pigs were obstructing people taking their horses to water at the Gullet, while in 1498 the dyer John Clerk was putting out his pigs to wander in Brocholeslane, and throwing out into the lane the dung from his 'hoghouse'. In 1500 the court reverted to the sterner provisions of 1488; the churchwardens were to value pigs found in the churchyard, sell them, and 'put the pence so taken to the use of the church', while the bailiff was to sell those taken in the highways on behalf of the lord.

In spite of the by-law passed in 1388 against river pollution, the rivers continued to be fouled by waste disposal. The innkeepers near the stone bridge were the worst offenders. The Gullet backwater behind the Boar's Head inn was used by the inhabitants as a washing place and watering place. This did not deter Robert Snell, landlord of the Cock inn by the stone bridge, and later of the Boar's Head, from tipping all his refuse on the bank there; indeed in 1471 he completely blocked the entry to the Gullet from Springfield Lane, so that no one could reach the bank to fetch water, and in 1480 he virtually dammed the course of the water with dung. Two years later his widow, far from removing the obstruction as ordered, 'continually day by day adds to it', and she was warned that failure to comply would cost her a fine of 20s. William Carr, successor to Robert Snell as landlord of the Cock, was said in 1482 to have dumped no less than eighty cartloads of muck in the river behind his house, that is, in the gullet, and Nicholas Hyde, the landlord of the Lion on the opposite side of the road, had dumped forty cartloads in the Great River (the Can). Besides dung and rubbish, Robert Snell had thrown into the river meat and fish offal, butchers threw in the guts of their slaughtered beasts, a white tawer (white leather dresser) threw in the trimmings of his skins, and William Browning washed sheepskins in it.

Horrifying as these conditions seem today, they were no worse than those in most market towns of the period, although in Chelmsford they were concentrated in a cramped site far too small for an expanding urban community. But successive leaders of the townsmen sought persistently, according to the standards of their day, to prevent life and work in such a crowded environment becoming intolerable. At least the dirt underfoot provided a livelihood in 1494 for Francis 'patynmaker', whose pattens enabled pedestrians to step out boldly through the mire and garbage in the street.

The town officers who supervised the quality and price of goods and victuals carried out a thankless task unpaid. Some of the aletasters, meat and fish tasters, and leather searchers, held those offices many times. Thomas Rygdon, who was not a chief pledge, was one of the two aletasters at least fourteen times between 1462 and 1480, assisted by ten different partners, and though he was often fined for poor performance of his duties, yet plenty of offenders were brought before the court and fined as a result of his activities. From the 1480s, when hops were introduced into local brewing, the aletasters had to sample both ale and beer. The pioneers were John Playford and his wife; in 1485 she was the first to be fined as a 'byre' brewer, and he was fined the next year. There were at the time about thirteen people being fined for offences connected with the brewing and selling of ale, including Guy Harling's widow Joan, and the wife of Richard Pratt. By 1495 over thirty people were selling both ale and beer.

The office of aletaster was hardly ever served by a chief pledge. The other annual offices enjoyed a higher social standing, for they were mainly, though not entirely, filled by chief pledges; even Richard Pratt served as a meat and fish taster. Between 1461 and 1504 the office of leather searcher was almost monopolised by three shoemakers, Robert Chever, who served at least nine times between 1461 and 1475, John Biggemore, who served at least eight times between 1469 and 1490, and Richard Biggemore, who served at least nine times between 1481 and 1504. In the whole period of over forty years only eleven men, two of them each year, served that office. Victuallers and innkeepers were prominent among the two meat and fish tasters, including Geoffrey Scott at the Lion; Robert Downham served the office seven times between 1488 and 1501. This office, like that of constable, had its risks; in 1468 a butcher forcibly recovered from Thomas Waryn the meat he had just condemned and confiscated; and in 1498 a fishmonger struck Thomas Buxston on the mouth with his cudgel to recover his forfeited wares. But however often the officers themselves might be fined for failing in their duty, the court rolls record repeated condemnation and seizure of food unfit for human consumption: badly salted eels, a bad 'codfyssh' offered for sale by John Gybbe of Billericay, and stinking saltfish offered by Andrew, servant of the prior of Hatfield Peverel; from John Golding of Moulsham it was stinking mackerel seized, and from Thomas Gros of Maldon four whole casks of rotten red herring. The offence committed by Robert Daysy and four others in 1474, when they tried to sell off decomposing and stinking saltfish and red and white herring, was the more blameworthy in that they did so during the forty days' fast of Lent, when meat was forbidden. The dishonest practices of butchers had also to be checked, when they offered for sale such unhealthy flesh as a stinking quarter of beef, a rotting sheep's carcass or measled pork. An extreme case was that of Geoffrey Waryn, who was fined 6s 8d in 1498 for killing a sick cow and sheep, 'plene de Pokkes' (full of the pox, probably tuberculosis), 'knowing them to be so and unwholesome for man'. He was warned that repetition of such an offence would cost him 100s.

The court had also to prevent food prices being raised artificially by forestallers, who bought up supplies before they crossed the threshold of the market, to sell at a profit, and by traders' malpractices within the market. Between 1464 and 1470 a notorious offender of the first kind was Thomas Rygdon, whose activities 'at the end of the town', buying up produce coming in to the market, included at one time or another chickens, cocks, capons, eggs, geese, doves, butter, fish, and other victuals. Another culprit was Robert Snell, who, as landlord of the Cock beside the stone bridge, was conveniently placed to preempt poultry and victuals as they crossed the bridge from Moulsham.

A common malpractice within the market was the marking up of prices as goods became scarcer during the day. Although the court rolls contain regular long lists of butchers and fishmongers fined for overcharging, details of their offences are rarely given. But Robert Daysy was fined in 1474 for selling five red herring before noon for 1d, but in the afternoon offering only four a penny. John Elys, the servant of William Fayrer (who was a chief pledge), was fined in the 1470s for selling two mackerel for 1d at daybreak, but raising the price to 1½d or 2d later, and finally to 3d. He was also caught selling four herring for 1d when the market opened, but within two hours raising the price to 1d each. Whether his master connived in this, or whether Elys was making something on the side for himself is not clear, but it seems more likely that Elys was the scapegoat for his master, who was regularly fined between 1461 and 1477 for selling bad fish and overcharging. William Fayrer was a man of considerable substance, with property in the high street, including fish stalls, and served three times as constable; but as a chief pledge he was conspicuously negligent, fined five times between 1463 and 1482 for dereliction of duty.

In 1506 a copyhold stall in the Shoprow was the subject of dispute. It had been acquired by a newcomer to the town, without recourse to the customary manorial procedure of surrender and admission, from Anne, second wife and by then widow of the mercer John Cornish the elder, who was Guy Harling's son-in-law. The newcomer was also a mercer, 'a certain Thomas Mildemay'. With the coming to Chelmsford of the 'certain Thomas Mildemay', the death three years later of King Henry VII, and the accession of his son, King Henry VIII, a new chapter was opening in the history of the town.

CHAPTER EIGHT

The Rise of the Mildmays

THOMAS MILDMAY, MERCER

Thomas Mildmay's venture into business in Chelmsford as a mercer dated from the deal made in 1506 with the Cornish family, who were not only mercers like himself, but also his kinsmen. Much of the recorded ancestry of the Mildmays is untrustworthy, based as it is on documents forged in the late 16th century (and accepted then by the College of Arms) to provide an ancient lineage for the family. But the Cornish family connection is supported by independent sources. The Cornishes were established in Chelmsford by 1446, when Thomas 'Cornesshede' of Chelmsford was one of the collectors of the subsidy in Essex. They also held land in Great Waltham. According to the *Essex Visitation* of 1612, two sisters, Mary and Margery Cornish of Great Waltham, married respectively Thomas Everard of Great Waltham and a Thomas Mildmay; subsequently Thomas and Mary Everard's daughter Mary (or Margery) married her cousin Walter, the son of Margery and Thomas Mildmay; their son was Thomas Mildmay the mercer, who thus had two Cornish grandmothers. A Walter Mildmay (Meeldemay) and his wife Margery were granted a tenement in Great Waltham, at Church End near the church, in 1472, and in 1483 they bought eleven acres of pasture in Great Waltham. In 1492 Walter partnered John Cornish, senior (the Chelmsford mercer who married as his first wife Guy Harling's daughter Joan), as witnesses to a Great Waltham transaction. In 1531 two pieces of land in Great Waltham were described as 'sometime bought of Thomas Mildmay'.

Members of both families served the Staffords, dukes of Buckingham, in Essex in the 15th century. In 1467 a John Cornish, parker of Hatfield Park, was granted by Anne, duchess of Buckingham, an annuity of £6 13s 4d during her lifetime out of the revenues of Hatfield Broadoak, 'for his good service before and to come'. He was still receiving the annuity in 1469. Walter Mildmay, was bailiff of Fobbing, a Buckingham manor, in 1477-8, and in 1481 presented his accounts for that year, including his own wage of £3 10s 8d, to the late duke's steward, receivers, and auditors, sitting at Writtle, also a Buckingham manor. In 1484 a Walter Mildmay, the same or another, was paid a fee of 30s 4d as keeper of the park of 'Morlewode' in the Stafford lordship of Thornbury in Gloucestershire. This lends some support to the Mildmay family tradition of roots in Gloucestershire.

When Thomas Mildmay appeared in Chelmsford in 1506, he had recently acquired a market stall from Anne Cornish, the widowed second wife of old John Cornish the mercer. In 1515 old Cornish's heir John, and John's brother Humphrey, agreed that Mildmay should have the 'quiet enjoyment' of Mayes, the Cornish family house facing the fishmarket (site of New London Road gap), with an option of buying it. In 1520 they leased him the house, in which he was then living, for twelve years; at the end of the lease in 1533 John Cornish sold it to him.

Thomas Mildmay prospered in Chelmsford. By 1524 he was one of the two wealthiest men in the town; only the draper, Richard Humfrey, was richer. Mildmay and his wife Agnes (Read) brought up a family of five sons, Thomas,

William, John, Edward, and Walter, and three daughters, Joan, Margaret, and Thomasin. His kinsman John Cornish had sold Guy Harlings in 1516; after several changes of ownership, in 1530 Thomas Mildmay bought it from the executors of Geoffrey Markday, and moved in. It was a hall house, with a chamber built over the hall, a great chamber, a parlour, a buttery and kitchen, each with a chamber above, and a gatehouse with a bedchamber over it. There are no Chelmsford court rolls extant for the years when Mildmay was establishing himself in business in the town, but the position he rose to in the community is suggested in a fragment of a roll of 1532, which names him as one of the homage at a general court, together with John Wallinger and other senior householders. In 1538 he was one of the two churchwardens, the office reserved for the most prominent inhabitants.

Three of Mildmay's sons, William, John, and Edward, followed their father's trade of mercer; Edward, who was apprenticed in London and became a London citizen, died in 1549, before his parents. Thomas, the mercer's heir, and his youngest brother Walter, took a different path, making careers for themselves not in trade but in government employment. The convulsion of the Reformation, and in particular the survey and management of religious property confiscated by the Crown after the breach with Rome, offered them the opportunity to advance themselves and their family in rank and wealth.

THE REFORMATION AND THOMAS MILDMAY, Esq.

In May 1533, in the face of Papal opposition, a court convened by Archbishop Cranmer pronounced the marriage of King Henry VIII to Queen Catherine void, and his secret marriage earlier in the year to Anne Boleyn valid. Catherine's daughter, Princess Mary, was living then at 'Beaulieu' — New Hall, Boreham — near Chelmsford. On 7 July 1533 the princess's household accounts recorded that thirty women from Chelmsford 'came to dinner' at New Hall, and a fortnight later another sixty women 'of Chelmsford and elsewhere'. But after the birth of Anne's daughter Elizabeth in September, the title 'Princess' was taken away from Mary, who wrote to her father in October vigorously objecting to the new title of 'the Lady Mary' imposed upon her. In 1534 Parliament passed the Act of Succession, excluding Mary in favour of Anne's child, and also an Act of Supremacy which declared Henry to be the Head of the Church. The clergy were required to subscribe to the royal supremacy, and to recognise that the 'Bishop of Rome has no greater jurisdiction given him by God in this realm of England than any other foreign bishop'. The thirty-five signatories in the Chelmsford deanery were headed by Hugh Taylor, the Chelmsford curate, and included Peter Wyley, the chaplain of Mounteney's chantry, but not William Tate, the rector since 1522; Tate, as a canon of Windsor (where he was buried in 1540) and a canon of York probably signed elsewhere.

Before the divorce, in 1532, while Henry still pressed for papal acquiescence, the payment of first fruits to Rome had been stopped as a warning. After the breach became final, in 1534 Parliament granted both first fruits and tenths to the king, and in 1535 commissioners were appointed to make a survey and valuation for him of all benefices in England and Wales — the *Valor Ecclesiasticus*. One of the commissioners was the mercer's eldest son, Thomas Mildmay, styled in the commission, 'Auditor'. In the same year, the smaller religious houses worth less than £200 a year were dissolved, and their revenues placed under the control of a newly created 'Court of Augmentation of the Revenues of the Crown'. In 1536 Mildmay was appointed one of ten auditors of the new court, with an annual fee of £20 and 'profits'. He became distinquished thereafter from his father, Thomas Mildmay, senior, mercer, as 'Master Auditor', or 'Thomas Mildmay, esquire'.

In the years which followed Master Auditor surveyed, valued, and inventoried, the lands and goods of religious houses. From June 1536 to February 1537 with three fellow commissioners he was busy in Essex, Suffolk, and Norfolk, claiming daily expenses for breakfast, dinner, supper, and lodging. He carried on in 1537-8 in Hertfordshire, Northamptonshire, Middlesex, London, Cambridge, and Huntingdonshire. In 1539 he was one of the commissioners who took the surrender, among other houses, of St Osyth's priory in Essex, in which matter Thomas, Lord Audley, remarked that Mildmay and his fellows had served the king well. In 1539-40 he became involved in certifying pensions for redundant monks and nuns.

The seizure of monastic lands and buildings launched the greatest property boom since the Norman Conquest, with the whole authority of the Crown behind it. A minimum purchase price of twenty times the annual rental values (normal for the period) was laid down in December 1539. Any indiscreet comment on the Crown's policy was tantamount to treason. A sombre note in the Chelmsford parish register records that on market day, Friday, 1 December 1542, James Mallett, rector of Great Leighs, was drawn, hanged, and quartered for high treason on Chelmsford market hill. The unhappy Mallett, a former chaplain of Queen Catherine, and rector of Great Leighs for twenty-eight years, 'when the news was of the great Commotions in several parts of the Nation, upon and after the Dissolution of Religious Houses', had said openly: 'Then hath the king brought his hogs to a fair market'. Among the first to invest in the spoils were the royal agents, such as Master Auditor, who were employed in the process of confiscation.

The hospital of St Mary, Elsyngspitell, in London, was among the smaller houses suppressed. Their property in Chelmsford was Master Auditor's first acquisition. In partnership with his father, the mercer, he bought it from the Crown in 1537 for £79 6s 8d. Their purchase included the Crane inn and its meadow in Tunmanmead, and four adjoining houses (sites of 4-8 High Street), two of which were already leased to the mercer. Five years later in 1544 the father and son were licensed to transfer the whole property to the mercer's youngest son, Walter.

The Dominican priory of Black Friars in Moulsham was also among the smaller foundations suppressed. In the early 15th century the house had continued to prosper, presenting a steady flow of applicants for ordination to the bishop. One of the friars, Thomas Langton, about 1420, had been a noted scholar, who wrote a universal chronicle from the beginning of the world to his own time. In 1437 the English Dominicans held their Chapter General at Moulsham. Such was the reputation of the Moulsham preaching friars that they were in demand as chaplains to great lords; in 1453 one of them, Robert Toppyng, confessor and household chaplain to Humfrey Stafford, duke of Buckingham, was given papal dispensation to hold for life any one secular benefice, with or without cure, even a parish church, and to resign or exchange it as often as he pleased. Such opportunities for personal advancement and profit may well have sown the seeds of the future decline of the house. The phrase used in 1503 by John Stokwell of Moulsham, in his will giving five marks to 'the pour and devout of the freeres in Mulsham' to pray for his soul, hardly suggests an affluent community at that date. During the episcopate of Richard FitzJames (1506-22) Moulsham friars only appeared three times in diocesan lists of ordinees, in 1508, 1515, and 1518, with only five applicants presented. In 1535 the income of the house was no more than £9 6s 5d; there were only seven brothers in occupation when the house was 'taken for the king' in 1538. It was in debt, many of its possessions were pledged, and what remained was mostly old and 'poor'.

The furnishings of the chambers and dorter, which were 'very poor stuff' and not worth selling, were given, with the exception of one featherbed, to the remaining friars. Everything else was sold: the vestments in the vestry, including six old chasubles without albs; the domestic equipment, such as pots, kettles, spits, cobirons, and an old furnace, in the buttery, kitchen, and brewhouse; 'certain old pewter' in the prior's chamber; seven tables in the frater or refectory; the pavements, iron, and glass, in cloister, chapter house, chapels, choir, and church; the stalls, altars, organs, and organloft, even the gravestones; and the timber, tiles, and lead. The whole sale raised £13 14s 6d. The friars were given £1 11s 8d between them for their subsistence until they should find some other living. One of them, William Wynter, died not long afterwards, and was buried at Chelmsford in 1540. When all the debts had been paid and pledges redeemed, the balance handed over by the royal visitor to the auditor, Thomas Mildmay, was no more than 6s 1d.

Shortly afterwards, in 1539, Master Auditor leased from the Crown the house and site of the priory, with its crofts in Moulsham, Writtle, and Great Baddow, for twenty-one years, at a rent of 32s 6d. His tenure was threatened in 1542 when the king granted the reversion of the property, and its rent, to Antonio Bonvix, a merchant of Lucca, settled in London. But before the end of the lease, and not later than 1551, the freehold was acquired by the Auditor, and the 'Friars' was to remain in Mildmay hands until 1839.

The Auditor soon secured a better bargain than some stripped friary buildings and a few crofts. Westminster Abbey surrendered on 16 January 1540, and on 21 January Mildmay was one of those who signed the certificate for the monks' pensions. Six months later he bought the abbey's former manor of Moulsham, an estate of over 1,300 acres, with some two hundred tenancies, a watermill, and valuable woodland called Moulsham Frith, for £622 5s 8d. With the manor went the so-called 'manor' of Bekeswell (Bexfields) which had been given to Westminster Abbey in 1392. Mildmay successfully negotiated a reduction of £80 in the price, to allow for the cost to Moulsham's lord of 'the contynualle reparaciones of the brydge of Chelmysford'. The valuation of the woods of Moulsham Frith made allowance, too, for 200 oaks of sixty to eighty years' growth, and 200 sapling oaks of forty years' growth, reserved for repairs to buildings and mill, and to the bridge, which was claimed to be 'all of tymber and dayly in charge to be repayred with tymber'. This was not quite true; only the gravelled carriage way of Chelmsford's 'stone bridge' was of timber. In 1520 the abbot of Westminster had employed a master mason on repairs to the bridge, besides three carpenters and a man for hewing and lashing of timbers. But there is no doubt of the constant burden maintenance of the bridge laid on both manors.

The Auditor had married well; his wife Avice was the daughter of William Gunson, the paymaster of the king's ships. How much influence Gunson had had on his son-in-law's entry into government service is not known, but on occasion the Auditor relied on his father-in-law for advice. When he was commanded in 1542 to raise footmen equipped with bows, arrows, and bills, probably for the Scottish campaign, Mildmay wrote to Gunson to ask how he should act. Gunson replied from Deptford, 'Loving son ... Although the preparation of twenty men be much, you must needs do it, and so for bows, etc., I am compelled to buy for myself and so must you; and I suppose you must prepare coats. Mr Chancellor ... can best inform you'. Gunson himself had acquired in 1540 the reversion of the Crown lease of the site of a chapel and lands in Moulsham, with a share of the Moulsham tithes, which had belonged to St Osyth's priory. The chapel, its yard, land, and field (shown on John Walker's Moulsham map of 1591) in due course passed to his son-in-law. At Moulsham the new lord of the manor, as befitted his changed status, pulled down the decayed old house, which had been good enough for the abbot's farmers of the manor, and about 1542 began to build a new 'manor place' — Moulsham Hall. It was to be accounted by his contemporaries 'the greatest esquire's building' in Essex.

With Moulsham manor, the Auditor acquired the leper hospital. The hospital had been ill managed by a recent keeper, William Meriwether, who held it with the adjoining two-acre garden and croft for life; in 1529 it was said to be ruinous and in disrepair. But in 1530, after Meriwether's death, it was rehabilitated; Robert Jaxson, a poor man, was appointed keeper for life, but under strict conditions laid down by Westminster Abbey. Jaxson was to maintain the buildings, which the abbey treasurer would inspect from time to time; he was to treat the inmates well, particularly men and women of Chelmsford and Moulsham; and he was not to admit suspicious characters. The inventory drawn up of the furnishings of the hospital handed over to Jaxson reveals its poverty after Meriwether's neglect. The only bedding was five sheets, two coverlets, two mattresses, and two bolsters, and the only utensils a great brass pot, a little brass pot, three pewter plates, two dishes, two saucers, and a pewter salt-cellar. A little table with four feet and an old chest were all the furniture, and in the 'chapel' were three candlesticks, a chest containing two vestments, and a 'crewett'. With the meagre furnishings Jaxson took over a cock and five hens. The hospital relied on charity; 8*d* was left to 'the lazar house at Chelmsford' in a will of 1534.

The hospital's work continued after Master Auditor's purchase of the manor. The Chelmsford parish registers from time to time recorded burials from the 'lazar-house' or 'spittle house'. In 1540 Laurence Baker, a leper brought from Mucking to Chelmsford, was buried. But with leprosy an increasingly rare disease, the hospital became a refuge for the destitute sick and infirm of every condition, and in particular for the poor of Chelmsford parish. In 1545 the keeper was fined for taking in vagrants from other places. Burials from the hospital were usually nameless, 'a poor wench' (1558, 1560), 'a poor fellow that was dumb' (1561), 'a poor maid' (1562), 'a lame woman' (1563), 'two boys', 'a child', and 'another child' (1566), and 'a poor woman' (1568). By the 1570s the hospital was more usually known as the 'poor house'.

In the same year that he acquired the Moulsham manor, 1540, Master Auditor Mildmay bought a house called Rynged Hall in the parish of St Thomas the Apostle in London, and four small tenements next to it. He now had a London town house as well as a country seat. He had already, at some date in King Henry's reign, gained the right for himself and his posterity to bear Arms: Three greyhounds' heads couped with collars.

A ROYAL MANOR

While Master Auditor established himself as an 'esquire' in Moulsham, across the river in Chelmsford his father continued to trade as a mercer. The manor (and town) of Chelmsford remained in the bishop of London's possession until 1545, when Bishop Edmund Bonner, 'moved by certain causes and considerations', gave the manor, with the advowson of the rectory, and the Southwood estate, to Henry VIII. What those 'considerations' were was not explained. Bonner was a more conservative bishop than some of his fellows, but had served both the king, and his Vicar-General, Thomas Cromwell, well before he became bishop of London in 1539. Indeed, as ambassador at the French court he had helped to forward the negotiations in Paris in 1538-9 for the printing there of the Great Bible, the first authorised translation into English. But considering King Henry's attitude towards ecclesiastical property, and his urgent need of money for his French campaign of 1544-6, Bonner may have been pressured by 1545 into a politic 'voluntary' relinquishment of some of his episcopal estates. Chelmsford was an outright gift, in contrast to Clacton, which the bishop handed over in exchange for some other lands in Worcestershire. Bonner retained his see for the time being, but after Henry's death, unable to accept the policies of the young king, Edward VI, and his counsellors, he was deprived of his bishopric in 1549 and replaced by the reformer, Nicholas Ridley. In 1535 Thomas Mildmay as Auditor had valued the bishop of London's Chelmsford estate for the *Valor Ecclesiasticus*. When he bought Moulsham Mildmay may well have coveted Chelmsford too, but the bishop's manor, Bishop's Hall, was to remain in the hands of the Crown until after the accession of Elizabeth I.

Bishop's Hall itself and the demesne lands were still being farmed out. In 1514 Bishop Richard FitzJames (1516-22) leased them to John Markday for nineteen years, at the usual rent of £40. Markday, like his predecessor, the bailiff Thomas Tendring, was a Chelmsford innkeeper and had been a chief pledge since 1503. His lease included the bishop's watermill, the Tollhouse where the market tolls were collected and the manor courts sat, and the profits of markets, fairs, customs, heriots, fines and tolls, up to a limit of 20s in each case. He had to pay the expenses of the bishop's surveyor, receiver, steward, and auditor, and their servants, when they came to hold courts or settle the manor accounts, and he was forbidden to lease the manor or any part of it to anyone above his own degree of yeoman. As the mill and millhouse were at the time 'olde, feble and utterly in alle poynts distroyed' the bishop agreed to give him £40 to rebuild the mill, millhouse, and milldam, and to replace the millstones when necessary. For repairs Markday could cut timber at Southwood. With the lease he took over the manor farm store of corn, wheat, barley, and oats, and its livestock, four horses, twenty-four cows, and eighty ewes. Each year he was allowed 'a gowne of the sute of yomen of the said Bisshop's houshold lyvere', or 6*s* 8*d* for the price of it.

Markday died before 1524, and his lease was inherited by his son Geoffrey (who bought Guy Harlings in the town in 1528). In 1530 Geoffrey, 'sick in body', made his will, leaving the remaining years of his lease of Bishop's Hall to his wife Joan, and died soon afterwards. It was Geoffrey's widow and executor who sold Guy Harlings to Thomas Mildmay the mercer that same year. When the Bishop's Hall lease ran out in 1533, a fresh twenty-one-year lease at the usual £40 rent was granted to John Taylor by Bishop John Stokesley (1530-9). After Edmund Bonner became bishop of London in 1539, a survey made of his estates noted that Taylor, 'bayly ther', had still fifteen years of his lease to come. The survey also noted that the bishop and the abbot of Westminster were 'bound to repayr the bridge in Chelmsford, which is in great decay, 100 marks will not repair it'. When the manor passed from the bishop to the king in 1545 Taylor as bailiff accounted to the Crown for the customary payment of palfrey money (6*s* 8*d*) in recognition of a new lord, but offset against it the 6*s* 8*d* due to himself as farmer and bailiff for his annual suit of household livery. He also deducted from his £40 rent £5 16*s* 1*d* spent that year, on repairs to both the stone bridge and the bridge in Springfield Lane dividing Chelmsford from Springfield, on thatching manor farm buildings, and on the purchase of a new millstone in London, its hoisting and carriage by sea to Maldon, and thence to Chelmsford.

Taylor's term as farmer of Bishop's Hall and the demesne lands did not long survive the passing of the manor to the Crown. In 1548 that notoriously grasping opportunist, the chancellor, Richard, Lord Rich, was given a fresh twenty-one-year lease of them by the new young king, Edward VI, at the rent of £40 which had not altered since the 14th century. Rich seems to have leased them back to John Taylor, who continued to serve as bailiff of the manor and occupied Bishop's Hall up to his death in 1560, when his widow Elynor inherited the remaining term of his lease. Taylor's long service as bailiff, through all the vicissitudes of the Reformation, must have contributed much to the stability of the town's government during those disturbed years.

Although for the time being Chelmsford itself eluded Master Auditor Mildmay, in June 1546, six months before King Henry's death, on the recommendation of the court of augmentations he did secure from the Crown a twenty-one-year lease of the Southwood estate which, though at Writtle, was in the lordship of Chelmsford. A year later on 22 June 1547 Edward VI gave Southwood to John Dudley, earl of Warwick, from whom Mildmay finally acquired it four days later.

CHELMSFORD AND THE GREAT BIBLE

While shrewd 'new men' made fortunes in a nationwide property market, popular support for the Reformation was stirred by the liberation of religious thought and belief which accompanied it. Once Henry VIII had authorised the printing of a revised edition of Coverdale's translation of the Bible into English, and Thomas Cromwell had told the bishops in 1538 to urge the laity to read the 'Great Bible', and see that a copy was placed in every parish church, all who wished could read or hear the Old and New Testaments in their own tongue and interpret 'God's Word' for themselves. Five editions of the Great Bible, sold at 10*s*, were published by 1541, and a cheaper edition for private reading in 1540. So avidly was it read and debated that by 1543 it was considered advisable to restrict the new freedom, by an Act of Parliament 'For the Advancement of True Religion', to discreet and reliable classes of people; thus women, artificers, apprentices, journeymen, servingmen of the degree of yeomen or under, husbandmen, and labourers, were forbidden to read the New Testament in English, and English Bible-reading in church was stopped. But by then it was too late to halt the spreading flood of religious argument. In his last speech to parliament in 1545 King Henry complained that 'that most precious jewel, the Word of God, is disputed, rhymed, sung, and jangled in every alehouse and tavern'.

At the time of Cromwell's injunction in 1538 a youth called William, son of the haberdasher John Maldon, had been living with his parents in Chelmsford, where he was born. On Sundays he used to listen to some poor men reading aloud an English New Testament at the back of St Mary's church, where, he said, 'manye wolde flocke aboute them to here theyr reading'. But his father would fetch him away to say the Latin Matins with him. So William taught himself to read English from an English primer, and he and his father's apprentice, Thomas Jeffery, pooled their money to buy an English New Testament, which they hid under their bedstraw to read in secret when they could. After he was put in charge of a haberdashery and grocery shop about 'a bowshot' distance from his father's house, he was able there to 'ply his book' in safety. He also acquired, and hid, a copy of John Frith's book on the Sacrament, first published in 1533. Soon reading was not enough; he began 'to speke of the scryptures', even daring to argue with his mother one evening, while his father sat asleep in his chair. He reasoned that kneeling to the crucifix, knocking the breast, and 'holding up our handes to it when it cam by on precessyon', was plain idolatry, against the commandment, 'Thou shalt not make to thyself anye graven image, thou shalt not bowe downe to it nor worshippe'. His mother reproached him: 'A, thou thefe, yf they father knewe this, he wolde hang the[e]. Wilte not thou worshippe the Crosse, and it was aboute the[e] when thou weare crystened and moste be layed one the[e] when thou arte deade'. After William had gone up to bed his father awoke, and his wife reported the conversation. John Maldon took a great rod up to the bedchamber where his son slept between his brother Richard and the apprentice Thomas, three to a bed, and demanded: 'Serra, who is your schoolmaster, tell me'. 'Forsooth, father', replied William, 'I have no schoolmaster but God'. Dragged from his bed by the hair, and beaten, the youth rejoiced to suffer for Christ's sake, 'and wepte not a tear'. His father said, 'Surely he is paste grace for he wepeth not', and went downstairs in a rage to the shop to fetch a halter, saying, 'As good I hange hym up as another shoulde'. Returning he put the halter around William's neck, dragging him from the bed, until, entreated by the cries of his son Richard, and the pleas of his wife, who pulled at her husband's arm, he let him go. Six days later William's neck still 'greved' him. The rift between father and son was never healed. The father, who was buried in Chelmsford in 1561, before his death revoked all previous wills, leaving all he had to his wife Bridget, and his other two sons, Richard and John. William, who shed tears of grief for his parents' 'lake of knowledge', left Chelmsford, and later, after meeting John Foxe, who was compiling his 'Boke of marters', at Foxe's request wrote from 'Newington' the account of his ordeal.

THE END OF THE CHANTRIES

Henry VIII died on 28 January 1547. A precocious nine-year-old boy, Henry's son by his third wife, Jane Seymour, succeeded him as Edward the Sixth. The boy's uncle, Edward Seymour, was designated Protector on 31 January and created duke of Somerset in February. Under the new government the protestant reformers led by Archbishop Cranmer had free rein. The statute of 1543 restricting reading of the English Bible was repealed by Edward's first parliament, which sat from 4 November to 24 December 1547, and went on to annex the revenues of the surviving chantries, religious guilds, and obit-lands, to the Crown. An earlier statute of 1545-6 directed against them had not yet been effectively applied. The 1547 statute roundly condemned 'superstition and errors in christian religion' and the 'phantasying vain opinions' of purgatory and masses sung for the dead. The will drawn up by Master Auditor's father, Thomas Mildmay the mercer, on 7 January 1548, three years before his death, reveals an old man's dilemma in the face of the condemnation of beliefs he had held for a lifetime. His wish, whenever he should die, was for an honest priest to be paid £6 13s 4d, 'to singe for my soule and all Christian soules' in Chelmsford parish church for one whole year after his death. But he felt compelled to add that his wish should be honoured only 'if it so may stonde by thorders hereafter to be taken'; otherwise the money was to be distributed among the poor.

The commissioners who were appointed in 1547 to investigate and certify details of the foundations, value, and possessions of the chantries, described Chelmsford as a very great and populous market town, and 'a great thorughfare for the kynges people'; in one tabulation of their certificates there were said to be eight hundred communicants 'and more' in the parish; in another, a thousand 'at the least', the parish having 'but one priest'. The commissioners found that though the guilds of Corpus Christi, St John, and Our Lady, had all been founded to provide priests to say divine service in the church, the only guild with a priest fulfilling that duty in 1548 was the Corpus Christi or Morrowmass guild. St John's guild had had no incumbent for three years, and Our Lady guild for over a year. The incumbent of Mounteney's Lady chapel in the churchyard celebrated mass in that chapel.

According to Newcourt, Dr Henry Cole, who had been rector of the parish since 1540, a Doctor of Civil Law and warden of New College, Oxford, 'resigned' his Chelmsford living in 1548; but according to the parish register he was 'dysgraced'. Cole had been at first 'altogether for the Reformation', but later became a zealous Catholic and dean of St Paul's under Queen Mary, only to be deprived as dean when Elizabeth became queen, so the parish register may well be right. Thomas Eve, the Corpus Christi priest who was officiating in the church, was described by the commissioners as being over forty years of age, literate, and 'of good conversation and usage'; he was also teaching a school. He had been one of the canons of Little Leighs priory who took the Oath of Supremacy in 1534, before the suppression of the priory in 1536. Peter Wyley, the Mounteney chapel priest, was described as being fifty-six years old, a Master of Arts, and of good conversation; he held no preferment but the chapel in the churchyard, and for sixteen years 'and more' had been teaching a grammar school there. Peter had graduated B.A. at Cambridge in 1519-20, M.A. in 1523, and probably B.D. in 1531-2. Whether Thomas Eve assisted him in the grammar school, or taught his own school was not stated.

The gross annual value of all the houses, market stalls, gardens, meadows, and crofts of land, mainly in Chelmsford and Moulsham, with a few in Writtle and Great Baddow, which belonged to the four chantries, was about £36; the most valuable single property was the manor of Benedict Otes in Writtle, worth £11 a year, owned by Mounteney's chantry. None of the chantries possessed any ornaments, jewels, goods, or chattels. A good deal of this chantry property was already leased to members of the Mildmay family, including the mercer himself. The commissioners also listed the values of rents charged on nineteen properties for the observance of obits, including those of Robert Glover dating from 1411, of Geoffrey, father of the butcher John Biglon, and of Thomas Chalke and Richard Pratt. These obit rents, with the properties of the guilds, now went to swell the revenues of the Crown.

The greatest beneficiaries of the Crown's takeover of the Chelmsford chantry property and obit rents were undoubtedly the Mildmay brothers. Master Auditor and his mercer brother John bought from the Crown all the property of the guild of St John, most of it in Moulsham, but including the priest's house on the north side of Chelmsford churchyard. They also bought jointly a croft of land worth 12s a year which belonged to the Corpus Christi guild. Most of the more valuable town properties of the Corpus Christi guild, to an annual value of £6 6s 8d, were bought by their mercer brother William. Of the Corpus Christi guild's remaining six small tenements, together worth annually £1 16s 10d, one by the churchyard was sold to three Londoners (a gentleman, a fishmonger, and a skinner), but the rents of the other five were still in the hands of the Crown more than a century later. Master Auditor and his brother John also bought small parcels of land and meadow which had belonged to the guild of Our Lady, but most of that guild's property remained in the hands of the Crown, except for two small houses in the town occupied by a surgeon and a tailor, which were sold to outsiders. The Writtle manor of Benedict Otes which had belonged to Mounteney's chantry was also sold to outsiders; but the ten shilling rent of the small house in Duke Street where Mounteney's priest, Peter Wyley, had lived, was reserved for the king's sister, Lady Mary, for life. Another house in Duke Street (site of former 79 Duke Street), which had belonged to the Writtle chantry of St John the Baptist, was bought in 1549 by Robert Wood, gentleman, of the Inner Temple. The Wood family, newcomers, were soon to make their mark in the town. Seven of the nineteen properties charged with obit rents were sold to Thomas and William Mildmay. The obit rent of 10s 4d charged on the three high street tenements called Glovers Obit (site of 28-30 High Street) was sold to the occupant, John Turner, at twenty years purchase: £10 6s 8d. All the others were retained by the Crown.

Sir John Mounteney's Lady chapel in the churchyard did not survive the suppression of the chantries. Built before 1365, and in need of repair in 1497, it had been demolished or fallen down by 1569, when the haberdasher Nicholas Eve asked to be buried in the churchyard, 'near where the late chappel was'. Its site is not known. But the little chapel of St John the Baptist, built on to the north aisle, survived for over three hundred years, to become the repository from the late-17th century of the Knightbridge Library. Much decayed by 1801, but still standing in 1863, it was finally pulled down when the outer north aisle was built in 1873. The two chapels built for the fraternities of Our Lady (north) and Corpus Christi (south), on either side of the chancel, form an integral part of the present building.

King Edward's government did, however, acknowledge that some chantries had provided local services which were worth continuing. It was at this stage that Master Auditor's youngest brother, Walter Mildmay, became involved in the fortunes of his birthplace.

THE NEW GRAMMAR SCHOOL

Walter, born about 1520, was the first Mildmay to have a university education, as a student of Christ's College, Cambridge, about 1538. He was probably brought into the court of augmentations by his eldest brother, Master Auditor; an unsigned letter attributed to 1538, addressed, 'To my brother Mr Thomas Myldemay', provided measurements of the buildings of Badwell Priory, near Bury in Suffolk, and estimated how much lead remained on the roofs. By 1540 Walter was serving in the office of John Eyer, one of the receivers of the court of augmentations: an entry that year in the receivers' accounts is signed in Walter's hand: 'per me Wa. Mildmay'. By 1542, in seeking advancement, he had the goodwill of patrons close to the king, Anthony Denny of the Privy Chamber, Keeper of Westminster Palace, and John Gates, Groom of the Privy Chamber. In 1543 he was appointed one of the two auditors of the King's Prests, auditing the accounts of the king's works and ships, and of all money advanced on the king's affairs, including his wars; his salary was £40 a year. This office took him to Calais in 1544-5, involved in the finances of the French campaign. He was still in 1545 known to his superiors as 'Young Myldemaide', but was rapidly overtaking his eldest brother in reputation and standing, and moving out of his shadow. Indeed, in June 1545 Thomas Mildmay resigned as auditor, to be reappointed joint auditor with Walter of the augmentations for Norfolk, Suffolk, Cambridgeshire, Huntingdonshire, Essex, Hertfordshire, Middlesex, and London. In 1546, like his brother before him, Walter married well. His wife, Mary, was the sister of (Sir) Francis Walsingham, who became a life-long friend.

Shortly before his death King Henry reorganized the court of augmentations. One of the reconstituted court's two General Surveyors, appointed on 2 January 1547 for life, with a salary of £200 a year, was Walter Mildmay. On 28 January the king died. Edward VI was crowned on 20 February, and two days later Walter Mildmay was knighted at the first investiture of the new reign. He was not yet thirty years old. A year later he became one of the two commissioners appointed to determine which functions formerly supported by chantry endowments should be continued.

In Essex Sir Walter and his colleague Robert Keilway found five parishes with chantry objects worthy of support. At Harwich it was the upkeep of the sea walls, at Witham provision for the poor, at Romford a travelling preacher, and at Rayleigh a grammar school. At Chelmsford they approved of two objects. They agreed that an assistant was needed to serve the cure in the parish church, and recommended that Thomas Eve, the former priest of the Corpus Christi guild, become curate, with a stipend of £7 12s 10d a year, the same as he had enjoyed as guild chaplain. They also agreed that

> '... a grammar school has been continually kept in Chelmsford with the revenues of the late chantry of Our Lady otherwise Mownteneye chantry in Chelmsford, and that the schoolmaster there has had for his yearly wages £9 12s, which school is very meet and necessary to continue'.

Walter may have had his early education in that same school.

On 10 February 1551 an order of the court of augmentations, signed by Thomas Mildmay the Auditor, allocated the rents of former guild property in Great Baddow, Hatfield Peverel, and West Tilbury, totalling £20 17s 10d, to the support of a free grammar school in Chelmsford. The royal foundation charter was sealed on 24 March. The school was to be managed by a corporation of four governors: Master Auditor's friend and neighbour, Sir William Petre, knight; his brother, Sir Walter Mildmay, knight; his brother-in-law, Sir Henry Tyrell, knight; and Master Auditor himself, Thomas Mildmay, esquire. The governorships were to descend to their heirs.

Master Auditor took charge of the new foundation. His son and heir, Thomas, remembered in 1606 how his father had appointed a 'wholesome and gentlemanlike house' of his own in the parish, 'somewhat remote from the common street', with two acres of garden and orchard, and adapted it at his own cost as a dwelling for the master and usher, and schoolhouse to teach and instruct the scholars. The house stood on the site of the former friary in Moulsham; it was said to have been the friars' refectory. The Auditor also appointed a 'learned' schoolmaster, Thomas Ithill, later Master of Jesus College, Cambridge, and put his son Thomas, then aged nine years, 'to be his scholler'. There was, at first, no provision for the appointment of an usher, but the master of the former chantry grammar school, Peter Wyley, may have assisted in the early years of the school. Certainly Peter remained in Chelmsford. He witnessed the probate of old Thomas Mildmay the mercer's will in January 1551, and when he died in 1566 he was the owner and occupant of the St John's chantry priest's house on the north side of the churchyard, which had been bought by the Auditor in 1548.

Thomas Ithill left the school about 1554, when young Thomas Mildmay was twelve years old, and was succeeded by Mr Richard Kitchen, M.A., '... a very learned and painful schoolmaster ... one that made many good scholars'. Under Kitchen, who stayed until about 1565, there were over sixty scholars in the school. One of them was Philemon Holland. Holland's parents, John and Barbara, were married in Chelmsford in 1551; their son Philemon was born in 1552, reputedly in Chelmsford, though there is no record of his baptism. From the grammar school he went on to matriculate at Trinity College, Cambridge, in 1566, graduating B.A. in 1570, and M.A. in 1574. The grounding in Latin that Holland gained under Kitchen served him well, for he became renowned as a translator of the classics, including Livy's *History of Rome* (1600), Pliny's *History of the World* (1601), Plutarch's *Morals* (1603), Suetonius's *History of twelve Caesars* (1606), and in 1632, at the age of eighty, Xenophon's *Life of Cyrus*. In 1610 his translation of his friend William Camden's *Britannia* was published. Dr Fuller later called Holland the 'translator general of his age', adding that 'these books alone, of his turning into English, will make a country gentleman a competent library'. Holland's parents died in Dunmow, his father, rector there since 1564, in 1578, followed by his wife Barbara in 1580. Philemon, their eldest child, was remembered in both their wills. He never returned to Chelmsford, but became a schoolmaster and physician in Coventry, after taking his degree in medicine in 1597. His career was a testimonial to the quality of the schooling to be had in the early years of Chelmsford's grammar school.

Kitchen's immediate successor as master, Thomas Rust, conscientiously attended to his duties, brought his scholars to church on Sundays, and was respectfully accorded the status of 'gentleman'. His salary was £24 a year and he lived with his family in the schoolhouse. His premature death in 1584 left his widow Grace homeless with five small children and little to support them. But her dilemma was solved when she married her husband's successor, Mr Stephens, M.A., who held the post until his death in 1594.

THE DEATH OF THE MERCER

Thomas Mildmay the mercer was buried on 17 November, 1550, four months before the grammer school was established. By then his eldest son Thomas the Auditor was an esquire, and his youngest son Walter a knight; they were land-owners, lords of manors, and justices of the peace; Sir Walter had already sat in parliament as member for Lostwithiel. Their two surviving brothers, William and John, both of them mercers, styled themselves, 'gentleman', and William was lord by purchase of the manor of Springfield Barnes near Chelmsford, once the property of Coggeshall Abbey. But their father was content to be titled in his will plain 'merchant and yeoman'. He owned no manors, and apart from some market stalls in Braintree, all his property in houses, market stalls, crofts, barns, and oxen stalls, lay in Chelmsford and its neighbour Springfield. He was buried, as he wished, in the Lady chapel in the parish church. Guy Harlings he gave to his heir, Thomas the Auditor; Mayes was left to William, and to John the house next to the Crane where John was living, a cottage in New Street, and other small properties. One of his stalls in Chelmsford market he gave to William, 'to occupy in every Friday at his pleasure', and also his two stalls in Braintree, 'now made one, which I have used to stand in every Wednesday'. His other Chelmsford stall and a second double stall in Braintree went to John. His wife Agnes was provided for for life, and his two surviving daughters, Joan Peyton and Thomasin Bourchier, his nine grandchildren, and two Read relatives of his wife, received gifts of money. On his son John he laid the duty of providing five loads of firewood every year for the poor.

The mercer's youngest son, Sir Walter, was an overseer of his father's will, but not personally a beneficiary. Sir Walter's son Anthony, however, on reaching the age of twenty-four years, was to be paid by his father the sum of £20 which Sir Walter owed the old mercer at the time of his death. Thomas the mercer was a business man, and his sons, however distinguished, were expected to pay their debts.

The mercer's widow, Agnes, did not long survive her husband. She died in April 1552, a kindly woman, thoughtful for her family, her household, and the poor. She left 3s 4d to buy 'pore folks boks' in church, a shilling apiece to forty poor householders of Chelmsford and Moulsham, and a featherbed, mattress, bolster, and blankets, canvas (coarse linen) sheets 'of my awne cloth', and a tablecloth, all from the room over the kitchen, to 'the gerle called Jone yt I browght uppe of Almes'. To each of her maids, Denise and Agnes, she gave the mattress and featherbed 'she lies in', with two pairs of sheets and two canvas tablecloths. She asked her executors to give to 'poor folks ... where they think most need' the beds her men servants had lain on, each with a pair of coarse worn sheets. Her other possessions were shared among her sons, daughters, and grand-children. They included her best 'trusse' bed in the great chamber at Guy Harlings, with the best bedding and her six best cushions; her own featherbed that 'I lie on in the chamber over the hall', and another bed with hangings of red and yellow say standing in the room over the gateway; more hangings in the great chamber; her best carpet; and another carpet and curtains of red and green say in the parlour. She shared out cupboards, tables, and stools; pots of brass and a great pewter basin; chargers, platters, and porringers, cauldrons and candlesticks, and a chafer 'to sethe in water by the fire'. The choicest items, a dozen silver spoons, a silver pot, and the gilt pot which had belonged to her dead son Edward, she left to her daughter Thomasin, and to her grandson Richard Bernard, son of her dead daughter Margaret.

After the death of his father, Thomas Mildmay, Auditor, took his place as head of the Mildmay family. The family, in his person, were already entitled to bear Arms featuring three greyhounds' heads, but in 1552 his ambitious youngest brother, Sir Walter, applied for a grant of Arms on his own behalf. Sir Walter had acquired a fine manor house and country seat at Apethorpe in Northampton-shire in 1551 (a seat which was to be the home of his descendants until the present century), and he submitted his application the following year. His peti-tion did not refer to his father, the mercer, or name any of his forbears or kindred, but claimed simply that Sir Walter was descended

'... of a house unedefemyd and hath of longe tyme used hymself in feats of armes and warks vertuous so that he is well worthie to beare the tokens and ensignes of honnoure, that is to say, armes'.

The coat granted bore a winged horse on a silver bend.

Master Auditor, for his part, as a government official, justice of the peace, esquire, lord of Moulsham, and governor of the new grammar school, was now the personage of the greatest local consequence in the county town of Essex. In 1558 he became sheriff of Essex. When his wife Avice died in October 1557 her burial at Chelmsford was solemnized with fitting ceremony; the procession was described with professional interest by Henry Machyn, a London merchant tailor and furnisher of funerals, as one attended

'... with ij whytt branchys, and ij dosen of grett stayffe torchys, and iiij dosen of skochyons, and mony mornars in blake'.

Master Auditor might be lord of Moulsham, but Chelmsford was still in the hands of the Crown. In parish matters, however, this was no disability, for Chelmsford was already progressing towards a delicate balance in local govern-ment between the town and hamlet and the parish which embraced them both. This was encouraged by Tudor policies which increasingly laid local civil duties upon the parish rather than upon the manor, and by the residence in the parish of a lord of the manor in Moulsham of Master Auditor's standing, while only a manor bailiff lived in Chelmsford. The oldest surviving assessment to a

Chelmsford parish rate, raised in 1557 to pay the parish clerk's wages, listed the ratepayers of Chelmsford and Moulsham separately. But Mildmay was not listed among Moulsham's ratepayers; his name headed the whole list, above the four senior householders of Chelmsford, the draper 'Master (William) Reynolds', the Auditor's brother, 'Master William Mildmay', 'Old Mr Ayer' (William Ayer), 'gentleman', who occupied the White Horse inn (formerly known as Wendover-shall) at the top of the high street, and 'Master Baylye' himself, John Taylor, the Crown's manorial agent in the town.

The assessment named ninety-five rateable householders in Chelmsford at that date, and only thirty-seven in Moulsham. Thomas Mildmay, rated at 5s a quarter, bore the heaviest burden in the parish, followed by his brother William and Master Reynolds at 3s 4d each, Geoffrey Scott of the Lion inn at 2s 6d, and the bailiff, John Taylor, the occupant of Bishop's Hall, at 2s. The Auditor's other brother, mercer John Mildmay, paid 1s 8d a quarter, as did Richard Putto of the Cock inn, William Wigglesworth of the Crown (*alias* New) inn, Nicholas Eve of the Rose (site of former 12-13 Tindal Street), and John Bridges of the Boar's Head. No one else paid more than a shilling a quarter. In all, twenty-five of Chelmsford's ninety-five ratepayers paid 6d a quarter or more, the rest of them paid from a penny to fourpence. This parish assessment exposes the widening economic gulf between the town and the hamlet: in Moulsham the highest assessment was fourpence a quarter, and only two householders paid as much as that; Clark the cobbler only paid ½d.

QUEEN MARY'S TOWN

King Edward VI died on 6 July 1553. In the course of the six and a half years of his reign, while rival aristocratic families, such as the Seymours and Dudleys, competed for influence with the young king and control of his council, reaction had set in against the increasingly extreme Protestant policies of his government. In Chelmsford dissidents were active in November 1550, when the Privy Council sent Master Auditor down from London as a justice of the peace, with Sir John Gates, to investigate a seditious bill which had been thrown in the streets. In April 1551 the parish register recorded the burials of a tapster and three other men hanged at Chelmsford for a 'conspiracy', or, as the clerk originally wrote, then struck out, an 'uprore'. The clerk was surely familiar with the English Bible, for 'uproar', in the sense of an insurrection, was first used in English by Tyndale and Coverdale.

Once Edward was dead, conspiracy and rebellion erupted on a national scale. Indeed, while the king was dying John Dudley, the Protestant duke of Northumberland, was plotting to exclude the legitimate heir, Edward's half-sister Mary, a devout Catholic, in favour of his own daughter-in-law, Henry VIII's great-niece, Lady Jane Grey. But the plot collapsed, and on 19 July Mary was proclaimed queen, amid general rejoicing and hopes of more settled times. Power shifted from the extreme Protestant reformers to those who had clung to the old Faith, whether openly, like Mary herself, or privately; and to the more conservative reformers, whose loyalty to the Crown or self-interest bound them to Henry's elder daughter.

As the manor of Chelmsford was still a Crown possession, Queen Mary became the town's new Lady. When Sir Richard Rich and six other Essex notables sent her a letter of support on 3 February 1554, at the time of Sir Thomas Wyatt's rebellion against the queen's proposed Spanish marriage, they wrote to her 'from your Towne of Chelmysforde', to wish her 'most honerable vyctoryes and good successe in your Graces affayers'. Thomas Mildmay was not one of the signatories, but this need not imply any lack of loyalty; it more likely indicates his lower county rank as a newcomer among the Essex landed gentry, compared to the members of the longer-established Rich, Capel, Wiseman, Berners, Tyrell, and Josselin families, who signed. Mildmay continued to hold office as an auditor of the court of augmentations until that court was dissolved in 1554, when he became an auditor of the Crown's land revenues.

Queen Mary could not hope to find support for any attempt to undo the Reformation's dispersal of eccliastical property and wealth. As Simon Renard, ambassador to England of Mary's cousin the Emperor Charles V, reported to his Catholic master: 'The Catholics hold more Church property than do the heretics'. The new owners, such as the Mildmays, were reassured by an Act of Parliament passed in January 1555, which confirmed their title to their acquisitions. But the changes made by Henry VIII and Edward VI in religious practice and belief were not universally acceptable to her subjects, and Mary's own fervent wish, her mission as she saw it, was to bring about England's reconciliation with Rome. This was accomplished in November 1554. The Latin Mass was restored, in place of the new English service for administration of the Sacrament, drafted by Cranmer for the 'book of common prayer' published in 1549, and revised in 1552. With the return to favour of church ornaments and images, proscribed in Edward's reign, the crown on the figure of Our Lady on the high altar of Chelmsford church was repaired and her hands mended, and the angels holding up the roof of the nave and displayed upon it were repainted.

Ominously, the medieval laws against heresy, condemning unrepentant heretics to 'be burnt, that such punishment may strike fear to the minds of other[s]', and abolished in Edward's reign, were revived in December 1554. Mary's initial popularity, undermined by her marriage in July 1554 to Philip of Spain, was to be destroyed by the persecution of 'heretics' which began in 1555, and continued to the end of her reign nearly four years later.

On her accession Mary deprived Nicholas Ridley of the see of London, and restored Edmund Bonner as bishop. His diocese, including Essex, was one of those most harassed by the pursuit of heretics. In London sixty-seven were burned, in Middlesex eleven, and in Essex thirty-nine. Over the inhabitants of Chelmsford, where the justices of the peace met to investigate informations and rumours, and the assize judges sat to pronounce sentence on those whom the persuasions of the Church failed to move, hung the shadow of the persecution. The town became a stage in the journey of suspects, where they halted for the night under guard, on their way up to London for interrogation. One of them, in February 1555, was the revered and popular Dr Rowland Taylor from Hadleigh in Suffolk. On his return journey, condemned to the stake, it was at Chelmsford that the sheriff of Essex handed him over to the sheriff of Suffolk, to conduct him to Hadleigh for execution of sentence. In April 1555 Thomas Wats, a Billericay linendraper, came before the justices, including Thomas Mildmay, at Chelmsford, charged with not saying mass, and holding conventicles in corners.

He was sent up to London, condemned, and brought back to Chelmsford. There he was lodged in Geoffrey Scott's inn, the Lion, by the stone bridge, where he dined with four fellow victims, Thomas Hawkes, Nicholas Chamberlain, Thomas Osmond, and William Bamford, and three reprieved men on their way to Coggeshall to make public recantation. Wats's companions were sent on to Coggeshall, Colchester, Manningtree, and Harwich for burning, but the execution of Wats himself took place at Chelmsford in June. The occasion cost the ratepayers of Harwich 14s for the expenses, including hire of a horse, of sending a representative to Chelmsford, to attend, as ordered, upon Lord Rich and the other heresy commissioners and justices, at the public spectacle of Wats's burning.

The border-line between heresy and treason was sometimes a fine one. In July 1555 the privy council were investigating 'a conspiracy of late intended in Essex and Suffolk'. This was probably the subject of the letter of thanks sent to Thomas Mildmay, William Berners, and Edmund Tyrell on 3 August, 'for thier travail in apprehending such lewd persons as intended a conspiracy of late in Essex'. But whether a man was a traitor or a heretic could be a matter of opinion. John Foxe extolled George Eagles as a martyr for religion, but the privy council regarded him as a dangerous agitator, and his death at Chelmsford was the one prescribed by law for traitors.

Eagles was a tailor of Moze in north-east Essex, popularly known as a Trudge or Trudge-over-the-World. In 1556 a Mersea husbandman and a Dedham clothier were indicted at Chelmsford sessions for assembling with twenty others in Mersea and Dedham and other places on many occasions to hear Eagles's 'heresies and schismatic sermons and preachings'. His wanderings were such that a reward of £20, offered by the authorities in the summer of 1556 for his capture as a runagate who 'dothe what he maye to persuade the people to rebellion', was advertised in Essex, Suffolk, Kent, and Norfolk. He evaded capture for a year, until he was taken near Colchester in July 1557. He was held in the county goal there until brought to trial at Chelmsford, on the charge, 'that thou didst such a day make thy prayer that God should turn away Queen Mary's heart or else take her away'. He was condemned as a traitor, to be executed at Chelmsford.

The townsmen were divided in their sympathies. The choice by the town's leaders in 1556 of Thomas Jeffery as one of their constables may suggest that in religion they were at least tolerant. Thomas Jeffery, by then a grown man and a ratepayer, was the former haberdasher's apprentice who in King Henry's day had shared with his bedfellow, William Maldon, the English New Testament hidden under the straw mattress. Some of the townsmen who witnessed Eagles's execution took the trouble to send a full report of it to John Foxe, for inclusion in his record of Protestant martyrs. Foremost among them was the draper William Reynolds, who was at pains to deny rumours that Eagles under interrogation had betrayed 'honest men' who had succoured him in his wanderings. Their report implicitly condemns the brutality of the proceedings.

But others in the town, and most notably Richard Putto, the landlord of the Cock inn beside the stone bridge, were zealous for the old Faith restored by Mary, and the conversion of heretics. After conviction Eagles was taken to the new inn called the Crown on the corner of Springfield Lane, where the sheriff sometimes lodged his prisoners. While Eagles was being bound and laid on a sledge with a hurdle on it, to be drawn to the gallows place upland of the town,

Putto assailed him with religious argument. When the procession reached the gallows, Putto was still importuning him to recant as he mounted the ladder, until the sheriff ordered Putto 'to trouble him no more'. Then followed the sickening legal formalities of the traitor's death; turned off the ladder to hang, Eagles was cut down alive and laid on the sledge, where William Swallow, a Chelmsford householder who was one of the sheriff's bailiffs, 'did hackle off his head ... with a cleaver, such as is occupied in many men's kitchens and blunt'; the body was cut open, the heart plucked out, bowels burned, and body quartered. The quarters were exposed on the fishstalls before the door of Swallow's own house in the fishmarket, while a cart was made ready to carry three of the quarters to Colchester, Harwich, and St Osyth, for display. The head was set up on Chelmsford market cross on a long pole, 'and there stood, till the wind blew it down, and lying certain days in the street tumbled about, one caused it to be buried in the churchyard at night'. A letter of 3 August from the Privy Council to Anthony Browne, serjeant-at-law, officially approved the diligence of his conduct of the proceedings against Eagles, and commended the decision made 'towching the distribution of Trudge's hed and quarters', which the council said was 'well liked'.

Anthony Browne was well known in the town in a different capacity, as Queen Mary's manor steward, who presided over Chelmsford's manor court. In that rôle his authority was not unchallenged; at a court held two months before Mary's death he was openly opposed by one of the Chelmsford constables, William Browning, who was fined 40s for his insolence. When Browning refused to pay the fine, the bailiff John Taylor seized his bay gelding in distraint for it, but Browning attacked him with a sword and recovered it. The fine was not paid until 1560.

Mary's death in November 1558 lifted the shadow of terror. She was succeeded by her half-sister Elizabeth, whose first parliament, which met on 23 January 1559 and sat until 8 May, reversed Mary's policy, and laid the foundations of a moderate and lasting religious settlement. In August 1559 the earl of Oxford administered to the Essex justices at Chelmsford sessions the oath acknowledging the abolition of all foreign powers. In the same month, all the clergy were required personally to accept the restoration of the 'Auncyaunte Jurisdiccion over the state Ecclesiasticall and spyrytuall of the Realme of Ynglande and abolisshing of all forayn power repugnaunte to the same', together with the order for administering the sacrament and performing divine service 'as it is set furthe in a Booke comonly called the booke of common prayers'. Seventy-two of the Essex clergy signed their 'confession' in Chelmsford parish church; others signed at South Weald, Bishop's Stortford, Dunmow, and Colchester. Among those who signed in the county town was its new rector, Christopher Tatem, presented to the living by Mary as patron only a few months before her death. Other signatories there were Peter Wyley, the former chaplain of Mounteney's chantry, and Hugh Taylor, parson of Woodham Ferrers, who had been curate at Chelmsford in 1534 when he and Peter Wyley had together subscribed to the Act of Supremacy. James Bilney, the vicar of Chigwell, who was the first of the clergy to sign at Chelmsford, did so with evident relief. Beneath the terms of the declaration, which were set out in full at the head of every page of signatures, he wrote after his name: 'Ore non tantum sed ab intimo corde subscribo' [Not only with my mouth but from the depth of my heart do I subscribe].

CHAPTER NINE

The Elizabethan Town

MASTER AUDITOR'S TOWN

On Queen Mary's death, her half-sister Queen Elizabeth I became Chelmsford's new lady of the manor and patron of the living. Elizabeth claimed from the manor's copyholders the customary 6s 8d due as Palfrey Money at every lord's first court keeping; she exercised her right as patron in 1561, after Christopher Tatem resigned, to present William Ireland as rector in his place; and when she passed through the town in 1561 on one of her royal progresses the ringers, fortified by twelve pennyworth of beer, pealed St Mary's church bells for the queen who was also their lady and patron.

Under Queen Elizabeth, Thomas Mildmay of Moulsham continued to hold office as an auditor of the Crown's land revenues. Elizabeth was the fourth Tudor sovereign he had served, and within five years of her accession he won his reward. On 24 July 1563 the manor of Bishop's Hall in Chelmsford and advowson of the rectory of Chelmsford, with the rent and reversion of the manor house and nearly three hundred acres of demesne lands (leased since 1548 to Richard, Lord Rich, for twenty-one years), were granted by Elizabeth to 'Thomas Mildmay of Moulsham, the queen's servant'. He paid £1,202 2s 9d for them. The deal must surely have represented the achievement of a long-held ambition. A week later, on 31 July 1563, the 'First Court of Thomas Mildmay, esquire', was held for the manor of Chelmsford, and the tenants acknowledged him to be their lord.

Mildmay's purchase included the watermill on the Chelmer called the Bishop's Mill, the market in the town, the Tollhouse 'to keep court in', and the Cross of Chelmsford. He claimed the customary Palfrey Money as new lord, and the town's chief pledges, emboldened by the arrival of a lord known to them from his youth, and the first lord ever to be resident in the parish, lost no time in petitioning him in 1564 to restore the roof of the 'Great Cross called Le Market Cross', said to be 'in great ruin', and to provide a bushel measure for the market, both these matters being by custom the lord's charge.

Master Auditor's enjoyment of his new status in Chelmsford as lord of town, upland, and hamlet, and patron of the living, was brief, for he died three years later. In his short term as lord perhaps his single most beneficial act on behalf of the town was his appointment of William Sidey as manor steward in place of Anthony Browne, the unpopular serjeant-at-law who had pursued George Eagles with such ruthless efficiency. At the first court presided over by Sidey, in February 1564, a determination to enforce good government in the town was immediately evident. For the convenience not only of the residents, but also of 'foreigners' coming into the town, the court reaffirmed its by-laws, and set them down formally in a schedule in the keeping of the bailiff. The schedule was, moreover, written for the first time, not in Latin like the rest of the court record, but in English, 'for the better and more redy understandying' of the bailiff himself, as also of those he had to warn to observe them. This was a good augury for the town's future under the Mildmays.

Master Auditor was buried on 25 September 1566. His will had been drawn up

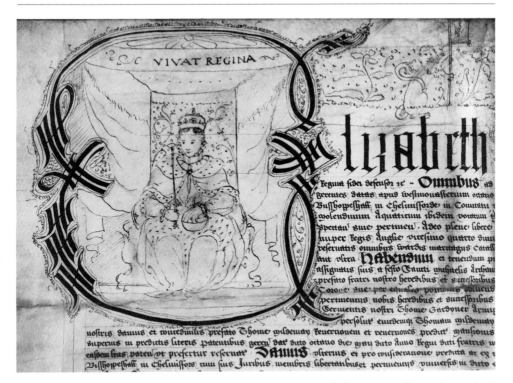

Initial portrait of Queen Elizabeth I on the Crown grant of the manor of 'Busshoppeshall in Chelmisforde' to Thomas Mildmay of Moulsham, 1563

with care in the January of that year. Only five of his fifteen children survived him: a married daughter, Elizabeth Waldegrave; his heir Thomas, twenty-six years old; and three younger sons, Walter, Henry, and Edward, who were still being educated. Their father was determined that the estate which he had so carefully built up in Moulsham and Chelmsford should remain the capital seat of the newly-arrived Mildmay family. The estate was entailed on his eldest son Thomas and his male heirs, with successive reversions, failing such heirs, to his other three sons and their male heirs in turn. In default of any heir at all of his line, the estate was to revert successively to the male descendants of Master Auditor's own brothers, Sir Walter of Apethorpe, William of Springfield Barnes, and John of Chelmsford and later of Terling, in that order. The London house, with its great garden and stables in the parish of St Thomas the Apostle, was to descend with the Chelmsford and Moulsham estate, so that the family should always have a 'handsome house' to occupy when there was occasion to resort to London.

The rest of Master Auditor's extensive estate, including manors, lands, parsonages, and leases, in Essex, Norfolk, and Hertfordshire, were to remain for seven years in the hands of his executors — his son Thomas and brother Sir Walter — to provide for the education and support of the three younger sons; later they would be shared among the four brothers.

The personal bequests of the will reflect the rewards of the Auditor's long years in government office. Individual gifts of money totalled £1,653, and annuities for life charged on the estate some £92 a year. There were gold rings engraved *Remember me* for his three brothers, his son-in-law William Waldegrave, and his brother-in-law, Benjamin Gunson. There were hangings and napery, brass and pewter vessels, plate worth £100, jewels and brooches, to be shared out. To Thomas, his heir, went Master Auditor's personal armour, a flagon and gold chain which his mother-in-law Mistress Bennet Gunson had given him, and the ring with his seal which he always wore on his forefinger; and to his son-in-law Waldegrave choice of two of his best geldings. For his daughter Elizabeth there was the little silver gilt salt-cellar which he had given to her mother Avice as a New Year's gift in the year of her death, and for his grand-daughter Avice Waldegrave a gold chain on the day of her marriage. His servants were all remembered, according to their service, with his maid Isabel and Nurse Sabian receiving £10 each provided they remained with his children for two years after his death.

Master Auditor provided generously for the poor. A bias in favour of the poor of Moulsham, which had been his home for over twenty years, was to be expected. This was one of the few occasions when Chelmsford came off second best. Immediate alms of £8 to be distributed in Moulsham were matched by only £2 for 'the poverty' of Chelmsford. The executors were to give £4 a year to the Moulsham poor out of the profits of both manors for seven years, then, when all legacies in the will had been paid, to distribute a further £40 in Moulsham from what remained. Every year 66s 8d was set aside to buy three barrels of white herring and four casks of red herring during Lent, for the poor of both manors; but only the Moulsham poor were to enjoy the roasted ox or bullock provided each Christmas eve at a cost of 40s.

The will's most outstanding provision for the Moulsham poor was the creation of an almshouse charity. The sum of £6 a year was allotted to support six aged impotent poor people of Moulsham, three men and three women, to be called 'the Bedefolkes' or 'poor alms people' of Moulsham. This provision was amplified in a codicil added to the will only a month before Master Auditor's death; this devised in trust to the bishop of London six separate houses in Moulsham (two of them next to the Friars' Gate and another next to the Greyhound), 'to the end that the six poor folkes called Bedefolkes or alms people of Moulsham shall be assured of their certain dwelling places in Moulsham'. The almsfolk were to be chosen by the owner of Moulsham Hall, who was to deliver to them each year six loads of firewood.

Finally, Master Auditor did not forget the free grammar school which he had helped to establish in the old friary building, and to which he had entrusted his heir's education. By his will he increased its endowment by 40s a year, towards the salary of an usher to assist the master. The usher was to be nominated by the owner of Moulsham Hall.

Master Auditor asked his executors to bury him in the parish church, 'hard by or within' the grave of his wife Avice, and to spend £40 soon after his death on 'a comely tomb or monument of hard stone' near his wife's burial place. His own and his wife's arms were to be engraved on it, with

'... pictures of us both and fifteen children, the one half men children and the other half women children, as a remembrance of our being here together upon the earth, and for a remembrance to our children and friends left behind us, without any pomp or glory or other respect'.

The monument was erected in 1571, in the north (Lady) chapel of the parish church. It stands now at the east end of the outer north aisle. Tall, richly embellished with fluted columns, friezes, pinnacles, and pediments, and surmounted by a noble fluted capping of ogée form topped by a gilded ball, it probably displays greater pomp than Master Auditor would have wished. But otherwise his specification was faithfully observed. The Latin epitaph reads:

> 'Here are seen engraven the effigies of Thomas Mildmay and Avice his wife, but within their remains lie in peace. He was a renowned Esquire, she a daughter and lovely branch of William Gunson, Esquire, and they had fifteen pledges of their prosperous love'.

The kneeling figures of Avice at the head of their seven daughters, and Thomas at the head of their eight sons face each other, in two panels on either side of a third panel which bears the achievement of the Mildmay Arms granted to Thomas and his posterity in the reign of Henry VIII — three greyhounds' heads couped with collars. The Gunson Arms of Avice's family are incorporated in another shield on the side of the monument.

THE FIRST SIR THOMAS MILDMAY

The new lord of Chelmsford, Master Auditor's son Thomas, had been knighted only three months before his father's death. Besides being well educated — at Chelmsford grammar school, Christ's College, Cambridge, and Lincoln's Inn — he was well connected, with his uncle, Sir Walter Mildmay, Queen Elizabeth's chancellor of the exchequer. Indeed, in 1583 Sir Walter procured a new Coat of Arms for the family. As Sir Walter's previous petition for a grant of Arms in 1552 had been unaccompanied by any evidence of ancient lineage, it was curious that his 1583 application was supported by a bundle of 'auntient credible and authenticall deedes, charters, recordes, wrytinges, evidences and letters'; these purported to prove the Mildmay descent from an otherwise unknown Hugh de Mildeme said to have lived in King Stephen's reign. It was also curious that the documents were produced by Sir Walter in Northamptonshire, and not by his nephew, Sir Thomas, the head of the family, in Chelmsford. In fact the documents, now housed in the Northamptonshire Record Office, have been revealed to be forgeries, as J.H. Round suspected in 1930. Nonetheless Robert Cooke, Clarenceux Herald, accepted the evidence, and granted Sir Walter a new coat of three blue lions rampant in a silver field, the device subsequently adopted by the family. In a codicil to the grant, however, Cooke confirmed that the Arms granted to Master Auditor and his posterity in the reign of King Henry VIII, and depicted on his tomb (three greyhounds' heads couped with collars), might still lawfully be borne by the family, as well as the new Arms.

In 1580 Sir Thomas married into the peerage; his first wife, Frances, was the daughter of Henry Radcliffe, second earl of Sussex, whose family held the barony of Fitzwalter. Unlike his father and uncle, who had profitable careers in central government, Sir Thomas made his mark as a county magnate, deeply involved, unpaid, in the conduct of local affairs. He was a leading Essex justice of the peace, the county's *custos rotulorum* from 1576 to 1608, sheriff in 1572-3, member of parliament in 1584-5, and deputy lieutenant in 1603. Between 1569 and 1603 he attended ninety-two sessions of the peace, more than any other Essex magistrate, the next most diligent member of the bench, with sixty-seven attendances from 1573 to 1603, being Sir John Petre. When invasion from Spain threatened in 1588, and King Philip launched his 'invincible armada', it was Sir Thomas Mildmay who, with Sir Henry Gray of Pyrgo, was responsible for reporting to the earl of Leicester, commander of the army mustering at Tilbury to resist the invaders, on the state of readiness of the forces in Essex. It was Sir Thomas and Sir Henry who told the earl how 'the gentlemen of the shire', assembled at Chelmsford, had agreed voluntarily to furnish thirty-eight horsemen and ninety-four footmen, in addition to their usual complement, and who asked for the earl's directions on the equipment of a two thousand contingent of the trained bands who were to form the queen's bodyguard on her visit to Tilbury to review the troops.

For forty-two years Sir Thomas presided over the two Chelmsford manors of Bishop's Hall and Moulsham. The manor house and demesne farm of Bishop's Hall he leased to a yeoman tenant; he himself continued to live in Moulsham Hall, the great courtyard house built by his father, which by 1591 Sir Thomas himself had 'much bettered, augmented, and beautified'. His jealousy of his position as proprietor of the county town of Essex, which became his with the manor of Bishop's Hall, was revealed in a letter which he wrote in 1604. The occasion was the election of the members of the first parliament of King James I. Whenever Essex's two knights of the shire were to be elected, the sheriff of Essex was required, 'according to the ancient custome', to assemble the county's freeholders 'at Chensford and not elsewhere for that purpose'. At such times candidates and their patrons vied in taking up inns in the town for the refreshment and encouragement of their supporters. Before the 1558 election the privy council had had to intervene in a dispute when Geoffrey Scott, owner of the Lion inn by the stone bridge, after promising his inn to Lord Rich, withdrew his consent in favour of Sir John Raynsforth. A similar wrangle arose in 1604, when Robert, Lord Rich, tried to secure the Crown (New) inn on the north corner of Springfield Lane, the Dolphin in the back street behind the Middle Row, and the Lion (which belonged to Sir John Petre), for his chosen candidate, Sir Francis Barrington. It appeared, however, that Sir Thomas Mildmay had already 'taken up almost all the inns and houses in Chelmsford, and, as it is given out, for Sir Edward Denny,' Denny being a rival candidate, favoured by the Court, Barrington, who had expected Mildmay's support, wrote to Mildmay to protest. Mildmay's reply was blunt: 'If you have heard that I have taken up sundry inns in Chelmsford, you have heard it truly, for I have done so, and I know not who hath authority to except against me in so doing in mine own town'. Chelmsford's new lord was a man to be reckoned with, one who, as he added in his letter to Barrington, 'neither would be led nor driven to any man's pleasure'. So far as the town was concerned his authority was paramount. From time to time he chose to be 'present in person' when the manor court sat, and presided at the annual 'assembly' of the chief inhabitants of the parish.

Under the Mildmays, Bishop's Hall, with 283 acres of demesne farmland in the Upland, was no longer tenanted by the lord's bailiff, but by prosperous yeomen

112

like Richard Long (d.1588), and his son Edward, at a rent of some £130 a year. John Taylor (d.1560) was the last bailiff to occupy the hall. Nor were any profits of the manor leased to the Mildmay bailiff, whose duty it became to gather them up as agent on his master's behalf. Sir Thomas Mildmay employed four bailiffs: Richard Marion, who had served his father, to *c.*1570, then Richard Parker (who had been Marion's deputy) to *c.*1575, followed by John Rison to 1591, and John Reeve to 1607. Sir Thomas's profits included manorial rents amounting to £21 a year, manor court fines and dues, including heriots, worth some £20 a year, other customary entitlements such as felons' goods and fines imposed on residents in the manor at Quarter Sessions or higher courts, worth £18 a year, and tolls for traders' standings at the annual fairs and weekly Friday market, worth some £20. By the end of the century two fairs were being held each year, on May Day, and on Holymas Day (1 November). As the lord's agent the bailiff had to distrain on defaulters' goods for rents in arrears or court fines unpaid, and to confiscate movable stalls set up in the market without proper title.

As lord of the town Sir Thomas had certain responsibilities. One of them was the Great Cross. In 1564 the chief pledges had drawn his father's attention to the ruinous state of its roof, but Master Auditor died before anything was done. Immediately after Sir Thomas became lord in 1566 he, too, was petitioned to restore the Cross. The date 1569, discovered in 1709 carved on one of its oak timbers, was accepted then as the date of its rebuilding; this was stated to have been done 'at the publick charge of this county at above £1,000 expence'. This is not unlikely, for the Market Cross or 'Cross House', although privately owned by the Mildmays, was also, as described in 1531, the shire court house used by the justices of the peace and the assize judges; manor court business was conducted in the Tollhouse behind the Cross, near the south gate of the churchyard. The rebuilt Cross was an open-sided building, with eight oak columns supporting upper galleries and a tiled roof. The galleries, which overlooked the open 'piazza' below, were lit by three dormer windows in the roof. In 1590, at a parish assembly presided over by Sir Thomas, the principal inhabitants agreed to spend a surplus of £6 10s 8d on the parish surveyors' account on repairs to the Cross, as far as it would go, and on 'setting the same wythin wyth stonne', that is, paving the floor of the court.

The Cross was described in 1591 by Edward Moryson, Sir Thomas Mildmay's professional surveyor, as a 'faire building ... verie convenient and necessary both for the Justices themselves, their under officers and ministers, and also for all sortes of subjects to be attendant there ...', where all might 'commodiously' serve at their 'convenient ease'. The description, probably calculated to please a patron, was perhaps over-optimistic. The magistrates and judges sat in open court, which measured only 26 feet by 24 feet, with the officers of the law, counsel and clerks, plaintiffs and defendants, jurors, sureties, witnesses and prisoners, before and around them, while spectators, hangers-on, and those awaiting their turn, crowded into the galleries above or thronged the street outside. They had to contend with the noise of passing wheeled traffic and droves of cattle, the stifling heat of the sun in summer, the chill draughts of the wind in winter, and the all-pervasive dust and odours of the street. It fell to the manor court to uphold as best it could the dignity of a public building so exposed to the daily squalor of its surroundings. Nearby householders were discouraged by fines from sweeping their domestic rubbish and ashes out into the street around the Cross; a by-law totally forbade the disposal of 'stable dung' on the common town dump near the Cross at the top of the Middle Row. In 1574 the court threatened a fine of 20s for anyone who should 'presume' to use the Cross as a convenient place for easing nature; a serving man or maid, or apprentice, who did so, was to be beaten with blows or whipped through the town.

The open form of the Cross did, however, suit the corn buyers in the market, for while it sheltered them, it let in plenty of light to judge the quality of the grain. The standard market bushel was supposed to be kept chained in the Cross, 'that thereby the buyers and sellers of corn may measure and try measures by'. In 1605 complaint was made to Quarter Sessions that the chained bushel was missing, and that five regular corn buyers or 'loaders' used their own measures; these were kept for them in the houses of the bailiff, John Reeve, and the innkeeper John Dudsbury of the new Bell inn (on the west side of the market, facing the conduit), and suspected to be larger than the standard. The provision of the town's bushel measure had been regarded in 1564 as the lord's responsibility, but in 1605 it was the inhabitants who were ordered by the magistrates to restore the chained measure to the Cross.

Sir Thomas as lord was required by custom to provide the law's instruments of punishment, stocks, pillory, and cucking-stool. When the manor lacked a cucking-stool in 1596 Sir Thomas was asked to pay for one to be made. The stocks and pillory stood near the town dump at the upper end of the Middle Row. The justices of the peace ordered two dishonest brewers to be put in the stocks in 1576, and in 1586 condemned a labourer who had passed false tokens to stand in the pillory in the open market and to lose an ear as well. In 1594 the manor court ordered that thieves who stole their neighbours' wood, to sell in bundles for fuel, be fined 12d and put in the stocks for four hours, and the purchasers fined 20d. With the county gaol in Colchester castle, prisoners brought from Colchester to Chelmsford for trial at Quarter Sessions or the Assizes were lodged at one or other of the town's inns. Local petty malefactors were thrown into the town Cage, which stood near Poultry Hill at the lower end of the Middle Row (part of the site of 76 High Street), until it was moved to the top of the town (site of 1 Tindal Street), opposite the White Hart inn.

As lord of both manors, Sir Thomas Mildmay bore sole responsibility for the three-arched stone bridge over the Can which linked Chelmsford with Moulsham; this was alternatively known as the Great Stone Bridge, Chelmsford Bridge, or Moulsham Bridge. The bridge had been described in 1539 as greatly decayed, but in 1545, while Bishop's Hall was in the hands of the Crown, the bailiff and farmer of the manor, John Taylor, had carried out some repairs on the Chelmsford side. The bridge must have been in fair condition in Elizabeth's reign, for no complaint of it was made to Quarter Sessions in Sir Thomas Mildmay's lifetime.

The crossing of the Chelmer in Springfield Lane was another matter. The flood-prone area of the ford lay at the mercy of the tenants of Moulsham mill, who could alter the level of the river above the mill by penning up the water and releasing it as they chose. In 1547 Master Auditor's miller had been accused of penning up the water 'more high' than he should, so that the flow of the river between Springfield mill above the crossing and Moulsham mill below it was 'not as it hath byn accustomed'; this had caused the water to 'swell and drown' Springfield mill, flood Springfield Lane, and overflow into the houses in the lane. Similar problems were caused in 1572 by the miller's wharf, when he heightened it below the crossing, and in 1581 by flash-boards he set up at the sides of the channel to deeepen it.

Even without the intervention of the Moulsham miller, the complicated Springfield Lane crossing of the Chelmer ford was dangerous. It involved three bridges. The first was the 'Treen Bridge', a high wooden cart bridge at Chelmsford 'town's end', marking the boundary between Chelmsford and Springfield, and customarily repaired by the lords of Chelmsford and Springfield. Beyond the Treen bridge lay an island swamp between two arms of the river, called 'Tyrell's marsh'; this was forded by horsemen, carts, and cattle, but a ramshackle wooden causeway about forty yards long was provided for travellers on foot. The causeway led on to the third bridge, called the 'Stone Bridge', or 'Springfield Bridge'. The footbridge and stone bridge both lay wholly in Springfield, and controversy over who was responsible for them seriously prejudiced their maintenance. There was still a ford alongside the Springfield stone bridge.

All three bridges were in poor condition in the latter part of the 16th century, 'in decay', 'in great ruin', 'dangerous to foot and horse passengers'. In 1568 the Treen Bridge was 'like to fall down and that shortly'; Sir Thomas Mildmay and Sir Harry Tyrell of Springfield were ordered by Quarter Sessions to see to it, an order repeated in 1571, when the puzzled justices noted: 'Query if there be two bridges?'. They might well be confused, for the wooden Treen Bridge at the town's end and the stone bridge in Springfield were both freely referred to as 'Springfield Bridge'. The stone bridge in 1582 was in such a bad state that 'there was one drowned and a horse and cart fell in'. But Sir Henry Tyrell, lord of the stream on both sides, resolutely denied responsibility for it. He was supported by the evidence of one of his tenants, who quoted a former ancient inhabitant, who had told him in 1578, 'as they walked by the way', that he remembered when there was no bridge there at all, and that when it was built it was paid for 'by the country', that is, at public expense. In 1586 Sir Henry, through his Chelmsford attorney, Thomas Wallinger, pleaded that he was 'greatly vexed' that the magistrates should indict him for neglect of the bridge. By 1587 the bridge was said to be in such ruin that it could not be crossed without danger. Sir Henry died in 1588, and in 1589 a jury diplomatically declared that, 'if his worship (Mr Thomas Tyrell, Sir Henry's son and heir) has cleared himself that he ought not to make it, then we find that the country should make it', and left it to the lawyers to continue the wrangle. The bridge was still 'in decay' at the end of the century. The footbridge which linked the two bridges was the victim of similar arguments, although in 1576 it was stated that the timbers, when they were rotten in 1556, had been repaired with money gathered by the high constable in the Chelmsford hundred. Finally, in 1596 the justices ruled that householders living near the footbridge, and those who had most benefit from it, be rated for its repair.

The rivers were dangerous enough without the added risk of broken-down bridges. The parish register records in 1543 the burial of one stranger drowned at night in the old Bell Mead (now King's Head Meadow), and another, by misfortune 'and his own lewdness', behind the Lion; a maidservant at the Lion was drowned in 1557. In 1546 two men 'by mysfortune as they wesshid themselfes yn the ryver were drownyd'; a twelve-year-old boy was drowned in 1570 washing with other boys in the Chelmer; and in 1600 a butcher, who stepped into the 'main river', the Can, at 8 p.m., to cleanse himself after his day's work, was swept away by the current and drowned. Would-be suicides were fatally drawn to the river; in 1574 an elderly carpenter threw himself into the Chelmer in the early hours of the morning.

SIR THOMAS'S TOWN

The town which Sir Thomas Mildmay inherited was still growing. Medieval timber-framed halls, cottages, and shops, were crammed together on both sides of the high street, with parlours and solars, jettied upper rooms, gabled cross-wings, exterior galleries and stairs, built on; attic windows poked through the roofs, and gatehouses bridged the cartways and larger passages leading through to the 'backsides'. On both sides of the south gate of the churchyard a two-storey row of buildings faced the market. Only in the backsides, and on the street itself, was there ground space left for new building. Wings, gable-end to the street, were spreading down the backsides at right angles to the frontage, with cottages and workshops, forges and stables, lofts and sheds, privies and pigsties, flanking the courtyards. The gateways of the town's three greatest inns, the Lion (site of 52-4 High Street), with the medieval Hart (site of 55) annexed, the Boar's Head on the opposite side of the street (site of 40-1 High Street), and the Crown (or New) inn (site of 37-8 High Street), led through into great enclosed quadrangles. The street frontage was broken only by its dark covered passageways and alleys, beneath the angular profile of the town's red-tiled pitched roofs, tall brick chimneys, pointed gables, and dormer windows.

As the sixteenth century advanced property values in the town had leaped forward. Roger Alford bought Guy Harlings from John Cornish in 1516 for £30. His widow Elizabeth and her second husband sold it to William Eve in 1522 for £54. Six years later William sold it to Richard Rich for £75. By 1563, when Geoffrey Scott bought it, the price had risen to £213. John Ayliffe of London, esquire, who bought it from Geoffrey Scott in 1574 for £220, left it by his will in 1580 to his younger son George, who sold it in 1596 for £400.

The rising price of property, and competition for position on the prized frontage of the high street, encouraged the sub-division of sites. John Living the saddler's property (site of 47-8 High Street), next to the Cock inn, was split up by his son John and sold in two parts in 1574 and 1587. In the 1580s Biglands, *alias* The Bull (site of 31-2 High Street), next to the Falcon inn (site of 28-30 High Street), was demolished, and reported in 1591 to be 'nowe at this daye newly builte by Edward Makin, gent., ... and devided into two tenements'. In New Street, Maynetrees became divided into three properties, still owned as one, but described in 1566 as 'Mannynges, a tenement and two other tenements adjoining', and in 1591 as 'a messuage called the Lamb and two adjoining messuages called Manningtreyes' (sites of 54-7 New Street).

The high street backsides belonged to the freeholders of the frontage sites, who could build on them what they chose, provided they did not annoy their neighbours. But the waste soil of the street belonged to the lord of the manor.

116

Opportunists who took over a few feet of the street to stack firewood, or set up a stall, salt-bin, shed, or lean-to against the house, were usually reported to the manor court sooner or later, fined, and ordered to vacate the space occupied or pay a fixed annual manor rent for it. Thomas Gylder was fined 20*d* in 1560 for building a little buttery in the street, joined on to the west side of his house on Poultry Hill (site of 81 High Street) facing the fishmarket, without permission; at the same court John Eve, who had built a gatehouse, was fined 20*d* and ordered to pull it down before the next court or face a fine of 40*s*. It was not necessary for an illegal erection to stand on the ground to constitute a manorial encroachment — to overhang the street was enough. In the early 1590s the apothecary Thomas Watson built on to his house called Brettons on Poultry Hill, at the end of the Middle Row (site of 77-8 High Street), two galleries or balconies, overhanging the street, the 'new-built eves' projecting beyond the 'old eves' to the extent of just over two feet at the front of the house and just over a foot at the back. Such a conspicuous alteration could not hope to escape detection. In 1594 he was given a date to pull down the galleries, which were 'an evil and pernicious example to all the other inhabitants of the town and a nuisance to his neighbours', or pay a fine of £20. He 'reformed' part of the addition in time, but 'not entirely as ordered', and the court doubted 'whether that which still stands is within the law'. In 1596 the court ordered Watson to pay the £20 penalty and pull down the galleries. Defeated, he admitted the encroachment, threw himself on the lord's mercy, and offered to pay £12 in compensation. This was accepted, the remaining £8 of the fine was pardoned, and the galleries allowed to remain. But an annual manorial rent of 6*d* was laid on 'the evesdropp of the two galleryes fixed to his freehold tenement'.

The vigilance of steward, bailiff, and court, against encroachments was not prompted by any zeal to conserve open space, or ease the flow of traffic through the town, but by their duty to uphold the lord's legal rights in the soil, and to gather the manorial fees and rents which were his due in return for licensed occupancy. No one, not even Sir Thomas Mildmay himself, foresaw the problems which would arise from the progressive narrowing of the high street and market-place. At least eighteen new grants of high street waste were enrolled between 1568 and 1599, most of them in the vicinity of the Middle (Shop) Row. Hitherto the Middle Row had spread from the neighbourhood of the Great Cross downwards towards the Great Stone Bridge on the east side of the gutter which flowed down the hill from the conduit. Now the first recorded grants were made of parcels of ground behind the Middle Row, on the west side of the gutter, narrowing the back lane which ran between the Middle Row and the former west side of the high street. Most of these plots were used as woodyards, but it was not long before some of them were built upon. Waste ground there measuring 72 feet long by 3 feet wide was granted to the brewer Walter Baker (*alias* Wilkes) in 1568; by 1591 three butchers' shops had been built upon it on either side of the Shambles. Another parcel, 20 by 12 feet, opposite the Dolphin inn (site of former 14 Tindal Street), was granted in 1570, in return for an annual manorial rent of 12*d* and a court fine or fee of 13*s* 4*d*; five years later its owner, Edward Bigland, landlord of the Dolphin, was licensed to build a shop on it and had done so by 1591. One of the largest grants, of space behind the roper John Pamplin's Middle Row house, Copt Hall (site of 94 High Street), was made in 1585, and measured

West Side of the Manor

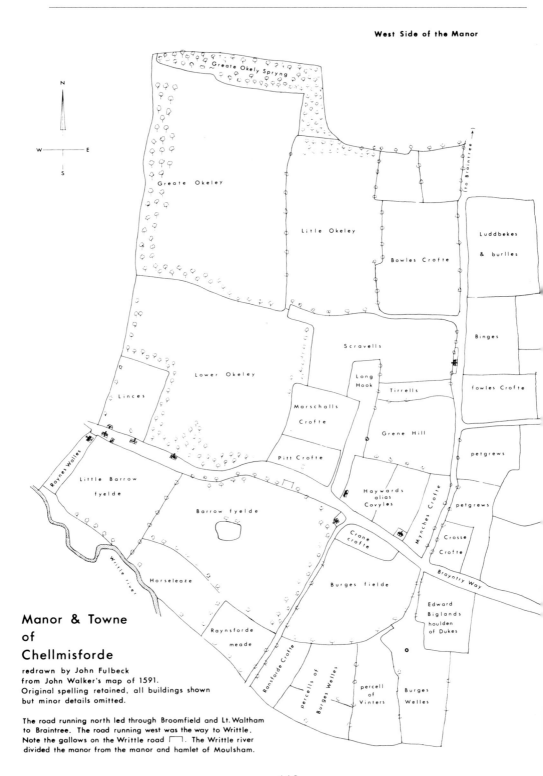

N
W — E
S

Greate Okely Spryng

Greate Okeley

Litle Okeley

Bowles Crofte

Luddbekes & burlles

to Braintree

Binges

Scravells

fowles Crofte

Long Hook

Tirrells

Lower Okeley

Marschalls Crofte

Grene Hill

petgrews

Linces

Pitt Crofte

Haywards alias Coyles

Mynches Crofte

petgrews

Roynes Walles

Little Barrow fyelde

Barrow fyelde

Crane crofte

Crosse Crofte

Writtle river

Horseleaze

Burges fielde

Brayntry Way

Edward Biglands houlden of Dukes

Manor & Towne of Chellmisforde

Raynsforde meade

Ransforde Crofte

Percells of Burges Welles

percell of Vinters

Burges Welles

redrawn by John Fulbeck
from John Walker's map of 1591.
Original spelling retained, all buildings shown
but minor details omitted.

The road running north led through Broomfield and Lt. Waltham
to Braintree. The road running west was the way to Writtle.
Note the gallows on the Writtle road ⌐⌐. The Writtle river
divided the manor from the manor and hamlet of Moulsham.

no less than 43 by 8 feet. The steady transformation of the Middle Row from stall space to permanent buildings is illustrated by the medieval 'Spycerestall' in the Fish Market; this had become a 'shed' or 'shop called Spicer's stall' by 1584, and a 'shop called Spicer's stall with a chamber newly built over it' by 1595 (site of 83 High Street).

Sir Thomas had no reason to reject requests for grants of parcels of his manor waste; they increased his annual rental income from the town, and won the goodwill of his tenants. Indeed, at a court in 1594, which he attended himself, he 'personally ... of his grace' allowed George Gylder to keep (subject to an extra rent of one penny) 10½ by 5 feet of ground in The Poultry on which Gylder had already built an illegal extension to the same buttery for which his father Thomas Gylder had been penalised in 1560.

Sir Thomas even encouraged development between the Middle Row and the east side of the high street, on the highway between the church and the stone bridge. A number of 'built stalls' (permanent stalls with tiled canopies), known as the Middle Stalls or Little Middle Row, had already sprung up there, divided from the Middle Row by a narrow passage called Potterslane (*alias* Potter Row or Shoprow Lane). In 1594 Sir Thomas allowed John King, who had recently acquired one of those built stalls, to extend the north end of it over an extra nine by three feet of the highway, for a fixed annual rent of 2*d*. On the other hand, when the surgeon, Thomas Parkins, built an outside stair on to his house facing Potters lane (site of 89 High Street), leading up to his gallery, he was peremptorily ordered in 1606 to pull it down, as it was a nuisance to nearby shops. Galleries were useful in the confined space of the Middle Row for hanging out the household washing to dry; some of Thomas Parkins's linen was stolen from his gallery in 1589.

Sir Thomas permitted another unfortunate intrusion on the highway lower down the high street. Towards the stone bridge a forge had once stood in the middle of the street, opposite the Boar's Head inn. This was pulled down towards the end of the 15th century, leaving the ground on which it stood 'open to the highway'. But the space remained privately owned, and by 1566 was occupied again, by a small butcher's shop, measuring ten by five feet, built subject to a proviso that the lord might pull it down if he wished. By 1591 three shops stood on the plot. Yet in 1596 Sir Thomas gave their owner, Richard Terrett, permission to enlarge the three shops by building upon 36 by 5 feet of the surrounding highway 'near, in front of, and on the east part of them'. The little row became known as the 'Shophouses'.

Sir Thomas continued to approve new building in the town to the end of his life. In 1605, three years before his death, he granted Thomas Dalton a patch of ground at the back of the new Cross, 38 by 11 feet, 'to build on'. It was a prime site, and Sir Thomas made Dalton pay for it, with a rent of 4*s* a year. It may have helped to keep the draught off the magistrates and judges in session, but it severely restricted passage between the Cross and the buildings behind it alongside the churchyard, including the Tollhouse near the south gate.

While the town became ever more congested, the Upland remained almost unpopulated. Outside the town some 306 acres of arable and pasture, meadow and copse, were the lord's manorial demesne lands, cultivated by the tenant of Bishop's Hall farm. Almost as many acres again, freehold or copyhold, were in the hands of individual owners, cultivated by them or their lessees; most of the landowners were townsmen, but some of them were outsiders like the Wisemans of North End in Great Waltham, who owned the Burgeyswell lands. Apart from the Bishop's Hall manor complex of hall, farm buildings, and watermill, and the rector's impressive two-storey parsonage house nearby, the only upland buildings were a few scattered cottages and barns, built alongside the highway on the road-side waste. A conspicuous isolated feature in the landscape was the gallows, standing by the highway where the road broadened out just beyond Burgeysfield and 'Rainsfordes Lane', on the 'way leading to Writtle'. But the precursors of upland development appeared in the early 1580s, when Sir Thomas began to grant as copyholds small parcels of roadside waste on both sides of the Writtle road, between the gallows and the Writtle boundary, specifically for building. Between 1581 and 1608 he granted sixteen plots, each large enough for a cottage and garden. The first five plots, granted before 1591, and the farthest from the gallows, had all been built on by that date. These cottages, and those built later, became described as 'at Gallows End'. One of the first of the cottages was built by Seth Andrews. It comprised a hall, a parlour, a room next to the hall, and a kitchen. Firewood was stacked in the yard, and pigs and chickens were kept in the garden. In the cottage lived Seth, his wife Sara, two adult sons, and five younger children. For some years to come, however, the only upland residents of substance were the lessees of Bishop's Hall and the mill, and the occupants of the rector's parsonage house. A rate assessment of 1587 listed some 124 rateable householders in the town, but only four, including Richard Long, the tenant of Bishop's Hall, in the whole of the Upland and Southwood.

THE CONDUIT

The Upland continued to provide the town's public water supply, from the Burgeyswell spring in Burgeysfield. The field's early ownership is only documented from the late 14th century to 1516. But an exchequer commission of 1565 claimed that the Burgeyswell lands had been given to the Black Chapel at Ford End, Great Waltham (at a date unknown) to support the stipendiary priest officiating there, and had hitherto escaped confiscation by the Crown by being 'concealed'. The Crown accordingly sold them to Nicase Yetsweirt, a speculator in 'concealed lands'. But he may never have succeeded in establishing his title, for in 1571 Thomas Wiseman of Ford End (whose family had been benefactors of the chapel in 1500 and 1559) as legal owner of the Burgeyswell lands granted an annual rent charge of £5 6s 8d out of them to trustees for ever, 'for needful works of charity in Ford End'. When Wiseman died in 1580 he devised the Burgeyswell lands to his son, Thomas, subject to the rent charge, which by 1685 (and thereafter) was enjoyed by the trustees of the Black Chapel. It was not to be redeemed until 1974.

Whatever the vicissitudes of the fields in which the spring lay, underground its piped water flowed unhindered to the town. It rose to the surface on the west side of the open market, beyond the Cross, and opposite the house of the barber Roger Webb. From there the water ran in the 'common gutter' down the back lane behind the Middle Row, past the Blue Bell and White Hart inns, the 'Capital Messuage or Place' of Mr John Pake, gentleman, called The Heath, the

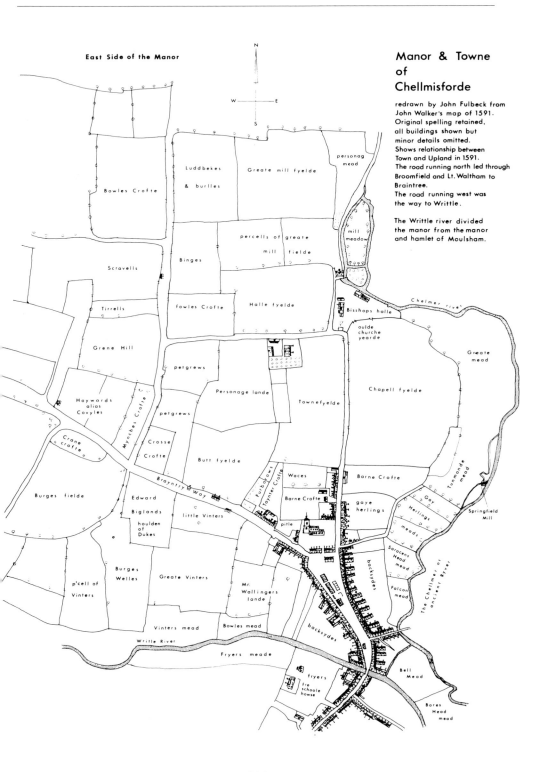

East Side of the Manor

Manor & Towne
of
Chellmisforde

redrawn by John Fulbeck from
John Walker's map of 1591.
Original spelling retained,
all buildings shown but
minor details omitted.
Shows relationship between
Town and Upland in 1591.
The road running north led through
Broomfield and Lt. Waltham to
Braintree.
The road running west was
the way to Writtle.

The Writtle river divided
the manor from the manor
and hamlet of Moulsham.

Bowles Crofte

Luddbekes
& burlles

Greate mill fyelde

personag
mead

mill
meadow

percells of greate
mill fielde

Scravells

Binges

Chelmer river

Tirrells

fowles Crofte

Halle fyelde

Bisshops halle

oulde
churche
yearde

Greate
mead

Grene Hill

petgrews

Personage lande

Townefyelde

Chapell fyelde

Haywards
alias
Covyles

petgrews

Crane
crofte

Crosse
Crofte

Butt fyelde

Mynches Crofte

Brayntry Way

Furbolows

Toynter Crofte

Waces

Barne Crofte

Tunmonde
mead

Burges fielde

Edward
Biglonds
houlden
of
Dukes

little Vinters

Barne Crofte

gaye
herlings

Gay
Herlings

Springfield
Mill

meads

pitle

Saracens
Head
mead

p'cell of
Vinters

Burges
Welles

Great Vinters

Mr.
Wallingers
lande

backsydes

Falcon
mead

The Chelmer or
ancient Ryver

Vinters mead

Bowles mead

backsydes

Writtle River

Fryers meade

fryers
fre
schoole
howse

Bell
Mead

Bores
Head
mead

smaller house of Pake's neighbour, Matthew Rudd, gentleman, Walter Baker's brewery and his adjoining inn, the Bear, the house of John Monk, tippler and tallow-chandler, called Sharparrows, and the Dolphin and Rose inns, as far as the Mildmay house, Mayes, opposite the fishmarket (Tindal Street, west frontage, from former Corn Exchange site to New London Road gap). There the channel changed course; it crossed the fishmarket towards the leather stalls outside the Woolsack inn (site of 15-17 High Street), and turned between The Poultry and the Woolsack leather stalls to run down the street. It flowed in front of some of the most valuable properties on the east side of the high street, owned or occupied by London citizens, such as Alderman Benedict Barnham who owned the Falcon inn (site of 28-30 High Street), and the haberdasher John Stafford who owned the Crown; by leading townsmen such as Robert Wood senior, woollen-draper (site of 21-2 High Street), and his son Robert junior, mercer (site of 26 High Street); and by gentlemen and esquires of the quality of John Pynchon of Writtle and Springfield (who owned the Woolsack), and Edward Makin, lawyer (site of 31-2 High Street).

Just past the Crown inn, at the corner shop of linen-draper Richard Carsey, the gutter turned off the high street, between Carsey's shop and the opposite 'Cornerhouse', into Springfield Lane, which was then no more than half the width of the present Springfield Road entrance. The water flowed only a short distance down the lane before turning right, into the alley dividing the house of the glover Richard Neale in the lane from the backside of the 'Cornerhouse'. There, behind the 'Cornerhouse' and Toppies (site of 39 High Street), where grocer John Bridges and his wife Anne lived, and at the back of the Boar's Head inn, the water from Burgeyswell finally flowed into The Gullet.

In Elizabeth's reign the parish took responsibility for the conduit head, where the water surfaced in the market. In 1570 the churchwardens' accounts record 5s paid to set up a gate, two posts, hinges, hooks, rails and pales 'against the well', probably to protect it from passing traffic and prevent its use by animals as a drinking trough. But it was the manor court and chief pledges who attended to the state of the open gutter flowing through the town. The principle adopted by the court, declared in 1560, and repeated in the tabulated by-laws of 1564, was that each inhabitant whose house faced the gutter, from Roger Webb's house to Springfield Lane, should, 'for his part against his house', scour and cleanse it once a month as it came through the town, on pain of a fine of 12d for default. In 1576 the inhabitants of the Middle Row were ordered to share the scouring of the gutter where it ran past the back of their houses. The by-laws cannot have been effective, for in 1584 the penalty for default was raised to 10s, and after a warning in 1591 that all inhabitants on both sides of the street should maintain the gutter 'as they used to do', the court in 1592 took a firmer line. All those living by it were forbidden to throw dung or filth into it, and were required to contribute towards its cleansing and 'good keeping ... according to a rate made for this'. Fines imposed in future were to be levied at once, if necessary by distraint on the offender's goods.

MANOR AND PARISH

The management of the conduit and conduit stream was typical of the partnership of manor and parish in the government of the town in Elizabeth's reign. There was no rivalry in the relationship. Since the middle ages the leading townsmen as chief pledges of the manor court had ruled the town, and the same individuals, described in a parish context as 'the chief inhabitants of the town' (1559), 'the best and ancientest of the town' (1583), 'the chiefest of the parish' (1589), 'the better sort of the inhabitants' (1591), or 'the principal neighbours' (1608), conducted the affairs of the Elizabethan parish. The élite of the manorial chief pledges, who were chosen to the key offices of constable or affeerer, were also chosen to the important parish posts of churchwarden, overseer of the poor, or surveyor of highways. This being so, the spheres of responsibility were often blurred, with the manor court found underpinning the authority of the parish.

No Chelmsford parish records have survived earlier than 1538 (parish registers) and 1557 (churchwardens' accounts), so it is impossible to assess the rôle of any medieval parish meeting in the lay affairs of the town. But with Tudor governments imposing civil responsibilities on the parish, in particular the care of the poor and maintenance of highways, with power, supervised by the magistrates, to gather money in the parish to meet local obligations, the balance in town government between parish and manor began to shift.

Although the manor court enacted the by-laws which governed the high street gutter, its 'good keeping' might well be regarded as a parish duty, since the Highways Act of 1555 laid responsibility for highway maintenance upon the parish. This act also established the unpaid office of surveyor of the highways, to be chosen, not by the manor court, but by the parishioners. One of the first of Chelmsford's surveyors, Geoffrey Scott, landlord of the Lion inn, was a senior manorial chief pledge, and subsequent known surveyors were of similar standing. But though the surveyor was a parish officer, it was the manor court which dealt with defaulters like Thomas Hubbard, who refused in 1569 to do his statutory work on the highways, and incurred the heavy fine of 6s for his intransigence. Although the 1555 act provided for unpaid personal labour on the highways, or the provision of substitutes, as early as 1558 the Chelmsford surveyors, including Geoffrey Scott, were accounting to the parish for highway money gathered from parishioners. But it was the manor court which enforced parish demands for highway rates: in 1574 the court forbade any inhabitant to refuse to pay the tax demanded of him by his neighbours to mend the street, on pain of a fine of a shilling or distraint on his goods. The court's authority was also exercised in 1589 in support of contributions demanded from householders on the east side of the town, 'each according to his share', to pay for cleansing the common ditch behind the Falcon inn, which ran between their backsides and the water-meadows, and discharged into the Chelmer. Thus the 'rate' made in 1592 for the 'good keeping' of the common gutter was made by the parish, though the manor court enforced it and fined the defaulters.

TOWN GOVERNMENT

Topographically Chelmsford's local government structure in the reign of Elizabeth I remained divided. Only Sir Thomas Mildmay, as lord of both manors (the town manor of Chelmsford or Bishop's Hall, and the hamlet manor of Moulsham), and as patron of the parish, united all the inhabitants. The separation

Transcript of entry in Churchwardens' Book in handwriting of Myles Blomefylde (see opposite), recording parish proceedings of 7 June 1590

Anno. 1590. Junij. 7º.

At the Assemblye of the pryncypall
Inhabytantes of the parysshe off
Chelmesforde   And the hamlet
of Mulsham   whose names are
here underwrytten In the Church
on Wytsondaye, the 7th of June
it is Agreed as followeth etc

1. Fyrst it is requyred, that John Seaman and Wylliam
Heddyche, nowe collectors for the poore shall Remayne
theyr Collection styll, for the hole yeare to come
wch shall ende, at the feast of the Annuntiation next
And they to contynewe theyr place accordynglye,
And Mr Wallenger to contynewe overseer for
that tyme, as before

2. It doth appere that the Churchwardens John Grene,
Rychard Bateson & Mr Blomefylde have dysbursed
for the parysh, wythin theyr tyme The Summa of
Vli. iiijs. xjd as perticulerlye appereth by theyr
severall bylles now cast up and delyvered wherof
they have receyved in Rentes — xviijs. iiijd. due
to the parysh   And they are more to be allowed
by Mr Wallenger, As part of a legacye, geven
by hys brother, towardes the Reparations of ye Church

R. of Mr Wa
lynger the
some of 33s
4d

The Summa of — xxxiijs. iiijd. wch allowaunces beyng
made the parysh is Indetted to the sayd Churche
wardens, In the summa of — liijs. iijd. whych ys
agreed to be payd unto them by a generall
levye made upon the parysh.

3. Towchyng the Choyse of the Churchwardens
It is agreed That George Martyndale And
Edward Byglond, shall take upon them the
offyce for Chelmesforde & Mr Rudd for Mulsham
In wch choyse of Churchwardens, If the parsun had
any voyce, yet he beyng suspended as we are informed the paryshe
holdeth it theyr ryght absolutelye to make ye full choyse

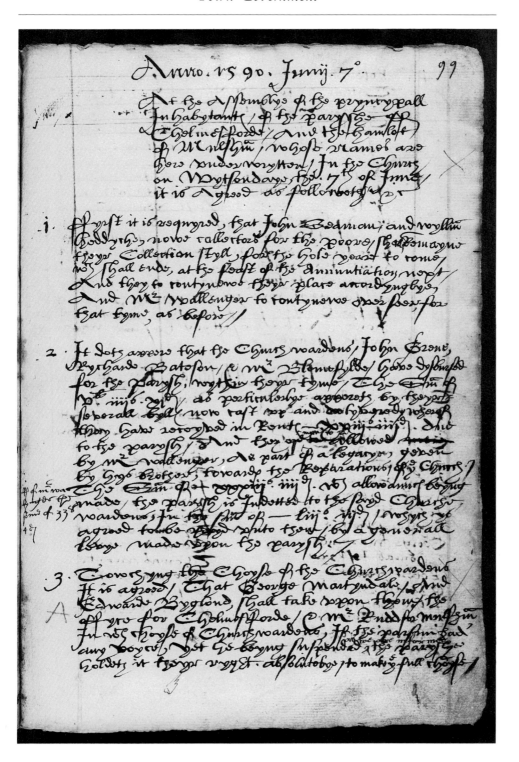

Anno. 1590. Junij. 7°   99

At the Assemblye of the principall
Inhabytants of the parysshe
Chelmesforde And the hamlett
of Mulsham, whose names are
here under wrytten In the Churche
on Whytsonday the 7th of June
it is Agreed as followeth

1. Fyrst it is requyred, that John Bedman and wyllm
Pollyth, nowe collectors for the poore, shall contynue
theyr Collection styll, for the hole yeare to come
wch shall ende, at the feast of the Annuntiacion next
And they to contynewe theyr place accordyngly
And Mr Wallenger to contynewe ... ... for
that tyme, as before

2. It doth appere that the Churchwardens, John Browne
Rychard Bateson, & Mr Blenerhasset have dysbursed
for the parysshe, wythin theyr tyme, the summ
of iiijli ... as particulerlye apperth by theyr
severall byll nowe cast vp and so togydy wherof
they have receyved in Rent — xiiijli iiijd. And
to the parysshe And the ... followed
by Mr wallenger, as part of a loyarye, geven
by the brother, towards the Reparations of the Churche
The summ of ... iij d. wch allowances beyng
made, the parysshe is indetted to the sayd Churche
wardens, in the summ of — liij li. xij d. wch is
agreed to be payd vnto them by a generall
leavy made vppon the parysshe

3. Concernyng the Choyse of the Churchwardens
It is agreed, That George Martyndale, And
Edwarde Byglond, shall take vppon them the
office for Chelmysforde, & Mr Pudd for Mulsham
In wch choyse of Churchwardens, If the parysshe had
any power, that he beyng suspended the parysshe
holdeth it theyr vyst. absolutelye, to make full choyse

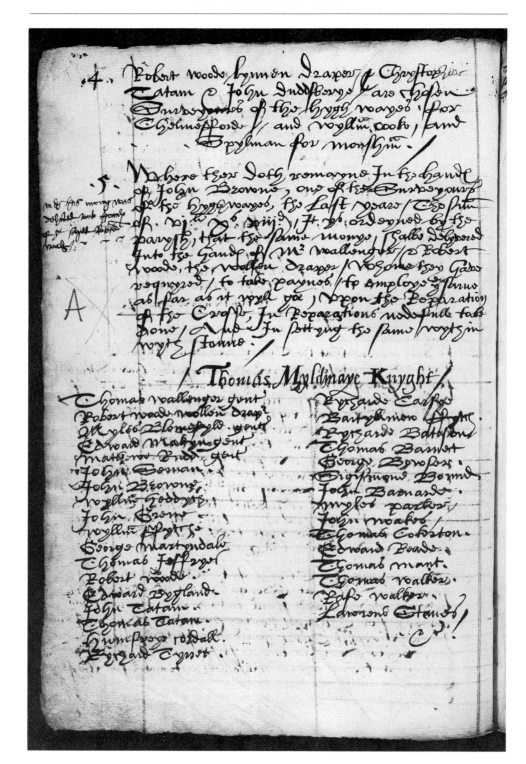

Transcript of reverse page in Churchwardens' Book in the handwriting of Myles Blomefylde (see opposite), completing the parish proceedings of 7 June 1590, and listing the parishioners present

4. Robert Wood lynnen draper & Chrystopher Tatam & John Duddsberye are chosen Surveyoures of the hyghwayes for Chelmesford and Wylliam Cooke and [*Blank*] Spylman for Mousham

5. Where ther doth remayne In the handes of John Browne, one of the Surveyours of the hyghwayes, the Last yeare The summa of. vj^{li}. x^s. viij^d. It ys ordeyned by the parysh, that the same monye shalbe delyvered Into the handes of Mr Wallenger & Robert Wood, the woollen draper, whome they have requyred to take paynes to employe ye same as far as it wyll goe, upon the Reparation of the Crosse. In Reparations nedefull to be done And In settyng the same wythin wyth stonne.

Md. this mony was delyvered unto thandes of ye saydd Roberte Wood

Thomas Myldmaye Knyght

Thomas Wallenger gent
Robert Wood woollen draper
Myles Blomefyld gent
Edward Makyn gent
Mathew Rudd gent
John Seman
John Browne
Wylliam Heddych
John Grene
Wylliam Fytche
George Martyndale
Thomas Jeffryes
Robert Wood
Edward Bygland
John Tatam
Thomas Tatam
Humfreye Cordall
Rychard Tyrret

Rychard Carsye
Bartyllmew Fytch
Rychard Bateson
Thomas Barnet
George Bowser
Sigismond Bound
John Barnard
Myles Parker
John Noakes
Thomas Cokerton
Edward Reade
Thomas Mant
Thomas Walker
Rafe Walker
Lawrens Stanes
etc

of town and hamlet was complete, and the hamlet had no part in the government of the town. The two manor courts chose their own manorial officers. Bishop's Hall regularly chose three constables, two aletasters, two meat, fish, and victual tasters, two leather sealers, four affeerers of fines (two for the lord and two for the tenants), and from time to time supervisors of the town's by-laws, wine tasters, scavengers, water bailiffs, and swineherds. Moulsham chose two constables, two bread, victuals, and ale tasters, and supervisors of nuisances in the river and in the 'high street called Moulsham street'. The authority of all manorial officers, including the constables, was limited to their own side of the river Can. At the annual parish meeting, styled in 1590, 'The Assemblye of the pryncypall Inhabytantes of the parysshe of Chelmesforde and the hamlet of Mulsham', separate parish officers were chosen for town and hamlet, two churchwardens for Chelmsford and one for Moulsham, three surveyors for Chelmsford and two for Moulsham, and, by 1589, when officers for the poor are first mentioned, two collectors and one overseer for Chelmsford, and two overseers for Moulsham. The parish officers' spheres of operation, like those of the manorial officers, were demarked by Moulsham bridge.

The town's governors were to be found among the Bishop's Hall manor chief pledges, with one notable exception, Mr Thomas Wallinger. The Wallingers (Waryngers) were an old-established family in the town. They had appeared in Chelmsford in the 1390s, when a Clement Warynger married Joan Taillour, joint heiress with her sister Isabel to Maynetrees in New Street, through their mother Margaret, sister of John Mayntre. In 1478 Stephen Warynger, son and heir of Joan and Clement, also inherited Isabel's half share of Maynetrees, after the death of his cousin, Agnes Skinner, daughter of Isabel and John Sparew. The Wallingers owned the Maynetrees estate until 1566, when Clement's great-grandsons, the brothers John and Thomas Wallinger, sold it to William Shether. Clement Warynger's wife had also inherited her father John Taillour's property, prominently sited on the west side of the market facing the conduit (site from 1857 to 1969 of the Corn Exchange), with about nine acres of free and copyhold land behind it running down to the river. This was where the Wallinger family had lived and prospered since the early 15th century, in a hall house with a frontage of thirty-seven feet. Some six feet of waste ground in front of the hall door and hall and parlour windows, granted for a rent of 6*d* in 1585, formed a forecourt, fenced off from the market traffic and cattle by posts and rails. Thomas Wallinger succeeded to the family property in 1579 when his elder brother John died unmarried. Thomas's first wife Avice, whom he married in 1568, was the daughter of the draper William Reynolds (d.1572), who was a senior chief pledge; his second wife, Bennett, was the daughter of Benjamin Gunson (d.1577) of Great Baddow, treasurer of the Navy and Sir Thomas Mildmay's uncle, a marriage which brought Wallinger into the family circle of the Mildmays; his second son Benjamin married a Mildmay. Although he was a tenant of Bishop's Hall manor, and one of the recognised leaders of the town, he did not serve as a chief pledge because, trained in the law, he acted as the court's deputy steward. Wallinger had other manorial stewardships, including the stewardship of the Tyrell manor of Springfield with Dukes. He was intimately involved in the property and probate affairs of Chelmsford's inhabitants, and as a parishioner was an inevitable choice for parish office, serving as churchwarden in 1573 and 1580, and in 1589-91 as the town's first recorded overseer of the poor. Between 1590 and his death in 1614 he was present at eight of the only ten parish meetings for which there is a record of attendance in the churchwardens' book. Thomas Wallinger was the first of the professional gentry, mainly lawyers and physicians, who were to play leading rôles in the town's affairs in the future.

The manorial chief pledges still formed the nucleus of the town's governors after the Reformation, and the rolls of the annual manor court leet continued to record their payment of the ancient common fine 'for them and their deciners'; but the phrase was a formality, for there were no longer deciners in organised tithings. With no court rolls extant between 1508 and 1560 the final stages of disintegration of the tithings cannot be followed, but by 1560 the system, which was already breaking down in the late 15th century, was obsolete, and reports of residents in the town 'out of tithing' had ceased.

The medieval court rolls sometimes recorded elections of chief pledges, but the Elizabethan rolls did not. Chief pledges still held office for life, so it may well have become the practice for them to renew their numbers informally from the more substantial householders by agreement among themselves. It was not unusual for a father's place to be filled by his son; John Monk became a chief pledge in 1591, after the death of his father, the tallow-chandler John Monk, in 1589. There was no fixed number of chief pledges; the juries sworn in at the annual Whitsun court leets between 1560 and 1603 varied in size between 10 and 29. Both those figures were extremes, the more usual number lay between 15 and 26. But a few pledges were regularly sworn. John Wallinger, Thomas Wallinger's elder brother, was one of the leet jury every year from 1572 until his death in 1579. The haberdasher Thomas Jeffery was sworn one of the jury at eighteen of the twenty-five courts of which record survives between 1563 and his death in 1592. Less influential pledges might not be sworn more than once. The regulars formed the core of the town's government.

The distinction of being 'First sworn' of the jury of chief pledges when the court proceedings opened was enjoyed by only the most senior of them, men of the standing of William Mildmay, Master Auditor's brother, in 1560 and 1563, and William Reynolds. Old William Reynolds (who had married the daughter of Richard Humfrey, the richest man in the town in 1523) had served as churchwarden in partnership with Thomas Mildmay the mercer in 1538; his daughter Avice was married to Thomas Wallinger. In the decade before his death in 1572 William Reynolds was 'First sworn' at the annual leet four times. By 1576 most of the older generation of senior pledges had died, including William Mildmay (d.1571), William Reynolds, John Bridges of the Boar's Head (d.1575), Geoffrey Scott of the Lion (d.1576), and William Wigglesworth of the Crown. But a new younger leader was emerging, the wool and linen draper Robert Wood the elder. The first occasion when Wood headed the swearing in was in 1569; from 1574 to 1601 he dominated the chief pledges, 'First sworn' thirteen times in the twenty-three years of which there is record. He served as constable in 1568 and 1576, and as an affeerer, always on the lord's behalf, nine times between 1569 and 1600. His standing as a leader of the Bishop's Hall tenants is implicit in the preamble to the great survey of the manor commissioned by Sir Thomas Mildmay in 1591. This states that the survey was conducted before Sir Thomas's professional agents (his Surveyor, Edward Moryson, esquire, his Steward, John Lathum, gentleman, and his Measurer, John Walker), and before 'Robert Wood and other tenaunts and scutors there'. Wood's standing in parochial matters was comparable; he served the key office of churchwarden in 1554-6, 1580-1, 1587-9, and 1596-9. In 1587 he was High Constable of the Chelmsford Hundred.

In 1584 the parish élite openly displayed their status when they separated themselves from the rest of the congregation on Sundays; at their own expense they set up a partition between the chancel and the body of the church, with seats for themselves in front of the chancel. There were eight of them: Mr Thomas Wallinger, Mr John Pake, gentleman, Walter Baker, beerbrewer, Robert Wood the elder, woollendraper, Richard Long (the yeoman tenant of Bishop's Hall), William Heditch (Herrytch), haberdasher, George Martindale, fishmonger, and John Browne of the Boar's Head. All except Richard Long were townsmen. Wallinger, Pake, and Wood, were three of the four highest rated parishioners (the fourth was a woman, Anne, widow of John Bridges); all eight of them were among the most heavily assessed ratepayers. All (except Richard Long) served one or both of the principal offices of churchwarden and town constable; Baker, Wood, Martindale, and Heditch, were four of only six chief pledges ever to be 'First sworn' between 1574 and 1601.

No Chelmsford manor court rolls have survived from the reigns of Henry VIII, Edward VI, or Mary, a gap of nearly half a century, but the Elizabethan rolls, dating from 1560, show the procedures of the court intact, and its authority undiminished, after the momentous changes of the previous reigns. Its officers were facing much the same sanitary and social problems as had preoccupied its officers in the late middle ages. Armed with the town's by-laws, firmly stated in English in 1564, the court continued to attack 'commen annoyances and other disordred thynges ...', and in 1564 elected three of the chief pledges, the haberdasher Nicholas Eve, the mercer Henry Somersham, and the saddler Edmund Sebright, to be sworn to a new office, as 'Surveyors, Serchers, Reprovers, Reformers, and Presenters' of the by-laws. When this office lapsed thereafter, the duties reverted to the whole body of chief pledges.

The stiffest penalty prescribed in the 1564 by-laws was 20*s*, for any inhabitant who used his own house as a slaughter house, instead of the 'New Shambles' in Shamble Lane in the Middle Row, where a house had been pulled down to create a place to kill beasts and butcher meat (site of Crown Passage and 91 High Street). Butchers, or anyone else, who threw horns, bones, or any other 'filth' into the street or river risked 3*s* 4*d*. This by-law could be invoked against all kinds of offenders, including fishmongers who did not clear up the fishguts and straw beneath their stalls, housewives who swept their dust, ashes, and refuse out of the front door into the street, followed by pailfuls of dirty slops, or townspeople who dumped dung in the churchyard or dead dogs and cats in Shytburye Lane (Waterloo Lane).

For keeping 'blokkes or logges' under the eaves of the house or before the door from Michaelmas to Easter, a practice dangerous to traffic and passers-by in the dark winter months, the fine was 20*d*. Swine put out to roam in the street cost their owners a penny a piglet or twopence a pig. The town pigs were a constant nuisance, and the officers who had to round them up faced the resentment of pig-keepers like Robert Glascock, who was fined in 1562 for his 'evil conduct' towards the manorial swineherds. In 1568 Walter Baker's fines for pigs and piglets wandering unringed, rooting up the soil, totalled 6s 8d. By 1576 the by-law had been extended to cover horses and cattle as well as pigs allowed 'daily and often' to go at large in the open places in the town without a keeper. Yet the offences persisted; in 1579 seventeen townsmen, including Walter Baker and other chief pledges, were fined between 2d and 12d each for pigs at large. In 1604 the court set a basic fine of 2s 4d.

The 1564 by-laws also penalised those who cut firewood from the lord's or his tenants' hedges. They were to be put in the stocks by the constables, with the stolen wood set before them, and for a second offence be punished again in the stocks, then expelled from the town. This by-law was revised in 1594, to deter dealers in bundles of stolen firewood; the purchasers became liable to a fine of 20d, and the vendors to four hours in the stocks and a fine of 12d. By 1597 it was necessary to raise the purchasers' fine to 20d for every bundle bought, and the vendors' punishment to six hours in the stocks for every bundle sold.

New by-laws were promulgated, or existing ones renewed, whenever necessary. In 1594 a special penalty of 10s was set for dumping rubbish or filth close to the salt-bins in the fishmarket, and the fishmongers were reminded to wash down their fishstalls by noon on Saturday. In 1603 the butchers were reminded to remove their chopping blocks on Friday night.

Marketing practices continued to be supervised by the manor court and its officers, but under increasing scrutiny by the magistrates. In 1570, a Ramsden Bellhouse grocer who offered rotten plums for sale at Chelmsford was fined 3s and his plums were burned in the market; a shoemaker was fined 3s for faulty shoes; and a butcher 2s for measled pork. But the chief target of manor court and Quarter Sessions alike was excessive prices. Year after year Sir Thomas Mildmay's income was boosted by the fines regularly imposed in his court on butchers, bakers, victuallers, and innkeepers, for overcharging. Many of the town's senior chief pledges appeared from time to time among the offenders: in 1580 John Green, Edward Bigland, William Parker, and John Browne, were among eleven innkeepers fined for overcharging for bread, ale, and victuals for men, and hay, oats, and horsebread, for horses. The tallow-chandler, John Monk, was fined in 1579 for overcharging for the communion candles. In 1600 the manor court warned all brewers of ale that, whether it was to be sold 'within their doors or without', their ale must be sold at such a price that all buyers could enjoy a full quart for a penny; in 1601 five brewers, one of them John Dudsbury of the Bell, were fined 10s each for ignoring this obligation.

Dealers who engaged in regrating victuals and grain (buying to re-sell in the same market), engrossing (buying up large quantities to command the market), or forestalling (buying up supplies on the way to market) were widely blamed for forcing up prices. The manor court could penalise offenders operating within the town's market, as they did in 1577, but only Quarter Sessions could discipline dealers active county-wide. It was the magistrates who handled a case in 1576 of malt bought on a Wednesday in Braintree market, to be re-sold two days later in Chelmsford market. In 1595 the Privy Council warned the Essex justices about engrossers and forestallers of poultry, butter, and eggs, who were swarming in markets, and in particular the markets of Braintree, Chelmsford, Dunmow, and Billericay, as well as buying up stocks directly from farmers' houses by the way. Twenty of these dealers, none of them Chelmsford men, were named in 1595, one of whom had engrossed 20,000 lb. of butter worth £300 in twelve months.

In 1608 twenty 'poore handicraft men' of Chelmsford complained to Quarter Sessions that the price of corn, which had already risen so high that poor tradesmen did not know how to live, was likely to rise still more if abuses were not reformed; without reform, they said, they and all poor men would feel 'the smart thereof and be utterly undone'. Their petition explained that as soon as the Chelmsford market bell rang, loaders, badgers, and millers, bought up all the corn and carried it off to their 'chambers', so that the smaller tradesmen 'cannot gett any corne or meale but att such a reconinge as yt maketh the hartes of us all could within our belles thinking uppon yt'; and they begged the magistrates to place some restraint upon these wholesale buyers.

A new trading offence had been created in 1552, when Edward VI made attendance of the laity at the parish church on Sundays and Holy Days compulsory. This Act, repealed by Mary, was restored by Elizabeth's first parliament. The manor court accordingly ordered in 1560 that in future no inhabitant should have his shop window open on Sunday after the last ringing of the bells to matins. The rule also applied to the sale of food and drink. The penalty for non-observance, originally set at 20*d*, was soon raised. Richard Studley was fined 3*s* 4*d* in 1562 for keeping his tippling house open on Sundays in service time, and threatened with a future fine of 40*s*. In 1579 an innkeeper, Bartholomew Fitch, was fined 3*s* for offering oranges for sale on Sunday before morning prayers.

The magistrates alone exercised control over wages, under the Statute of Artificers of 1562. Better wages were to be had in the town than the maximum permissible rates fixed by the Essex magistrates; in 1572 the wage of 53*s* 4*d* a year paid to their journeymen by the shoemaker John Furley, the glover Richard Burles, and the saddler John Cowland, was judged excessive and penalised. Another shoemaker, John Stockes, who paid his three men £3 a year each, and the butcher Christopher Wilson, whose man, Henry Andrews, earned £5 4*s* a year, were also fined; as Wilson was only fined 2*s*, the equivalent of one week of his man's wages, the fine was hardly likely to deter him in future. Walter Baker, probably one of the largest employers in the town in his brewery, also paid excessive wages: two of his men earned £4 a year; Cornelius Derycke, who kept an alehouse for him, £3 6*s* 8*d* a year; and a third employee as much as £6 13*s* 4*d* a year. Among craftsmen employed by the churchwardens and paid by the day, a bricklayer, tiler, or carpenter, was paid 12*d* a day, and their 'man' or 'labourer', 8*d*. This was without meat and drink, for the tiler John King and his man Covyll, who were paid together 20*d*, 'found themselves'. Goodman Barnes and his son, both plumbers, could earn more (the father 16*d* a day, and the son 14*d*), finding themselves in meat and drink. Among women servants, Joan Fynche, employed at Bishop's Hall by the tenant, Mr Edward Long of Terling, had been paid £2 a year for the last four years before her death in 1597. She was a responsible servant, entrusted since the death in 1593 of her mistress, Judith Long, with her master's keys, which she kept locked in her chest at the hall. Her wage was well ahead of that assessed by the Essex magistrates as the suitable maximum for 'the best woman servant, able to take charge of a household'; even a suggestion made to the justices in 1599 that the wage rates they had set in 1598 were too small, recommended no more than 26*s* 8*d* a year, with 6*s* 8*d* for livery, for the best woman servant; and in 1611 the relevant maximun wage was only amended to 33*s* 4*d*.

Regulation of wages was not the only field in which the town was becoming aware of increasing intervention by the magistrates in local life. In 1552 the Tudor government had enacted that keepers of alehouses must be licensed by the justices of the peace. Twelve Chelmsford tipplers were charged at Quarter Sessions in 1568 with selling ale and beer unlicensed; three of them kept brothels. The manor court, supporting the magistrates in enforcing this legislation, fined six unlicensed tipplers 8*d* each in 1570, raised the fine for nine offenders in 1570 to 20*d*, and when this did not prove sufficient deterrent, warned in 1576 that any inhabitant of the town 'presuming to tipple without licence from the justices' might be fined as much as 6*s* 8*d*.

The legislation was timely, for the number of places in the town where ale, beer, and victuals, were sold grew steadily in the late 16th century. All the late medieval inns continued to flourish, except the Robin Hood, and the (White) Hart which had become annexed to the adjoining Lion. But by 1570 the Hart's sign had been taken over by a new White Hart (site of former 27 Tindal Street) higher up the west side of the town, facing the conduit. The 'New' inn, which became known as the Crown, had appeared before 1556. By 1591 there were eleven major inns: on the west side of the town the Lion and old Hart near the bridge, the Dolphin by the fishmarket, and the White Hart near the conduit head; on the east side, the Cock at the bridge, the Boar's Head, the New inn or Crown, the Falcon farther up the high street, the Woolsack (also called the Woolpack) opposite the leather stalls and fishmarket, the Crane and the Saracen's Head facing the Market Cross, and the White Horse on the corner of Shytburye lane leading to Tunman Mead. By the turn of the century these had been joined by John Dudsbury's (Blue) Bell next to the White Hart, then the Talbot (site of former 24 Tindal Street; later called the Dog or Spotted Dog) and the Rose, both of them behind the Middle Row in the back street, the Star (site of 2 High Street) between the Saracen's Head and the White Horse, the Chequer in Duke Street (site of former 79 Duke Street), and the Greyhound in New Street (site of 58-9) next to Maynetrees, and once, two centuries before, part of it.

Besides inns, alehouses of varying size and repute were scattered throughout the town, in the high street, in Springfield Lane, up New Street, and in Duke Street. Some were run as a sideline to another trade; Zachariah Purchas the fletcher tippled ale, so did Thomas Wood the surgeon. An enterprising alehouse-keeper could achieve in time the status of an inn for his house, as did James Scrafton of the Black Boy (site of 69-70 High Street) on the west side of the high street. An alehouse-keeper by 1575, he was named for the first time among the town's innkeepers in 1589, and by 1603 had managed to buy the freehold of the inn from his former landlord. In 1602 the Whitsun manor court named no less than eighteen innkeepers and twenty minor alehouse-keepers and victuallers in the town.

In spite of licensing, dishonest and disorderly tipplers were to present a problem to both Quarter Sessions and the manor court for many years to come. Some offenders were incorrigible. George Blacklock, a servant of the brewer Walter Baker, was one of the unlicensed tipplers indicted at Quarter Sessions in 1568; he also ran a bawdy house, allowed his customers to gamble with dice and cards, sold victuals on Sundays in service time, and enticed servants and children 'to play all they can get to come by' at all hours of the night. The manor court, finding in 1571-3 that

Blacklock obstinately refused to reform, finally ordered in 1574 that 'henceforward he does not presume to tipple, licensed or unlicensed, on pain of £5.'

Unlike George Blacklock, who was another man's servant, Henry Coe was self-employed. He owned the freehold of his house called Chandlers on the west side of the high street (site of 65 High Street), and some land in the Upland. A tippler of ale and baker, he was indicted at Quarter Sessions in 1568 for tippling unlicensed, and for creating a public scandal by his visits to one of several suspect houses listed that year, Mother Bowden's brothel. Coe's wife had had her suspicions of these visits; the 1568 indictment told how,

'... on a time she went to the brothell house of Mother Bowden to se yf her husbande ware there (which before was ofte denied) and he sliped out of the howse thorowe the backside; and his wyf beate bothe the olde woman and the harlott her daughter, and pulled her aboute the house by the hare of the heade, which daughter came runninge into the street and made annawtes that Cooe his wyf woulde kill her mother; and this was in the eveninge as the people came from churche beinge about the hower of vi of the clocke being darke; and on the 19 day of December last, being Friday, worde came that Henry Cooe was at this foreseyde brothell howse and after viij of the clocke the howse was besette to take hym; and as they dyd knocke at the dore on the foreseyde of the sayd howse he went out at the backeside, and when he was in the yearde feared that some ware at the backe gate, lept over the pale into another man's yearde thinkinge so to escape; but he was taken or he coulde gette any fourther and was carred to the constablz to use thier office upon hym'.

Coe never reformed. He managed to keep clear of the magistrates, but was penalised regularly in the manor court: in 1571, 1576, and 1583 for tippling without licence, in 1574 for tippling at unsuitable times and entertaining undesirable customers, in 1578 and 1579 for selling ale in unsealed measures, in 1580, 1582, 1590, 1593, 1594, for overcharging, and again in 1596 and 1597 for selling beer in unsealed measures and cups not approved by the clerk of the market. He died in 1598, unrepentant, and his widow, who took over, continued to use the unapproved measures and be fined in her turn.

Besides dice and cards, such illicit games as 'shovyll aborde and slyde grote', and tables, also called 'Tick-tack' (backgammon), were popular in alehouses and inns. One enterprising tippler, Henry Stuck, was operating a bowling alley in 1600. Gambling was one means of passing counterfeit money. Robert Lodge, tapster at the Boar's Head, confessed to the magistrates in 1569 how the tailor, Thomas Hall, who then owned a shop (site of 56-7 High Street) opposite the Boar's Head, gave him a counterfeit gold sovereign and asked him to 'play it away or put it otherwyse awaye and ... theye would be parteners in the moneye theye culd gett for it'. Lodge also admitted borrowing another counterfeit coin, a gold angel worth ten shillings, which the under-ostler at the inn had found in the river at the back of the inn. A fortnight later, playing at Tick-tack, Lodge lost four shillings he had borrowed from a sailor who was passing through the town; the sailor, 'being importunate ... to have his 4s againe', Lodge gave him the counterfeit angel, taking six shillings change from him. But the sailor was too smart for the tapster; suspecting that the coin was counterfeit he took it to the constables, and the tapster was arrested and brought before Sir Thomas Mildmay.

Magistrates and manorial officers alike were concerned about the allurements of tippling houses for servants and apprentices. An alehouse in Springfield, where minstrels gathered, attracted many young men of the neighbourhood to noisy revels, and kept them on Sundays and Holy Days from the practice of 'artyllery which by that meanes is lytle used'. One night in 1571 a 'prevy watche and serche' at midnight discovered among the revellers at Springfield the servants of two of Chelmsford's leading townsmen, the brewer Walter Baker and fishmonger George Martindale. The manor court in 1573 forbade innkeepers and tipplers to entertain servants or apprentices in their houses at night after nine o'clock, and in 1598 embodied this prohibition in a by-law, coupled with a warning about forbidden games. Masters were expected to check rowdyism among their servants; in 1580 the mercer William Fitch, haberdasher Thomas Tatem, and innkeeper Bartholomew Fitch, were fined a shilling each for allowing their apprentices to keep ill rule and 'bear themselves ill among honest men, both in the town and villages outside', and ordered to see that this did not happen in future.

URBAN PROBLEMS

In Elizabethan Chelmsford, windows which overlooked the common street and backside yards, and thin interior wattle and daub walls which divided room from room, and even house from house, allowed little personal privacy. Living at such close quarters, the business and domestic circumstances of each individual, of whatever station, were known to the neighbours. It was common knowledge in 1567 that Henry Coe 'lived in great disorder with his wife'. In 1584 Den Parker and Harry Strowde were picked by the churchwardens as 'a cople of sobre men' worthy to be paid 6d to remove the dung heaped on the pightle side of the churchyard fence, to stop the hogs climbing over on it into the churchyard. It was sufficient record for the churchwardens to enter in their accounts sums paid to 'Christopher the butcher', 'Polle the tiler', 'Lince the locksmith', 'Brookes the mason', 'Michael the joiner', or 'Todman the glazier'; and for the manor court rolls to identify town locations as 'Path's corner', or 'Burtenwood's corner'; and to order John Salmon to make a bucket for his well 'between Wilcok's and Somersham's'.

Such 'disordred thynges' as broken gutters, neglected chimneys, leaking wells, unsavoury privies, rotten gates and fences, and disputed backside garden boundaries and rights of way, were threats to neighbourly harmony, and the manor court sought to remove such 'annoyances' before they led to blows. It was a formidable task as, year by year, a stream of small, and not so small, neighbourly confrontations were brought before the steward and chief pledges for reconciliation, warning, or punishment. Robert Glascock was warned in 1560 to remove his jakes overhanging Shytburye Lane, and to cease offending his neighbours with the stench of the animal offal which he fed to his pigs. The taverner, William Wigglesworth of the Crown, was warned in 1566 to block up his stable windows opening towards tailor William Boxford's house and yard. Nicholas Adams was ordered in 1584 to set up his paling and posts correctly on his own soil next to John Seaman's garden, and in future not to encroach on John's soil with its supports. In 1589, Henry Coe was ordered to remove his logs and firewood, which he had stacked against Henry Clarke's house, Humphrey

Cordall to allow the rainwater running off his neighbour Edward Makin's roof to escape as it always used to do by Cordall's drains, and Humphrey Bowsie to make a gully to carry away surface water on his yard which overflowed into William Shether's property, Maynetrees.

The gentry and chief inhabitants were as subject to warning as anyone else. William Gainsford, gentleman, who owned the White Horse inn (site of 1 High Street) on the corner of Shytburye Lane, was ordered in 1591 to remove the paling he had erected in the lane, from the bottom of his apple orchard towards Tunman Mead way, so that people could safely pass down the lane with horses and carts. John Ayliffe (Oliffe), esquire, of Guy Harlings, was ordered to take down a similar paling which he had set up on his side of the lane. If gentry palings, set up 'without right', were a nuisance to neighbours, so were unsavoury trade practices, such as Robert Geste's storage of stinking fish baskets in his house. The glover and leather dresser, Thomas Lawrence, who worked at his trade next door to the Cock inn, was ordered in 1592 to fill up the lime pits by his house, and remove the drench tub in which he steeped his skins for fifteen days in a fermenting mixture of bran and water, which was 'most offensive to his neighbours'.

If warnings to amend 'disordred thynges' were disregarded, the culprits forfeited the prescribed fines, renewed warnings were given, and penalties increased. Robert Whale forfeited 3s 4d in 1590 for continuing to stack his wood so as to obstruct William Hewitt's kitchen, after being warned not to do so in 1589. Robert Platt, landlord of the Crown inn, who ignored for three years warnings, first given in 1569, to mend his gutter 'towards' his neighbour Richard Nicholls of Holdens (site of 36 High Street), forfeited in 1572 a penalty of £5.

When neighbourly differences or disputes with 'foreigners' ended in violence, the manor court dealt with minor brawls fought with fists, or with such weapons as pewter pots, even when blood was drawn, by inflicting a standard fine of 3s 4d. A heavier fine of five shillings was imposed for a breach of the peace, or 'ill behaviour both in words and deeds', while the manor court was sitting, even if, as in 1571, the culprit was a senior chief pledge, Walter Baker. But more serious incidents were referred to the magistrates.

If there was one kind of quarrel which was liable to escalate beyond the powers of the manor court, it was disputes over rights of way, which had multiplied as the street frontage closed up. Many frontagers, usually the occupants of buildings 'once part of' a larger divided property, had become dependent on prescriptive rights 'to carry and recarry as of old' through neighbours' cartways and alleys to reach their backside gardens and yards. The property called Olivers on the east side of the market (site of 9-12 High Street) had no opening to drive carts and carriages through to its backside yard and garden. The owner in 1574, Thomas Knott, the county coroner, claimed that he and his ancestors 'had been wont to use' a cartway by 'a certain gateway' to carry and recarry as necessary. The occupants of the property with the gateway, the nearby Crane inn, prevented Knott from using it. Knott sought redress from the court of quarter sessions, without recourse to the manor court.

Henry Andrews and John Tatem were neighbours in the confined area of the Middle Row. Henry Andrews, a butcher's ill-tempered servant, was well known to the manor court, fined on many occasions for assault, for selling measled flesh

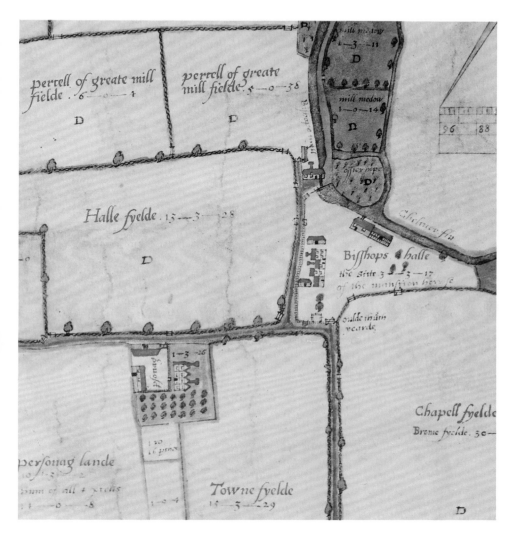

Bishop's Hall, mill, and parsonage, mapped by John Walker in 1591. (Reduced)

and overcharging for it, and for slaughtering, butchering, and disembowelling beasts openly in the high street, contrary to the by-laws. John Tatem, grocer and fishmonger, as occupant of Samptons, an Eve family house (site of 84-5 High Street), had the misfortune to live next door to Henry Andrews and share a common entry. In 1584 the manor court tried to settle disputes between them, ordering Tatem to repair his garden doorway leading into Andrews's garden, and always keep it closed, and Andrews to clear away the mire obstructing the way from his own door to Tatem's garden, and keep it continually clear in future. But the court was too late to keep the peace. The dispute reached the magistrates in the same year, after Andrews attacked Tatem in Tatem's back yard,

> '... and by whorlinge his dagger at the sayd John Tatem, hym the sayd John uppon his heade did hitt, greaveously wounde, beate, and evill entreate, and in greate peryll of his lyffe then and there putt; and the common highwaie of hym the said John, belonginge to the freehoulde tenemente or meess of one Johane Eve, gent., did deney, interrupt, and lett, and other hurtes and damag to hym then and there did, contrarie to the peace of our Soveraigne Ladye the Queenes Maiestie, her Crowne and dignytye'.

Tittle-tattle was alway dangerous in a small closely-knit community. The manor court fined Robert Glascock 6s 8d in 1566 '... for eavesdropping and carrying news and tales to excite contention among neighbours in the town, contrary to the Queen's peace and the tranquillity of the town'. The vendetta of Elizabeth (Whale) and her second husband, Hugh Barker, barber, scrivener, tooth-drawer, and blood letter, against her brother, the tailor John Whale, and his wife Mary, Elizabeth's sister-in-law, disturbed the tranquillity of the town for fifteen years. The trouble may have originated in the trust created under the wills of their brother Robert Whale of Great Baddow and his wife Sybil (who both died in 1598) to protect the inheritance of their four orphaned children. The sole trustee was Robert Whale's brother-in-law, Elizabeth's first husband, the glover Clement Pope. When Pope also died, later in 1598, his will transferred the trust, not to his brother-in-law, John Whale, who was the children's uncle and overseer of their father's will, but to his widow, their aunt Elizabeth; a proviso in Pope's will, in the event of Elizabeth's remarriage, required her and her future husband, before marriage, to put in bonds to the bishop of London's commissary for the due payment of the children's legacies. About 1600 Elizabeth was married again, to Hugh Barker; within a year she was the defendant in a suit in the bishop of London's consistory court, brought against her by her brother, John Whale, almost certainly involving the trust set up by their late brother Robert. While the Whale family trust can account for the trouble between brother and sister, the malevolence shown towards Whale's wife Mary seems to have arisen from Elizabeth's suspicions, no doubt shared with her new husband, Barker, of her first husband Clement Pope's relationship with her sister-in-law Mary Whale. As for Hugh Barker, he joined in the imbroglio with all the zest of the habitual troublemaker.

The bad blood between the Barkers and the Whales, became an open scandal in 1601. That autumn, Thomas Chitham, a Boreham schoolmaster, who was poor, fond of a drink, and happy to earn a little here and there by writing letters and love songs to order, on a visit to a sick friend at the Crown inn crossed the street to Barker's shop (Hoses, site of 71 High Street) to have his hair cut. Barker begged a favour of Chitham, saying, 'It is nothing, but to have you pen a fewe verses for mee, upon a pretty jest which I shall tell you.' Chitham agreed when Barker said he 'would take no money' for his trim. According to Chitham, Barker then retailed 'a tedyous discourse' about Clement Pope and one Whale's wife, 'and with such lacyvious termes and undecent speeches did he intermingle his discourse as I am ashamed to thinck on, much lesse can I with modesty dare (for feare to offend the vertuous and chast mynded) once presume to sett them downe'. Barker assured Chatham that the verses were for his private use, to sing to on his 'citron' (a cithern, a guitar-like instrument often kept in barber's shops for the use of customers), and 'to laughe at when he was melancholie'. Barker fetched paper and ink, and 'in most vyllanous sorte plotted how he wold have it donne'; Chitham protested that he 'wold not write so beastly, but wold cover the fylthiness of the fact under as cleanly tearmes as I could'.

Naming no names, Chitham composed on the spot twenty-four lines of verse, embellished with much classical pedantry, such as allusions to 'Cerberus' and 'Charon's flood'; he disguised John Whale as 'mightie Cetus', and as 'Huge Leviathan aryved in brave Albion's Eastern partes', and Clement Pope as 'the Pope did practise glover's art'; he referred elegantly to Leviathan's mate's romps with the Pope as 'Venus maigames'; and lightened the tale with a jocular touch:

'And if hir husband takes hym at the Fray
Upp goes his hoose and fast he runnes away'.

Barker read over the verses to his wife Elizabeth, asked Chitham to explain 'Leviathan' and 'Albion', then revealed that the verses were about the wife of the tailor John Whale, and the late Clement Pope, whose widow Elizabeth was now Barker's wife. Chitham, alarmed, asked Barker to give him back the verses, but Barker refused.

On his next market day visit to Chelmsford, Chitham was drinking with, among others, Richard Fitch the apothecary, of Colmans (site of 27 High Street), and Fitch's landlord, the jerkin-maker John Long, when he heard talk of libels, said to be by Barker, which were circulating in the town. On the following Friday Chitham was accosted in the high street by John Whale himself, who showed Chitham, not only a copy of his own verses, but also a copy of 'certain lacyvious, villainous, and beastly rhymes', which Chitham was vehemently to protest, 'before God I never saw, before Goodman Whale shewed them me'. These were some thirty-eight scurrilous rhyming couplets, implicating more than a dozen well-known townspeople, including William Shether of Maynetrees, and endorsed: 'He that findes this song lett hym make coppyes and give to his freindes'. The target of his slanderous ballad was

'... Mary Whale that bonnye lasse.
But hir husband is a very asse
For if that he weare very wyse
He would shoore open both his eyes
And se the doinges of his wyfe
And learne her to amend her lyfe
For if she doe not tell hym trew
Both hedd and hornes shalbe his due'.

Monument to Thomas Mildmay, Esquire, and his wife Avice, erected by their son, Sir Thomas Mildmay, in 1571

Panic-stricken, and urged on by Whale, Chitham hurried to Moulsham Hall, where he told the whole story to the nearest magistrate, Sir Thomas Mildmay.

On 15 October 1601 Hugh Barker was bound over to appear at Quarter Sessions on a charge of libel, with four sureties for his appearance — the blacksmith Richard Tye, the tailor George Knightbridge, and the saddler John Goose, all of Chelmsford, and Valentine Turner of Writtle. John Whale stood bail for Chitham to appear. At the January Sessions following a true bill was found against Barker, described as 'a very troublesome and dangerous fellow, and a raiser of great seditions amongst his neighbours'. But the case was postponed to the next sessions, and in February John and Mary Whale were bound over in the meantime to keep the peace towards Hugh Barker, with the innkeeper John Little and the glover Thomas Lawrence as their sureties.

The postponement was unfortunate for Chitham. Daily the Barkers tried to cajole, bribe, or intimidate him, to withdraw his evidence, or to disappear. They were supported by Barker's two sisters (the wives of Simon Cawdell who kept a tippling house, and one Boxford of Moulsham), and their cronies. On Friday 5 February, while Chitham was 'penninge a lovesonge' for a young musician at Boxford's house, Boxford's wife sent secretly to fetch Barker, who warned Chitham that if he gave evidence against him, he, Barker, would be 'utterly undone', yet Chitham do himself no good. Barker promised Chitham gifts of money from time to time, and 'sent his boy to Boxford's house to trim mee, and wold take no money for his labour'. On Saturday the 6th Barker 'wished mee to forsake my greate charge of children, and my poore wife, and to shift for myself, alleadging that I was fytt to live anywhere'. On Sunday, 7th, Barker changed his tactics, and suggested that Chitham should write a letter admitting some wrong he had done Barker. When the demoralised schoolmaster complied, an elaborate charade was enacted to compromise him before witnesses. A stranger sitting before the fire at Cawdell's carried the letter to Barker's, and had a pot of beer from Cawdell's wife for his pains. Barker then sent for Chitham to come to his house, 'where wee supt togither in an upper chamber, being hung round about with painted cloath whereon was described the history of Hammon and his sonnes'. After supper Barker made Chitham write another letter, asking for a meeting, and said, 'I thinck yt meete to talk with you before some of my frendes'. While Chitham remained in the upper room, Barker went down to the shop, sent for three or four of his friends, told them that Chitham had written to him 'to desyre to speake with him', and pretended to send for him. Chitham waited upstairs with Elizabeth Barker until, as he told later, she

> '... ledd me downe the stayres (for it was darke) and openinge the streete dore softly, byd mee goe forth and knock.'

He went out, knocked, and was admitted to the shop. In the presence of his friends Barker 'repeated certaine speeches' to which the unhappy schoolmaster 'soothed him upp with yea and nay'. Finally on Monday, 8 February, at a meeting at the house of the shearman Richard Brewer in Springfield Lane, Barker made Chitham write a third letter, a petition to the justices of the peace, 'to collor' Barker's cause; this done, Barker's wife rewarded Chitham with 10*s* all in groats — silver fourpenny pieces — and 2*d* for a drink. Harassed and confused, Chitham then fled to an uncle in Oxfordshire, for advice and help.

Chitham stayed in Oxfordshire until 11 March, when he returned to Chelmsford, arriving on the 13th. When Barker's wife discovered him at Boxford's, 'she wondred to see mee', but 'sent her boy to Boxford's to trym mee, and wold lett mee pay nothing, but did give me 6*d* to drinck, and told me her husband had a doublett for mee; and that I shold want nothing if I wold stick to her husband'. She also told Chitham of 'divers practices which goodman Whale had practised against mee in my absence, which afterwardes I proved to be meere fictions, only to make mee fly the country and forsake my wife and children'. In spite of all the Barkers' efforts, in April Chitham appeared as witness at the Easter sessions, where Barker tried to discredit him by producing the letters he had made Chitham write. But Barker was bound over to appear at the assizes, with two more sureties for his appearance and his good behaviour in the meantime, the grocer John Blanck and the glover Jonas Carsey. John and Mary Whale continued to be bound to keep the peace towards Barker.

In the interval between the April sessions and the July assizes Barker brought a bill of perjury against Chitham, and took out writs against Chitham, the tailor John Phillips (who was named in Barker's verses), and John and Mary Whale. Meeting Chitham by chance one night in the town in the dark, Barker cried, 'God's wounds, you are Chitham', and drawing a 'dudgeon dagger, without a hilt', struck at his head. But Chitham escaped to tell all to the Midsummer assize judges in July. Barker was found guilty, sentenced to a year's imprisonment, to stand in the pillory in four markets, Chelmsford, Witham, Braintree, and Billericay, to pay a fine of £40, and at the end of the year to find security for good behaviour. The witnesses against him were John and Mary Whale, Thomas Chitham, and the scrivener Richard Browne, whose wife Dorothy was Mary Whale's kinswoman. John Whale was discharged from his bond to keep the peace towards Barker.

This was not, however, the end of the town talk caused by this family disharmony. In October 1607 the scrivener Richard Browne was bound over to keep the peace towards Elizabeth Barker. A new dispute had come to a head between Richard Browne and Hugh Barker and their wives, and had been referred to the rector, William Pasfield, and Mr Thomas Wallinger, to settle. In January 1608 the rector and Wallinger reported to Quarter Sessions that they had taken pains with the aid of other 'principal neighbours' for the better avoiding of scandals, and 'yet they can draw them to no unity and peace', Barker being altogether recalcitrant and refusing to stand to their order. The court then referred the matter to old Sir Thomas Mildmay of Moulsham Hall, Sir Thomas Mildmay of Barnes, and Humphrey Mildmay of Danbury, esquire, to determine.

The result of the 1608 Mildmay arbitration is not known, but Barker continued to trim hair in the town, and to be employed as scrivener by such respectable townspeople as the apothecary Richard Fitch, and John Dudsbury of the Blue Bell inn and his wife Philippa (the sister of Walter Baker), on such delicate matters as the writing of their wills. In 1612 he was still in business, when he set up posts and benches and built a trapdoor entrance to his cellar on the street in front of his house without permission from the manor court; this matter was regularised in 1613 by the grant of a three-foot strip of highway waste along the eighteen-foot frontage of his house, for a proper rent.

But in 1614 Barker was before the magistrates again, as 'a sower of discord among neighbours, disturber of the peace, and stirrer up of suits between party and party'. The costs of his tangles with the law were catching up on him. In January 1615 his apprentice, Abraham Graye (bound to Barker two years earlier), with his mother Margaret, of Writtle, petitioned the magistrates for redress; Barker, in debt, with no place to live, had returned the boy to his mother, allowed nothing for the boy's keep, and refused without payment to release him from his indenture. The justices immediately discharged the boy from his apprenticeship, and allowed him to keep his clothes.

In the same year that Barker lost his apprentice, and, apparently, his house, a writ of attachment was issued against him to appear at the assizes to answer undisclosed transgressions and contempts. He never appeared, and after being returned 'Not found' at successive assizes for three years, in January 1618 was formally outlawed by the court. The town was well rid of him.

THE POOR

A new element appeared in the government of the town in 1584, when the manor court suddenly chose twenty-four townsmen 'to serve the office of headborough of this town'. No reason was given for this appointment, but the twenty-four individuals chosen were of the highest calibre. Twenty-two of them were chief pledges, all of whom continued to be sworn, some of them regularly, as members of the annual manor court leet jury. The two headboroughs who were not chief pledges were Mr Thomas Wallinger, and his near neighbour at the upper end of the town, Mr John Pake, gentleman. Pake's wife Anne was the daughter and heiress of the former town bailiff, Richard Marion (d.1576), whose property included the White Hart inn (site of former 27 Tindal Street), and the 'capital messuage or Place' next door to it called The Heath (site of former 25-6 Tindal Street), where the Pakes lived. The twenty-four headboroughs, who were all high ratepayers, included the seven townsmen who occupied private pews in church on Sundays in front of the rest of the congregation. They comprised two gentlemen, a lawyer, two woollendrapers, two linendrapers, two mercers, two haberdashers, a beer brewer, the landlords of the Lion, Boar's Head, Dolphin, Falcon, and three other inns, a saddler, a fishmonger, and two lampmakers and tallow-chandlers. The status of only one is not known. The headboroughs did not replace the manor chief pledges, or the constables (who continued to be chosen annually, and sometimes included individual headboroughs among their number); but they may have been appointed to reinforce the chief pledges' and constables' authority, particularly in the control of one increasingly intractable Tudor urban problem. This was the intrusion into the town of undesirable 'inmates', strangers lodging in the town, without property, master, honest trade, or any means of support.

By the 1560s there were manorial by-laws in force against landlords 'that take in undertenants which are likely to be noisome, and burdenous to the township'. A number of townsmen were fined in 1568 and 1569, among them John Salmon, owner of the Robin Hood, no longer an inn, for disregarding orders to remove lodgers. In 1573 the townsmen were reminded that the by-law applied to 'all, great and small', and that the term 'landlord' meant 'as well the owners of the freehold as others', that is, the freeholders' lessees. The by-laws were enforced against both the harbouring householder and the lodger. In 1574 Thomas Jackson was fined for lodging the whole Tibbold family in his house, a barber was ordered to quit the town, a minstrel to remove himself to Woodham Ferrers where he was born, and a subtenant of the grocer William Pamplin to remove himself to the place where he last lived for three years, or where he was born. In the same year the by-law was strengthened. In future, no one, on pain of a fine of 40s, was to take in any strange or unknown tenant without a testimonial letter from the place where he last lived for a whole year; the letter was to be kept by the constables and officers of the town. Townsmen who disobeyed orders to remove lodgers did indeed forfeit the penalties: in 1584 William Shether of Maynetrees forfeited 40s for not removing a lodger as ordered.

The headboroughs survived for at least sixteen years, for in 1600 the manor court ordered that no one in future be permitted to receive an inmate into his house without the consent of 'six of the chiefest of the headboroughs'. But there is no later mention of them. If reinforcement of the control of 'inmates' was indeed the reason for their appointment, their responsibilities probably lapsed in 1603, when a manor court by-law transferred the duty of licensing lodgers to the constables, churchwardens, and overseers of the poor. With the appointment of parish overseers of the poor under the poor law acts of 1597 and 1601, backed by the authority of the justices of the peace, the surviving members of the manorial 'twenty-four' probably became redundant.

Intruding 'inmates' were not Chelmsford's only 'burdenous' problem; the town was haunted by vagrants and beggars. Some of them died in the parish. The registers record 'two pore weman buryed that laye in the strete' (1557), and many burials thereafter of unnamed strangers, 'a poor travelling man', 'a poor fellow', 'a poor wench', 'a poor strange boy', or 'a poor strange child'. In 1559 two 'walkyng peple' were married in the church, and 'the son of a wayfaring man' baptised. Tudor law, enforced by the justices, required that vagabonds and unlicensed beggars be whipped and sent back to their birth-place or last place of work. After 1587 they could be committed to the newly-built county house of correction at Coggeshall. A Kentish man taken at Chelmsford in 1568 was whipped by order of the magistrates and sent back to Maidstone, and an Essex woman was returned to Witham. Only indigent travellers carrying passes authorising their journey were exempt, and entitled to be helped on their way. Forged passes made at Chelmsford's May fair could be bought for a shilling in the 1590s. In one year, 1582-3, fifty-four vagrants were arrested in Chelmsford and taken before the magistrates, thirty-three of them in mid-winter, when casual work was hardest to find. Usually only the able-bodied, including runaways from their masters, were whipped; those who were lame, or deranged ('franticke'), were moved on without punishment. Indeed, by the end of the century the Chelmsford constables showed reluctance to inflict punishment; in 1601 the magistrates charged them with 'suffering incorrigible rogues to beg in the parish'. In 1602 the town itself was charged at the assizes with 'suffering rogues and wandering persons to beg and pass through the town unpunished'. The 1603 constables admitted this charge, as did the Moulsham constables, and all of them were fined by the magistrates for it. No help was to be had from the town's neighbours in controlling the flow of homeless pauper traffic. The constables of Great Baddow in 1603 were harbouring beggars and rogues 'in great flockes in a barn' in the parish, unpunished, and the Springfield constable refused to receive rogues and beggars carried to him from Chelmsford, even with passes, 'saying he would neither meddle with them nor their passports, but cast them out of his doors'. The sore straits of some of this human flotsam is illustrated by the unfortunate woman who, 'journeying' across the fields to Moulsham Hall in 1588, 'hoping to be given food for herself and her family', slipped climbing over a fence, impaled herself, and died of the wound.

The town's own resident poor were a different matter. Tudor legislation on the treatment of the settled poor had progressed from the general exhortation in 1549 that the 'maimed, sore, aged, and impotent poor' be relieved, cured, and habitations provided for them 'by the devotion of good people', to the Act of 1553, which laid the onus of 'charitable devotion' on all parishioners in each parish. In 1563 compulsion began to creep in: 'That which every person will of their charity give weekly' was to be gathered by parish 'collectors' and distributed weekly; but parishioners who refused to 'pay reasonably' could be taxed by the justices of the peace to 'a reasonable weekly sum'. In 1572 voluntary parish contributions for the poor were superseded by formally assessed parish rates. Finally, Acts of 1576, 1597, and 1601, required that the able-bodied poor be 'set on work', that houses of correction be provided in every county, and that the churchwardens in each parish, together with 'substantial' householders nominated annually as parish overseers of the poor, raise money from the inhabitants according to annual parish rate assessments. The money was to buy stocks of materials such as flax and hemp for those able to work; to assist the 'lame, impotent, old, blind' and other poor who could not work; and to place pauper children as apprentices.

In Chelmsford a parish 'book of account for the poor' was begun before 1582; the names written in the churchwardens' account book of the recipients that year of the sum of 11s 8d, gathered for the poor at communion, were endorsed: 'To be entered in the book for the poor'. The book, which was listed in the church inventory of 1589, has not survived, but the importance attached by the parish to the proper management of the relief of its own poor is implicit in the high standing of the officers chosen to administer it. The earliest names recorded occur in 1590, when the 'continued' appointment was agreed of Mr Thomas Wallinger as overseer, and the woollendraper John Seaman and haberdasher William Heditch as two collectors. All three of them were among the twenty-four manorial headboroughs chosen in 1584, and were former churchwardens and constables.

The able-bodied poor in the town and their families had always been expected to work. Edmund Carpenter, a poor man, presented in 1569 at the manor court for keeping two sons idle at home, up to no good, and outraging the neighbours, was ordered to put them out to service forthwith. But Dumb Bessie, Lame Bucket, Old Father Button, and Mother Agnes Richold, the former sexton's widow, were proper objects of the town's care, as were the town's licensed beggars, such as 'Richard at the Bell, a man that beggyd for his lyving', buried in 1544, and Ellen Perkin, 'a woman that livyd by the almes of the towne', buried in 1555. The policy of the parish is evident from comments in the churchwardens' book. Relief was to be given '... when and to whom it shall be thought most meet by the parishioners', to those 'that shall have most cause for relief', or 'where we thought most need'. Mr Thomas Williamson, gentleman, churchwarden from 1593 to 1596, was most precise when he drafted his will later, leaving an annual endowment of 30s to the poor of Chelmsford and Moulsham. It was to be distributed to the poor of good behaviour, to those who 'do their endeavour to lyve honestly by their work and labour', to the lame, blind, aged, and sick, and to those 'who resort to Church to hear service and God's word read and preached, to learn their duty towards God and men'. His gift was not, he wrote, for the idle who would not labour, or for those who lived 'wickedly in filtching and stealing, in filthiness of life, and in drunkenness, whoredome, prophaning of the Lord's Sabbath, swearing, and quarreling'.

The sources of relief (besides rates) available to the parish officers, and dependent on the 'devotion of good people', were varied. A somewhat insecure poor man's box was kept in the church. It needed two new keys in 1560, had to be mended in 1582, and was robbed in 1583 when all three locks were torn off it and the money, 'which was but little', taken. Nevertheless, the box reminded the congregation of their Christian duty, and made a small but steady contribution to the funds available; 4s paid to Smith's wife in 1588 to look after a sick woman's children for eight weeks, was taken from the poor box. The sum of 5s 8d paid to Anne Haggett by the churchwardens in 1591, 'in her sickness', was raised by collections in church. The Haggett family's misfortunes had been alleviated by casual payments since 1585, and by their admission to a town almshouse by 1586. A further 2s was paid to Anne 'in her great necessity at sundry times' in 1591, the year she died.

Many wills included gifts for the poor, to be distributed according to the testators' instructions, often at the funeral, by the executors, parson, or churchwardens. A legacy of 23s 11½d in 1591 was shared out in carefully graduated amounts from fourpence to one shilling among fifty-four parishioners, among them Mother Mason, who received the maximum; in 1585 the parish had spent 2s on 'Healing Mother Mason's eyes'. A charity endowed by the shearman William Davey in 1520 provided £8 a year as a rent charge on Swayns barn in Springfield, which he had acquired in 1498 under the will of his father-in-law, the dyer Richard Corall. The money was to buy firewood for the poor; it was enough in 1574 to pay for four loads of 'billets' or logs. When John Ayliffe, who bought Guy Harlings from Geoffrey Scott of the Lion in 1576, died in 1580, 40s left by him to buy faggots for 'my poor neighbours' was distributed among '30 persons or more'.

Simon Scraffeild's concern was for 'the lame and bedrid' of Chelmsford; he left them by his will of 1557 a rent charge of 26s 8d a year on Millfield in Springfield the money to be distributed on Good Friday. His will raised the query among the churchwardens whether 'Chelmsford', in a bequest, meant 'Chelmsford and Moulsham'. In the churchwardens' book 'and Moulsham' was struck out of the entry recording the first distribution of Scraffeild's gift. Benefactors had to specify 'Chelmsford and Moulsham' to ensure that the hamlet shared in their generosity. Thus in 1607 the tailor George Knightbridge's will stated unambiguously that 30s to be given in alms was for 'the oldest and best disposed of the poor of Chelmsford and Moulsham'. The withholding from Moulsham of any share in 'Chelmsford' bequests became a bitter source of grievance in the hamlet.

Every year at Michaelmas the parish received the 'Queen's Gift' for the poor, a variable sum, with 'portage' and 'quetance' deducted as charges. The origin of this annual gift is unknown. In 1663 the parish could only explain it as the 'gift of a former queen'. In 1562, when the payment is first recorded, the sum was over £6, but by 1574 it had fallen with deductions to some £3 5s 4d, distributed at the discretion of the churchwardens.

In the churchwardens' book many of the same names recur between 1585 and 1592 as the recipients of casual doles: Sparrow and his wife Joan 'in their long sickness'; Father Whiting and William Springfield, both in their 'last sickness', and Joan Whiting, also sick; Old Button, who died in December 1592; and Lankashire's wife, 'in her great sickness'; all these lived in town almshouses. Robert Marsh, on relief since 1587 and 'on his deathbed' in 1592, died that year. Lame Bucket, assisted in 1588, was still receiving relief in 1596. When King's wife was sick in 1588, she was given sixpence, and a shilling was paid for her child to be nursed; in the same year Coffyld's wife was given 2s for the relief of her sick daughter, while Smith's wife was paid 13s 4d over a period of twenty-two weeks to keep the daughter's two children, and 11d to buy a pair of shoes for the boy. Besides such doles, whenever possible the churchwardens employed and paid the poor for casual parish tasks, such as washing the surplices, gathering flags and rushes to strew the church on special occasions, killing the starlings in the church and sweeping away the cobwebs, and repairing the almshouses.

There was housing for the poor in both Chelmsford and Moulsham. The medieval leper hospital in the hamlet had become known by the 1570s as the 'poor house'. The frequent register entries of burials 'from the poor house' suggest that it mainly received the sick and infirm; it was described in 1591 as a 'hospital or poor-house for ... poor leprous and lazer people', and marked as 'Hospitalle' on John Walker's 1591 map of Moulsham. The hospital, managed by a 'Guider' or 'Governor', was still receiving benefactions: in 1570 Leonard Sandell of Hatfield Peverel left 10s to the poor people of the Spittle House of Moulsham. Like the six Moulsham 'Bedefolkes' who occupied the six separate almshouses provided by Master Auditor in his will, the sick poor in the hospital were 'put in and out' by the lord of the manor, Sir Thomas Mildmay. In 1586 Dumb Bessie was one of those registered as 'buried from the poor house'.

In the town the two almshouses in the Shoprow given by Robert Daysy about 1481, were said in 1564 to have been 'lately dismymbered' and the site sold. The site was never recovered for the poor. In Duke Street the churchwardens claimed as almshouses, and 'tenements for the relief of the poor', four cottages opposite the churchyard, 'supposed in right of their church'. They included former property of the guild of Corpus Christi, and the almshouse next to the Blue Boar known in 1527 as William Heyward's almshouse. Some of this property was still in the hands of the Crown in 1591, when investigation of the churchwardens' title found the tenements to be 'almshouses by sufferance, having no warrant from the Prince or the Lord of the Manor', and occupied 'without any licence, corporation, or other warrant'. By 1605 three of these tenements had been 'detained away'; by 1639 only the 'house given to the use of the poor' next to the Blue Boar was still in the hands of the church. The Crown's property had been sold to the Wallinger family to enlarge their estate in the town, which adjoined it.

Even the remaining almshouse in Duke Street had not survived intact. Its occupants, old Father Springfield until his death in November 1591, and the widow Springfield thereafter, had only the ground floor room. The upper room, known as 'the chamber over the almshouse where William Springfield dwells' (1579), 'the chamber at the Blue Boar' (1585), or the 'church chamber' (1608), had become annexed to the Blue Boar. But at least the parish poor benefited from an annuity of 5s charged on it. This was paid from 1576 until his death in 1585 by the owner of the Blue Boar, the brewer Walter Baker, and from 1585 by Walter's father-in-law, the haberdasher Thomas Jeffery, who was overseer of Walter's will, until 1590. From 1591 it was paid by William Gainsford, after his marriage to Walter's widow Joan, until the Blue Boar and church room with its rent charge were taken over by George Knightbridge about 1596.

But no one challenged the parishioners' right to the 'church house' and four almshouses on the west side of New Street, or the row of five almshouses at the back of the churchyard, the end house facing New Street. The New Street church house and almshouses originated as William Skinner's almshouse, dating from about 1478. The churchyard almshouses are not mentioned before 1570 and the origin of the row is unknown. The churchwardens maintained the church house and these almshouses, renewing groundsills, roof and gutter tiles, laths, and daub, doors, locks, keys, staples, and brick chimneys. To build a new chimney for the church house in 1585 cost the parish £1 14s 4½d, including 450 bricks at 20d a hundred, 50 tiles for 6d, and nine days' labour for 15s. The church house occupants, usually widows or widowers, paid rent if they could; Widow Robinson paid 4s a year in 1584, but Widow Lawrence only paid 2s 8d, because Widow Robinson 'hath the greatest and best part'. The churchwardens allocated all the town almshouses; when Mother Fletcher was buried in 1583, Father Button was 'set into the same house by me Myles Blomefylde with the consent of the rest of the churchwardens'.

Occasionally Sir Thomas Mildmay as lord of the manor intervened to house the poor. In 1582, 'of his grace and mercy, at the humble request of divers tenants', he granted a small piece of waste, sixty feet by twelve, 'to build a cottage on, or place to live', to Edward Nicoll, a poor man; and another piece, 'of his charity', seventy-two feet by fourteen, to Thomas Brooke, a poor mason, to build a dwelling on 'for the relief and comfort of him and his family'. In both cases the usual court fine for admission was pardoned.

THE CHURCH

The new civil duties imposed on the churchwardens by Tudor legislation had to be borne alongside the traditional responsibilities of their ancient office. In marked contrast to the manorial structure of the town, the Church in Chelmsford emerged from the middle years of the 16th century in some disarray. After the 'disgrace' of one rector, Dr Henry Cole, in 1548, his successor, Thomas Crook, as soon as he became rector began to lease the glebe, tithes, profits, and mansion house of the parsonage to laymen; one such lease, made in 1551, of the mansion house for twenty years, reserved to Crook and his successors as rector no more than 'sufficient lodging' within the parsonage. These leases, which became the subject of an obscure legal wrangle between William Mildmay, Master Auditor's younger brother, and Geoffrey Scott of the Lion inn, must have proved a sore incumbrance to Crook's successors. The living was served by curates, such as

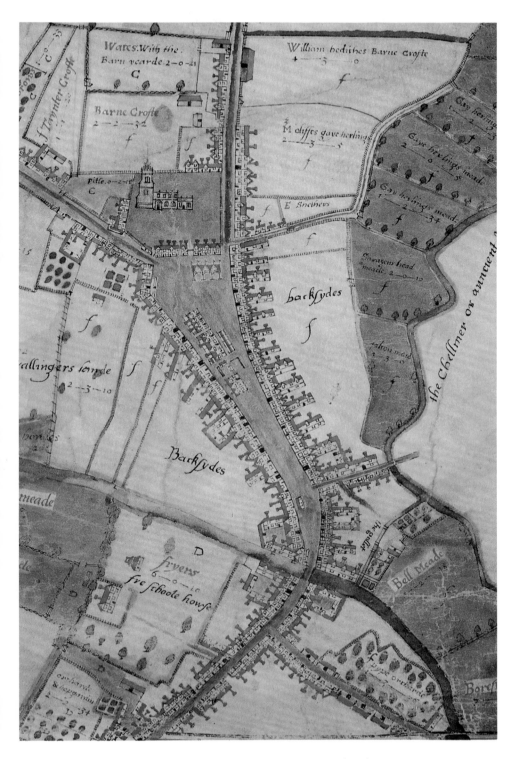

Chelmsford Town mapped by John Walker in 1591. (Reduced)

Thomas Eve, the former chantry priest, from 1548 until he became rector of Mashbury in 1555. Christopher Tatem, who became rector in 1558, was a member of a local family and served the cure personally, contributing 6s towards the purchase of a bible and a book of paraphrases, and witnessing the wills of parishioners, including the will of the bailiff John Taylor. But Tatem moved in 1560 to Writtle, and in September that year Elizabeth Utton of Chelmsford, 'for lake of a pryst' in her own parish, had to be married to William Skelton at Springfield.

From 1561 to 1571, when William Ireland, presented to the living by the Crown, was rector, there is no evidence that he lived in the parish, which was served by curates. Among these, Thomas Howlatt was particularly diligent, visiting the sick, witnessing their wills, or writing down the last wishes of the dying. In 1571, when the twenty-year lease of the parsonage expired, Howlatt, on the presentation of Sir Thomas Mildmay, succeeded Ireland as rector, and for twelve years the parish enjoyed the rare experience of a resident rector active in pastoral work, until April 1583, when the register records, 'Mr Thomas Howlatt parson departed out of this miserable life'. During the vacancy a Mr Pynchbeck of Writtle sometimes said service, at a fee of a shilling a time, until the arrival in June of Mr William Stone, the new parson, who 'made a famous sermon'. Apart from a second sermon a year later, Mr Stone made no mark in the parish, and in December, 1584, a Mr Gabriel Holt suddenly appeared, who told the churchwardens that 'he was our curate, and hired the benefice of Mr Stone'.

The casual commitment to the parish of most of its incumbents left the management of parish affairs in the hands of the churchwardens and leading parishioners. Not only were the resources of the parsonage impaired at the beginning of Elizabeth's reign, but the parish was burdened by debt, and the church itself, as revealed in the churchwardens' accounts, dilapidated. So serious was the financial position in 1559 that 'the chief inhabitants of the town to the number of twenty-four' agreed to sell silver-gilt church plate weighing 110 oz., a cross, pyx, cup, and chrismatory, to a London goldsmith, to settle debts owing to various parishioners, and to pay for urgent repairs to the building. The sale raised £29 6s 8d. A gilt chalice and paten of 23 oz. were sold later, to a Lombard Street goldsmith for a further £6 4s.

At the same time as the church plate was sold, money was raised by the disposal of everything saleable, old brass, stones, iron and lead, surplus wax, pieces of carved timber, pillars, a door, chests (including a long torch chest), a press, an 'altar stone' and 'St George's table'. A 'great' bell weighing over 22 cwt. was sold to the Queen for £10, the Roodloft to John Bridges for 13s, and a small bell to the bailiff, Richard Marion, for the market. A set of pewter 'vessels' which had belonged to the Corpus Christi guild, comprising some sixteen dozen pieces, large and 'middle sort' platters, dishes, and saucers, was leased to John Mildmay for 12s a year.

It is tempting, but not realistic, to link the twenty-four chief inhabitants of 1559, who took the weighty decision to sell the church plate, with the twenty-four headboroughs elected in 1584. But the headboroughs were a manorial body, their authority and membership restricted to one only of the two manors which comprised the parish of Chelmsford, Bishop's Hall. There is no evidence that at this time Chelmsford as a parish had adopted a system of government by select vestry similar to the 'Twenty-Four' of Braintree.

It was the leaded roofs of the church which were in the worst condition. In 1558-60 timber, lead, and nails, were bought 'for leading the church', and a London plumber paid £1 9s 8d for casting lead, laying new and old lead, and soldering, about the church. Cast lead, tiles, and corner tiles, left over from this early work, were sold to build up the repair fund. In 1565-7 masons were employed mainly on restoring the battlements of the 'high roof' (nave) and Corpus Christi guild (south chapel) which had been 'overthrown' during a heavy thunderstorm in July 1565, and the stonework of the chapel. In spite of this restoration work, by 1580 a rate of £40 15s 4d had to be gathered for church repairs; the 'decayed' roof was shored up, and timber and carpenter's work on the south aisle roof near the porch cost £5. But still the church was not water-tight. In November 1584 Myles Blomefylde, churchwarden, wrote:

> 'Goodman Pepper and his sonne wrought thys daye on the church, and with leade, lyme, sand, and heare, made mortar to stoppe the craneys and ryftes and hooles wheras the rayne ded dryve in all the length of the sowth syde of the church, and also the north syde, wheras yt rayned yn lykewyse.'

In 1562 the bishop of London authorised a diocesan contribution of £5 to Chelmsford church, 'to be stowed in repairing of glass windows', with 'other things' at the churchwardens' discretion. Robert Drane the glazier was usually the craftsman in greatest demand by the churchwardens, whether to carry out government orders to deface window glass with superstitious pictures, to mend minor 'holes and faults' which let in draughts, rain, and starlings, or to repair storm damage, particularly after the tempest of 1565. The west window in the belfry was broken by 'a great vehement wind' in 1575, and in 1590 the picture of St George in the east window of the south chapel was 'blown down by the wind and shaken all to pieces'.

Refurbishing and re-arrangement of the interior of the church accompanied the structural restoration. The floor was paved in 1560-2, and in 1566-70 the walls were 'whited'; some parts, including the pillars, were 'redded' with red lead. A panelled wooden canopy, the gift of Widow (Anne) Bridges, was set up over the pulpit in 1583, new stairs built up to the pulpit in 1584, a smooth white staff made for 'a stay to go up into the pulpit' in 1585, replaced in 1593 by a 'wrought pillar post', and a 'desk' made about the pulpit in 1591. Then the pulpit and font cover were varnished and 'coloured' by Davy Palmer the painter with white lead in oil. The pulpit was the platform for the 'famous' and 'worthy' sermons which became a popular feature of church life from the 1580s. These were delivered by every kind of visiting preacher, from Master Edgeworth, one of the earl of Leicester's chaplains, to a stranger who preached and was given 2s, 'being a poor man'. In 1588 fourpence was invested in an hour-glass for the preacher. Two lecterns were set up in 1586 for Erasmus's Paraphrases of the Gospels and Epistles. In 1583 the chamber over the church porch was prepared to house the parish armour, hitherto stored in the room above the vestry. When five panes of glass had been inserted in the windows over the porch, and 'crosses' made to hang the harness on, twenty-eight corselets and head-pieces were moved up into the little room.

In the 1580s, too, the churchwardens began to reorganise seating arrangements in the church, removing 'stools' (pews) and seats by the north chapel aisle and

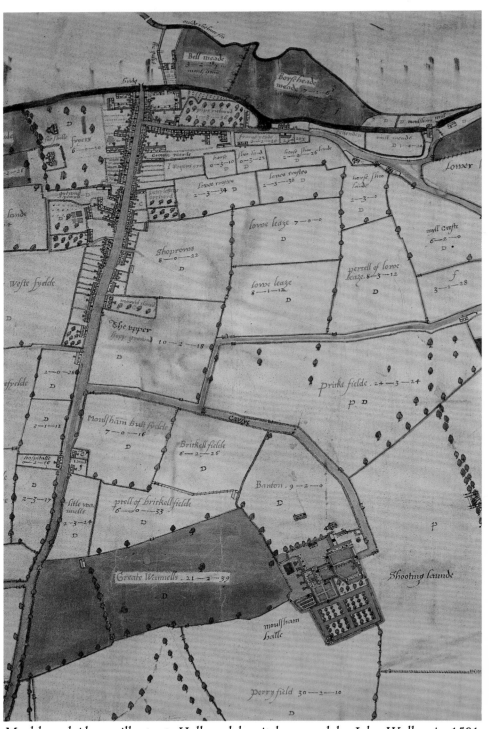

Moulsham bridge, mill, street, Hall, and hospital, mapped by John Walker in 1591. (Reduced)

setting them 'orderly'. Re-arrangements did not always proceed smoothly. In 1583 Myles Blomefylde and the other churchwardens, who had decided, 'with the consent of the best and ancientest of the town', to move Jane Scot to another seat, 'after evensong ... went to her and talked with her neighbourly and friendly in that behalf and she answered us gently. But ... when we were all out of the church, she brought a carpenter and reaved off the door of the stool and rent up the mat and carried away all out of the church'. The churchwardens, however, prevailed, for a marginal note adds: 'But it was restored'.

Meanwhile the 'best and ancientest of the town' were building private pews for themselves before the chancel. The first two pews for men were built in 1584 for the seven leading townsmen of the day and the tenant of Bishop's Hall. By 1593 private pews, approved on the grounds that they left more room in the nave and aisles for the rest of the congregation, were subject to clear rules. When a 'room' or seat in one of the men's pews became vacant by an occupant's death or departure from the parish, the surviving occupants or their successors chose who should fill it, all newcomers paying 6s 8d towards church repairs. A male heir, provided he was a householder of honest condition and behaviour, could inherit a seat free of charge. Between 1593 and 1601 the woollendraper John Seaman (1593), Mr Richard Nicholls (1596), Mr Edward Makin (1598), and the inn-keeper Michael Fox (1601), managed to buy vacant seats in the original men's pews. Three of them were headboroughs chosen in 1584; all of them, including the youngest, Michael Fox, had already served as churchwardens by the time they acquired their seats.

Three private pews for women had also been built by 1593, in the south aisle, one of them by John Reynolds, oatmealmaker, and Thomas Wallinger, and another by John Pake, Robert Wood, and Richard Long, for their wives; the third was built by two widows, Anne Bridges of Toppies (site of 39 High Street), and Elizabeth Browne of the Cock. The privilege of acquiring a vacant seat in the womens' pews was accorded only to those 'thought meet' to sit with them by the original occupants or their successors; the husbands of newly-admitted wives, other than daughters-in-law of sitting occupants, paid 3s 4d to the church. The innkeeper John Browne of the Boar's Head paid 3s 4d in 1593 for his wife to move into the pew where Mrs Long and the others sat.

The grammar school master had a pew at the east end of the south aisle, where his scholars and other children sat on long forms. But there were private seats for the children of the élite. In 1591 Mr Edward Makin paid for a little bench to be built alongside the pew where Mr Wallinger sat, for his own children to sit, and the children of the occupants of Mr Wallinger's pew, and a similar little children's bench beside the pew where Mr Robert Wood sat. No doubt this generosity was not forgotten in 1598, when Mr Makin applied for, and was granted, a vacant pew seat for himself.

The church was described in 1591 as 'goodlye, seemely, and large ... meete for the receipte of two thousand people or more ... scituate in one faire church yarde ... furnished with manie goodlye pues, one goodlye steeple ymbattelled ... and a convenient ringe of foure belles'. The churchyard of two and a half acres was walled in in 1601, the parish rate to pay for it raising £10 15s 2d in Chelmsford and £5 1s 10d in Moulsham. In 1602 two new bells were hung, a tenor bell weighing over 18 cwt. and a treble bell over 7 cwt. The treble bell, cast by a

Colchester bellfounder, cost over £21. The tenor bell, a former bell re-cast with nearly a hundredweight of 'new metal that she was made heviar', cost over £8. When Queen Elizabeth came to the throne the church already had a clock, little bells on the altar called chimes, and two organs. Clock and chimes survived to the next century, but when the church was robbed in 1579 and 1583 most of the organ pipes were stolen. Those that were not taken, broken and whole, were sold, as were the 'spoiled and broken' cases of the Great and Little Organs.

THE PLAYS

A festival of plays was undertaken by the parishioners in 1563, administered and audited by the then churchwardens, the brewer Walter Baker, his father-in-law Thomas Jeffery, and Thomas Hunwick; the festival may have been designed to raise funds to support the mounting cost of renovation of the church. The performances revived a pre-Reformation dramatic tradition first recorded in 1490. The medieval players' garments, which had been borrowed by Dunmow in 1539 for their Corpus Christi plays, had remained in the custody of the Chelmsford churchwardens, stored in chests, and inventoried with the parish vestments and vessels, including a black velvet gown noted in 1564 as 'very muche worne'.

The only clues to the nature of the four 'plays' or 'shows' given in 1563, with performances in Braintree and Maldon as well as in Chelmsford, are the stock of 'garments' and the production expenses entered in the churchwardens' account book. The players performed in the pightle beside the churchyard, in the church itself, and on a mobile pageant carried by ten men. There were parts for Christ, Aaron, Prophets, Shepherds, Vices, Devils, and a painted Giant. Scenes required stages built for Heaven, Hell, and a Temple, and fifty fathom of line to manipulate 'clowds'. Special sound effects were provided by a brass cannon called a 'Falcon', weighing 239 lb., with an ample supply of gunpowder to fire it, and by minstrels playing on drum, flute, and trumpet. Among the stage properties were daggers, whips, and 'sheephooks'.

Most of the 'garments' listed could have been adapted to dress up any stage character. There were long and short gowns of red, blue, and black, velvet, satin, and silk; 'jornets' or cloaks, and sleeved and sleeveless jerkins, of blue velvet, and mantles of red brocade. Some garments were enriched with ornamental borders, green, gold, and silver tinsel, and 'cloth of tyshew' (a rich gauze often interwoven with gold and silver thread). There were beards, 'hares' or wigs, and caps of fur and velvet. Christ was distinguished by a leather coat, Aaron and the Prophets by their caps, Shepherds by their crooks, Vices by their coats and 'scalps' (? skull-caps), and Devils by baggy trousers called 'slops'.

Exciting and popular as these performances must have been, whatever the plot, financially they were not a success, the costs exceeding the takings by over £9, leaving the parish indebted to the churchwardens, and to local sponsors who had advanced money or furnished properties and materials. It took a decade to clear the debts. Between 1564 and 1574 play garments were hired from time to time to other places, to Billericay, Colchester, Saffron Walden, and Bishop's Stortford, to the children of Great Baddow and the men of Little Baddow, to Boreham and Brentwood, even to Lavenham and Sawbridgeworth, and to the earl of Sussex's players; in 1572 they were hired to John Walker of Hanningfield, father of the famous Essex mapmaker John Walker, Architector. In 1568 the churchwardens began to sell off garments and properties. All that remained by 1576 were sold that year to raise £6 13s 4d for church repairs, leaving only one sheephook and the brass falcon. The falcon was sold in 1579 to a London pewterer for £3 1s 9d, and the sheephook was finally struck out of the church inventory in 1582.

Dr John Coldewey of the University of Colorado, in a Ph.D. thesis presented in 1972, explored the possibility that the Chelmsford performances in 1563 might have included some early 16th-century plays preserved in the Bodleian Library in Oxford (Digby MSS. 133). These are plays of 'The Conversion of St Paul', of 'Mary Magdalen', of 'Wisdom, who is Christ' (a morality play), and of 'Candlemes Day and the Kyllyng of ye Children'. The evidence from the churchwardens' accounts is insufficient to support positive identification with any of these plays. But suspicion is justifiably aroused by the fact that three, and possibly four, of the Digby manuscript plays were formerly owned by a Chelmsford townsman. The 'Conversion' bears his autograph, 'Myles Blomefylde'; the 'Magdalen', and 'Wisdom', are initialled by him in his distinctive fashion, 'MB'. Only the 'Candlemes Day' play is not marked by him, but it is bound up between the 'Magdalen' play and 'Wisdom' in the manuscript.

At the time of the 1563 performances Blomefylde was not living in Chelmsford, where he settled about 1566. The 'play books', which had cost the parish £4, were in the custody of George Martindale in 1573, who also held a parish bond for £20 as security for the return to him of 'certain parcels used about the plays by him delivered out'. This entry was later struck through, with a marginal note — 'The parcels redelivered' — implying a parish settlement with Martindale. At this time Blomefylde, who was by then well-established in the town, could have bought the play books from the parish. But there is no record of such a transaction in the churchwardens' accounts.

MYLES BLOMEFYLDE

Myles Blomefylde was a notable bibliophile of his day. Books known to have been in his collection, bearing his autograph or initials, included works on alchemy, philosophy, geography, and history. On the last leaf of his copy of Wynkyn de Worde's, 'Information for pilgrims into the holy land', published in 1524, he wrote in his bold Elizabethan secretary hand:

'I Myles Blomefylde of Burye Saynct Edmunde in Suffolke was borne ye yeare followyng, after ye pryntyng of thys book ...'

After seven years' study at Cambridge he was licensed in 1552 to practise as a physician, and probably practised in Sudbury, where his daughter Elizabeth was baptised in 1559.

When Blomefylde appeared in Chelmsford, about 1566, he had acquired the house next to the almshouses on the north side of the churchyard. This priest's house which once belonged to the guild of St John, had been seized by the Crown in 1548, and later sold to Thomas Mildmay the Auditor, to be held of the Crown 'by fealty only'. Later it became the property of the former Corpus Christi priest, Thomas Eve, perhaps as a gift from the Mildmays. Eve's will, proved in 1565, devised it to the former rector of Chelmsford, Christopher

Tatem, vicar of Writtle, to be disposed of by him, let or sold, for the benefit of the 'eldest and most honest' of the poor. This was when it came into Blomefylde's possession. As a newcomer to Chelmsford, from the first mention of him in 1566, when he sold the parish a book of homilies, he was respectfully addressed as 'Mr Blomefild'. By 1572 he was numbered among the chief pledges.

In the years which followed Blomefylde gained a reputation as a 'cunning man', a gift which brought him to the notice of the magistrates in 1577, when a man from North Ockendon went to 'one Mr Blomefild dwelling at Chelmsford', for help to recover a lost mare. Blomefylde suggested that if his client searched in the north-east, 'peradventure he should have his mare again', and took a shilling as fee for his advice. The mare providentially turned up. In 1578 a North Ockendon maidservant, 'making her moan' to the mare's owner about some washing — a smock, a neckerchief, a shirt band, and a pair of ruffs — stolen from her master's garden, hearing about the mare, sent a friend called Lynford to Chelmsford to question Blomefylde at his house 'hard by the churchyard'. Blomefylde fetched a looking glass, hung it on a nail over the bench in the hall, and told Lynford to 'look in yt and said as far as he could gesse he shulde see the face of him that had the said lynnen'. Lynford looked, saw a face like that of a North Ockendon acquaintance, and asked, 'Hath this man whose face I see here the said lynnen or not?'. Blomefylde said 'he would not say that he had yt, nor accuse him, but as farre as he coulde judge he had yt'. Lynford paid Blomefylde 8*d*, and promised 'that he shulde tell no man what he had shewed him'. But the story came out; Blomefylde found himself up before the magistrates, charged under the laws against conjuration, witchcraft, enchantment, or sorcery for gain. There is no evidence that he was convicted, or penalised, and the incident did no harm to his standing in the town, for four years later, in 1582, he was chosen churchwarden.

Blomefylde served as churchwarden in 1582-4, and 1586-7; in 1589 he agreed, in his own words, 'at the request of the Chefest of the parysh', to help the other churchwardens in place of one of the chosen wardens, Richard Nicholls. To the office of churchwarden Blomefylde brought all the zest of his extrovert personality, keeping the churchwardens' book himself in his unmistakable sprawling hand, embellishing the entries with rubricated headings and capitals, and the same personal monogram 'MB' with which he marked the treasures of his library. He recorded the Monday in April 1582 when there 'came a prynce of Polonia (as they saye) into this towne, at whose commyng we were requested to ryng out our belles'; and the collection that 'I, Myles Blomefylde and John Stuck, churchwardens, ded gather in the Church for xv Englishmen in pryson in the Turkes dominion and must paye for theyr Rawnsome 900 li or yei be Released'. He told how in 1583 robbers broke into the church, took the money from the poor man's box, the communion table cloth, and both surplices, and 'attempted to have broken into the vestry, but they prevailed not, to have had the communion cup; thanks be to God, they missed of that'. He noted the night in 1584 when the clapper of the Great Bell was 'broken asondre in the myddest', and the purchase in 1586 of a five-foot length of board, fifteen inches deep, to mend the north door of the church, 'all the length below at the nether edge to keep out dogs'.

At Whitsun 1590 Blomefylde was the first churchwarden ever to enter formally in the account book full details of the annual parish meeting, when parish officers were chosen and the retiring officers' accounts examined. He called the meeting, 'The Assembly of the pryncypall Inhabitantes of the parysshe of Chelmesford And hamlet of Moulsham', and named the thirty-three parishioners present, headed by Sir Thomas Mildmay and including thirteen of the town's headboroughs and thirteen representatives from Moulsham. He revealed the simmering controversy, which was to come to a head twenty-one years later, over the parson's rights in the choice of churchwardens: 'If the parsun had any voyce, yet he beyng suspended, as we are informed, the paryshe holdeth it theyr ryght absolutelye to make ye full choyse'. The suspended rector at the time was George Burghley, who had succeeded William Stone in 1586, and been charged at the assizes in 1588 with breaking into the house of John Elliot and raping his wife, Joan. Although found not guilty, in 1589 he was still facing proceedings before the ecclesiastical authorities.

WITCH TRIALS

The credulity which prompted resort to cunning men like Myles Blomefylde to resolve such harmless mysteries as lost or stolen stock or linen, was only one symptom of the prevailing superstition, which found other more sinister outlets. In 1580 the privy council ordered the sheriff of Essex to apprehend, 'using secresie lest they escape', suspects said to be 'deply touched with detestable practises of conjuration'; the suspects included a tapster at Chelmsford's New (Crown) inn, whose dwelling-place was to be searched 'for bookes and wrytinges concerning conjuring'. Under a statute of 1563 conjuring evil spirits carried the death penalty on first conviction; so did murder by 'Witchcrafte, Enchantment, Charme, or Sorcerie'. A harsher statute of 1604 made the death penalty also mandatory for the first conviction (instead of the second) of injury to people or property by witchcraft. There were some 163 prosecutions of 'witches' at the Essex Assizes between 1560 and 1599. Most of the trials were held at Chelmsford, and those convicted were hanged on the gallows near Rainsford Lane. None of those accused at that time were Chelmsford people. But in 1607 there was a sudden outbreak of witchcraft hysteria in Moulsham. One woman, Blanche Worman, was accused by six families, two of them next-door neighbours, of practising witchcrafts and sorceries on three women, who all survived, and three males, possibly children. Two of the males had died before the trial; the third, still living, was 'consumed, mutilated, and wasted' in body at the time of the trial, and died later. Blanche was convicted at the assizes and hanged on the evidence of the fathers of the males and the husbands of the women.

Sensational printed and illustrated pamphlets — 'The Examination and Confession of Certain Wytches at Chensford ... before the Queens maiesties Judges, the xxvi day of July Anno 1566'; 'A Detection of damnable driftes, practized by three Witches arraigned at Chelmisforde ... at the late Assizes there holden, which were executed in Aprill, 1579'; and 'The Apprehension and Confession of three notorious Witches Arreigned and by Iustice condemned and executed at Chelmesforde ... the 5 day of Julye last past, 1589' — expose the avid public appetite for the sensational claims made by witnesses, and even confessed by the 'witches' themselves, at these trials. At the 1566 trial there was talk of a white spotted cat called Sathan which could be turned into a toad and spoke in a strange hollow voice, and of a thing like a black dog with a face like an ape, a short tail, a chin, and a pair of horns on its head. The 1579 trial discovered a fiend called Tom, a rat which ran up the chimney and fell down again in the likeness of a toad, and three spirits, Great Dick who was kept in a wicker bottle, Little Dick kept in a leather bottle, and Willett in a wool pack. The court's investigators who searched the suspect's house found the bottles and the wool pack, 'but the Spirites were vanished awaie'.

POLITICS AND RELIGION

Sir Thomas Mildmay outlived Queen Elizabeth I, who died in 1603. Her successor, her kinsman King James VI of Scotland, was the son of Mary, Queen of Scots, and great-grandson of Henry VIII's sister Margaret. As King James I of England he united the two Crowns. Sir Thomas regarded the political rivalries which surfaced during the elections to King James's first parliament in 1604 as an ill omen for the future. He wrote to Sir Francis Barrington about Lord Rich's election manoevres in Essex:

'I am sorry to understand of the extraordinary courses holden in this business, which I wish may not end with the discontentment of very many, and make this country, that hath in the whole course of my poor service therein, been ever reputed peaceable and quiet, now to become factious, wherunto you are both bound as good patriots to have a singular regard'.

Mildmay himself was responsible for negotiating the compromise whereby one of Robert, Lord Rich's candidates, Sir Gamaliel Capel, withdrew, leaving the field to Barrington and Sir Edward Denny, thus avoiding a contested election.

If the growth of political factions among the upper echelons of society filled Sir Thomas in his last years with foreboding, as a magistrate he cannot have been unaware of the religious differences within his own town. In religion, Elizabeth's government had shown at first tolerance to those who clung to the Old Faith, so long as they lived peaceably and posed no threat to the State. But after Pope Pius V excommunicated the queen in 1570, making her a legitimate target of Catholic rebellion, and rumours spread of plots, real or imagined, to displace her in favour of her Catholic cousin Mary, Queen of Scots, the official attitude hardened. Adherence to Rome became treasonable. In particular, missionary priests trained at seminaries on the continent, who clandestinely entered the country to say mass and teach in Catholic houses, were sought out.

One of these priests, John Payne, succoured by the Catholic Petre family of Ingatestone Hall, arrested there in 1577, and briefly imprisoned before returning to Douai, was back in England within a year to continue his mission, only to be arrested again in 1582. After being tortured on the rack in the Tower of London, he was handed over to the sheriff of Essex, tried for treason at the March Assizes in Chelmsford, and on the unsupported evidence of one informer of singularly ill repute, found guilty and condemned to hang. He was drawn on the traitor's hurdle to the execution place to the north of the town, where he mounted the ladder to the gallows, and there made a final statement denying any treason, before the halter was fitted to his neck, and the ladder turned away by the Newgate hangman. A bystander's account of the execution was published the

158

same year in Rheims. He wrote: 'All the town loved him exceedingly, so did the keepers and most of the magistrates of the shire. No man seemed in countenance to dislike him, but much sorrowed and lamented his death'. But it was not safe to speak up locally for Payne. A yeoman of Margaretting was closely questioned by the privy council about speeches he was said to have made in defence of 'Payne the traytor, lately executed at Cheinsford'.

In spite of the stricter enforcement of the penal code on Catholics, a remnant survived in the town and hamlet. In 1588 a Moulsham labourer affirmed before witnesses that he 'was a papyste, and that he wolde praye for the Pope, and that the Quene's Majesty did love the Pope better than any of them', and went to gaol for it.

A greater threat than popery to the future tranquillity of the town lay in the growing number of Puritan objectors to the ceremonies of the 1552 Prayer Book. This had been adopted in the 1559 Act of Uniformity as the only authorised liturgy of the Elizabethan settlement. But 'God's Word', as revealed in the English Bible, had become for many the touchstone of personal belief and practice. In 1561 a Chelmsford labourer, Robert Taylor, was accused of causing a public scandal by saying 'that service that the Quene hadd and did use in her Chappell was but palterye'. In 1586 Thomas Glascock, shoemaker, 'did rend certain leaves out of the said Book of Common Prayer conteyning Public Baptism, being the book of one Collen'; when Collen asked him why he did so, he replied, 'because it is naught; there is in it named the water of Jordan for the washing away of our mystical sins; if that water washeth away sins, then Christ died for us in vain'. Glascock was referred by Quarter Sessions to the Assizes, charged with uttering these words, abetted by other locals, and saying 'that he utterly myslyked' the prayer book service of baptism which 'was not agreeable with Godde's word'. But no one could be found to give evidence against him. In the same year John Pake complained that at the baptism of his own son in Chelmsford parish church the officiating minister, one Ralph Halden of Margaretting, did not make the sign of the Cross over the child, as prescribed by the Book of Common Prayer.

By the 1590s the churchwardens were pursuing deliberate absentees from church; in 1591 they paid 2s 10d to the clerk at the assizes 'for framing the indictment against Puritism'. As a result, eleven parishioners from the town and hamlet appeared at the July assizes on this charge, a cooper and his wife, three smiths and two of their wives, a shoemaker, a saddler, a haberdasher, and a collar maker. The cooper's wife, Bridget Seaton of Moulsham, was indicted again in 1592, at Quarter Sessions; she had not attended her parish church for over a year. A Moulsham turner was indicted with her, for refusing to bring his child to be baptised in the parish church. A nucleus of nonconformity was emerging, particularly in the hamlet.

THE TOWNSPEOPLE AT HOME

Whatever the religious or political storms looming in the future, Sir Thomas's town was moving towards the next century in good shape. In 1591 he commissioned a professional survey of his manor of Chelmsford. The manor, its customs, demesne lands, and 209 freehold and copyhold holdings, were exhaustively researched by Sir Thomas's steward, John Lathum, gentleman, by examination of its manorial records since the 14th century, and of 'other materiall escriptes', in particular the deeds of each holding, which the tenants had to produce in court as evidence of title, or be fined for default. Edward Moryson, esquire, supervised the survey, and his 'measurer', John Walker, also described as 'architector', drew the magnificent map which accompanied the written volume. The introduction to the survey declared:

> 'Chelmersforde is one ancient goodlye manor scituate in the harte of the countye of Essex in good and holesome aire, convenientlie and well housed and well builte for timber and tile ... Within this manor, uppon parcell of the same, uppon the common roode waye, is scituate the towne of Chelmesforde, sometime written the Burrowe of Chelmesforde, well scituated with moe than three hundred habitacions, divers of them seemelye for gentlemen, manie fayre innes, and the residue of the same habitacions for victuallers & artificers of cytie like buildinges ... This town is called the Shire towne ... It is alsoe a greate thorowefare, and markett towne weekely uppon the Friday, in which markett are to be sold abundance of victualles and wares ...'

Chelmsford's Elizabethan inhabitants are revealed in their wills in the privacy of their homes, knit together in an intricate pattern of personal relationships. Charles Dabbes, the public notary, appointed his wife Tamisan as his executrix in 1588, but relied on the discretion of his cousin, Mr John Pake, gentleman, and his brother-in-law, Edward Bigland of the Dolphin, to arrange for his son Thomas at fourteen to be suitably bound apprentice; while the loyal service of 'Mathew, my man' was rewarded with 10s, and the black doublet, black galligaskens, and black netherstocks, which were doubtless the livery Mathew had worn attending the notary upon his business. Walter Baker, the brewer, who died in 1585, was the son of a Springfield miller; he married the daughter of the Chelmsford haberdasher, Thomas Jeffery. With his marriage, Walter gained one Jeffery sister-in-law and three brothers-in-law in the town; of his own seven sisters, one, Joan, was the wife of Thomas Scott, landlord of the Blue Boar, which Walter owned, and another, Philippa, was the wife of John Dudsbury of the Bell; Walter's daughter Joan married one of the Chelmsford Woods. Besides his family circle, there were the servants of his household, and the workpeople of his brewery. One of Walter's employees, George Blacklock, who had died, unmarried, five years before his master, had divided his assets, about £13, between his sister, his master and mistress and their daughter Joan, the brewers and carters 'of my master's house', three of their maidservants, a dozen friends, and the poor. He named his master as executor of his will. As the major owner of property in the town, a large number of under-tenants were dependent on Walter Baker's goodwill. His testament required that after his death none of them be put out, or their rents raised.

Husbands showed their concern for their families, each in his own way. Alexander Tornor in 1565 encouraged his mother with a legacy of 3s 4d 'to be good to my wife and toue cheldare'. Robert Leonard in 1576 left his lease of the Crane inn to his son, to see 'his mother kept as a childe ought to do'. John Graveley in 1576 gave the lease of his house jointly to his wife Amy and to their daughter and son-in-law, 'that they shall together, inhabyt, and joyntly ... occupy the same ...

wylling them ... to help and ayde one another, and especially to be good to my wyfe and diligent to helpe her in all her bysines'. Richard Carsey, besides the joined bed he had shared with his wife in the chamber over the shop, with its bedding and curtains, and the household stuff she had brought at marriage, left her £4 a year in 1591, and her 'dwelling, diet, and lodging' with his son Jonas for life, to help Jonas 'in the oversight and governance of his family, so long as she is willing and shall please to remain'. The joiner William Wyther, who had built the stages for the plays, was childless. In 1595 he divided his inn, the Chequer in Duke Street, between his wife Sara and his friend or kinsman, the yeoman George Studley, for life, with reversion after their deaths to his cousin, a Moulsham carpenter. Sara's share was the parlour, the loft called the 'appell chamber', the garret chamber, the loft over the shop, the little room under the stairs leading up to the loft, and a little garden, with rights of access to wash and bake in the kitchen, and to draw water from the well; she also received an annuity of 20s, and sufficient household goods, clothing, beehives, pigs, poultry, growing fruit, cheeses, and firewood. Studley had the rest of the inn for life, provided he honoured Sara's share. In the event, the widow in 1596 leased to Studley her small annuity and share of the premises for forty years, for an annual rent of £4 6s. The Moulsham cousin in 1597 sold his reversionary interest for over £46 to Thomas Mildmay of Barnes, who then persuaded Studley in 1600 to sell out to him his whole interest in the inn. After Mildmay gained possession of the freehold, the inn's name was changed to the George (site of former 79 Duke Street). Studley himself took over the wine tavern in the high street (site of 23 High Street) and named it the Chequer.

It was expected that a widow would carry on her late husband's business. The tallow-chandler John Monk of Sharparrows (site of former 15-17 Tindal Street) arranged in 1589 that if his widow did not do so, his son John should have his implements. Apprentices were encouraged to support their masters' widows. A smith in 1569 left 40s to his apprentice on condition he 'serve out the yeares for which he is my covenaunt servant with my wife, or with some honest man at the appointment of my wife.' A Moulsham wheelwright in 1604 left his apprentice his best doublet and hose, and all the timber in his shop except two pairs of cart wheels, one already made, the other not fully finished, on condition that he 'truly serve' his master's widow for a year after his apprenticeship expired for a wage of £3 a year.

Provision for the widow was closely tied to the upbringing of the children. Many children never reached maturity. Eighteen out of forty-eight burials in 1582 were of children. In the space of six weeks in 1603, a plague year in Chelmsford, John Harrison lost not only his wife, but three sons and two daughters. Yet some surprisingly large families survived. When the haberdasher William Heditch died in 1597, eight sons and four daughters still lived from his two marriages. When the cutler Thomas Almon died in 1593, his widow Joan was left with their ten children to bring up on her own; nine of them were still minors when she died herself ten months later in 1594. Apart from her eldest son William's legacy of a leather-covered black trunk and tools, her childbed linen earmarked for her eldest daughter Joan, and legacies of £10 each for the nine youngest children (the sons at twenty-one years, the daughters at eighteen years or marriage), and 40s to her brother-in-law Robert Almon, all the family possessions were to be sold, the proceeds to remain in the hands of her 'beloved friends' and executors, John Hayward her brother-in-law and Richard Terrett, presumably for her children's upbringing. Any overplus when the trust was fulfilled was to be divided among the eight youngest children.

When Anne Neale, widow of the well-to-do glover Richard Neale who died in 1597, died two years after him, ten children were orphaned, one of them, Edward, born after his father's death. Because 'her dear children, William, Richard, Margaret, Ursula, Avice, Bridget, Anne, Elizabeth, and Sara' had been, as Anne said, 'sufficiently provided for' by her late husband's will, she set aside in her own will an equal portion for Edward, with the qualification that if the baby died, his share be applied to the 'good placing, education, and bringing up' of her daughters. She entrusted the charge of the children to be a formidable group of executors, her 'good friends' Thomas Wallinger and Matthew Bridges, gentlemen, her cousin Edward Bigland of the Dolphin, Jonas Carsey (whose wife was a Wallinger), Thomas Glover, and William Neale, her kinsman. Parents who died in poorer circumstances, with less fortunate connections, foresaw a bleak future. A Moulsham man, leaving all he had in 1605 to his wife, to bring up his only child, confessed to the bedside witnesses, 'hee thoute ite was note enowe toe bring him up bute he sed she coulld have nomore thene that he had'.

Husbands expected their widows to carry out their wishes in the upbringing of their children, sometimes making this a condition of the widow's portion. In 1559 Elynor, widow of the bailiff John Taylor, was given the remainder of his lease of Bishop's Hall so long as she supported his two sons at the grammar school. In 1575 the Chelmsford innholder Ralph Neale left his wife Margaret all his property in Springfield for a small annual rent until his eldest son William came of age, provided she brought him up 'with all things for a child to be brought up withal according to his age', until he was bound apprentice or put out to service. Robert Glascock, maltman, in 1571 left everything to his wife Denise, 'to releiffe herself, susteyne and keepe my mother, and bryng upp my thre children vertuously and in the fere of God so fare furthe as she can'. Thomas Gylder in 1574 left it to his wife Rose's discretion whether to pay to their son Thomas £6 13s 8d when he 'cometh forthe of hys prentysheship ... so that the said Thomas wylbe ruled by hir, or ells she to be in choyse whether he shall have yt or not'. Nicholas Adams in 1586 charged his wife to bring up his three sons until she could 'bestowe them in godly exercise to gett their lyvinge'. Joan, widow of Thomas Wood the surgeon (1602), was to keep his son Tiberius at school to 'perfectlie understand the Englishe and the Lattine tonge'. Once this was achieved, Tiberius might have his father's instruments and books. The five youngest children of Seth Andrews at Gallows End became dependent from 1600 on their eldest brother to bring them up 'in honest education, and to fynd them with fit necessaries until they come to lawful yeares to help themselves'.

Petty family differences sometimes surfaced when sick people were questioned about the disposal of their possessions. Joan Fynche, the servant at Bishop's Hall, had a brother who owed her 10s, yet would not come to see her when she was sick, 'but would content himself to howld that which he had in his hands'; so she said she would give him nothing, and left all she had, including the wages for three years' service owed to her by her master, to those 'that tooke paynes about her then in the tyme of her sicknes'. Another single woman told the two women tending her to be sure to give her possessions to two of her sisters, 'or her brother Robert would have them'; when they reminded her of her third sister, she agreed that they might give her 'somewhat for remembrance, some trifelyng thing'. One wealthy testator may have feared that his family would fall apart after his death. When Mr John Bridges of the Boar's Head and Toppies died in 1575 he left £4 a year to pay for his widow Anne, and his well-provided-for sons, Thomas, John, Matthew, and William, 'to meet together' twice a year, at Christmas and Whitsun.

The wills reveal the growing domestic comforts and refinements enjoyed by those of Chelmsford's inhabitants prosperous enough to afford them. The town's windows were being glazed; the annalist John Stow recorded in July 1565 a thunderstorm 'so terrible', with showers of hail, that at Chelmsford the glass windows on the east side of the town were 'beaten down'. The walls of 'old' and 'new' parlours and chambers, of upper 'hall chambers' formed by division of the central hall, and of the 'great chamber over the shop', were being hung with fashionable 'painted cloths' and covered with panelling. Edmund Sebright the saddler in 1576 left his house by the stone bridge (site of 51 High Street) to his wife Mary for life, with its windows, doors, and glass, 'as it now is'. Opposite Sebright's, at the Cock, Widow Elizabeth Browne, making her will in 1605, disposed carefully of the inn's 'waynscotts, seelinges, portalls, benches, settles, lockes, dores, keyes of dores, glasse', and 'glasse windowes'. A successful Moulsham haberdasher in 1594, proud of his improvements, left his house to his wife rent free for life, on condition that she did not remove the wainscoted 'portolls' and 'backesettles' nailed to the walls, the painted cloths nailed and painted on the walls, and the glass about the house, so that 'portolls, backesettles, painted cloths, and glass shall be alwaies standers with the said house forever'.

Alongside the basic beds and truckle or trundle beds pushed under them by day, the stools and settles, tables and forms, and chests and hutches, appear standing wainscot bedsteads, with iron rods and bed-curtains of fine say cloth, coverlets of tapestry work, stools covered with silk 'wrought with gold', wicker chairs, chairs 'with bottoms of bullrushes', and chairs covered with needlework, cushions of needlework and Turkish tapestry work, window hangings, and striped carpets. Conspicuous among the usual household pots, platters, and dishes of brass, copper, latten, and pewter, and the occasional clock or warming pan, was the array of silver and silver gilt plate, the 'Maindenhead' spoons, the fruit dishes, the silver salts with gilt covers, the maple-wood mazer 'done about with silver and gilt on the brymmes', and the 'nests' of silver goblets and bowls 'all gilt with covers'. The innholder John Browne of the Cock, who died in 1573, had a special chest covered with leather and barred with iron to keep his plate in.

As for clothing, besides the homely 'workaday apparill', 'small wearing lynen', red petticoats, best and second best kirtles and gowns, aprons, doublets, shirts, and hose, the wills expose such extravagances of the wealthy as women's taffeta hats, gowns laid with broad purl lace, or guarded with velvet, and girdles embroidered in red and gold. Men flaunted Venetian velvet hose and silver buckles, hats lined with velvet, cloaks of broadcloth and capes of velvet. Personal finery ranged from gold rings, chains, and buttons, gold rings set with stones, such as a 'table diamond' or a 'ruby stone', to a necklace of red amber beads with silver 'gaudies', bracelets of red coral or jet beads, and handkerchiefs 'wrought with gold'.

Among the furnishings of the home and items of personal adornment, the wills note less usual possessions that some owners set great store by. For the Southwood husbandman John Shotylworthe (1558) it was his white cow called Almylke and her companions Jolyeharte and Brownesnowte; for the mercer Henry Somersham (1574) it was his Bible, Testament, and Prayer Book, and for the linendraper Richard Carsey (1591) Foxe's Book of Martyrs. The prized possession of John Browne (1573), landlord of the Cock, was his 'stillatory of tynne, and lymbeck (alembic) to make Aquavite.'

The town was alert to changing fashions, including styles in barbering. William Harrison in 1577 quoted a Chelmsford barber, Cornelius, as the exponent of contemporary taste in beards:

'If a man have a lean and strait face, a Marquis Otto's cut will make it broad and large; if it be platter-like, a long slender beard will make it seem the narrower; if he be weasel-becked [beaked], then much hair left on the cheeks will make the owner look big, like a bowdled [ruffled] hen, and so grim as a goose, if Cornelius of Chelmsford say true ...'

SPORT AND ENTERTAINMENT

The personal bequests of the notary Charles Dabbes in 1588 included his longbow, quiver, arrows, buckler, and gauntlet. Archery equipment featured from time to time in Elizabethan wills, but the townsmen as a whole were not over-enthusiastic about its practice. The lord of the manor allowed the use of the field called Butt Field off Duke Street (area of Railway Station and Townfield Street) for practice, but the townsmen, who had to maintain the butts, neglected to do so, and were ordered in 1560 to make new ones or face a heavy fine. Again, in 1596 the inhabitants admitted that they did not possess the bows and arrows they were required to keep by law, and were fined. A more popular outdoor exercise was the practice of 'artillery'. This could be lethal. In 1596, during training at Writtle, the grocer John Wortley, appointed a 'gunner or caliver shot' by the captain of the Chelmsford Hundred trained men, while holding another man's caliver for him, and unaware that it was loaded, discharged it for a lark behind a horse to startle it, and shot dead a bystander, Christopher Tatem, innkeeper of the Rose. A robust but equally risky sport was wrestling. In 1572 a bout between two Moulsham men, 'for the sport of it and without any malice or discord between them', ended in tragedy when one of them died of concussion after a throw when they fell together one on top of the other. Ill-tempered football also had its perils. In 1582, 'some falling out at a football play', between players from Chelmsford and Writtle, was blamed by one player for the spiteful accusation made against him by another player of the criminal offence of defending 'Payne the traytor'.

The high street was the centre for much entertainment. Some householders had the right to set up a 'quintain' in the street, a post in front of the house with a swivelling crosspiece, to be tilted at. If the tilter, on horseback or afoot, was too slow away after striking the target on his side of the crosspiece, he was clouted, to the delight of onlookers, by a bag of sand swinging round from the far side. In the middle ages the target on the post was often the carved bust on a pivot of a Turk, Saracen, or Blackamoor. The figure's brandished scimitar swung round to smite the tilter if the lance did not strike the target in the centre. This sport may be the origin of the Saracen's Head and Black Boy as local inn signs. In the increasingly congested area of the high street tilting at a quintain became a nuisance. In 1569 the manor court ordered the bailiff to penalise unlicensed tilters, who endangered passers-by, and ruled that in future townsman licensed to tilt on market day were to tilt no farther than four feet from the house.

The most popular high street sport was bull-baiting. Indeed, it was illegal for a butcher to sell the flesh of a bull slaughtered before being baited by dogs. Queen Elizabeth took foreign ambassadors to bull-baiting for their entertainment. The law was rigorously applied by the Chelmsford manor court, but, from the number of fines imposed on butchers, often ignored. The Chelmsford 'bull ring' was in front of the Market Cross, where a stake was set up with a ring to which the bull was chained or roped. Butchers were fined 3s 4d for each bull slaughtered unbaited, a fine equal to that for a brawl or assault in which blood was drawn. In 1593, among ten butchers fined for this offence, Henry Andrews was fined 10s for three unbaited bulls; in 1600 Edward Hindes was penalised 16s 8d for five bulls slaughtered unbaited.

Any market day could produce lively episodes for the diversion of onlookers. In 1590 a servingman, with a grudge against a London upholsterer, 'did verie malissiously cutt thre holes' in the booth where the upholsterer displayed his wares, threatened to burn it down, and drew his knife on the constables who came to arrest him. Rose Hearse of Maldon had long suspected that the dealer from Wickham Bishops, who usually bought her fish and oysters in Chelmsford market, used a false measure. In 1609 the dealer complained that Rose had attacked him unprovoked, 'misused him in flinging about his ware, in flinging of dirt and other filth in his face and upon his apparel ... calling him thief and not suffering him to be in quiet'. He said that strangers and townsmen alike tried to persuade her to desist; that the whole market cried out against her, saying it was 'a great shame for us to suffer such abuses in our own town'; and that, 'with his face and apparel all besmeared with dirt', he had appealed to the constable to restrain her, so that he might 'be in quiet to sell'. The constable and five supporters, finding her 'more like a mad woman (indeed more like a drunken woman) than one that was fit to remain in a market, not knowing what else to do with her, she disturbing the whole market', put her in the stocks, where she became so distraught that they provided someone 'to look to her'. Rose's version was rather different. She said that, being a 'very orderly' woman, in the past she had been repeatedly 'misused in words' by the dealer; and on this particular occasion, after her husband had complained to the trader about her treatment, she had been beaten and misused by the trader for 'bewraying' his measure; she had then been put in the stocks without a justice's warrant, in the scuffle had been lamed, had lost her purse with a shilling and 'odd money' in it, had been reported to the magistrates for being mad and drunk, and no longer dared go out to market.

A unique market day entertainment was provided one Friday in 1599 by Will Kemp, the comic actor who performed in Shakespeare's plays at the Globe, and wrote to Queen Elizabeth that he had 'spent his life in mad Iigges and merry iestes'. One of these mad jigs was to dance the morris from London to Norwich, a feat which he accomplished in nine days, and recounted in *Kemps nine daies wonder*. He set out accompanied by his taborer, Tom Slye, with pipe and drum, his servant, and an 'overseer' of the undertaking, peddling gee-gaws by the way. On the third day of his dance, Friday, he reached Widford bridge and approached Moulsham,

> '... where a number of country people, and many Gentlemen and Gentlewomen were gathered together to see mee. Sir Thomas Mildmay, standing at his Parke pale, receiued gently a payre of garters of me; gloves, points, and garters, being my ordinary marchandize, that I put out to venter for performance of my merry voyage.
>
> So much a doe I had to passe by the people at Chelmsford, that it was more than an houre ere I could recouer my Inne gate, where I was faine to locke my selfe in my Chamber, and pacifie them with wordes out of a window instead of deeds: to deale plainely, I was so weary, that I could dance no more.'

Next day he 'footed' it three more miles towards Braintree, but finding himself too exhausted to continue, returned to Chelmsford, to rest until Monday. There he found the 'good cheere and kind welcome ... much more than I was willing to entertaine; for my onely desire was to refraine drinke and be temperate in my dyet'. He did, however, give one display over the weekend, when 'a Mayde not passing foureteene yeares of age, dwelling with one Sudley, my kinde friend, made a request to her Master and Dame that she might daunce the Morrice with me in a great large roome'. Her master, Edward Sudley, a shoemaker, and his wife

> '... being intreated, I was soone wonne to fit her with bels; besides she would haue the olde fashion, with napking on her arms; and to our iumps we fell. A whole houre she held out; but then being ready to lye downe I left her off; but thus much in her praise, I would haue challenged the strongest man in Chelmsford, and amongst many I thinke few would haue done so much'.

The presence of Sir Thomas Mildmay 'standing at his Parke pale', enjoying with his neighbours the spectacle of Kemp's dance, and purchasing a pair of garters, presents an unusually happy picture of the local magnate relaxing at home, in the place where he was born and had his schooling. He died in 1608, and his obituary may be read in the Chelmsford parish register:

> '... A most worthy gentleman for the service of his Prince and Countrie, for which he had done many honorable services — noe man of his rank like unto him. He died very penitently and patiently ... and the towne of Chelmsford lost a most worthy governor'.

Sir Thomas, who four years earlier had warned good patriots to avoid factious divisions, was to be spared the mounting discord in both town and kingdom in the years ahead. How his town, his two sons, Thomas and Henry, and his grandson Robert, faced that test, is another story.

STREET
DIRECTORY OF
THE 1590s

A STREET DIRECTORY
OF THE 1590s

This directory identifies the town sites of the 1590s with the street names and numbers of 1876, when 'house numbering' was first adopted. The numbers have hardly altered since, except in the vicinity of the entrance to New London Road, and in Springfield Road. Unless otherwise stated, all sites were held of the manor of Bishop's Hall in Chelmsford.

Identification of late Tudor sites with 1876 street locations and house numbers

THE HIGH STREET (1463, 'Alta Strata')

East side from North to South

Waterloo Lane	SHYTBURYE LANE leading to Tunman Mead and Springfield Mill. The 'way which leads to Tunemanemedue' existed by 1261.
High St. **1**	WHITE HORSE inn, owner Wm. Gainsford, esq., in right of w. Joan, widow of Walter Baker; landlord Wm. Rogers. It was called Wendovershall after Jn. of Wendover acquired it in 1261, from Rob., vicar of Gt. Baddow.
2	COVILLS (by 1603 the STAR inn); Wm. Heditch, haberdasher. Rob. Colvyle had this in 1469; in 1381 Jn. Pye, mason, lived here, and in 1256 Walter Trygg, his w. Amphilise, and their son Walter.
3	SARACEN'S HEAD inn, owner and innkeeper Ric. Brett. This was SPICERESTENEMENT, associated in 1345 with Nic. the Spicer, and in 1381 with Jn. Spicer. It was known as the Saracen's Head by 1539.
4-6	CRANE inn, held of the Crown. Owner Thos. Mildmay of London, gent. Former property of London hospital of St Mary, Elsyngspitell. It was known as the Crane by 1470.
7-8	Once part of the adjoining site (4-6); held of the Crown. Owner Thos. Mildmay of London, gent. Former property of London hospital of St Mary, Elsyngspitell.
9-12	OLIVERS, Jn. Jegon, yeo., in right of w. Mary, dau. and heir of late coroner, Thos. Knott. Rob. and Jn. Oliver fl.1382.
13-14	Owner Susan Ford, widow, occ. Wm. Fitch, mercer. Former Corpus Christi guild property, held of Honor of East Greenwich.
15-17	WOOLSACK (WOOLPACK) inn, with shops and outbuildings, stables, and orchard, owner Jn. Pynchon, gent., in right of w. Fran. (Brett); landlord Jn. Higham. It was known as 'Le Wulsak' by 1478.
18	Wm. Mundes, house, yard, and garden.
19	CHANDLERS, owner Leonard Aylett, yeo., house, garden, yard, and orchard. Jn. Wright, chandler (d.c.1414) owned this.
20	CHANDLERS, owner Jn. Brown, innkeeper at the Lion (52-54), occ. Thos. White, vintner. Held of the manor of Springfield. Jn. Wright, chandler (d.c.1414) owned this.
21-2	DAYSIES, owner Rob. Wood, sen., woollendraper. Rob. Daysy, fishmonger (d.1481) owned this.

168

NYCOLLES, later the CHEQUER, owner Jarvis Cole, cit. and clothworker of London. This was the WINE TAVERN. It had been charged with a religious obit in memory of Thos. Chalke (d.1498), and was held of the Honor of East Greenwich. Jn. Nicoll held this in 1428.

PLOMERS, occ. Mr Thos. Williamson and w. Martha. He was widely read in the classics and a formidable polemic writer against popery. Thos. Plummer had this in 1441.

Rob. Wood, jun., linendraper; held of the Honor of Beaulieu or New Hall, Boreham.

COLMANS, owner Rob. Wood, sen., woollendraper, until 1595, then Jn. Long's, jerkin-maker, who sold it soon after to Ric. Fitch, apothecary. Named after Thos. Colman (fl.1414), whose mother Isabel inherited it as the heir of Sir Jn. Mounteney (fl.1370s), founder of the Mounteney chantry.

FALCON inn, formerly GLOVERS; owner Benedict Barnham, esq., cit. and alderman of London; landlord probably Humph. Cordall. Not named in sources as the FALCON until 1567. Its owner in 1381, Nic. Cook, was an innkeeper selling wine and victuals. Rob. Glover bought the property from Nic. Cook in 1384 as a house, 4 shops, house for pigs, garden, and yard.

BIGLANDS or the BULL, owner Geo. Kekewich, esq., occ. Edw. Makin, gent., who rebuilt it as two houses. This belonged to Jn. Biglon, butcher (d.1521).

NEWLANDS, owner Thos. Jeffery, haberdasher (d.1592). In 1603 it was in hands of Wm. Gainsford, esq., in right of w. Joan, dau. of Thos. Jeffery, and widow of Walter Baker, brewer. Jn. Newland acquired this about 1415, and his family were still living here in 1499.

HOLDENS, owner Ric. Nicholls, gent.; held of the manor of Springfield. The Holden family owned this in the 1520s.

NEW inn or CROWN (so called by the 1550s); owner Eliz. Stafford, widow of Jn. Stafford, cit. and haberdasher of London. Also called the QUEEN's (later KING's) ARMS until c.1642, when it became the (GREAT) BLACK BOY. The site was once the property of Jn. of Thorpe (fl.1327).

CORNER HOUSE, Jonas Carsey, glover, son of Ric. Carsey, linendraper. Its outbuildings spread down Springfield Lane, incl. a kitchen, two stables, and a garden; held of the manor of Springfield. Part of Joan Wendover's share of the 14th-century Wendover estate, held by her two husbands, Wm. Nafferton (fl.1384) and Sim. Bodenham, a London vintner (fl.1403), before it was bought by the Duke family; *and see* 39-46, and Springfield Lane (south side).

SPRINGFIELD (Colchester) LANE.

CORNER HOUSE (partly pulled down c.1820 to widen Springfield Lane), and TOPPIES, occ. Anne Bridges, widow; both held of the manor of Springfield. Wm. Topy (fl.1511) gave his name to Toppies. This was part of Joan Wendover's share of the 14-century Wendover estate; *and see* Corner House (38 part).

BOAR's HEAD inn, occ. Anne, widow of Jn. Bridges, grocer; held of the manor of Springfield and known from c.1633 as the KING's HEAD. Known as the BOAR's HEAD by 1469; Gilbert the Taverner owned the site in c.1284. This was part of Joan Wendover's share of the 14th-century Wendover estate; *and see* Corner House (38 part).

HIGH STREET
East side

42   PARKERS, with a shop called the SMYTHES FORGE; Thos. Beane. Part of Joan Wendover's share of the 14th-century Wendover estate; *and see* Corner House (38 part).

43   NAFFERTON'S, Nic. Clarke, gent., occ. Anne Clarke, widow. Part of Joan Wendover's share of the 14th-century Wendover estate; her first husband was Wm. Nafferton; *and see* Corner House (38 part).

44-5   NAFFERTONS, Jn. Nookes, glover. Wendover estate, *see* 43 and Corner House (38 part).

46   NAFFERTONS, Jn. Cowland, saddler. Wendover estate, *see* 43 and Corner House (38 part).

47   LIVINGS, formerly the BELL (in the 1540s); Joan, widow of Jn. Hindes, butcher. Jn. Living sold it in 1574 to Jn. Hindes.

48   LIVINGS, once part of the Bell; Thos. Lawrence, glover. Jn. Living sold it separately in 1587 to Thos. Lawrence.

49-50   COCK inn, next to the bridge, owner Alice Aleston, widow, landlady Eliz. Browne; known as 'Le Cok' by 1470.

    MOULSHAM (Great Stone) BRIDGE of three arches, 1372

THE HIGH STREET
West side from North to South
MIDDLE (SHOP) ROW

    Undeveloped open space, partly occupied by saltbins and the town midden. This was probably where the MAYPOLE 'once stood'; it had been taken down by 1474.

    Footway leading from the WHITE HART in the Back Street to the CROSS in the Market Place.

    THE HEAD, so called because it stood at the head of the Middle (or Shop) Row. It comprised two shops with two solars built over, a parlour annexed, and a yard with a kitchen built on it. Owner Jn. Wharton. This site was manorial waste, not yet built on, when it was granted in 1381 to Thos. Roper and Adam Gynes, roper.

95-6   RAMMESTENEMENT otherwise Gyneses, split between RAMMES, and WOLSTON'S PARCEL of Rammestenement; Thos. Amatt had RAMMES, a house, and a yard with a kitchen built on it; Wm. Pamplin, grocer, had WOLSTON'S PARCEL, a shop with a room built over it and a plot of ground in front of the shop. Jn. Ramme fl.1351; Adam Gynes d.1423; Rob. Wolston fl.1485.

94   COPTHALL, with yards at the back and a little workhouse; owner Jn. Pamplin *alias* Arundell, ropemaker. In 1384 this was a shop with a solar built over it, belonging to Adam Gynes, roper.

92-3   BRETTONS, otherwise DALBIES, with a yard and garden plot, owner Wm. Gainsford, esq., occ. Chris. Nash, musician. This was still an undeveloped 'parcel of ground', 40 by 14 feet, when Wm. Breton died holding it in *c*.1483.

    SHAMBLE LANE.

91

NEW SHAMBLES, a tenement 'lately dismembred' to make a new shambles, with three butchers' shops on either side of the shambles, owner Wm. Gainsford, esq.

90, 89
(part)

THREE TUNS inn, with yard, stables, and kitchens, and a 'rosteting house' and 'romes of ease' on the backside; owner Wm. Gainsford, esq., occ. Ric. Browne. In 1401 Ralph Watyer, cook, and w. Christine, acquired this, and in 1404 more ground with licence to build a 'rostynghous'.

89 (part)

WALMISFORD, a house with a yard; occ. Thos. Parkins, surgeon. This house, like DALBIES, the NEW SHAMBLES, the THREE TUNS, and other property in the town, was in the hands of Wm. Gainsford, esq., in the right of his w. Joan, widow of the brewer, Walter Baker *alias* Wilkes, in trust for Walter's young son, And. Baker *alias* Wilkes. In 1387 Thos. Walmisford, chaplain, owned this, and the two adjoining sites, with the 'shops' built on them.

88

WALMISFORD, a cottage where Thos. Free, the owner, was living; there was a yard behind, and a plot with a shop newly built on it.

86-7

WALMISFORD, two houses 'lying together', each with a yard behind, owner Thos. Watson, apothecary, occs. Nic. Dawbney, alehouse-keeper, and Jn. Browne.

84-5

SAMPTONS, the corner house of the Middle Row, owner Ant. Loveden in right of w. Joan (dau. and heir of Nic. Eve), occ. Jn. Tatem, fishmonger, bro. of Thos. Tatem, haberdasher. Hen. Sampton fl.1461.

LITTLE MIDDLE ROW OR MIDDLE STALLS

A row of built stalls with tiled roofs stood in the street, divided from the Middle Row by POTTERSLANE, also called SHOPROW LANE. Potterslane is first mentioned in 1466. These built stalls belonged to Jonas Carsey, glover, Geo. Martindale, fishmonger, Wm. Shether, yeo., and Wm. Gainsford, esq. The row developed in the 17th century into a terrace of shops and a coffee house, narrowing the high street to nine feet, until 1725, when the row was pulled down to widen the street.

Way leading from the DOLPHIN in the Back Street to the WOOLSACK in the High Street, between SAMPTONS and the FISH MARKET.

FISH & LEATHER MARKETS , & SALTBINS

83

A standing for a moveable leather stall, once a spicer's stall, held of the manor of Springfield; by 1584 it had become a 'shed called spicer's stall', and by 1595 a 'shop called spicer's stall with a chamber newly built over it'. It stood between SAMPTONS and the FISH & LEATHER MARKETS, half on one side of the conduit channel flowing down the Back Street, and half on the other. It belonged to an innkeeper, Bart. Fitch, who sold it in 1595 to Wm. Monk.

82 & New
London Rd.
gap

Ground-space for four FISH STALLS held of the manor of Springfield, formerly owned by the Eve family, but from 1593 by Jn. Tatem, grocer. The Mildmays, Thos. Taylor, and Geo. Ballard, each had a standing for one fish stall. Samuel Some owned the three SALTBINS. In the LEATHER MARKET, located east of the fish stalls, Jn. Pynchon had almost a monopoly, with space measuring 57 by 4 feet for seven stalls, besides 50 by 50 feet from the front of his inn, the WOOLSACK, to the conduit channel. Thos. Whitbread had space for one leather stall, but space for another three, held by the butcher, Hen. Andrews, had been built upon as a permanent roofed stall.

The separate stall sites of the open FISH and LEATHER MARKETS were to be progressively merged and built on in the 17th century, until by 1703 a house with a shop, and the HALF MOON inn, stood there.

1876 site
identities
High St.
77-81

HIGH STREET
West side

POULTRY HILL OR POULTRY MARKET

81   House at Poultry Hill with a little buttery built on; Wm., s. of Thos. and Rose Gylder.

79-80   House, once the property of Corpus Christi guild, Anne Wigglesworth, widow.

77-8   BRETTONS, the corner house and LAST OF THE ROW, with a saltbin on Poultry Hill; its owner, the apothecary Thos. Watson, found himself in serious trouble in the 1590s when he added on to it two galleries or balconies with eaves projecting beyond the bounds of the site, to overhang the highway on the east, south, and west. Wm. Breton d.*c.*1483.

76   Very confused sites, former property of the Corpus Christi guild and split up at the Reformation. David Palmer, painter, owned a little house where the old CAGE once stood; next to him, the tailor Wm. Hewitt and mercer Wm. Fitch each had a small house; Thos. Mildmay of Barnes owned the next, and largest, house, called CHANDLERS, occ. Rob. Bates, next door to SHARPES; it was held of the Crown. Jn. Wright, chandler, owned CHANDLERS in 1381.

74-5   SHARPES (once part of THORPES), held of the Crown, owner Thos. Mildmay of Barnes. Sewal Sharp, chaplain, owned this in 1315. By 1428 it belonged to the Corpus Christi guild.

73   ROBIN HOOD, anciently THORPES, owner Thos. Writtington esq.; formerly an inn. Jn. of Thorpe fl.1327.

72   House, once part of THORPES; occ. Edw. Stane. Former property of Our Lady guild.

71   HOSES (Hosiers), owner Hen. Coe. baker, occ. Jn. Barker; by 1603 Hugh Barker, barber, owned it. Former property of Our Lady guild. It had probably belonged to Jn. Colvyle, hosier (fl.1406).

69-70   BLACK BOY inn, owner Ant. Radcliffe, esq., landlord Jas. Scrafton, formerly an alehouse. About 1642, after the CROWN (37-8 High St.) took the name (GREAT) BLACK BOY, this became the LITTLE BLACK BOY. It belonged until he died in 1384 to Jn. Peyntour, whose son Jn., chaplain, then sold it to Thos. Roper and Adam Gynes.

67-8   House, garden, and yard, owner Jn. Seaman, woollendraper; once the property of the guild of Our Lady.

66   Mich. Adams; a house once held by a hosier (Jn. Colvyle, fl.1406), later the property of the guild of Our Lady. It had belonged to Wm. Prentys, innkeeper, shop owner, and stallholder (fl.betw.1351 and 1389).

65   CHANDLERS, Hen. Coe, tippler of ale and baker. Known as Chandlers by 1428; this may have belonged to Elias the Chandler fl.1323, 1342.

63-4   WYMONDS, Eliz. Somersham, widow of Hen. Somersham, mercer. Jn. Wymond (d.bef. 1381) and his widow Mabel (fl.1381) were innkeepers.

60-2   COCKSAYES and PATCHINGS, two tenements 'lying together'; Thomasine Bodye. Wm. de Cogeshale (fl.1324) and Jn. de Pacchingge (fl.1327) may have been kinsmen.

59   SHARPES, Wm. Boxer (Boxford), tailor, previous owner an apothecary. This could be named from Sewal Sharp (fl.1315), Jn. Sharp (fl.1316) or Christine Sharp (fl.1327).

HIGH STREET
West side

FELSTEDS, the only copyhold site among the original freehold high street frontage sites; owner Thos. Hawes. About 1324 Hen. of Felsted and his s. Rob. bought a shop in Chelmsford.

Three little shops stood out in the street in front of FELSTEDS and opposite the BOAR'S HEAD (40-1); they became known as the SHOPHOUSES. They were enlarged by their new owner, Ric. Terrett, in 1596. They were still there in 1687, but pulled down by 1703.

MARYES otherwise LIGHTFOOTS, owner Ric. Neale, glover; let to tenants. Ric. and Marg. Lightfoot, fishmongers (fl.1362) owned two shops, a plot with a house on it, and fishstalls. After Ric. died (bef.1381), Marg. carried on the business until c.1388. Later, for a short time, the Corpus Christi guild owned this, but without permission, so it was confiscated by the bishop.

LION inn (52-4) with the medieval (WHITE) HART inn (55) annexed; owned by the Petre family since 1566, when Sir Wm. Petre of Ingatestone bought them; landlord Jn. Brown.

House and shops next to the bridge, formerly part of the LION; owned by Jn., son of Edm. Sebright, saddler.

51-54, next to the bridge, were two of the 'new places' in the bishop of London's new town. He granted them in c.1205 to two of his officials, Wm. Glunde, and Jn. of Witham. The two sites had been merged by 1371, when Thos. Osteler acquired them, with the house and three shops built on them. Thos. Osteler and his w. Nichola kept an inn on the combined site, carried on by their son Rob., and known by 1455 as the LION.

55 was owned from c.1315 for over a century by the Gybon family. Jn. Gybon, who also owned the site of 74-5, stalls, and other property in the town, kept an inn here from c.1377 or earlier, until after 1409; by 1416 it was known as the HART.

51-55 were acquired by the Tyrell family in the late 15th century, when the HART inn became annexed to the LION inn. By 1618, when the LION was described as 'an antient Inne time out of mynde', its name had changed to the RED LION.

51, the part of the LION closest to the bridge, and projecting into the street, at some date before 1561 became permanently separated from the inn as an independent site.

MOULSHAM (Great Stone) BRIDGE of three arches, 1372

THE MARKET PLACE
North side from East to West alongside the churchyard

House at New St. corner, owner Thos. Standish, knacker, occ. Humph. Dale.

The TOLLHOUSE, where manor court business was conducted; Jn. Rison (d.1597), former bailiff of the manor, continued to hold this after Jn. Reeve succeeded him as bailiff in 1591. The TOLLHOUSE, mentioned by name from 1392, was one of the 'two houses where the courts are held' which existed by 1382.

Two little houses between the TOLLHOUSE and the SOUTH GATE of the churchyard, were Crown property, confiscated from the guild of Corpus Christi.

SOUTH GATE of the churchyard.

1876 site
identities
Tindal Sq.

1-2 CURDES, by the south gate, Wm. Pamplin, grocer.

3 Two small houses, Ric. George.

4-5 Two more small houses, former property of the guild of Blessed Mary, in the hands of the Crown.

West side from North to South

91 *Duke* JOSEPPES, Wm. Clarke, gent. In the late-14th century this belonged to Master Jn.
St., partly Scolemayster.
demd. 1879 to make Market Road.

Corn Thos. Wallinger, attorney, and his large family, lived in the hall house with 37-ft
Exchange frontage, which had been the Wallinger home since the early 15th century. A
(demd. forecourt in front of the doorway, hall, and parlour windows, was enclosed by posts
1969) and rails. Next to Wallinger's house was BRESONS, Jn. Webb, innkeeper, and Rog.
Webb, barber.

Bell Hotel BLUE BELL (BELL) inn, Jn. Dudsbury, innkeeper, and w. Philippa, sis. of the late
(demd. Walter Baker, brewer. In 1381 the owner was Jn. Gybon, innkeeper; he was the col-
1948) lector of the 1377 poll tax in Chelmsford and he and his w. Joan were both taxed in
1381.

South side

6 *Tindal* Still part of the undeveloped open space where the water from BURGESS WELL surfaced
Square at the CONDUIT, and where the CATTLE MARKET was held. The south built-up frontage on the market was formed by THE HEAD (site of 97-8 High Street).

East side

Pavement THE MARKET CROSS or SESSION HOUSE, stood on CORNHILL; it was rebuilt in 1569, and
in front of pulled down in 1789 when the Shire Hall was built farther back, alongside the church-
Shire Hall yard. The CROSS belonged to the lord of the manor; the tenant in 1591 was Jn.
Rison, bailiff of the manor until that year; the CORN MARKET was held in it, as well as
the ASSIZES and QUARTER SESSIONS. The CORN MARKET is named in 1382, the CROSS in
1403, and CORNHILL in 1479. The 'two houses where the courts are held' (i.e.,
TOLLHOUSE and CROSS) are mentioned in 1382.

Tindal
(Conduit)
Street

THE BACK LANE (STREET)
West side from North to South

27 *(demd.* WHITE HART inn, owner Jn. Pake, gent. First recorded as an inn in 1570. Site docu-
1969) mented from 1385.

25-6 THE HEATH, a capital messuage or 'Place', with barns, stables, and malthouses, owner
(demd. Jn. Pake, gent., in right of his w. Anne (Marion). By the 1620s this had become the
1971) ANGEL inn. Site documented from the 1380s.

24 *(demd.* Bought by Jn. Bird of Moulsham, yeo., from Jn. Pake, gent., in 1575. Occ. Mat.
1971) Rudd, gent. By 1601, still in the possession of the Bird family, it had become the
TALBOT inn, later known as the DOG or SPOTTED DOG.

21-3 Formerly SHAWES or the BULL, but by 1591 the BREWHOUSE, Wm. Gainsford, esq., in
(demd. right of his w. Joan, widow of Walter Baker *alias* Wilkes, brewer. 'Shawes' from
1971) Sir John Shaa, mayor of London, 1502.

18-20 The BEAR, Wm. Gainsford, esq., in right of w. Joan; occ. Wm. Holforth.
(demd. 1971)

*1876 site
identities
Tindal St.*

15-17
*(demd.
1971)*

SHARPARROWS or the THREE ARROWS, Thomasine Monk, victualler, widow of Jn. Monk, sen., tallow-chandler and alehouse-keeper. Also called BENNIDITTES, from Ric. Benette (fl.1381).

14 *(demd.
1971)*

DOLPHIN inn, Edw. Bigland, innkeeper, in right of w. Margaret (widow of Ric. Marchall). Also called BRYDDES, from Jn. and Alice Brydde (fl.1382).

12-13 & 1
*New Lon-
don Road
(demd. 1969, 1971)*

ROSE inn, owner Ant. Loveden, esq., in right of w. Joan (Eve); occ. Chris. Tatem, innkeeper. This belonged to Rob. of Writtle in 1383, then to Jn. Parys of London; in 1421 it was called PARYSSHOPPE.

*New Lon-
don Road
gap*

MAYES, with a right of way down to the river through the neighbouring gate and yard. Owner Thos. Mildmay of Barnes, occ. Geo. Martindale, fishmonger, and w. Agnes. MAYES faced the Fishmarket. By 1603 it had become the UNICORN inn. All the buildings on the site were demolished when New London Road *alias* New Bridge Street was cut through in 1839-40. When Emma, widow of Geof. Priour, sold the property in 1383, the conveyance incorporated elaborate provisions to protect the purchaser's right of way with horses and carts through the gate and yard of PARKERS, without any payment of rent.

*10-11 and
part of
New Lon-
don Road
gap*

PARKERS, also called SCRAVELLS, owner Thos. Writtington, esq. All the buildings on this site were pulled down in 1839-40, and only part of the site was rebuilt, as the ROYAL OAK inn. Jn. Wright, chandler, owned this in 1383, with the gateway and yard through which his neighbours at MAYES had right of way. Sim. Scraffeild (d.1557) was a benefactor of Chelmsford's poor.

*Tindal
(Conduit)
Street*

THE BACK LANE (STREET)

East side from North to South

1

Undeveloped open space, where the STOCKS, PILLORY, and new CAGE stood.

2-9, *and
backsides of
84-9 High
St.*

The CONDUIT CHANNEL (watercourse, sewer, or gutter) flowed the whole length of the east side of the Back Street, down to the FISHMARKET, forming the street's east frontage. On the other side of it were the back yards, outbuildings, woodstacks, privies, and leanto hovels of the MIDDLE ROW. By the 1590s there was not enough development west of the Middle Row 'beyond the gutter' to create a built-up east frontage in the Back Street, but a few plots had been granted here and there to stack wood or put up a shed; on one of these plots opposite the DOLPHIN inn a tiny 'shop' had already sprung up, and Middle Row householders were beginning to extend their properties across and beyond the gutter. Tiny open yards which survive to this day in the centre of the Middle Row mark the former course of the channel, which flowed on down the high street into Springfield Lane, to its outlet in the Gullet.

*Springfield
Road*

SPRINGFIELD (COLCHESTER) LANE

North side from the High Street corner to the TOWN'S END
at the TREEN BRIDGE

38 *High
St.*

CORNER HOUSE facing High St., with a kitchen, two stables, and a garden down the lane; Jonas Carsey, glover; held of the manor of Springfield.

*Black Boy
(demd.
1982),
former tap*

Outbuildings, barns, stables, yards, and garden of the NEW inn or CROWN (*see* 37-8 High St.), with two little houses called CANTLEYS (held of the manor of Springfield) incorporated in the inn; all in the occ. of the Widow Stafford. CANTLEYS had belonged to the guild of Our Lady.

*of Great Black Boy demd. 1857; Malthouse; Horse & Groom Beerhouse; Springfield Road Brewery (Gray
& Son), & Brewery House.*

Iron Bridge 1819-21

TREEN (Wooden) BRIDGE

SPRINGFIELD (COLCHESTER) LANE

South side from the High Street corner to the TOWN'S END at the TREEN BRIDGE

Springfield Road **39 High St.**	CORNER HOUSE facing High St. (partly pulled down *c.*1820 to widen the lane); Anne, widow of Jn. Bridges, grocer; held of the manor of Springfield; *and see* 39 High St.
Alley leading to the GULLET	Alley leading to THE GULLET and BELL MEAD (later KING'S HEAD MEADOW) off Springfield Lane; the conduit water flowed down the alley into the GULLET at the WASHING and WATERING PLACE.
8-11: *four shops and French's Sq.*	House of Ric. Neale, glover; he lived in half of it with his w. Anne, letting the other half to a tenant, Ric. Burles, glover.
6-7: *Scale-maker and Cabinet-maker*	Two houses owned by Wm. Prowe, gent;. held of the manor of Springfield. In the 14th century part of Joan Wendover's share of Wendover estate, *see* 38 (part) High Street.
5: *Coach-builder's workshops*	House at the bridge foot, Wm. Boxer (Boxford), tailor; held of the manor of Springfield. In 14th century part of Joan Wendover's share of the Wendover estate, *see* 38 (part) High St.
	5-11: The numbering of all Springfield Road sites has been altered at least twice since house numbering was adopted in 1876. No. 5 was changed to No. 11, and later to No. 38. Nos. 6-7 were changed to 7-6, then 9-10, and later to 30/36 (evens). The Alley, former sites 8-11, and French's Square (1-16) disappeared altogether when the Gullet channel linking the Chelmer and the Can was filled in in 1960-2 under a flood relief scheme; the whole site was then redeveloped, and a new entry made out of Springfield Road into King's Head Meadow, now called French's Square.
Iron Bridge 1819-20	TREEN (Wooden) BRIDGE

BROCHOLESTRATE *alias* BRANKETREWEY *alias* CHURCH STREET *alias* DUCK (DUKE) STREET

Duke Street

South side from East to West

91	JOSEPPES (*see* MARKET PLACE)
88-90	MAYES, former property of the guild of Corpus Christi, in the hands of the Crown. Divided from the adjoining property by a chaseway leading round the back to JOSEPPES.
Passage betw. **87 & 88**	CHASEWAY
87	Part of MAYES, former property of guild of Corpus Christi, in hands of the Crown.
86	Part of MAYES, former Corpus Christi property, taken over by Chelmsford church-wardens as an Almshouse, and Luke Whale, weaver, put in it. The churchwardens' right to it was being challenged by the Crown.
85	Part of MAYES, former guild of Our Lady property. Owner Jn. Webb, innkeeper, occ. Ric. Adams.
	85-91 all belonged in the late-14th century to Jn. Scolemayster, from whom Jn. May acquired them. Later they were Ric. Joseppe's. Sometimes referred to as SCHOOL-MASTER'S up to 19th century, particularly No. 85; *and see* MARKET PLACE.
84 (part)	ALMSHOUSE room acquired by the churchwardens when the Corpus Christi guild was dissolved, and occ. by Father Wm. Springfield, labourer.

84   (BLUE) BOAR inn, owner Wm. Gainsford, esq., landlord Thos. Scott, brother-in-law of the late Walter Baker, brewer. The Church owned an upper room at the inn above the adjoining almshouse room; it was let for 5s a year for the poor, and was called the CHURCH CHAMBER. In 1344 this belonged to Ste. Sacristan.

83   Small house next to the BLUE BOAR, occ. Thos. Spety. Former property of Mounteney's chantry.

*Thread-
needle St.*   BROCHOLESLANE, named from Walter Brochole (fl.1344), as was Brocholestrate (Duke St.).

Duke St.
81-2   GYLDERS, owner Wm. Gylder, occ. Ric. Reynolds. This became the MAIDENHEAD inn c.1618. In 1344 it belonged to Walter Brochole.

80   SPRINGFIELDS, owner Ric. Springfield, occ. Zachary Purchas, fletcher.

79   CHEQUER inn, owner and innkeeper Wm. Wyther, joiner. Former property of the guild of St John the Baptist, Writtle. This inn changed its name to the GEORGE after it was bought by Thos. Mildmay of Barnes in 1600. It was bought in 1627 by the grammar school trustees, when the school was moved from The Friars in Moulsham to Duke Street.

78   GYLDERS, a freehold cottage and garden, occ. by Buttolph Roper, carpenter, owned by Mary, dau. of late Walter Baker, brewer, and held of the Tyrell manor of Ramseys in Stock and Buttsbury. It was bought in 1627 by the grammar school trustees, when the school was moved from The Friars in Moulsham to Duke Street.

77   GYLDERS, two copyhold cottages, newly built, owned by Mary, dau. of late Walter Baker, w. of Rob. Cresswell; held of the manor of Springfield.

BROCHOLESTRATE *alias* BRANKETREWEY *alias* CHURCH STREET *alias* DUCK (DUKE) STREET

North side from East to West

Duke St.
2-3   Roadside thatched cottage by south-west corner of the churchyard, held of the manor of Springfield by Thos. Burtonwood; site called 'Burtonwood's Corner'.

4-9 *(7-9*   Roadside waste alongside the churchyard, not yet built upon.
demd. 1930 to widen street)

10-12 *(in*   In a plot by the churchyard, enclosed in 1417 from the PIGHTLE, was the PRIEST'S
1928 10   HOUSE or VICARAGE, facing the west door of the church. The 'rector's house called Le
demd. and   Presteshows' already existed when the plot was enclosed. At the Reformation, as
rebuilt with   part of the endowment of the chaplain of the guild of Our Lady, it was taken by the
frontage set   Crown. On the street frontage of the plot Wm. Shether, yeo., had a cottage, 'builte
back to   of olde time upon the Lordes waste soil', close to the TOWN WELL; near the cottage
widen the   Thos. Mildmay, esq., of Barnes, had a house and garden plot by the VICARAGE WALL.
street; and 11 altered to set back the frontage).

13-20   The PIGHTLE, or CHURCH PIGHTLE, a small croft belonging to the lord of the manor, and not yet built upon. This frontage was not developed until 1741.

21-2   DOVEHOUSE HALL, occ. Wm. Gainsford, esq., in the right of his w. Joan, widow of Walter Baker, and as guardian of his stepson, And. Baker *alias* Wilkes. In 1428 'Doffehous Hawe' was held by Alice, widow of Adam Gynes.

23-5   House, garden, and malting house, Ric. Nicholls, yeo., occ. Jn. Hall, maltster.

26   House and garden, Rob. Paperell, in right of w. Joan.

27   Croft called FURBOROWS, not yet built upon. This croft was regarded in 1591 as part of the UPLAND, not the TOWN. Held by Joan Paperell.

NEW STREET *alias* MILSTRETE
(1386 'Le Newstret', 1560 'Milstrete')

West side from South to North

Shire Hall (1789-91)	House at corner of churchyard, owner Thos. Standish, knacker, occ. Humph. Dale.
Churchyard	Street bordered by churchyard.
Church St. entrance	ALMSHOUSE facing New Street, the end house of a row of five almshouses at the back of the churchyard. At the other end of the row of almshouses stood the small house (formerly provided for the priest of the chantry of St John), where Myles Blomefylde, bibliophile and churchwarden, lived from *c*.1566 until his death in 1603.
New Street 1-2	BLUE ANCHOR, held of the manor of Springfield.
2 (part)	MAWDLINS, owner Wm. Gainsford, esq., held of the manor of Springfield. This had belonged to Wm. Madyll (fl.bef.1515).
3	Two cottages, owned by Wm. Gainsford, esq., and given to the parish in 1609 by his widow Joan and stepson And. Baker *alias* Wilkes, for the poor.
4-9	The CHURCH HOUSE (two cottages let to the poor) and four ALMSHOUSE cottages.
Legg St.	An 'ancient way' into BARN CROFT; after Ric. Legg (fl.1620) who owned the croft began to develop part of it fronting the churchyard, the way took his name.
New St. 10-28	Roadside cottages with small yards and gardens between the gateway into BARN CROFT and the gateway into the croft called WACES. These cottages, which were owned by the well-to-do, such as Wm. Gainsford, esq., and Robert Wood, sen., woollendraper, were let to labourers, and became smaller and smaller as they were subdivided in the next century. In 1591 BARN CROFT and WACES were both still regarded as part of the UPLAND, not the TOWN, but the cottages were in the TOWN.
Cottage Place	Gateway to WACES CROFT
New St. 29	NICHOLLS BARN, Ric. Nicholls, gent., yeo. From Nicholls Barn the way continued as MILL LANE ('Mellelane', 1472) to BISHOP'S HALL and the MILL. In 1591 the barn was regarded as in the UPLAND, not in the TOWN.

NEW STREET *alias* MILSTRETE
East side from South to North

Waterloo Lane	SHYTBURYE LANE, leading to Tunman Mead and Springfield mill.
New St. 58-9	GREYHOUND inn, owner Jn. Wright, occ. Jn. Rison, victualler, former bailiff of the manor. In the 14th century this site was part of the inheritance of Jn. Manytre, but it had become detached by the late 15th century.
57	The LAMB, owner Wm. Shether, yeo., occ. Shether's son-in-law, Ric. Browne and his wife Dorothy; part of MAYNETREES site.
54-6	MANNINGTREYES, two houses with gardens and orchards, Wm. Shether, yeo. Jn. Manytre died before *c*.1381, when his sis. Marg. inherited 'Manytres'.
52-3	GUY HARLINGS, 'capital messuage or faireplace', with barns, stables, large malting house, orchards, and ponds; owner Jn. Ayliffe. Guy Harling, brewer, d.1470.
43-51	An orchard and ground with a barn built on it, owner Anne Wigglesworth. This was added to Guy Harlings about 25 years later.
From Victoria Rd. to 42 New St.	ARROWSMITH'S, also called BARN CROFT, Wm. Heditch, haberdasher. From Arrowsmith's the way continued as MILL LANE to BISHOP'S HALL and the MILL.

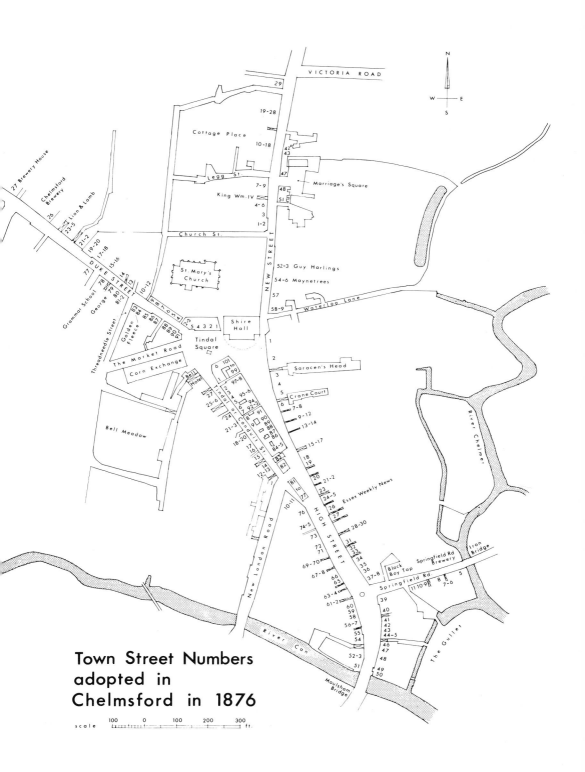

Town Street Numbers adopted in Chelmsford in 1876

scale 100 0 100 200 300 ft.

VICTORIA ROAD

Cottage Place

Legg St.

Marriage's Square

King Wm. IV

Church St.

St. Mary's Church

NEW STREET

52-3 Guy Harlings

54-6 Maynetrees

Waterloo Lane

Shire Hall

Tindal Square

Saracen's Head

Crane Court

Golden Fleece

The Market Road

Corn Exchange

Bell Hotel

Grammar School

George

Threadneedle Street

DUKE STREET

Tindal St.

Bell Meadow

Broomfield St.

HIGH STREET

Essex Weekly News

New London Road

River Chelmer

Springfield Rd Brewery

Iron Bridge

Black Boy Tap

Springfield Rd

The Gullet

River Can

Moulsham Bridge

27 Brewery House

Chelmsford Brewery

Lion & Lamb

179

SOURCES

Detailed footnotes to sources, paragraph by paragraph, are available in the Essex Record Office. This note summarises the sources (manuscript or in print) which have contributed to the narrative. The story of the early medieval years depends largely on printed transcripts, calendars, and abstracts of public and diocesan records. But the range of evidence widens as soon as long series of unpublished local manuscript sources become available. The most important of these for the history of Chelmsford town are:

1 *The archives of the Mildmay family of Moulsham Hall* deposited in the Essex Record Office (D/DM, D/DMs, D/DMy), and in particular the series of court records from 1381 (with a few gaps) of the manor of Bishop's Hall in Chelmsford. These manorial records underpin every aspect of the life of the town and its people from that date forward. The Mildmay archives are summarised in: F.G. Emmison, *Guide to the Essex Record Office* (2nd edition revised to 1968, published 1969), pp. 108-11; there is a detailed catalogue in the E.R.O.

2 Chelmsford residents' *Wills* from the 15th century. Most of these are indexed in *Wills at Chelmsford*, i. 1400-1619, ed. F.G. Emmison (Index Library, 1958). A few are indexed in *Wills proved in the Prerogative Court of Canterbury*, Index 1383-1558, ed. J.C.C. Smith (Index Libr. vol. ii), and Index 1558-1583. ed. S.A. Smith and L.L. Duncan (Index Libr. vol. iii).

3 *Chelmsford Parish Records* (D/P 94) from 1538, listed in the *Catalogue of Essex Parish Records, 1240-1894* (2nd revised edition 1966, prepared by F.G. Emmison).

4 *Essex Quarter Sessions Records* from 1556, in particular the Quarter Sessions rolls (Q/SR). Essex Quarter Sessions Records are listed in the *Guide to the Essex Record Office*, where the rolls are described on pp. 1-3. There is a typescript Calendar in E.R.O.

The TOPOGRAPHY of Chelmsford is based on collation of the John Walker maps of Chelmsford and Moulsham in Chelmsford drawn in 1591 (E.R.O., D/DM P1,2) with the Chelmsford Parish Tithe Map and Award of 1843 (E.R.O., D/CT 72), the late 19th century 1st and 2nd editions of the 6″ and 25″ O.S. maps, and, most valuable, the O.S. map of the town area published in 1874 on the scale of 120″ (10ft.) to 1m. This last splendid map is some compensation for the fact that the Tithe Map and Award omit the densely built up town area of the parish.

In building up the historical topography of a town artificially created at the end of the 12th century, it has been necessary to trace the descent of each medieval site to the point where it can be securely identified with the street and house numbers first adopted in the town in 1876. From the 13th century to the 19th the original frontage sites provided the constant element in the developing topography of the town. They could be divided, subdivided, reconstituted, or merged with neighbouring sites; the buildings on sites could be shared, pulled or burned down, rebuilt, enlarged, altered or refronted, and indiscriminately changed from one use to another, but in terms of the manor's tenurial structure and record their identities and relationship with their neighbours remained intact. They were still recognisable when street numbers were attached to them in 1876, and remained so until wholesale redevelopment of a block of sites, particularly after the second world war, obliterated them. The outstanding example of obliteration was the construction of the Shopping Precinct in the 1970s, which involved the demolition of the west side of Tindal Street and its 'backsides'.

The descents of Chelmsford town's sites to 1876 have been compiled from details of ownership, occupancy, abuttals, fixed manorial rents, and use, provided by manor court rolls, rentals and surveys (sometimes drawn up in street order), title deeds, wills, rate assessments, and tax assessments. Identification has been assisted by the persistent attachment to sites of the names of medieval or Tudor owners (at least in legal documentation if not in general use) up to the adoption of house numbers in 1876, and the consistency of that numbering to the present day. Inn signs, unfortunately, were the exception to this consistency, and were transferred disconcertingly from one site to another. The most important single document in establishing Chelmsford town's early historical topography is an ill-written, undated, but remarkably well-researched abstract of court rolls in the form of a survey, compiled in Latin *c*.1618-23, giving names of sites, tenants, and abuttals, and reciting earlier tenures in some cases as far back as 1392 (*E.R.O.*, D/DM M22). This abstract is a sounder guide than the more elegant English book of survey which partners the Walker map of 1591 (D/DGe M50 and D/DM P1), which can cause confusion because, though arranged in street order, it omits without warning any site in the town no longer at that date held of the manor of Bishop's Hall. The missing sites, scattered throughout the town, include most of the property confiscated from religious guilds by the Crown at the Reformation, and the many sites annexed in the 15th century by the acquisitive Duke family to the manor of Springfield with Dukes. The abstract of *c*.1618 allots most of these, and other strays from the parent manor, to their correct positions in street sequence. The Springfield sites must be traced in the records of the manor of Springfield with Dukes, dating from the 15th century (E.R.O., D/DGe M96-115).

PUBLIC RECORD OFFICE DOCUMENTS in chronological order

Class Key: C Chancery; C.P. Court of Common Pleas; D.L. Duchy of Lancaster; E Exchequer; K.B. Court of King's Bench; S.C. Special Collections; S.P. State Paper Office.

C 66/67 m.2d.	1253-4	Commission of goal delivery
E 372/108 m.15d.	1262	Pipe roll
E 32/13	1292	Forest Inquisition
C.P. 40/269	1327	Plea roll
E 179/107/13	1327	Lay subsidy roll, Essex
E 154/1/47	1339	Inventory of goods of Ric. Bintworth, bp. of London (d.1339)
C 143/259/15, 18	1341	Inquisition *ad quod damnum* (Moulsham friars)
C 66/204	1341	Licence to alienate *in mortmain* to Moulsham friars
E 137/11/2 rot.2d. mm. 23-4	1351	Exchequer estreats
S.C. 6/845/19	1351	Ministers' and Receivers' accounts
E 179/107/46	1377	Lay subsidy roll, Essex (Poll tax)
E 179/107/63	1381	Lay subsidy roll, Essex (Poll tax)

K.B. 9/166/2 1381 mm.2-4 Ancient indictments in the King's Bench. These are the Essex indictments incompletely and not always accurately transcribed by J.A. Sparvel-Bayly in 1878 (*E.A.T.* N.S. i.205) and A. Réville in 1898 (*Le Soulèvement des travailleurs d'Angleterre*, ed. C. Petit-Dutaillis), and since re-classified and re-numbered in P.R.O. For additional information on the activities of named Chelmsford rebels, locally and in London, from King's Bench indictments (K.B. 27/487, 145/3/5/1, and 145/3/6/1), and Common Pleas roll (C.P. 40/490), I am most grateful to Dr Andrew Prescott, who is preparing a new edition of Judicial records of the Revolt. For full details and a discussion of the nature of these sources, see A.J. Prescott, *The Judicial Records of the Rising of 1381*, London Ph.D. thesis, 1984, ch. 6.

E 136/77/1	1381	Escheats of Essex traitors and fugitives
C 67/29	1382	Pardon roll
C 47/39/53	1388-9	Returns on inquiry into guilds and brotherhoods
K.B. 27/514	1389	Plea roll, proceedings in court of King's Bench
K.B. 9/25	1389	King's Bench indictments
D.L. 25/3502	1394-5	Ancient deed
S.C. 6/1140 Nos. 18, 19, 20, 23	1394, 1408, 1437-8, 1458-9	Ministers' and Receivers' accounts
E 179/108 No. 151	1524	Lay subsidy roll, Essex (*and see* E.R.O., T/A 427/1/7)
K.B. 9/529/45	1531	Ancient indictments in the King's Bench
S.C. 2/171/37	1532-3	Fragment of Chelmsford manor court roll
E 36/64	1534	Signatures of clergy to renunciation of papal supremacy
S.P. 1/153	1539	Survey of bishopric of London
E 318/16/763 mm.1-2	N.D. *c.*1540	Valuation of Moulsham manor prior to sale
E 305/B 21	1545	Grant by Edm. Bonner, bp. of London, to King Henry VIII, of manor, advowson, mill (etc.) of Chelmsford
S.C. 6/Hen. 8 No.903	*c.*1545	Compotus of manor of Chelmsford, leased to Jn. Taylor
E 315/217	1546	Lease from Crown to Thos. Mildmay, of Southwood in Chelmsford
E 301/19, 20, 30, 83	1547-8	Chantry certificates
E 315/68	1548	Sale of chantry properties and obit rent charges
E 315/30 No.44	1548	Recommendation to continue a grammar school at Chelmsford
C 1/1247/4-6	Betw. 1547 & 1551	Dispute over lease of Chelmsford parsonage
E 319/7	1551	Endowment of grammar school
S.P. 11/3	1554	Letter of support written to Queen Mary from Chelmsford by Lord Rich and others
C 66/1012	1565	Grant of Burgess Well lands
C 66/1098 m.11	1572	Pardon for death caused by misadventure during a wrestling match

ESSEX RECORD OFFICE DOCUMENTS in chronological order

Q/ Court of Quarter Sessions
D/ Deposited Records:
      D/AB Court of Commissary of Bishop of London; D/AE Court of Archdeacon of Essex; D/CT Diocesan Records, including Tithe Appointments and Maps; D/D Estate and Family Archives; D/P Parish Records; D/Q Charities; D/Z Miscellaneous Archives.

Only the most important sources, which have contributed directly to the narrative in this volume, are listed here. The sources of incidental and isolated references which helped to fill in or confirm details of the descents of sites, the identities of individuals, or their occupations, are not included. The list has been arranged in chronological order.

D/P 50/25 Nos. 3-26	1344-1479	Deeds of Brocholestrate (Duke Street) sites
D/DM M72, 73, 79	1348,1350 1360	Manor of Moulsham (Westminster Abbey), bailiffs' account rolls
D/DM M1-3	1381-1422	Manor of Chelmsford *alias* Bishop's Hall in Chelmsford (Bishop of London), court rolls
D/DM M30	1381-1399	Moulsham manor court roll
D/DAv 1-16	1383-1520	Deeds of Mayes in Fish Market neighbourhood
D/DP O29, 30	1386-1627	Deeds of Duke Street sites, incl. the Chequer (later the George), bought in 1627 for the Grammar School
D/DM M95, 96	1391-1392	Moulsham manor bailiff's accounts
D/DM T32 Nos. 2,3	1411-1446	Endowment of Glover's Obits
D/DP Tl/946- 990	1426-1565	Deeds of the Hart and Lion
D/DM M20 (revised 1477)	1428	Rental of manor of Chelmsford
D/DTu 64-99	1433-1531	References in Gt. Waltham deeds to the Cornish and Mildmay families
D/DM M4-6	1461-1508	Chelmsford manor court rolls (with annotated drafts 1492-1504)
D/DTu 244	1462-1483	Court roll of manor of Gt. Waltham
D/DP M590	1477-1478	Manor of Writtle, bailiff's account
D/DM M35-6	1484-1543	Moulsham manor court rolls
D/DA T38	1485-1646	Deeds of Mayes in Fish Market neighbourhood

D/AE	From 1487	Chelmsford and Moulsham Wills proved in Court of the Archdeacon of Essex (Wills, D/AEW; Wills Registers, D/AER).
D/DGe M96, 97	1488-1505 1511-1547	Court rolls of manor of Springfield with Dukes
D/DM T33/1	1514	Lease of Bishop's Hall, the Tollhouse, Bishop's Mill, and profits of market and fairs, to Jn. Markday, yeoman
D/AB	From 1522	Chelmsford and Moulsham Wills proved in Court of the Bishop of London's Commissary in Essex (Wills, D/ABW; Wills Registers, D/ABR)
D/P 94/1/1, 2	1538-1564 1564-1638	Original paper parish register of baptisms, burials, and marriages to 1564; from 1564 transcript made on parchment in 1609 of paper original no longer extant; from 1609 register on parchment; *and see* modern transcripts from 1538 (T/R 5/1/1-3)
D/DM T28 No. 2A	1548	Crown grant to Thos. Mildmay of Moulsham, esq., of chantry properties in Chelmsford
D/DP O28	1551	Crown foundation grant of Grammar School
Q/SR 1-192	1536-1610	Essex Quarter Sessions Rolls
D/P 94/5/1	1557-1668	Chelmsford Churchwardens' book of accounts, including rates, inventories, nominations of officers, and a few resolutions
D/DM M7-9	1560-1639	Chelmsford manor court rolls
D/DM T28 Nos. 4,5	1563	Crown grant of reversion of manor of Chelmsford to Thos. Mildmay of Moulsham.
D/DGe M98-9	1572-1602	Court rolls of manor of Springfield with Dukes
D/DM P1,2	1591	Maps of manors of Chelmsford and Moulsham drawn by John Walker, 'Architector'
D/DGe M50	1591	Survey of manor of Chelmsford, Surveyor Edward Moryson, esq., Steward Edward Lathum, gent., Measurer John Walker
D/DGe 612	1603	Rental of manor of Chelmsford Sir Thos. Mildmay
D/DP O37/13	1606	Sir Thos. Mildmay's recollections of the early days of the grammar school
D/DM M22	*c.*1618-23	Survey and abstract of court rolls of manor of Chelmsford, reciting from *c.*1392, and including town properties not held of the manor of Chelmsford
D/DHt T59 No. 4	1622	Sale of Blue Boar and adjoining Church chamber
D/Z 6	N.D. *c.*1660	Crown rents from former Chelmsford chantry and obit properties
D/Q 2/1	1685	Black Chapel, Great Waltham, Trustees' Accounts
Q/AS 2/2/1; Q/SBb 288/44	18th cent.	Abstracts of entries in Quarter Sessions Order Books about Shire House, 1660-1776
D/DBe O1	1771	Evidence of witnesses in petition laid before Parliament on condition of old Shire House
D/P 94/25/18	1782-3	Legal case and opinions on inhabitants' right to watercourse from Burgess Well to Conduit
D/DOp E8	1818-24	Moulsham Bridge papers
D/CT 72	1843	Tithe Map and Award of parish of Chelmsford
Q/RDc 68A	1871	Writtle and Roxwell Enclosure Award

ESSEX RECORD OFFICE TRANSCRIPTS (T/)

Copies or catalogues of documents, or notes or extracts from them.
T/A Originals in public repositories; T/B Originals in private custody; T/P Parish collections; T/R Parish registers.

T/A 83	Transcripts made by B. Brownless from Westminster Abbey Muniments, including 1157 Bull of Pope Adrian IV, and Moulsham Bridge contract with Henry Yevele, 1372 (W.A.M. 19866)
T/A 122/2	Transcript of years 1550-1563 from Harwich Churchwardens' accounts, 1550-1619
T/A 139	Transcript by Professor C.R. Cheney of charters, *c.*1200-1605, relating to Mountpillers in Writtle and Chelmsford
T/A 221	1521 Will of John Biglon
T/A 427/1/7	Calendar of Essex Lay Subsidy Roll, 1524 (P.R.O., E 179/108/151)
T/A 428	Calendar of Essex Documents in King's Bench Indictments, 1558-1625 (P.R.O., K.B.9)
T/B 62	Photographs of Black Chapel, Great Waltham, Trust Deeds
T/P 70	Monumental inscriptions and notes on churches compiled by Thos. Martin (1647-1771)
T/P 157/1	Extracts from records in Chelmsford Cathedral Library: 1801-35, Mins. of Trustees for repairing Chelmsford Church
T/P 195/9/1	MS. History of Essex, compiled *c.*1710-30 by William Holman of Halstead.
T/P 238	Report on Moulsham in Chelmsford, *c.*1200-1900, compiled by Stephen Freeth from original sources, including court rolls of Westminster Abbey's manor of Moulsham, 1422-1543 (D/DM M33-6)
T/R 5/1/1-3	Transcripts of Chelmsford Parish Registers from 1538

DOCUMENTS IN OTHER REPOSITORIES

Bodleian Library Oxford

MS. J. Walker *c*.2   Destruction in 1641-3 of 15th century
    f.201   carved wooden angels on roof of nave,
and east window glass, in Chelmsford
parish church

MS. Harl. 590   William Maldon's narrative of
    f.77   persecution by his father for reading
the scriptures in English; sent to John
Foxe for 'the boke of marters'. I am
most grateful to Dr A. Macfarlane for
drawing my attention to this narrative,
and sending me a transcript. The account is printed in *Narratives of the
Reformation*, ed. J.G. Nichols (Camd.
Soc., lxxvii, 1859)

Lambeth Palace Library

Lamb. MSS. Cart. 1559   Signatures of Essex clergy
Misc. xiii pt.2   subscribing to the royal supremacy
No. 57

British Library

MS. Egerton 2644   1604 Letter from Sir Thomas Mildmay
to Sir Francis Barrington. I have to
thank Mr Arthur Searle for drawing
my attention to this important letter.

E 105 (25)   Bruno Ryves, *Mercurius Rusticus*. III, 3
June 1643

Greater London Record Office

Records of Bishop of London's Consistory Court

DL/C/14   1602 Civil Case, Eliz. Barker v. John
Whale

DL/C/332   1561-74 Vicar General's Book

Dean and Chapter of St. Paul's

A. Boxes 41/1521   1205 Grant of a new 'place' in
Chelmsford's new market

  ,,   60A   1290 *Quo Warranto* proceedings

  ,,   62A-64   1318 Manorial Compotus of Chelmsford
and Southwood

PUBLIC RECORDS IN PRINT

All series marked with an asterisk *, including publications of the Record Commissioners (Rec. Com.), are listed in *British National Archives*: Sectional List No.24 (H.M.S.O.). They have been systematically searched, but only the volumes covered by the dates given have directly contributed to the narrative. The sources are arranged in chronological order.

1086   *Essex Domesday*, edited J.H. Round, with introduction, translated text, and index.
(*V.C.H. Essex*. i. 1903)

1182-1422   *Feet of Fines for Essex*. i-iii, ed. R.E.G. Kirk,
R.C. Fowler, and S.C. Ratcliff. (*Essex Arch.
Soc.* 1899-1949)

1184-1230   *Pipe Rolls*. (Pipe Roll Soc.)

1189-1237   *Curia Regis Rolls*

1194-1199   *Rotuli Curiae Regis* (Rec. Com.) Vol. i

1198-1293   *The Book of Fees*

1199-1216   *Rotuli de Oblatis et Finibus in Turri Londinensi
asservati, temp. Regis Johannis* (Rec. Com.)

1199-1216   *Rotuli Chartarum in Turri Londinensi asservati,
1199-1216* (Rec. Com.); includes the enrol-
ments of Chelmsford's three town charters

1204-1227   *Rotuli Litterarum Clausarum in Turri Londinensi
asservati,* (Rec. Com.)

1216-1272   *Rotuli Selecti.* (Rec. Com.)

1216-1572   *Calendar of Patent Rolls*

1231-1264   *Close Rolls*

1240-1272   *Calendar of Liberate Rolls*

1257-1516   *Calendar of Charter Rolls*

1274   *Rotuli Hundredorum* (Rec. Com.) Vol. i

1285   *Placita de Quo Warranto.* (Rec. Com.)

1300-1364   *Calendar of Inquisitions Post Mortem*

1323-1396   *Calendar of Close Rolls*

1326-1327   *Memoranda Rolls*

1327   *The Lay Subsidy of Essex. 1327* (P.R.O., E
179/107/13; ed. J.C. Ward; Essex Record
Office, 1983)

1334   *The Lay Subsidy of 1334.* R.E. Glascock. 1975

1337-1509   *Calendar of Fine Rolls*

1340-1341   *Nonarum Inquisitiones in Curia Scaccarii.* (Rec.
Com.)

1351-1365   *Register of Edward the Black Prince.* pt.4

1377-1392   *Calendar of Miscellaneous Inquisitions*

1377-1399   *Index to Pardon Rolls.* (P.R.O.)

1381   *Rotuli Parliamentorum*, vol. iii

1423-1547   *Feet of Fines for Essex*, vol. iv, 1423-1547, ed.
P.H. Reaney, and M. Fitch (*Essex Arch. Soc.*
1964)

1485-1497   *Calendar of Inquisitions Post Mortem, Second
Series*

1532-3   *Ancient Deeds*. Series E. (List and Index Soc.
vol. clxxxi): Lease from J. Stokesley, bp. of
London, to Jn. Taylor, yeo., of Bishop's Hall
in Chelmsford

1533-1547   *Calendar of Letters and Papers, Foreign and
Domestic, Henry VIII*

1535   *Valor Ecclesiasticus, temp. Henrici VIII, auctoritate
regia institutus.* (Rec. Com.)

c.1538   'Essex Monastic inventories', R.C. Fowler
(*E.A.T.*, N.S. x. 14-18. Text of P.R.O.,
E 117/10/39 Inventory of goods of Moulsham
friars)

1547-1610   *Calendar of State Papers, Domestic*

1550-1589   *Acts of Privy Council of England*

1558-1603   *Calendar of Assize Records: Essex Indictments:
Eliz. I.* (Ed. J.S. Cockburn, 1978 H.M.S.O.).
This supersedes the earlier transcript calendar
in the Essex Record Office.

Dates   *Descriptive Catalogue of Ancient Deeds.* Series
before 1603   A, B, C. vols. i, ii, iv

Printed Sources

CHRONICLES

*Chronicles in the Rolls Series are listed in *British National Archives*: Sectional List No. 24

Anglo-Saxon Chronicle (trans. J. Ingram, 1823. Everyman edn. 1912.)
Annales Monasterii S. Albani a Johanne Amundesham conscripti (Rolls Series)
Annales Monastici, vol. iv (Rolls Series)
Anonimalle Chronicalle, 1333-1381, ed. V.H. Galbraith, 1927
Eulogium Historiarum sive Temporis Chronicon ... usque ad Annum Domini, 1366 ... (Rolls Series)
Froissart, The Chronicles of, trans. Lord Berners, ed. G.C. Macauley (1895, reprinted 1930)
*Knighton, Henry, *Chronicon*, 1377 to 1395 (Rolls Series)
*Paris, Matthew, *Historia Minor*, 1067-1253 (Rolls Series)
*Paris, Matthew, *Chronica Majora* (Rolls Series)
*Ralph of Coggeshall, *Chronicon Anglicanum*, to 1227 (Rolls Series)
*Walsingham, Thomas, *Chronicon Angliae*, 1328-1388 (Rolls Series)
*Walsingham, Thomas, *Historia Anglicana*, vol. i. 1272-1381; vol. ii. 1381-1422 (Rolls Series)

OTHER PRINTED SOURCES

(*E.A.T. Transactions of the Essex Archaeological Society; E.R. Essex Review*)

Benham, W.G. (ed.). *Court Rolls of Borough of Colchester*, vol. i. 1310-1352
Benton, G.M. 'Essex Wills at Canterbury' (*E.A.T.* N.S. xxi. 234)
Bliss, W.H. (ed.). *Papal Letters*, vol. ii. 1305-1342. (P.R.O., 1895); *and see* Tremlow
Bliss, W.H. (ed.). *Petitions to the Pope*, vol. i. 1342-1419 (P.R.O., 1897)
Bramston, Sir J. *The Autobiography of Sir John Bramston, K.B., of Skreens* (Camd. Soc. xxxii. 1845)
Calendar of Wills: Court of Hustings, London. vols. i, ii
Clark, A. 'Great Dunmow Revels, 1526-1543' (*E.R.* xix. 189)
Clowes, R.C. (ed.). 'St. Osyth's Priory Minister's Accounts, 1512' (*E.R.* xxx. 1-13, 122-7, 205-21)
Davis, F.N. (ed.). *Register of Jn. Pecham, Archbishop of Canterbury*, 1279-1292, vol. i (Cant. and York Soc. lxiv. 1908)
Dyce, A. (ed.). *Kemps nine daies wonder: performed in a daunce from London to Norwich* (Camd. Soc. xi. 1840)
Flower, C.T. (ed.). *Public Works in Medieval Law*, vol. 1 (Selden Soc. xxxii. 1915)
Fowler, R.C. (ed.). *Registers of Ralph Baldock, bishop of London, 1304-1313, and of Stephen Gravesend, bishop of London*, 1319-1338 (Cant. and York Soc. vii. 1911)
Fowler, R.C. and Jenkins, C. (ed.). *Register of Simon Sudbury, bishop of London*, 1362-1375. 2 vols. (Cant. and York Soc. xxxiv, xxxviii. 1927-1938)
Foxe, J. *Acts and Monuments* (also known as the *Book of Martyrs*)
Furber, E.C. *Essex Sessions of the Peace, 1351, 1377-9* (Essex Arch. Soc. 1953)
Gibbs, M. (ed.). *Early Charters of St. Paul's Cathedral* (Camd. Soc. 3rd series lviii. 1939)
Harrison, W. *A description of England*, 1587 (ed. G. Edelen; Folger Library. 1968)
Jeayes, I.H. 'Deeds from a Parish Chest' (*E.A.T.* N.S. xix. 38)
Johnson, C. and Cronne, H.A. (vol. ii); Cronne, H.A. and Davis, R.H.C. (vol. iii); *Regesta Regum Anglo-Normannorum* (Oxford Univ. Press, 1956, 1968)
Lees, B.A. (ed.). *Records of the Knights Templars in England in the 12th century* (1935)
Metcalfe, W.C. (ed.). *The Visitations of Essex.* 1552-1634 (2 vols. Harleian Soc. 1878-9)
Riley, H.T. (ed.). *Munimenta Gildhallae Londoniensis.* vol. i: *Liber Albus* (Rolls Ser.)
Nichols, J.G. (ed.). *Diary of Henry Machyn*, 1550-1563 (Camd. Soc. xlii)
Nichols, J.G. (ed.). *Narratives of the Reformation* (Camd. Soc. lxxvii, 1859). Includes pp. 345-51 the text of Bodleian Library, Oxford, MS. Harl. 590 f.77 (Wm. Maldon's statement)
Report of the Commissioners appointed ... for Enquiries concerning Charities (Essex). H.C. 216 (1835)
Sawyer, P.H. (ed.). *Anglo-Saxon Charters* (R. Hist. Soc. 1968)
Simpson, W.S. (ed.). *Documents illustrating the History of St. Paul's Cathedral* (Camd. Soc. N.S. xxvi. 1880)
Smith, J.C.C. 'Some Additions to Newcourt's *Repertorium* — vol. II' (*E.A.T.* N.S. vi. 228)
Tremlow, J.A. (ed.). *Papal Letters*, vol. x. 1447-1455 (P.R.O., 1915); *and see* Bliss

BIBLIOGRAPHY

(E.A.T. Transactions of the Essex Archaeological Society; E.R. Essex Review)

Anon, 'English towns and their characteristics, in the time of Edward II' (*East Anglian Notes and Queries*. i. 201)

Baker, D.C., and Murphy, J.L., 'The booke of Myles Blomefylde' (*The Bibliographical Soc.* 1976)

Benton, V.M. 'Colchester Lepers' (*E.A.T.* xxi. 143)

Beresford, M.W. *The New Towns of the Middle Ages.* 1967

Beresford, M.W. 'The Poll Taxes of 1377, 1379, and 1381' (*Amateur Historian.* iii, 271)

Blaauw, W.H. *The Barons' War* (2nd edn., ed. C.H. Pearson. 1871)

Bonnier, C. 'List of English towns in the 14th century' (*English Historical Review*, xvi. 501)

Britnell, R.H. 'The making of Witham' (*History Studies*, University of Durham, 1968)

Britnell, R.H. 'King John's early grants of markets and fairs' (*English Historical Review*, xciv. 90)

Camden, W. *Britannia* (6th Latin edn. 1607; English edn. trans. Phileman Holland, 1610)

Chancellor, F. 'The Architecture of Chelmsford church' (*E.A.T.* O.S. ii. 195)

Chancellor, F. 'Guy Harlings, New Street, Chelmsford' (*E.R.* xxv. 151)

Chancellor, W. *A Short History of the Cathedral Church of St. Mary ... Chelmsford.* 1938, revised edns. to 1971

Chelmsford Archaeological Trust, *Minutes*, 16 April 1982

Christy, (R.) Miller. Note on *Annales of England* by Jn. Stow, 1592 (*E.R.* xi. 236)

Clark, A. 'The Black Death, 1349-51' (*E.R.* xx. 189)

Coldeway, J.C. 'Early Essex Drama' (Ph.D. thesis, Univ. of Colorado, 1972; copy in E.R.O.)

Colvin, R.B. *The Lieutenants and Keepers of the rolls of the county of Essex.* 1934

Cokayne, G.E. ed. V. Gibbs and H.A. Doubleday. *Complete Peerage*, v (s.v. Fitzwalter). 1926

Cox, J.C. *The Cathedral church and See of Essex.* 1908

Davids, T.W. *Annals of Evangelical Nonconformity in ... Essex.* 1863

Dibben, A.A. 'Blackchapel, Great Waltham' (In *An Essex Tribute*: Essays presented to Frederick G. Emmison. Ed. K. Neale. 1987)

Dickens, A.G. *The English Reformation.* 1966

Dowell, S. *History of Taxes and Taxation in England.* 1888

Drury, P.J. *Chelmsford Excavation Committee: Excavations 1972-3: interim Report*

Drury, P.J. 'Chelmsford Dominican Priory: The Excavation of the Reredorter, 1973' (*Essex Archaeology and History*, vi. p.40. 1974.)

Edward, A.C., and Newton, K.C. *The Walkers of Hanningfield.* 1984

Emden, A.B. *Survey of the Dominicans in England.* 1967

Emmison, F.G. *Elizabethan Life*: i. *Disorder.* 1970

Emmison, F.G. *Elizabethan Life*: iv. *Wills of Essex gentry and merchants.* 1978

Emmison, F.G. *Tudor Secretary: Sir William Petre at Court and Home.* 1961

Essex Archaeological News. Spring, 1984

Essex Chronicle, 30 April 1982

Essex County Council. *Historic Towns in Essex: An Archaeological Survey.* 1983

Ewen, C.L. *Witch hunting and witch trials ... 1559-1736.* 1929

Fisher, J.L. 'The Black Death in Essex' (*E.R.* lii. 13.)

Fitch, E.A. 'Historians of Essex — i. Nicholas Tindal' (*E.R.* ii. 168)

Foley, B.C. 'Blessed John Payne, seminary priest and martyr — 1582' (*Essex Recusant*, ii. 48)

Fryde, E.B. 'Edward III's Wool Monopoly of 1337: A Fourteenth century Royal Trading Venture' (*History*, xxxvii. p. 8. 1952)

Gentleman's Magazine, vol. cl. (1862 pt.1). Notes on list of English towns in Bodleian MS. Douce 98 ff. 194^v-195^r

Gray, I. 'Footnote to an Alchemist' (*Cambridge Review*, lxviii, p.172. 1946)

Hardy, T.D. (ed.). *Itinerarium Johannis Regis Anglie* (in introduction to *Rot. lit. pat. in turri Lond. asservati*. Rec. Com. 1835)

Harvey, J.H. *Henry Yevele, c.1320-1400: the Life of an English Architect.* 1944

Hill, M. *The King's Messenger.* 1961

Hinnebusch, W.A. *The Early English Friars Preachers.* 1951

Jeayes, I.H. 'The Writtle Chantries' (*E.A.T.* N.S. xiv. 158)

Jervoise, E. *Ancient Bridges of Mid- and Eastern England.* 1932

King, E.W. 'Notes on Guy Harlings' (*E.A.T.* N.S. iii. 177)

Johnson, J.H. 'Chelmsford Grammar School' (*E.R.* liv. 45, 100, 146; iv. 1, 69, 113, 180)

Knowles, D. and Hadcock, R.N. *Medieval Religious Houses in England and Wales.* 1971

Lehmberg, S.E. *Sir Walter Mildmay.* 1964

Longnon, A. *Les Noms des Lieus de la France.* Paris. 1920-9

Lyte, Sir H. Maxwell. *Historical Notes on the use of the Great Seal of England.* 1926

Macfarlane, A. *Witchcraft in Tudor and Stuart England.* 1970

Mackie, J.D. *The Earlier Tudors, 1485-1558.* 1952

Maitland, F.W. *Township and Borough.* 1898

McKisack, M. *The Fourteenth Century.* 1959

Mildmay, H.A. St.J. *A brief memoir of the Mildmay family.* 1913

Morant, P. *The History and Antiquities of Essex,* vol. ii. 1768

Muilman, P. *A new and complete History of Essex ... by a Gentleman.* Vol. i. 1771

Newcourt, R. *Repertorium ecclesiasticum parochiale Londinense,* 2 vols. 1708, 1710

Newton, K.C. *The Manor of Writtle.* 1970

Nichols, J.F. 'Custodia Essexae' (Unpublished thesis on conventual property held by Priory of Christ Church, Canterbury, in the Counties of Essex, Suffolk, and Norfolk. 1930)

Norgate, K. *John Lackland.* 1902

Notes and Queries, 6th ser., viii. 223. (Notes on List of English Towns in Bodleian MS. Douce 98 ff. 194ᵛ-195ʳ)

Oman, C. *The Great Revolt of 1381* (1906; new edn. E.B. Fryde 1969)

P., M. 'John Payne, seminary priest. Executed at Chelmsford 1582' (*E.R.* xix. 21)

Palmer, C.F.R. 'The Friars Preachers ... of Chelmsford' (*The Reliquary,* N.S. iii. 141)

Parsons, E.J.S. *The Gough Map.* 1958

Phillimore, W.P.W. and others. *Essex Parish Registers, Marriages,* vols. ii and iii

Pollock, F. and Maitland, F.W. *History of English Law.* 2nd edn. 1898

Poole, A.L. *From Domesday Book to Magna Carta, 1087-1216.* 1951

Powell, W.R. 'The making of Essex parishes' (*E.R.,* lxii. 6.)

Powicke, Sir F.M., *The Thirteenth Century, 1216-1307.* 1953

Powicke, Sir F.M., and Fryde, E.B. *Handbook of British Chronology.* 2nd edn. 1961

Prescott, A. 'London in the Peasants' Revolt: A Portrait Gallery' (*The London Journal,* vii. (2). 1981)

Pugh, R.B. *Imprisonment in Medieval England.* 1968

Putnam, B.H. 'The transformation of the keepers of the peace into the justices of the peace, 1327-80' (*Trans. R. Hist. Soc.* 4th ser. xii. 19)

Rahtz, P.A. *Excavations at King John's Hunting Lodge, Writtle, Essex.* (Soc. for Medieval Archaeology Monograph Series: No. 3, 1969)

Reaney, P.H. *Dict. of British Surnames.* 1958

Reaney, P.H. *Place-Names of Essex.* 1935

Return of the Names of every member of the Lower House of Parliament, 1213-1874, vol. i (H.M.S.O., 1878)

Round, J.H. 'The Mildmays and their Chelmsford estates' (*E.A.T.* N.S. vol. x. p.1)

Round, J.H. 'The Mildmay Mystery.' (In *Family Origins and other studies;* ed. W. Page. 1930)

Royal Commission on Historical Monuments (England). An inventory of the historical monuments in Essex. Vol. ii (Central and South West). 1921

Salusbury, C.T. *Street Life in Medieval England.* 1939

Samaha, J. *Law and Order in Historical Perspective: the case of Elizabethan Essex.* 1974

Silvette, H. *Catalogue of the Works of Philemon Holland.* 1940

Smith, J.C.C. 'Some additions to Newcourt's Repertorium, vol. ii' (*E.A.T.* N.S. vi and vii)

Strutt, Joseph *The sports and pastimes of the people of England.* 1876

Tanner, N.P. 'Heresy Trials in the Diocese of Norwich, 1428-31' (Camd. Soc. 4th ser. xx)

Taylor, P. 'The estates of the bishopric of London from the 7th century to the early 16th century' (Lond. Univ. Ph.D. thesis, 1976)

Thompson, C. 'The third Lord Rich and the Essex Election of 1604' (*Essex Journal* xiv (1), 1979)

Tout, T.F. *The Political History of England*. vol. iii. 1216-1377. 1905

Victoria History of the County of Essex. Vol. i. ed. Page, W. 1903; vol. ii. ed. Page, W., and Round, J.H. 1907; vols. iv.-vii., ed. Powell, W.R. 1956-78

Warren, W.L. *Reign of King John*. 1961

Weever, J. *Ancient Funeral Monuments within ... Great Britaine ...* 1631

Willard, J.F. *Parliamentary Taxes on Personal Property 1290-1334*. (Medieval Academy of America, No.19, Monograph No.9); see also in *Historical Essays in honour of James Tait* (ed. Edwards, J.G.)

Willard, J.F. 'Edward III's Negotiations for a Grant in 1337' (*English Historical Review*, xxi. 1906, pp. 727-31)

Withycombe, E.G. *Oxford Dictionary of English Christian Names*. 1945

Wood, R.G.E. 'Essex Manorial Records and the Revolt' (In *Essex and the Great Revolt of 1381*; ed. Liddell, W.H. and Wood, R.G. 1982)

INDEX

(m) *indicates location on map or plan*